Property of :-
Rabin Ezra

Radiosity and Realistic Image Synthesis

About the cover images:

The cover image shows the interior of Le Corbusier's Chapel at Ronchamp, France. The illumination was computed using radiosity, with the sunbeams added by stochastic ray tracing during rendering [109, 110]. The model was created by Paul Boudreau, Keith Howie, and Eric Haines with Hewlett-Packard's ME30 Solid Modeler and rendered by Eric Haines at 3D/EYE, Inc. with Hewlett-Packard's ARTCore Radiosity and Ray Tracing library.

The image is a frame from the animation *The Key is Light* presented at the Siggraph '91 Electronic Theater. The video was produced by Hewlett-Packard Company TV, with extensive help from Becky Naqvi, John Fujii, and Ron Firooz at Hewlett-Packard Company.

The back cover image is a radiosity rendering from a scene of Luther's Tavern in the Opera *Tales of Hoffman*. The opera lighting design software used for this image is part of a PhD dissertation by Julie O'Brien Dorsey at Cornell University's Program of Computer Graphics [73].

Radiosity and Realistic Image Synthesis

Michael F. Cohen
John R. Wallace

Academic Press Professional
Harcourt Brace & Company, Publishers
Boston   San Diego   New York
London   Sydney   Tokyo   Toronto

Copyright © 1993 by Academic Press, Inc.

ACADEMIC PRESS PROFESSIONAL
955 Massachusetts Avenue, Cambridge, MA 02139

An Imprint of ACADEMIC PRESS, INC.
A Division of HARCOURT BRACE & COMPANY

United Kingdom Edition published by
ACADEMIC PRESS LIMITED
24–28 Oval Road, London NW1 7DX

ISBN 0-12-178270-0
Library of Congress Catalog Card Number: 93-72454

Printed in the United States of America
93 94 95 96 97 98 BC 9 8 7 6 5 4 3 2 1

Contents

Foreword *by Donald Greenberg*   **xi**

Preface   **xiii**

1 Introduction   **1**
  1.1 Realistic Image Synthesis 1
    1.1.1 Goals 2
    1.1.2 Limitations 2
  1.2 A Short Historical Perspective 4
    1.2.1 Raster Graphics 5
    1.2.2 Global Illumination Models 6
    1.2.3 Early Radiosity Methods 7
    1.2.4 The Rendering Equation 8
  1.3 Radiosity and Finite Element Methods 8
  1.4 The Radiosity Method and This Book 10

2 Rendering Concepts *by Pat Hanrahan*   **13**
  2.1 Motivation 13
  2.2 Basic Optics 14
  2.3 Radiometry and Photometry 15
  2.4 The Light Field 17
    2.4.1 Transport Theory 17
    2.4.2 Radiance and Luminance 19
    2.4.3 Irradiance and Illuminance 24
    2.4.4 Radiosity and Luminosity 25
    2.4.5 Radiant and Luminous Intensity 25
    2.4.6 Summary of Radiometric and Photometric Quantities . . 27
  2.5 Reflection Functions 28
    2.5.1 The Bidirectional Reflection Distribution Function . . . 28
    2.5.2 Mirror Reflection 30
    2.5.3 The Reflectance 31
    2.5.4 Lambertian Diffuse Reflection 32
    2.5.5 Glossy Reflection 33
  2.6 The Rendering Equation 36
    2.6.1 Local or Direct Illumination 37

| | | 2.6.2 | Global or Indirect Illumination | 38 |
| | | 2.6.3 | The Radiosity Equation | 40 |

3 Discretizing the Radiosity Equation   **41**

	3.1	The Radiosity Equation	41
	3.2	Making Image Synthesis Tractable	42
	3.3	The Radiosity Approach	46
	3.4	Approximating Radiosity across a Surface	48
	3.5	Error Metrics	53
		3.5.1 Point Collocation	55
		3.5.2 Galerkin Form of Weighted Residuals	56
	3.6	Constant Element Radiosities	57
	3.7	Higher-Order Basis Functions	60
	3.8	Parametric Mapping to a Master Element	61
		3.8.1 Master Elements	61
		3.8.2 Isoparametric Mapping	62
	3.9	Summary	63

4 The Form Factor   **65**

I. The Form Factor Integral   **65**

	4.1	The Coefficients of **K**	66
	4.2	The Differential Form Factor	67
	4.3	Three Formulations of the Form Factor	69
	4.4	Computing the Form Factor	70

II. Closed Form Solutions for the Form Factor   **72**

	4.5	Formulae for Simple Shapes	72
	4.6	Differential Area to Convex Polygon	72
	4.7	General Polygon to Polygon	74

III. Numerical Solutions for the Form Factor   **75**

	4.8	Numerical Integration in General	76
		4.8.1 Gaussian Quadrature	77
		4.8.2 Quadrature Points and the Form Factor Integral	77
		4.8.3 Monte Carlo Methods	77
	4.9	Evaluating the Inner Integral	79
		4.9.1 Hemisphere Sampling Algorithms	79
		4.9.2 Nusselt Analog	80
		4.9.3 The Hemicube	80
		4.9.4 Single-Plane Method	88
		4.9.5 Monte Carlo Ray Tracing	89
		4.9.6 Area Sampling Algorithms	90
	4.10	Full Area-to-Area Quadrature	94
		4.10.1 Monte Carlo Integration	94

4.11 Contour Integral Formulation 95
4.12 A Simple Test Environment 96
4.13 Nonconstant Basis Functions 98
    4.13.1 The Hemicube for General Form Factors 99
    4.13.2 Monte Carlo for General Form Factors 99
    4.13.3 Singularities in the Integrand 100
4.14 Acceleration Techniques 103
    4.14.1 Hemicube Acceleration 103
    4.14.2 Ray Tracing Acceleration 106

5 Radiosity Matrix Solutions   **109**
5.1 Qualities of the Matrix 110
5.2 Linear System Solution Methods 112
    5.2.1 Direct Methods 112
    5.2.2 Iterative Methods 112
5.3 Relaxation Methods 113
    5.3.1 Jacobi Iteration 113
    5.3.2 Gauss-Seidel Iteration 114
    5.3.3 Southwell Iteration 116
    5.3.4 Ambient Energy and Overrelaxation 122
5.4 Dynamic Environments 126
    5.4.1 Lighting Changes 126
    5.4.2 Reflectivity Changes 127
    5.4.3 Changes in Geometry 127
5.5 Parallel Implementations 129

6 Domain Subdivision   **131**
6.1 Error Metrics 132
    6.1.1 True Error 132
    6.1.2 Local Estimate of Approximation Error 132
    6.1.3 Residual of the Approximate Solution 134
    6.1.4 Error Based on the Behavior of the Kernel 135
    6.1.5 Image Based Error Metrics 135
    6.1.6 Perceptually Based Error Metrics 136
6.2 Mesh Characteristics and Accuracy 136
    6.2.1 An Example 137
    6.2.2 Mesh Density 139
    6.2.3 Element Order and Continuity 142
    6.2.4 Element Shape 144
    6.2.5 Discontinuities 149
6.3 Automatic Meshing Algorithms 152
    6.3.1 A Posteriori Meshing 154

6.3.2   Adaptive Subdivision: H-refinement for Radiosity . . .   157
6.3.3   Error Estimation for Adaptive Subdivision   159
6.3.4   Deciding How to Subdivide   165

7 Hierarchical Methods   **167**
I. Hierarchical Subdivision   168
7.1   A Physical Example   168
7.2   Two-Level Hierarchy   169
7.3   The **K** Matrix   171
7.4   Multilevel Hierarchy   176
      7.4.1   N-Body Problem   177
      7.4.2   Radiosity and the N-Body Problem   177
      7.4.3   Hierarchical Refinement   177
      7.4.4   Solution of the Hierarchical System   181
      7.4.5   The Oracle Function   182
      7.4.6   Progressive Refinement of the Hierarchy   184
      7.4.7   Experimental Results   187
II. Hierarchical Basis Functions and Wavelets   187
7.5   Hierarchical Basis Functions   187
7.6   Wavelets   190
      7.6.1   Haar Basis   190
      7.6.2   Vanishing Moments   194
      7.6.3   Vanishing Moments and Sparse Representations   195
      7.6.4   A Wavelet Radiosity Algorithm   198
III. Importance-Based Radiosity   201
7.7   Importance Meshing   201
      7.7.1   The Importance Equation   202
      7.7.2   Importance-Based Error   204
7.8   Hierarchical Radiosity and Importance   205
      7.8.1   Pseudocode   205
      7.8.2   Example Results   208

8 Meshing   **209**
8.1   Basic Subdivision Techniques   209
8.2   Mesh Template Methods   210
      8.2.1   Grid Superposition   210
      8.2.2   Template Mapping   211
      8.2.3   Multiblocking   212
      8.2.4   Adaptive Subdivision with Templates   214
8.3   Decomposition Methods   216
      8.3.1   Nodes–Elements–Together Decomposition   217
      8.3.2   Decomposition by Recursive Splitting   217

	8.3.3	Decomposition by Advancing Front	218
	8.3.4	Nodes-First Decomposition	219
8.4	Mesh Smoothing		221
8.5	Discontinuity Meshing		222
	8.5.1	Discontinuities in Value	222
	8.5.2	First and Second Derivative Discontinuities	224
	8.5.3	Shadow Volume Algorithms	229
	8.5.4	Critical Surface Algorithms	231
8.6	Topological Data Structures and Operators		234
	8.6.1	Data Structure Criteria	235
	8.6.2	The Winged-Edge Data Structure	235
8.7	Alternatives to Meshing		239

9 Rendering   **243**
9.1	Reconstructing the Radiosity Function		244
9.2	Interpolation Methods for Rendering		245
	9.2.1	C^0 Interpolation	245
	9.2.2	C^1 Interpolation	252
9.3	Two-Pass Methods		257
	9.3.1	Evaluating the Radiosity Equation per Pixel	259
	9.3.2	Multi-Pass Methods	265
9.4	Incorporating Surface Detail		266
	9.4.1	Texture Mapping	266
	9.4.2	Bump Mapping	267
9.5	Mapping Radiosities to Pixel Colors		267
	9.5.1	Gamma Correction	268
	9.5.2	Real-World Luminance to Pixel Luminance	268
9.6	Color		273
	9.6.1	Human Vision and Color	274
	9.6.2	Color Matching Functions and the CIE Chromaticity Diagram	276
	9.6.3	Color Spaces and Image Synthesis	280
	9.6.4	Direct Use of Spectral Data	283
9.7	Hardware Accelerated Rendering		284
	9.7.1	Walkthroughs	284
	9.7.2	Hardware-Supported Texture Mapping	285
	9.7.3	Visibility Preprocessing	286

10 Extensions   **289**
10.1	Nondiffuse Light Sources		289
	10.1.1	Form Factors to and from Light Sources	290
	10.1.2	Point Lights	293

10.1.3 Parallel Lights 293
10.1.4 General Luminaires 293
10.1.5 Spot Lights 295
10.1.6 Sky Light 295
10.1.7 Normalization 297
10.1.8 Light Source Data 298
10.2 Directional Reflection 299
10.2.1 Classifying Transport Paths 299
10.2.2 Tracing the Transport Paths 302
10.2.3 Implicit Methods 307
10.2.4 Explicit Methods 309
10.2.5 Non-Lambertian Reflection and Hierarchical Methods . 316
10.2.6 Transmission 317
10.2.7 Two-Pass Methods 319
10.2.8 Surface Reflectance/Transmittance Data 324
10.3 Participating Media 325
10.3.1 Path Integrals 326
10.3.2 The Zonal Method 327

11 Applications and Research   331
11.1 Applications 331
11.1.1 Architectural Design 332
11.1.2 Lighting Design 334
11.1.3 Remote Sensing 338
11.1.4 Visual Shape Understanding 338
11.1.5 Infrared Signature Analysis 339
11.1.6 Fine Arts 340
11.2 Experimental Validation 340
11.3 Future Research Directions 343
11.3.1 Error Analysis 343
11.3.2 Perceptually Based Error Metrics 343
11.3.3 Physically Based Emission and BRDF Data 344
11.3.4 Meshing 345
11.3.5 Hierarchy 345
11.4 Conclusion 347

Bibliography   349

Index   373

Foreword

For the past 25 years, researchers in the field of computer graphics have continuously striven for the production of realistic images of nonexistent environments. To attain this goal and its ultimate potential for design and aesthetic evaluations, it is necessary to accurately represent the appearance of objects and scenes as they look to us. This requires the knowledge of how to simulate both the physical behavior of light and the perceptual behavior of the human visual system.

The accurate simulation of physical processes is crucial for realistic image synthesis. Ad hoc procedures, despite the fact that they can produce pretty pictures, will not suffice. The radiosity method, originally based on principles of thermodynamics, provides this physical basis and establishes the foundations for future rendering and display systems.

More explicitly, the creation of photorealistic images requires four basic components, a local model of light reflection, a means for simulating the propagation of energy throughout an environment, the appropriate strategies for sampling the scene, and procedurally accurate methods for displaying the results. The radiosity method discussed in this book describes each of these steps in great detail.

Historically, a major argument against the use of radiosity procedures has been the excessive computing demands. Today these constraints are rapidly being eliminated. During the last decade alone, processing power of workstations and personal computers has increased by three orders of magnitude. However skeptical one might be, all indications are that the trend of almost doubling computer power each year will continue until at least the end of this decade. Memory and storage costs have also dropped, by approximately four orders of magnitude since the early 1970s. Most recently, new advances in network technology have improved the possibility for image transmission rates by six orders of magnitude from what was available two decades ago. Further advances in the technology will occur due to parallelism and compression schemes.

Display technology is also accelerating at a remarkable pace. The dot spacing in printing technologies has been vastly reduced. High-resolution display monitors are now commonplace. The advent of high-definition television will push video technology further, both in terms of refresh rates and display resolution, and ultimately in cost due to the economics of mass production. For normal viewing conditions, resolutions will have surpassed the visual acuity of the human eye. Intensity ranges will be increased, and the speed of displays is already sufficiently fast to imply continuous motion.

With these dramatic advances in computing and display technologies, the arguments against the computational complexity of image synthesis techniques fall hollow. Processing and storage will essentially be free, and transmission will be sufficiently fast to deliver high quality picture information and allow the use of remote computing nodes. The computing obstacles of the past will have been overcome.

What is now needed is the ability to mimic the complex physical behavior of light distribution, from microscopic to macroscopic ranges. The radiosity method for image synthesis provides the theoretical underpinnings and algorithmic techniques toward these ends. With future experimental measurements and comparisons, these methods can be continually refined to improve their accuracy.

This book is the most thorough treatise on the radiosity method yet to be published in the field of computer graphics. The text includes detailed descriptions of all of the major components required to create a system for displaying modeled environments. From the explanations of the fundamental scientific bases to the state-of-the-art algorithms for implementation, the topics are covered in a clear and comprehensive way. The authors are to be congratulated for their in-depth treatment of the subject and for the presentation of a text that can significantly influence rendering systems of the future. The quest for photorealism will continue!

Donald P. Greenberg
Professor and Director
Program of Computer Graphics
Cornell University

Preface

Over the past decade, computer graphics has exploded out of university re-search laboratories onto television and cinema screens, and into medical imag-ing, scientific visualization and computer-aided design systems. A persistent goal through much of the research that has contributed to these developments has been to recreate, with the computer, strikingly realistic images of environ-ments that do not (and often could not) exist. This field of endeavor has come to be known as *realistic image synthesis*. Radiosity provides one important ap-proach to evaluating a physically-based illumination model, which is a key part of image synthesis.

The number of papers published on radiosity and related techniques increases yearly. Although the field is by no means mature, it is at a transition point, with early intuitive methods being replaced by approaches based on more rigorous attention to underlying physical processes and numerical methods. Thus, this is a natural time to summarize the research to date and to present it in a uniform format.

Our goal in writing this book is to survey the state-of-the-art in radiosity and related image synthesis research, to explain the underlying theory, and to provide a framework that organizes the broad and growing literature surround-ing this field. The book is intended for those interested in pursuing research in global illumination and image synthesis. It should also provide a useful theoret-ical background and insight into many practical issues, for those implementing radiosity or other global illumination systems.

After a short introductory chapter, the book continues with a chapter by Pat Hanrahan that carefully defines the terminology and concepts of radiometry and photometry, the fields concerned with the measurement of light. This discussion ends with the derivation of the rendering equation and its specialization in the form of the radiosity integral equation. The following three chapters discuss the use of finite element methods to solve this equation, by first formulating an approximately equivalent set of linear equations, then evaluating the coefficients of the linear system (the form factors), and finally solving the resulting matrix equation.

This is followed by three chapters in which the topic of domain subdivision (or meshing) is discussed. The discussion begins with an overview of mesh-ing issues, then takes an aside to discuss new hierarchical formulations of the radiosity problem including applications of wavelet methods, and closes with a chapter on the practical issues in generating a good mesh.

Chapter 9 explores the final step in the image synthesis process, that is, mapping the results of the numerical simulation to a display device. In this context, the peculiarities of the human visual system are discussed, ranging from the nonlinear response of the eye to luminance, to the tristimulus theory of color perception. Chapter 10 then expands the scope of the radiosity methods by lifting many of the restrictions assumed in the earlier discussion, such as diffuse surfaces and non-participating media. Finally, the book concludes with a chapter that explores a number of developing applications of the radiosity method, and takes a moment to look towards the future.

The presentation in this book assumes a familiarity with the basic concepts of computer graphics. There are a number of excellent computer graphics texts that more fully explore some of the techniques that are called on in the algorithms described here [84, 97, 173, 195, 258]. The discussion also assumes an understanding of undergraduate calculus and linear algebra. Where more advanced mathematical concepts are required, an effort is made to provide the reader with enough background information to understand and appreciate the material.

Acknowledgments

We thank the many colleagues who have directly and indirectly contributed to the making of this book.

Without the dedication and persistent efforts of Prof. Donald P. Greenberg of Cornell University, neither author would be in a position today to write this text. His contributions to the development of the field of image synthesis are well known. We thank him personally for inviting us into Cornell's Program of Computer Graphics where both authors were introduced to radiosity and image synthesis, and for contributing the Foreword to this book.

Pat Hanrahan, beyond contributing a chapter to the book, is also largely responsible for providing the first author with the stimulating environment at Princeton University in which to work.

We would like to especially acknowledge the great efforts that went into reviewing chapters of this book by Ken Chiu, Robert Cross, Brian Curless, Stuart Feldman, Alain Fournier, John Fujii, Steven Gortler, Paul Lalonde, Marc Levoy, Robert Lewis, Dani Lischinski, Earlin Lutz, Holly Rushmeier, David Salesin, Peter Shirley, and Filippo Tampieri.

We thank Jutta Joesch for many hours of editing this text and for her enormous help in gaining a better understanding of how to explain many of the more difficult concepts presented. We would also like to thank Steven Gortler and Peter Schröder for many discussions leading to much of the material on wavelets in Chapter 7; Holly Rushmeier for numerous discussions that contributed materially to the content of this book; John Abel, Maged Tawfik, Paul Heckbert, Mark Reichert, Seth Teller, David Munson, and Stuart Feldman for valuable discussions; John Fujii for first pointing out the topological shadow test discussed in Chapter 8, and for many hours of enjoyable discussions of aesthetic and philosophical questions; Tamar Cohen for creating models used in some of the images; Emil Ghinger for the black and white photography; Kevin Stokker for software used to compute the error images in Chapter 6; Kim Wagner for help in obtaining the cover image; Eric Haines for providing the initial version of the Bibliography; Brian Rosen for help in compiling the Bibliography.

The authors would like to acknowledge some of the many additional collaborators through the past decade who have contributed to this work. These include Daniel Baum, Philip Brock, Rikk Carey, Shenchang Chen, Lisa Desjarlais, Stuart Feldman, Cindy Goral, Kevin Koestner, David Immel, Peter Kochevar, Alan Polinsky, David Salmon, Kenneth Torrance, Ben Trumbore, and many others at Cornell University; François Sillion and Claude Puech at the Ecôle Normale Supérieure, James Painter, John Kawai, and Gershon Elber at the University of Utah, Philipp Slusallek at Universität Erlangen, and many current colleagues at Princeton University.

We would like to thank Eric Haines and Kells Elmquist at 3D/EYE, Inc. for many years of collaboration in the pursuit of realistic image synthesis, Samir Hanna for providing the second author time to write this all down, and the many other people at 3D/EYE, Inc. and Hewlett-Packard who have jointly participated in the development of radiosity and rendering software.

Images were contributed by Daniel Baum, A. T. Campbell III, Julie O'Brien Dorsey, Shenchang Chen, Stuart Feldman, Monika Fleischmann, Cindy Goral, Eric Haines, Pat Hanrahan, Paul Heckbert, Keith Johnson, Dani Lischinski, Gary Meyer, David Munson, Mark Reichert, Holly Rushmeier, Brian Smits, David Salesin, Peter Shirley, François Sillion, Filippo Tampieri, Hewlett Packard, and Zumtobel Licht GmbH.

To Jenifer Niles, our editor at Academic Press, thank you for guiding us successfully through the process of creating an actual book.

Finally, the contribution of our wives, Jutta M. Joesch and Diane L. Wallace cannot be understated. Without their patience and support we could not have finished this.

Michael F. Cohen   John R. Wallace
Department of Computer Science   3D/EYE, Inc.
Princeton University   Ithaca, NY

"But something in the air sets me to thinking, there might be things not too far off, that I might tell a few stories about, someday myself. Though exactly how I'll do it's beyond me. It wouldn't be any too simple, just trying to describe this scene right here, how pretty a figure that bird cuts, sailing across the red horizon. And I took these sharp eyes to be a blessing. When they might, just as easily, turn out to be a curse.

Oh well, enough of these idle musings. They ain't gonna feed me. I'd better get down to business."

Alan Cohen
from *The Saga of Harry the Snake*

Chapter 1

Introduction

In the pursuit of lifelike images, artists have long attempted to understand the behavior of light and the characteristics of perception. Techniques that may appear obvious, like perspective, were developed through painstaking study and experimentation. The paintings of Vermeer and Rembrandt represent an understanding of illumination, color, and perception that evolved through centuries of such experience. More recently, the Impressionists made a particular study of the subtleties of light and shading; Renoir, for example, pointed out that "Shadows are not black; no shadow is black. It always has color."[1]

The connection between light and visual representation received its most concrete realization with the invention of photography in the nineteenth century. Because a photograph is the direct consequence of the physical propagation of light, the camera is an invaluable recorder of things that exist. The creation of realistic images of things that do not exist, or that are not normally perceivable as images, such as scientific data, has remained until recently the domain of the artist and illustrator.

1.1 Realistic Image Synthesis

Over the last few centuries physicists have developed mathematical models of the processes by which light interacts with surfaces and propagates through an environment. With the advent of the computer it has become practical to evaluate such models on a large enough scale to simulate complex phenomena. Using a computer, a model of light reflection and propagation can be evaluated for a scene whose geometry and material properties have been specified numerically. In effect, a photograph can be taken of a scene that does not exist in reality.

The ability to create images of nonexistent environments is important to applications ranging from industrial or architectural design to advertising and entertainment. Phenomena not accessible to normal visual experience can also be *vi-*

---

[1]The immediate source of this quotation, which comes close to reducing radiosity to a sentence, is Parker *et al.* [179], who in turn quote from [193].

1

sualized by applying the illumination model to other forms of three-dimensional data. For example, data from magnetic resonance imaging can be rendered to provide three-dimensional images of the inside of the body.

The creation of images by evaluating a model of light propagation is called *image synthesis* and has been studied extensively in the field of computer graphics since the 1970s. The goal of image synthesis is often stated as *photorealism*. However, although photography produces "realistic" images, it is a physical process subject to the constraints of camera optics and the chemical nature of film. Should image synthesis really attempt to simulate photography, or should it aim higher?

1.1.1 Goals

A clear understanding of the goal of image synthesis becomes increasingly important as algorithms and computational methods grow more sophisticated. In addition to the evaluation of competing approaches, more intelligent algorithms need a basis for deciding how to allocate computational effort and when to end the computation, which requires knowing when the goal has been achieved.

Perhaps the most far reaching goal for image synthesis is the creation a visual experience *identical* to that which would be experienced in viewing the real environment. The diagram in Figure 1.1 shows a simple model of the image synthesis process that provides a basis for discussing the issues involved in reaching this goal.

In the real world, as shown in the top half of the diagram, light propagates through the scene and eventually enters the eye with a particular directional and wavelength distribution. The eye and the brain process this information at increasingly higher levels of abstraction, leading ultimately to what is called the visual experience.

The bottom half of the diagram shows the modifications to the process required for image synthesis. Instead of the physical propagation of light, a mathematical model is evaluated to produce the required distribution of light energy. These results are then passed to a display device that physically realizes the computed light distribution and sends it to the eye. Image synthesis thus appears to require simply the exact reproduction of the distribution of light energy entering the eye. Given this, the process of experiencing the image will take care of itself.

1.1.2 Limitations

There are two problems with this apparently simple approach. First, the computation in step one is arbitrarily expensive. For all practical purposes, there is no end to the detail or accuracy with which reality might be simulated. How

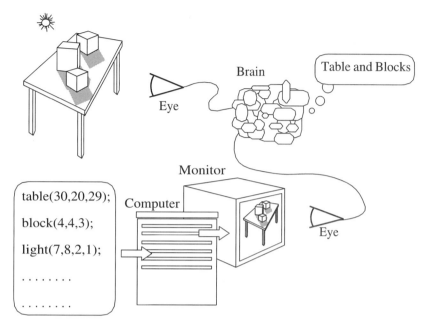

Figure 1.1: *The process of visual experience. The top half of the figure diagrams real-world experience; the bottom half displays visual experience based on computer simulation.*

should limited computational resources be distributed? When is the simulation done?

The second problem is with the display device. Even assuming that the first step is performed perfectly, there is no existing device that can correctly perform the second step! We can only imagine what such a device might be like – perhaps a descendant of current virtual-reality goggles, with extremely high spatial and color resolution, a field of view encompassing the entire range of our peripheral vision, and the ability to reproduce luminances ranging from starlight to the glare of snow on a sunny day.

In today's reality, the device will likely consist of a cathode ray tube (CRT), which generates a two-dimensional map of discrete picture elements with a spatial resolution of 1280 by 1024 pixels (often much less) and a color resolution of 256 values for each of three color channels. The range, or *gamut*, of reproducible colors will depend on the particular phosphors used in the CRT. Viewing conditions, such as the ambient light level in the room containing the CRT, will partially determine the eye's response to the light leaving the CRT. In most cases a single image will be presented to both eyes.

In part because of the limitations of available devices, the goal of image synthesis is, in practice, the reproduction of an *image* rather than of a direct visual experience. This goal maps more directly to the currently available 2D device (the CRT). The goal is similar but not identical to photorealism in that it does not necessarily include reproducing all the characteristics of photography.

The limitations of the display device provide one set of guidelines for the computation. For example, there is no point in computing a simulation with a spatial or color resolution greater than that reproducible by the device. An understanding of the final perceptual steps of the process is also important to guiding the development of image synthesis algorithms. Based on an understanding of perception one can focus computational resources on aspects of the simulation that contribute most to the final visual experience. For example, the eye is particularly sensitive to contrast in luminance while being relatively insensitive to absolute luminance levels.

The subject of this book is primarily the first part of the image synthesis process, the computation of the light distribution at an image plane. This requires developing a mathematical model of light propagation. The model may contain certain simplifying assumptions; the *radiosity method*, for example, is initially based on the assumption that all surfaces reflect light diffusely. Analytical or numerical methods can then be developed to evaluate the mathematical model. Algorithms that implement these solution methods must be written and, finally, the results must be displayed as an image. These steps will form the basic content of this book.

The evaluation of an illumination model cannot proceed until one has a mathematical description of the environment to be rendered. The specification of the scene geometry and material properties is itself a topic of active research and presents many difficulties. This problem will not be addressed in this book.

1.2   A Short Historical Perspective

The radiosity method emerged relatively recently in the development of image synthesis. Radiosity methods represent the development of several trends: the development of physically based shading models, the use of more rigorous computational methods, and the continuing tension between interactivity and realism in computer graphics. The historical development of image synthesis and radiosity will be discussed in this section.

CRTs were used as computer displays as early as the late 1940s. Such devices were capable of drawing dots and lines (vectors) on the CRT according to coordinates provided by the computer. Ivan Sutherland's *Sketchpad* program [228], an interactive 2D drawing application, provided an important demonstration of the potential of interactive computer graphics. Subsequent years saw many developments in vector graphics, including methods for representing and manipulating free-form curved surfaces for applications such as mechanical and industrial design.

1.2.1 Raster Graphics

By the late 1960s, the price of computer memory decreased to the point where *raster* graphics became practical. In raster graphics the computer specifies colors for an array of picture elements, or *pixels*, instead of drawing vectors, thus allowing the more realistic portrayal of surfaces. The seminal work of Bouknight [37], Gouraud [103], and Phong [182] explored the use of shading models to characterize surface shape visually. The models were *ad hoc*, in that they were not derived from physical models of light reflection. The models were also *local*, in that they computed shading based only on the relative positions of the light, the surface, and the eye. Illumination due to light reflected from other surfaces was ignored, as were other *global* phenomena such as the shadowing of one surface by another. In color plate 1, which contains six renderings of a simple environment computed using various algorithms, color plate 1a is rendered using a simple local shading model.

Another preoccupation of early researchers was the problem of determining the visible surfaces in an image; a wide variety of algorithms were developed for this purpose. Although visibility was originally posed as the problem of determining what is seen by the eye, visible surface algorithms turn out to be important to shading in general (e.g., in determining the surfaces that are visible to a light source).

Much of this early work was directed towards improving the information conveyed by *interactive* graphics. Thus, the primary objective was efficiency of computation as opposed to accurate physical simulation. As stated by Phong [182]:

> "We do not expect to be able to display the object exactly as it would appear in reality, with texture, overcast shadows, etc. We hope only to display an image that approximates the real object closely enough to provide a certain degree of realism."

The success of these early local illumination models and visibility algorithms is attested to by the presence of their direct descendants in the microcode and hardware of current graphics workstations. Such workstations are currently capable of displaying on the order of one million shaded polygons per second.

In spite of the focus on interactive graphics, the ultimate attraction of realism was not lost on early researchers. Appel [8] recognized that

" . . . many difficult problems need to be solved such as the effect
of illumination by direct and diffuse lighting, atmospheric diffusion,
back reflection, the effect of surface texture, tonal specification and
transparency of surfaces . . . "

Early steps toward solving these problems were taken with the development of techniques like texture mapping and bump mapping [31, 32, 44], which allowed the realistic representation of more complex surface properties. In addition, visible surface algorithms were applied to the problem of determining shadows [13, 36, 67].

1.2.2   Global Illumination Models

As Appel recognized, greater realism requires *global* illumination models, which account for the interreflection of light between surfaces. It was not until 1980 that the first global illumination algorithm was introduced by Whitted [265]. Whitted's innovation was the recursive application of *ray tracing* to evaluate a simple global illumination model accounting for mirror reflection, refraction, and shadows. The resulting spectacular images inspired growing interest in photorealism.

Whitted recognized that the evaluation of a global illumination model requires determining the surfaces visible in various directions from the point to be shaded. The heart of the ray tracing algorithm is thus the point visibility test provided by ray casting. Much of the subsequent innovation in ray tracing has consisted of faster algorithms for performing this visibility test.

The basic ray tracing strategy was extended to glossy reflection and soft shadows using stochastic ray tracing [63, 64] and cone tracing [7]. Color plate 1b was rendered using stochastic ray tracing to compute illumination from the area light source in the ceiling and glossy reflection on the floor. Although ray traced images continued to improve, the accuracy of the simulations was difficult to quantify since the reflection and illumination models were not based on physical principles and quantities. Also, ray tracing did not provide a practical strategy for computing diffuse interreflection.

More accurate physically based local reflection models were developed by Blinn [30] and Cook and Torrance [65], using results from the fields of radiative heat transfer and illumination engineering. This work contributed to a clearer understanding of the appropriate physical quantities for illumination, as well as an increased awareness of the results available in the engineering and the physical sciences.

1.2.3   Early Radiosity Methods

In 1984, researchers at Fukuyama and Hiroshima Universities in Japan and at the Program of Computer Graphics at Cornell University in the United States began to apply radiosity methods from the field of radiative heat transfer to image synthesis. These methods were first developed in the 1950s for computing radiant interchange between surfaces [216], for engineering applications ranging from radiator and boiler design to the analysis of radiative transfer between panels on spacecraft.

In image synthesis, radiosity [2] methods are applicable to solving for the interreflection of light between ideal (Lambertian) diffuse surfaces. Initial algorithms [100] were restricted to environments in which all surfaces could see each other. In following years, radiosity algorithms allowing occlusion were developed [60, 175], and efficiency was improved through the use of a hierarchical subdivision of the environment [61, 116].

Radiosity is a departure for image synthesis for several reasons. As opposed to the earlier empirical techniques, radiosity begins with an energy balance equation, which is then approximated and solved by numerical means. In contrast to ray tracing, which evaluates the illumination equation for directions and locations determined by the view and the pixels of the image, radiosity solves the illumination equation at locations distributed over the surfaces of the environment. This specification of the unknowns is *independent of the viewer position*, and thus radiosity methods are often called *view-independent* techniques. Of course, a final image is dependent on the viewer position and the screen resolution, but most of the computational effort is complete before the selection of viewing parameters. In this way, efficient interactive *walkthroughs* of simulated environments can be performed following the radiosity preprocess. Color plate 14 shows an early radiosity solution by Nishita and Nakamae. The effect of including indirect illumination by diffusely interreflected light is apparent when this image is compared to the image in color plate 11, in which only direct illumination is accounted for.

While the original radiosity method is based on the assumption of Lambertian diffuse reflection, subsequent work has included extensions of the radiosity approach to glossy and ideal (mirror) reflection [132, 217, 218, 246]. Rushmeier [200] has also extended the basic radiosity formulation to include participating media (e.g., smoke and haze). Color plates 1c–1e were rendered using variations of the radiosity method. Color plate 1c is the result of the original radiosity method for diffuse environments. Note that indirect illumination adds color to

---

[2]The term *radiosity* refers to a measure of radiant energy, in particular, the energy leaving a surface per unit area per unit time. Over time, *radiosity* has also come to mean a set of computational techniques for computing global illumination.

the shadows and the shadowed faces of the boxes. Color plate 1d is the result of extensions that provide glossy reflection on the floor, while Color plate 1e includes the effect of smoke within the environment.

More recent work has directly addressed the computational complexity of radiosity algorithms. In 1988, Cohen *et al.* [59] introduced a *progressive refinement* approach that allows fast approximate solutions to be displayed. In 1991, Hanrahan *et al.* [116] formulated a complete hierarchical radiosity system leading to a linear time algorithm. A great deal of work has also been devoted to the critical step of discretizing or *meshing* the surfaces [21, 43, 154, 230]. An important recent trend has been the incorporation of quantitative error estimates into the solution process. Examples include estimates of integration error [19] and the use of geometric- and energy-based error metrics in the hierarchical algorithm of Hanrahan *et al.* [116].

1.2.4   The Rendering Equation

Kajiya [135] unified the discussion of global illumination algorithms in 1986 with the general *rendering equation*. Kajiya applied Monte Carlo integration methods to solving the rendering equation and proposed a number of techniques for accelerating the convergence of the solution. Color plate 1f was rendered using a Monte Carlo solution to the rendering equation.

1.3   Radiosity and Finite Element Methods

Radiosity can be understood as a particular approach to solving the rendering equation under the assumption of Lambertian diffuse reflection. Heckbert and Winget [125] have shown that radiosity is essentially a finite element method.

Like Monte Carlo techniques, the finite element method is a broadly applicable approach to solving difficult integral equations, such as the rendering equation. The basic approach is to approximate an unknown function by subdividing the domain of the function into smaller pieces or *elements*, across which the function can be approximated using relatively simple functions like polynomials. The unknown function is thus projected into a *finite function space*, in which the approximated function is fully characterized by a finite number of unknowns. The resulting system can then be solved numerically.

The ideas underlying the finite element method were first discussed as early as the 1940s [66], although the term *finite element* did not become popular until the 1960s [57]. The development of the finite element method closely paralleled related work in approximating functions using piecewise polynomials or *splines* [205]. It was also recognized in the 1950s that finite element methods were a form of the more general Ritz variational methods.

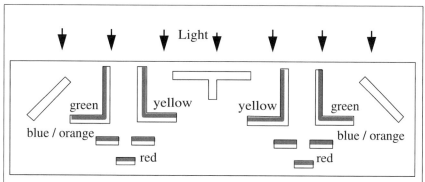

All visible surfaces, white.

Eye

A powerful demonstration, introduced by Goral [105], of the differences between radiosity methods and traditional ray tracing is provided by renderings of a sculpture, "Construction in Wood, A Daylight Experiment," by John Ferren (color plate 2). The sculpture, diagramed above, consists of a series of vertical boards painted white on the faces visible to the viewer. The back faces of the boards are painted bright colors. The sculpture is illuminated by light entering a window behind the sculpture, so light reaching the viewer first reflects off the colored surfaces, then off the white surfaces before entering the eye. As a result, the colors from the back of the boards "bleed" onto the white surfaces. Color plates 2–4 show a photograph of the sculpture and ray tracing and radiosity renderings of the sculpture. The sculpture is solid white in the ray traced image since illumination due to diffuse interreflection is ignored. The radiosity method, however, accounts for the diffuse interreflections and reproduces the color bleeding.

It was not until computers became more routinely available in the 1960s and 1970s that these methods became a common technique for engineering analysis. Since then, there has been considerable research resulting in many working finite element codes and in a better theoretical understanding of convergence and other mathematical properties of such methods. In addition, a number of excellent texts have also been written [23, 70, 273].

As Heckbert and Winget [125] point out, the heat transfer formulations upon which radiosity is based can be viewed as simple finite element methods.

Heckbert and Winget emphasize the need for quantitative error metrics and show that an explicit finite element approach considerably clarifies the understanding of the accuracy of the approximation. Radiosity will be presented in this book as a finite element method. However, this book cannot begin to do justice to the broad field of finite element methods in general, and the reader is referred to the above-mentioned texts for a wider theoretical background, as well as for a wealth of practical information.

1.4   The Radiosity Method and This Book

This book is structured as follows (see Figure 1.2 for a diagram of the book's structure). The first step is to derive a mathematical model of global illumination. This derivation is undertaken in Chapter 2, working from basic transport theory to the rendering equation, and finally making the assumptions that lead to the radiosity equation.

In Chapter 3, the basic principles of finite element approximation are used to cast the radiosity equation into a discrete form that is amenable to numerical solution. In particular, the original radiosity function is approximated by a sum of weighted *basis functions*. These basis functions are in turn defined by a *mesh* or discretization of the surfaces in the environment.

The finite element formulation of the radiosity integral equation produces a system of linear equations that must be solved for the weights of the basis functions. The coefficients of this linear system are formed by integrals over portions of the surfaces in the environment. These integrals can be solved using both analytic and numeric methods. Chapter 4 describes a variety of algorithms that have been developed for this purpose.

Techniques for solving the matrix equation once it has been formulated are described in Chapter 5. We will examine a number of linear equation solvers and discuss their applicability to the system of equations resulting from the radiosity problem.

Chapters 6, 7 and 8 cover the general problem of subdividing the surfaces of the model into the elements upon which the finite element approximation is based. The accuracy and the efficiency of the solution are strongly dependent on this subdivision. Basic subdivision strategies are described in Chapter 6. The use of hierarchical methods that incorporate subdivision into the solution process itself and accelerate the matrix solution is described in Chapter 7. Chapter 8 covers the basic mechanics of meshing.

Once a solution has been obtained, the final step is to produce an image, which is discussed in Chapter 9. This is less straightforward than it might seem, due to the limitations of display devices and the demands of visual perception.

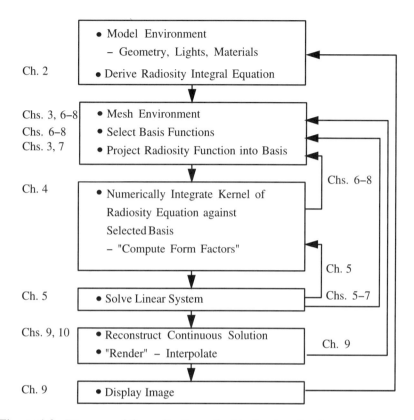

Figure 1.2: *Diagram of the radiosity method indicating the chapters where concepts are discussed.*

In Chapter 10 techniques for extending the basic radiosity method are described. These provide methods to handle more general global illumination models, including general light sources, glossy and mirror reflection, and participating media. With these more general approaches, the distinction between ray tracing and radiosity will become less clear.

Chapter 11 concludes this book with a discussion of applications that are already taking advantage of this technology. We also discuss current trends in the development of radiosity methods.

Another way to look at the organization of the book is to relate it to the flow of information in a generic radiosity algorithm. This view is provided by the diagram in Figure 1.2.

Chapter 2

Rendering Concepts

by Pat Hanrahan

2.1 Motivation

The progress in rendering in the last few years has been driven by a deeper and better understanding of the physics of materials and lighting. Physically based or realistic rendering can be viewed as the problem of simulating the propagation of light in an environment. In this view of rendering, there are sources that emit light energy into the environment; there are materials that scatter, reflect, refract, and absorb light; and there are cameras or retinas that record the quantity of light in different places. Given a specification of a scene consisting of the positions of objects, lights and the camera, as well as the shapes, material, and optical properties of objects, a rendering algorithm computes the distribution of light energy at various points in the simulated environment.

This model of rendering naturally leads to some questions, the answers to which form the subjects of this chapter.

1. What is light and how is it characterized and measured?

2. How is the spatial distribution of light energy described mathematically?

3. How does one characterize the reflection of light from a surface?

4. How does one formulate the conditions for the equilibrium flow of light in an environment?

In this chapter these questions are answered from both a physical and a mathematical point of view. Subsequent chapters will address specific representations, data structures, and algorithms for performing the required calculations by computer.

13

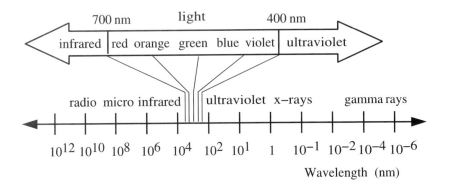

Figure 2.1: *Electromagnetic spectrum.*

2.2 Basic Optics

Light is a form of electromagnetic radiation, a sinusoidal wave formed by coupled electric and magnetic fields. The electric and magnetic fields are perpendicular to each other and to the direction of propagation. The frequency of the oscillation determines the wavelength. Electromagnetic radiation can exist at any wavelength. From long to short, there are radio waves, microwaves, infrared, light, ultraviolet, x-rays, and gamma rays (see Figure 2.1).

A pure source of light, such as that produced by a laser, consists of light at a single frequency. In the natural world, however, light almost always exists as a mixture of different wavelengths. Laser light is also *coherent*, that is, the source is tuned so that the wave stays in phase as it propagates. Natural light, in contrast, is *incoherent*.

Electromagnetic radiation can also be *polarized*. This refers to the preferential orientation of the electric and magnetic field vectors relative to the direction of propagation. Just as incoherent light consists of many waves that are summed with random phase, unpolarized light consists of many waves that are summed with random orientation. The polarization of the incident radiation is an important parameter affecting the reflection of light from a surface, but the discussion will be simplified by ignoring polarization.

The fact that light is just one form of electromagnetic radiation is of great benefit for computer graphics in that it points to theory and algorithms from many other disciplines, in particular, optics, but also more applied disciplines such as radar engineering and radiative heat transfer. The study of optics is typically divided into three subareas: geometrical or ray optics, physical or wave optics, and quantum or photon optics. Geometrical optics is most relevant to computer graphics since it focuses on calculating macroscopic properties of light as it propagates through environments. Geometrical optics is useful to understand shadows, basic optical laws such as the laws of reflection and refraction, and the design of classical optical systems such as binoculars and eyeglasses. However, geometrical optics is not a complete theory of light. Physical or wave optics is necessary to understand the interaction of light with objects that have sizes comparable to the wavelength of the light. Physical optics allows us to understand the physics behind interference, dispersion, and technologies such as holograms. Finally, to explain in full detail the interaction of light with atoms and molecules quantum mechanics must be used. In the quantum mechanical model light is assumed to consist of particles, or photons. For the purposes of this book, geometrical optics will provide a full-enough view of the phenomena simulated with the radiosity methods.

2.3 Radiometry and Photometry

Radiometry is the science of the physical measurement of electromagnetic energy. Since all forms of energy in principle can be interconverted, a radiometric measurement is expressed in the SI units for energy or power, *joules* and *watts*, respectively. The amount of light at each wavelength can be measured with a spectroradiometer, and the resulting plot of the measurements is the spectrum of the source.

Photometry, on the other hand, is the psychophysical measurement of the visual sensation produced by the electromagnetic spectrum. Our eyes are only sensitive to the electromagnetic spectrum between the ultraviolet (380 nm) and the infrared (770 nm). The most prominent difference between two sources of light with different mixtures of wavelengths is that they appear to have different colors. However, an equally important feature is that different mixtures of light also can have different luminosities, or brightnesses.

Pierre Bouguer established the field of photometry in 1760 by asking a human observer to compare different light sources [35]. By comparing an unknown source with a standard source of known brightness—a candle at the time—the relative brightness of the two sources could be assessed. Bouguer's experiment was quite ingenious. He realized that *a human observer could not provide an accurate quantitative description of how much brighter one source was than another, but could reliably tell whether two sources were equally bright.*[1] Bouguer was also aware of the inverse square law. Just as Kepler and Newton had used it to describe the gravitational force from a point mass source, Bouguer reasoned that it also applied to a point light source. The experiment consisted of the

---

[1]This fact will be used in Chapter 9 when algorithms to select pixel values for display are examined.

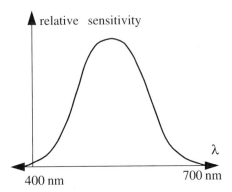

Figure 2.2: *Spectral luminous relative efficiency curve.*

observer moving the standard source until the brightnesses of the two sources were equal. By recording the relative distances of the two light sources from the eye, the relative brightnesses can be determined with the inverse square law.

Bouguer founded the field of photometry well before the mechanisms of human vision were understood. It is now known that different spectra have different brightnesses because the pigments in our photoreceptors have different sensitivities or responses toward different wavelengths. A plot of the relative sensitivity of the eye across the visible spectrum is shown in Figure 2.2; this curve is called the *spectral luminous relative efficiency curve*. The observer's response, R, to a spectrum is then the sum, or integral, of the response to each spectral band. This in turn is equal to the amount of energy at that wavelength, λ, times its relative luminosity.

$$R = \int_{380nm}^{770} V(\lambda)\, S(\lambda)\, d\lambda \qquad (2.1)$$

where V is the relative efficiency and S is the spectral energy. Because there is wide variation between people's responses to different light sources, V has been standardized.

Radiometry is more fundamental than photometry, in that photometric quantities may be computed from spectroradiometric measurements. For this reason, it is best to use radiometric quantities for computer graphics and image synthesis. However, photometry preceded radiometry by over a hundred years, so much of radiometry is merely a modern interpretation of ideas from photometry.

As mentioned, the radiometric units for power and energy are the watt and joule, respectively. The photometric unit for luminous power is the *lumen*, and the photometric unit for luminous energy is the *talbot*. Our eye is most sensitive to yellow-green light with a wavelength of approximately 555 nm that has a luminosity of 684 lumens per watt. Light of any other wavelength, and therefore any mixture of light, will yield fewer lumens per watt. The number of lumens per watt is a rough measure of the effective brightness of a light source. For example, the garden-variety 40-Watt incandescent light bulb is rated at only 490 lumens — roughly 12 lumens per watt. Of course, the wattage in this case is not the energy of the light produced, but rather the electrical energy consumed by the light bulb. It is not possible to convert electrical energy to radiant energy with 100% efficiency so some energy is lost to heat.

When we talk about light, power and energy usually may be used interchangeably, because the speed of light is so fast that it immediately attains equilibrium. Imagine turning on a light switch. The environment immediately switches from a steady state involving no light to a state in which it is bathed in light. There are situations, however, where energy must be used instead of power. For example, the response of a piece of film is proportional to the total energy received. The integral over time of power is called the *exposure*. The concept of exposure is familiar to anyone who has stayed in the sun too long and gotten a sunburn.

An important principle that must be obeyed by any physical system is the conservation of energy. This applies at two levels—a macro or global level, and a micro or local level.

- At the global level, the total power put into the system by the light sources must equal the power being absorbed by the surfaces. In this situation energy is being conserved. However, electrical energy is continuing to flow into the system to power the lights, and heat energy is flowing out of the system because the surfaces are heated.

- At the local level, the energy flowing into a region of space or onto a surface element must equal the energy flowing out. Accounting for all changes in the flow of light locally requires that energy is conserved. Thus, the amount of absorbed, reflected, and transmitted light must never be greater than the amount of incident light. The distribution of light can also become more concentrated or focused as it propagates. This leads to the next topic which is how to characterize the flow of light.

2.4 The Light Field

2.4.1 Transport Theory

The propagation of light in an environment is built around a core of basic ideas concerning the geometry of flows. In physics the study of how "stuff" flows

Figure 2.3: *Particles in a differential volume.*

is termed *transport theory*. The "stuff" can be mass, charge, energy, or light. Flow quantities are differential quantities that can be difficult to appreciate and manipulate comfortably. In this section all the important physical quantities associated with the flow of light in the environment will be introduced along with their application to computer graphics.

The easiest way to learn transport quantities is to think in terms of particles (think of photons). Particles are easy to visualize, easy to count, and therefore easy to track as they flow around the environment. The particle density $p(\mathbf{x})$ is the number of particles per unit volume at the point $\mathbf{x}$ (see Figure 2.3). Then the total number of particles, $P(\mathbf{x})$, in a small differential volume dV is

$$P(\mathbf{x}) = p(\mathbf{x})\, dV \tag{2.2}$$

Note that the particle density is an intrinsic or differential quantity, whereas the total number of particles is an absolute or extrinsic quantity.

Now imagine a stream of particles all moving with the same velocity vector $\vec{v}$; that is, if they are photons, not only are they all moving at the speed of light, but they are all moving in the same direction. We wish to count the total number of particles flowing across a small differential surface element dA in a slice of time dt. The surface element is purely fictitious and introduced for convenience and may or may not correspond to a real physical surface. In time dt each particle moves a distance $\vec{v}dt$. How many particles cross dA? This can be computed using the following observation: consider the tube formed by sweeping dA a distance $v\, dt$ in the direction $-\vec{v}$. All particles that cross dA between t and $t + dt$ must have initially been inside this tube at time t. If they were outside this tube, they would not be moving fast enough to make it to the surface element dA in the allotted time. This implies that one can compute the number of particles crossing the surface element by multiplying the particle volume density times the volume of the tube. The volume of the tube is just equal to its base (dA) times its height, which is equal to $v \cos\theta\, dt$. Therefore, as depicted in Figure 2.4, the total number of particles crossing the surface is

$$\begin{aligned} P(\mathbf{x}) &= p(\mathbf{x})\, dV \\ &= p(\mathbf{x})(v\, dt \cos\theta)\, dA \end{aligned} \tag{2.3}$$

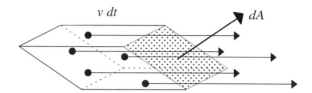

Figure 2.4: *Total particles crossing a surface.*

Note that the number of particles flowing through a surface element depends on both the area of the surface element and its orientation relative to the flow. Observe that the maximum flow through a surface of a fixed size occurs when the surface is oriented perpendicular to the direction of flow. Conversely, no particles flow across a surface when it is oriented parallel to the flow. More specifically, the above formula says that the flow across a surface depends on the cosine of the angle of incidence between the surface normal and the direction of the flow. This fact follows strictly from the geometry of the situation and does not depend on what is flowing.

The number of particles flowing is proportional both to the differential area of the surface element and to the interval of time used to tally the particle count. If either the area or the time interval is zero, the number of particles flowing is also zero and not of much interest. However, we can divide through by the time interval dt and the surface area dA and take the limit as these quantities go to zero. This quantity is called the *flux*.

More generally all the particles through a point will not be flowing with the same speed and in the same direction. Fortunately, the above calculation is fairly easy to generalize to account for a distribution of particles with different velocities moving in different directions. The particle density is now a function of two independent variables, position $\mathbf{x}$ and direction $\vec{\omega}$. Then, just as before, the number of particles flowing across a differential surface element in the direction $\vec{\omega}$ equals

$$P(\mathbf{x}, \vec{\omega}) = p(\mathbf{x}, \vec{\omega}) \cos\theta \, d\omega \, dA \qquad (2.4)$$

Here the notation $d\omega$ is introduced for the differential solid angle. The direction of this vector is in the direction of the flow, and its length is equal to the small differential solid angle of directions about $\vec{\omega}$. For those unfamiliar with solid angles and differential solid angles, please refer to the box.

2.4.2 Radiance and Luminance

The above theory can be immediately applied to light transport by considering light as photons. However, rendering systems almost never need consider (or at

---

Angles and Solid Angles

A direction is indicated by the vector $\vec{\omega}$. Since this is a unit vector, it can be represented by a point on the unit sphere. Positions on a sphere in turn can be represented by two angles: the number of degrees from the North Pole or zenith, θ, and the number of degrees about the equator or azimuth, ϕ. Directions $\vec{\omega}$ and spherical coordinates (θ, ϕ) can be used interchangeably.

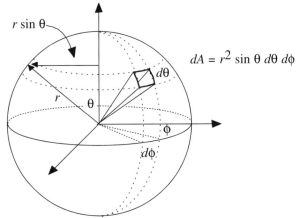

A big advantage of thinking of directions as points on a sphere comes when considering differential distributions of directions. A differential distribution of directions can be represented by a small region on the unit sphere.

---

least have not considered up to this point) the quantum nature of light. Instead, when discussing light transport, the stuff that flows, or flux, is the radiant energy per unit time, or radiant power Φ, rather than the number of particles. The radiant energy per unit volume is simply the photon volume density times the energy of a single photon $h\,c/\lambda$, where h is Planck's constant and c is the speed of light. The radiometric term for this quantity is *radiance*.

$$L(\mathbf{x}, \vec{\omega}) = \int p(\mathbf{x}, \vec{\omega}, \lambda) \frac{hc}{\lambda} \, d\lambda \qquad (2.6)$$

Radiance is arguably the most important quantity in image synthesis. Defined precisely, radiance is power per unit projected area perpendicular to the ray per unit solid angle in the direction of the ray (see Figure 2.5). The definition in equation 2.6 is that proposed by Nicodemus [174], who was one of the first authors to recognize its fundamental nature.

The radiance distribution completely characterizes the distribution of light

The area of a small differential surface element on a sphere of radius r is

$$dA = (r\,d\theta)\,(r\sin\theta\,d\phi) = r^2\sin\theta\,d\theta\,d\phi$$

Here $r\,d\theta$ is the length of the longitudinal arc generated as θ goes to $\theta + d\theta$. Similarly $r\sin\theta d\phi$ is the length of the latitudinal arc generated as ϕ goes to $\phi + d\phi$. The product of these two lengths is the differential area of that patch on the sphere.

This derivation uses the definition of angle in radians: the angle subtended by a circular arc of length l is equal to l/r. The circle itself subtends an angle of 2π radians because the circumference of the circle is $2\pi r$. By using a similar idea we can define a solid angle. The solid angle subtended by a spherical area a is equal to a/r^2. This quantity is the measure of the angle in *steradians* (radians squared), denoted sr. A sphere has a total area of $4\pi r^2$, so there are 4π steradians in a sphere.

A *differential solid angle*, indicated as $d\omega$, is then

$$d\omega = \frac{dA}{r^2} = \sin\theta\,d\theta\,d\phi \tag{2.5}$$

It is very convenient to think of the differential solid angle as a vector, $d\vec{\omega}$. The direction of $d\vec{\omega}$ is in the direction of the point on the sphere, and the length of $d\vec{\omega}$ is equal to the size of the differential solid angle in that direction.

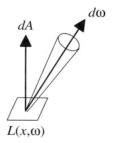

Figure 2.5: *The radiance is the power per unit projected area perpendicular to the ray per unit solid angle in the direction of the ray.*

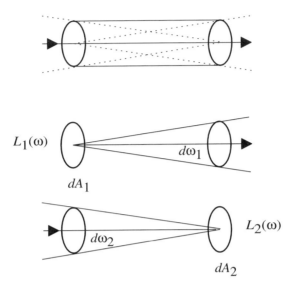

Figure 2.6: *Equality of flux leaving the first surface and flux arriving on the second surface.*

in a scene. Note that it is a function of five independent variables, three that specify position and two that specify direction. All other radiometric quantities can be computed from it. For example, the differential flux in a small beam with cross-sectional area dA and differential solid angle $d\omega$ is

$$d\Phi = L(\mathbf{x}, \vec{\omega}) \cos \theta \, d\omega \, dA \tag{2.7}$$

This follows immediately from the earlier discussion of particle transport.

To emphasize further the importance of radiance, consider the following two properties:

1. *The radiance in the direction of a light ray remains constant as it propagates along the ray* (assuming there are no losses due to absorption or scattering). This law follows from the conservation of energy within a thin pencil of light, as shown in Figure 2.6.

   The total flux leaving the first surface must equal the flux arriving on the second surface.

   $$L_1 \, d\omega_1 \, dA_1 = L_2 \, d\omega_2 \, dA_2 \tag{2.8}$$

   but $d\omega_1 = dA_2/r^2$ and $d\omega_2 = dA_1/r^2$, thus,

   $$T = d\omega_1 \, dA_1 = d\omega_2 \, dA_2 = \frac{dA_1 \, dA_2}{r^2} \tag{2.9}$$

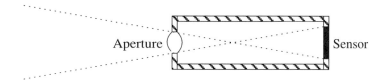

Figure 2.7: *A simple exposure meter.*

This quantity T is called the *throughput* of the beam; the larger the throughput, the bigger the beam. This immediately leads to the conclusion that

$$L_1 = L_2 \tag{2.10}$$

and hence, the invariance of radiance along the direction of propagation. *As a consequence of this law, radiance is the numeric quantity that should be associated with a ray in a ray tracer.*

2. *The response of a sensor is proportional to the radiance of the surface visible to the sensor.*

   To prove this law, consider the simple exposure meter in Figure 2.7. This meter has a small sensor with area a and an aperture with area A. The response of the sensor is proportional to the total integrated flux falling on it.

   $$R = \int_A \int_\Omega L \cos\theta \, d\omega \, dA = LT \tag{2.11}$$

   Thus, assuming the radiance is constant in the field of view, the response is proportional to the radiance. The constant of proportionality is the throughput, which is only a function of the geometry of the sensor. The fact that the radiance at the sensor is the same as the radiance at the surface follows from the invariance of radiance along a ray.

   This law has a fairly intuitive explanation. Each sensor element sees that part of the environment inside the beam defined by the aperture and the receptive area of the sensor. If a surface is far away from the sensor, the sensor sees more of it. Paradoxically, one might conclude that the surface appears brighter because more energy arrives on the sensor. However, the sensor is also far from the surface, which means that the sensor subtends a smaller angle with respect to the surface. The increase in energy resulting from integrating over a larger surface area is exactly counterbalanced by the decrease in percentage of light that makes it to the sensor. This property of radiance explains why a large uniformly illuminated painted wall appears equally bright over a wide range of viewing distances.

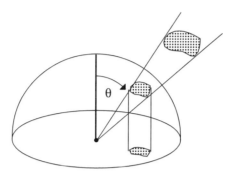

Figure 2.8: *Projection of differential area.*

As a consequence, the radiance from a surface to the eye is the quantity that should be output to the display device.

2.4.3 Irradiance and Illuminance

The two properties of radiance described in the previous section were derived by considering the total flux within a small beam of radiation. Another very important quantity is the total energy per unit area incident onto a surface with a fixed orientation. This can be computed by integrating the incident, or incoming radiance, L_i, over a hemisphere, Ω.

$$d\Phi = \left[\int_\Omega L_i \cos\theta\, d\omega \right] dA \tag{2.12}$$

The *irradiance*, E, is the radiant energy per unit area falling on a surface (the corresponding photometric quantity is the *illuminance*).

$$E \equiv \frac{d\Phi}{dA} \tag{2.13}$$

or

$$E = \int_\Omega L \cos\theta\, d\omega \tag{2.14}$$

The quantity $\cos\theta\, d\omega$ is often referred to as the *projected solid angle*. It can be thought of as the projection of a differential area on a sphere onto the base of the sphere, as shown in Figure 2.8.

This geometric construction shows that the integral of the projected solid angle over the hemisphere is just π, the area of the base of a hemisphere with unit radius. This result can also be derived directly by computing the following integral:

$$
\begin{aligned}
\int_{\Omega} \cos \theta \, d\omega &= \int_0^{2\pi} \int_0^{\pi} \cos \theta \, \sin \theta \, d\theta \, d\phi \\
&= -\int_0^{2\pi} \int_0^{\pi} \cos \theta \, d\cos \theta \, d\phi \\
&= -2\pi \frac{\cos^2 \theta}{2} \Big|_0^{\pi/2} \\
&= \pi
\end{aligned}
\tag{2.15}
$$

Note that if all rays of light are parallel, which occurs if a single distant source irradiates a surface, then the integral reduces to the simple formula

$$
E = E_0 \cos \theta
\tag{2.16}
$$

where E_0 is the energy per unit perpendicular area arriving from the distant source.

2.4.4 Radiosity and Luminosity

As the title of this book suggests, *radiosity* is another important quantity in image synthesis. Radiosity, B, is very similar to irradiance. Whereas irradiance is the energy per unit area incident onto a surface, radiosity is the energy per unit area that leaves a surface. It equals

$$
B = \int_{\Omega} L_o \cos \theta \, d\omega
\tag{2.17}
$$

where L_o is the outgoing radiance.

The official term for radiosity is *radiant exitance*. Because of the widespread use of the term radiosity in the computer graphics literature, it will be used in this book. The photometric equivalent is *luminosity*.

2.4.5 Radiant and Luminous Intensity

Radiance is a very useful way of characterizing light transport between surface elements. Unfortunately, it is difficult to describe the energy distribution of a point light source with radiance because of the point singularity at the source. Fortunately, it is very easy to characterize the energy distribution by introducing another quantity—the *radiant* or *luminous intensity*.

Note that this use of "intensity" is very different from that typically used by the computer graphics community. Even more confusion results because intensity is often used to indicate radiance-like transport quantities in the physics community. The radiant intensity is quite similar to that used in the geometric optics community.

The energy distribution from a point light source expands outward from the center. A small beam is defined by a differential solid angle in a given direction. The flux in a small beam $d\omega$ is defined to be equal to

$$d\Phi \equiv I(\vec{\omega})\, d\omega \qquad (2.18)$$

I is the radiant intensity of the point light source with units of power per unit solid angle. The equivalent photometric quantity is the luminous intensity.

The radiant intensity in a given direction is equal to the irradiance at a point on the unit sphere centered at the source. In the geometric optics literature intensity is defined to be the power per unit area (rather than per unit solid angle). In the case of a spherical wavefront emanating from a point source, the geometric optics definition is basically the same as the radiometric definition. However, in general, the wavefront emanating from a point source will be distorted after it reflects or refracts from other surfaces and so the definition in terms of solid angles is less general.

For an isotropic point light source,

$$I = \frac{\Phi}{4\pi} \qquad (2.19)$$

Of course, a point source may act like a spotlight and radiate different amounts of light in different directions. The total energy emitted is then

$$\Phi = \int_{\Omega} I(\vec{\omega})\, d\omega \qquad (2.20)$$

The irradiance on a differential surface due to a single point light source can be computed by calculating the solid angle subtended by the surface element from the point of view of the light source.

$$E = I\frac{d\omega}{dA} = \frac{\Phi}{4\pi}\frac{\cos\theta}{|\mathbf{x} - \mathbf{x}_s|^2} \qquad (2.21)$$

where $|\mathbf{x} - \mathbf{x}_s|$ is the distance from the point to the surface element. Note the $1/r^2$ fall-off: this is the origin of the inverse square law.

The distribution of irradiance on a surface is often drawn using a contour plot or *iso-lux* diagram, while the directional distribution of the intensity from a point light source is expressed with a *goniometric* or *iso-candela* diagram.[2] This is a contour plot of equal candela levels as a function of the (θ, ϕ).

---

[2] See Chapter 10 for details of lighting specifications.

Physics	Radiometry	Radiometric Units
	Radiant energy	joules $[J = kg\,m^2/s^2]$
Flux	Radiant power	watts $[W = joules/s]$
Angular flux density	Radiance	$[W/m^2\,sr]$
Flux density	Irradiance	$[W/m^2]$
Flux density	Radiosity	$[W/m^2]$
	Radiant intensity	$[W/sr]$

Physics	Photometry	Photometric Units
	Luminous energy	talbot
Flux	Luminous power	lumens $[talbots/second]$
Angular flux density	Luminance	Nit $[lumens/m^2\,sr]$
Flux density	Illuminance	Lux $[lumens/m^2\,sr]$
Flux density	Luminosity	Lux $[lumens/m^2\,sr]$
	Luminous intensity	Candela $[lumens/sr]$

Table 2.1: *Radiometric and photometric quantities.*

2.4.6 Summary of Radiometric and Photometric Quantities

In most computer graphics systems, optical quantities are simply colors denoted by red, green, and blue triplets. These triplets are used to specify many quantities including light sources, material properties, and intermediate calculations.[3] As noted, there is a small but finite number (six to be exact) of radiometric (photometric) quantities that characterize the distribution of light in the environment. They are the radiant energy (luminous energy), radiant power (luminous power), radiance (luminance), irradiance (illuminance), radiosity (luminosity), and radiant intensity (luminous intensity). These quantities and their units are summarized in Table 2.1.

---

[3]A more complete treatment of color specification is given in Chapter 9.

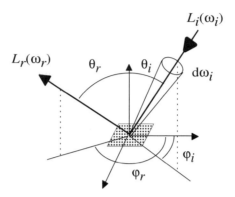

Figure 2.9: *Bidirectional reflection distribution function.*

2.5   Reflection Functions

The next question is how to characterize the reflection of light from a surface. Reflection is defined as the process by which light incident on a surface leaves that surface from the same side. Transmission, absorption, spectral and polarization effects, fluorescence, and phosphorescence are also important to consider in developing an accurate model of the interaction of light with materials, but will not be treated in detail here. Instead, this section will concentrate on nomenclature and the general properties that are satisfied by all reflection functions.

2.5.1   The Bidirectional Reflection Distribution Function

Consider the light incident on a surface from a small differential solid angle in the direction $\vec{\omega}_i$. The amount of reflected light in another direction $\vec{\omega}_r$ is proportional to the incident irradiance from $\vec{\omega}_i$ (see Figure 2.9). That is,

$$dL_r(\vec{\omega}_r) \propto dE(\vec{\omega}_i) \tag{2.22}$$

Equation 2.22 simply states that an increase in the incident light energy per unit area results in a corresponding increase in the reflected light energy. The incident irradiance can be increased by increasing either the solid angle subtended by the source or the energy density in the beam.

The constant of proportionality is termed the *bidirectional reflection distribution function*, or BRDF.

$$f_r(\vec{\omega}_i \rightarrow \vec{\omega}_r) \equiv \frac{L_r(\vec{\omega}_r)}{L_i(\vec{\omega}_i)\,\cos\theta_i\,d\omega_i} \tag{2.23}$$

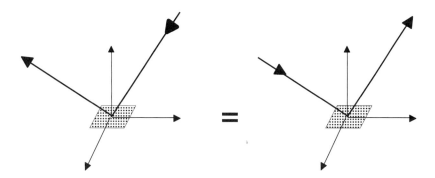

Figure 2.10: *Helmholtz reciprocity principle.*

More precisely, the BRDF is defined to be the ratio of the reflected radiance in the direction $\vec{\omega}_r$ to the differential irradiance from the incident direction $\vec{\omega}_i$ that produces it. The BRDF is bidirectional because it depends on two directions. Often, the dependence on the four angles is made explicit by writing the BRDF as $f_r(\theta_i, \phi_i; \theta_r, \phi_r)$. The BRDF is a distribution function because it is strictly positive. Since it gives the concentration of flux per steradian, it may take on any value between zero and infinity. The BRDF has units of inverse steradians.

The BRDF has several interesting properties:

1. If the BRDF is based on physical laws, then it will remain unchanged if the incident and reflected directions are interchanged. That is,

$$f_r(\vec{\omega}_r \rightarrow \vec{\omega}_i) = f_r(\vec{\omega}_i \rightarrow \vec{\omega}_r) \qquad (2.24)$$

This *Helmholtz reciprocity principle* is equivalent to saying that if a photon moves along a path, it will follow the same path if its direction is reversed (see Figure 2.10).

2. The BRDF is, in general, *anisotropic*. That is, if the incident and reflected directions are fixed and the underlying surface is rotated about the surface normal, the percentage of light reflected may change (see Figure 2.11). Examples of anisotropic materials are brushed aluminum or cloth [134].

Many materials, however, are smooth and their reflectivity does not depend on the surface's orientation. Thus, their reflection functions do not change if the surface is rotated, and

$$f_r((\theta_i, \phi_i + \phi) \rightarrow (\theta_r, \phi_r + \phi)) = f_r((\theta_i, \phi_i) \rightarrow (\theta_r, \phi_r)) \qquad (2.25)$$

This implies that the reflection function has only three degrees of freedom instead of four.

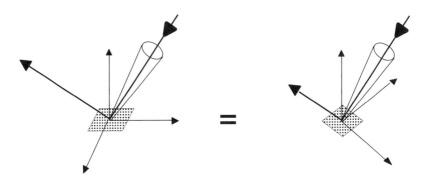

Figure 2.11: *The reflection may change with rotations of the surface due to anisotropy.*

Notice that adding light from another incident direction has no influence on the amount of light reflected from other incident directions. Thus, reflection behaves linearly, and hence the total amount of light reflected by a surface in a specific direction is given by a hemispherical integral over all possible incident directions. This leads to the *reflectance equation*:

$$L_r(\vec{\omega}_r) = \int_{\Omega_i} f_r(\vec{\omega}_i \to \vec{\omega}_r) \, L_i(\vec{\omega}_i) \, \cos\theta_i \, d\omega_i \qquad (2.26)$$

Put another way, the reflected radiance in a particular direction is due to the radiance arriving from all directions weighted by the BRDF relating the incoming and reflected directions and by the projected solid angle.

2.5.2   Mirror Reflection

As an example of a BRDF, consider a perfect mirror and the geometry of the reflection. For a mirror, the angle of reflectance is equal to the angle of incidence, and the reflected vector is in the plane determined by the incident ray and surface normal vector. This implies that

$$\begin{aligned} \theta_r &= \theta_i \\ \phi_r &= \phi_i \pm \pi \end{aligned} \qquad (2.27)$$

Second, consider the radiometry of reflection. For a mirror, the reflected radiance is exactly equal to the incident radiance.

$$L_r(\theta_r, \phi_r) = L_i(\theta_r, \phi_r \pm \pi) \qquad (2.28)$$

This physical fact can be mathematically expressed with a BRDF involving delta functions.

$$f_{r,m} = \frac{\delta(\cos\theta_i - \cos\theta_r)}{\cos\theta_i} \, \delta(\phi_i - (\phi_r \pm \pi)) \tag{2.29}$$

Recall that the delta function has the following three properties:

1. $\delta(x) = 0$ if $x \neq 0$

2. $\int_{-\infty}^{\infty} \delta(x)\,dx = 1$

3. $\int_{-\infty}^{\infty} \delta(x-y)f(x)\,dx = f(y)$

It can be verified that this leads to the correct reflected radiance by performing the hemispherical integral.

$$
\begin{aligned}
L_r(\theta_r, \phi_r) &= \int_{\Omega_i} \frac{\delta(\cos\theta_i - \cos\theta_r)}{\cos\theta_i} \, \delta(\phi_i - (\phi_r \pm \pi)) \\
&\qquad \cdot L_i(\theta_i, \phi_i) \cos\theta_i \, d\theta_i \, d\phi_i \\
&= L_i(\theta_r, \phi_r \pm \pi) \tag{2.30}
\end{aligned}
$$

2.5.3 The Reflectance

Recall that the delta function can be interpreted as an infinitesimally thin, infinitely high spike with unit area. This implies that the BRDF, although always positive, may be infinite. Often it is more intuitive to work with a quantity that is bounded between 0 and 1. This quantity is called the *biconical reflectance*, or simply *reflectance*.

Consider the ratio of reflected flux to incident flux. Since the reflected flux must always be less than the incident flux giving rise to it, the reflectance must always be less than 1.

$$
\begin{aligned}
\frac{d\Phi_r}{d\Phi_i} &= \frac{\int_{\Omega_r} L_r(\vec{\omega}_r) \cos\theta_r \, d\omega_r}{\int_{\Omega_i} L_i(\vec{\omega}_i) \cos\theta_i \, d\omega_i} \\
&= \frac{\int_{\Omega_r} \int_{\Omega_i} f_r(\vec{\omega}_i \to \vec{\omega}_r) L_i(\vec{\omega}_i) \cos\theta_i \, d\omega_i \cos\theta_r \, d\omega_r}{\int_{\Omega_i} L_i(\vec{\omega}_i) \cos\theta_i \, d\omega_i} \tag{2.31}
\end{aligned}
$$

Unfortunately, the reflectance depends on the distribution of incoming light, L_i. If it is assumed that L_i is uniform and isotropic, then L_i can be taken out from the integral in both the numerator and the denominator. This results in the relationship between the reflectance and the BRDF which forms the definition of the reflectance:

$$\rho(\vec{\omega}_i \to \vec{\omega}_r) \equiv \frac{\int_{\Omega_r} \int_{\Omega_i} f_r(\vec{\omega}_i \to \vec{\omega}_r) \cos\theta_i \, d\omega_i \cos\theta_r \, d\omega_r}{\int_{\Omega_i} \cos\theta_i \, d\omega_i} \tag{2.32}$$

The reflectance involves a double integral over the incident and reflected directions for which the limits of integration have not yet been set. Three choices for the limits are a differential solid angle, a finite solid angle, or the entire hemisphere. Since this choice can be made for both the incident and the reflected directions, there are nine different reflectances. These are shown in table 2.2.

	$\vec{\omega}$	$\Delta\omega$	2π
$\vec{\omega}$	$\rho(\vec{\omega}_i \to \vec{\omega}_r)$	$\rho(\vec{\omega}_i \to \Delta\omega_r)$	$\rho(\vec{\omega}_i \to 2\pi)$
$\Delta\omega$	$\rho(\Delta\omega_i \to \vec{\omega}_r)$	$\rho(\Delta\omega_i \to \Delta\omega_r)$	$\rho(\Delta\omega_i \to 2\pi)$
2π	$\rho(2\pi \to \vec{\omega}_r)$	$\rho(2\pi \to \Delta\omega_r)$	$\rho(2\pi \to 2\pi)$

Table 2.2: *The nine biconical reflectances.*

The names of these reflectances are formed by combining the following words: *directional* (for differential solid angle), *conical* (for finite solid angle), and *hemispherical* (for a solid angle equal to the entire hemisphere). Thus, $\rho(\vec{\omega}_i \to \vec{\omega}_r)$, $\rho(\Delta\omega_i \to \Delta\omega_r)$, and $\rho(2\pi \to 2\pi)$ are referred to as the *bidirectional*, *biconical*, and *bihemispherical* reflectances, respectively. Perhaps the most interesting reflectance function is the *directional-hemispherical reflectance*, $\rho(\vec{\omega}_i \to 2\pi)$. This is the amount of light scattered into the entire hemisphere from a single incident direction. Since this quantity is the ratio of fluxes, it must be less than 1. However, be aware that this quantity can change with the angle of incidence.

2.5.4 Lambertian Diffuse Reflection

To illustrate the relationship between the BRDF and reflectance, consider the case of Lambertian diffuse reflectance. Diffuse reflectance is modeled by assuming that light is equally likely to be scattered in any direction, regardless of the incident direction. In other words, the BRDF is constant. Thus,

$$
\begin{aligned}
L_{r,d}(\vec{\omega}_r) &= \int_{\Omega_i} f_{r,d}\, L_i(\vec{\omega}_i)\, \cos\theta_i\, d\omega_i \\
&= f_{r,d} \int_{\Omega_i} L_i(\vec{\omega}_i)\, \cos\theta_i\, d\omega_i \\
&= f_{r,d} E
\end{aligned}
\tag{2.33}
$$

This leads to two conclusions:

1. The value of the reflected radiance is proportional to the incident irradiance.

2. The reflected radiance is a constant and hence the same in all directions, since neither $f_{r,d}$ nor E depends on $\vec{\omega}_r$. This is true independent of the distribution of incoming light.

The fact that energy is conserved can be ensured by forcing the hemispherical–hemispherical reflectance to be less than 1.

$$
\begin{aligned}
\rho_d(2\pi \to 2\pi) = \frac{\Phi_{r,d}}{\Phi_i} &= \frac{\int_{\Omega_r} L_{r,d}(\vec{\omega}_r) \cos\theta_r \, d\omega_r}{\int_{\Omega_i} L_i(\vec{\omega}_i) \cos\theta_i \, d\omega_i} \\
&= \frac{L_{r,d} \int_{\Omega_r} \cos\theta_r \, d\omega_r}{E} \\
&= \frac{\pi L_{r,d}}{E} \\
&= \pi f_{r,d} \quad\quad (2.34)
\end{aligned}
$$

It thus immediately follows that if the BRDF is a constant, then the reflectance is also a constant. More importantly, this relationship can be used to parameterize the BRDF in terms of the reflectance: $f_{r,d} = \rho_d/\pi$. Often, it is more intuitive to describe materials using their reflectances because they are constrained to lie between 0 and 1. Whenever a ρ is used in this text, it can safely be assumed to lie between 0 and 1.

Since the outgoing radiance is constant, the radiosity

$$
B = \pi L_{r,d} \quad\quad (2.35)
$$

is related to the irradiance by the following equation:

$$
\rho_d = \frac{B}{E} \qu\quad (2.36)
$$

Equation 2.36 states that for diffuse reflection, the reflectance is equal to the radiosity divided by the irradiance.

2.5.5 Glossy Reflection

In practice it is often convenient to treat the general BRDF as the sum of three qualitatively different components: mirror (or ideal) specular reflection, Lambertian (or ideal) diffuse reflection, and *glossy* reflection (see Figure 2.12). The diffuse and mirror reflection laws, Lambert's law, and the law of reflection, were discussed in the previous sections.

However, real materials are not perfectly diffuse or perfect mirror specular. This is to be expected since these models of reflection are the simplest mathematical abstractions of the properties of surfaces and materials. Real surfaces

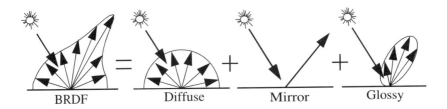

Figure 2.12: *Reflectance components.*

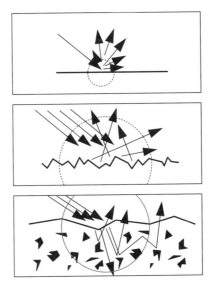

Figure 2.13: *Complex reflection distributions arise from rough surface and subsurface phenomena.*

are not planar and perfectly smooth and thus would not be expected to reflect light in just one direction. A real BRDF will thus contain a component between these limiting cases in which light hitting the surface from a certain direction is reflected into a complex distribution of outgoing directions.

The terminology for the various components is highly variable in the image synthesis literature. In particular, the intermediate component that we call glossy reflection is variously called specular, rough specular, wide and narrow diffuse, and directional diffuse. The term *glossy* has also been used in the surface reflection literature and has been selected instead for this work because its common usage is suggestive of the intended technical meaning.

Lord Rayleigh was the first to explain the effects of surface finish on the

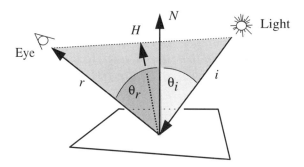

Figure 2.14: *Vectors for glossy reflection models.*

reflective properties of materials. He reasoned that a surface would become shinier if it were perfectly flat, or at least flat relative to the wavelength of the incident radiation. His theory is relatively easy to test because the wavelengths of common sources of radiation range from the macroscopic to the microscopic, and it can be verified that long wavelength radiation is more easily reflected from a surface. As shorter and shorter wavelengths are directed toward the surface, the ideal specular component decreases and the reflection becomes less focused. This transition occurs roughly when the wavelength of light becomes equal to the relative height changes in the surface. Thus, glossy reflection arises from the scattering of light from rough surfaces, an idea first proposed by Bouguer. The mirror specular term is considered to arise from perfectly smooth surfaces, while the Lambertian diffuse term arises from multiple surface reflections from very rough surfaces and from subsurface scattering (see Figure 2.13).

Another important optical effect is that glossy reflection increases at glancing angles of incidences and reflection. This is predicted by the Fresnel formula, which gives the relative percentage of light that is reflected or refracted across a planar boundary as a function of the angles of incidence and index of refraction.

In computer graphics glossy reflection from rough surfaces is typically modeled using the microfacet theory. This theory assumes the surface is made of little reflective facets, each behaving as a small mirror; that is, each reflecting light perfectly. This model predicts that the amount of light reflected from a light source toward the eye is equal to the relative number of microfacets oriented halfway between the eye and the light source. This model has been enhanced by many researchers [30, 65] and in its modern form consists of several terms

$$f_r = \frac{DGF}{4\cos\theta_r \, \cos\theta_i} \qquad (2.37)$$

- D is the microfacet distribution. This distribution function gives the number of microfacets oriented in a particular direction. This function is typically modeled with the following formula (see Figure 2.14):

$$D(H, N, \kappa) = (N \cdot H)^{\kappa} \tag{2.38}$$

  Note that this distribution is maximal when H equals N, implying that the maximum number of microfacets are oriented parallel to the surface. Note also that κ controls the rate at which the distribution of microfacets falls off, and is related to the roughness of the surface.

- G is a geometric attenuation term accounting for self-shadowing. This arises because a rough surface is actually a height field, and facets in the valleys are less visible at glancing angles as facets at the peaks. This is an important effect, but very difficult to model precisely with a simple formula.

- F is the Fresnel reflection term related to a material's index of refraction.

The modeling of reflection of light from real materials is an interesting and important subject; however, space does not permit us to cover it in detail in this book. Models that can be found in the literature range from Phong's simple empirical model [181], to models of the form given above [30, 65, 236] that differ primarily in the details of the D function, to more recent (and complex) models such as that proposed by He *et al.* [118]. A good summary and description of the earlier models is given by Hall[114]. Subsurface reflection (see Figure 2.13) that has typically been modeled as part of the Lambertian diffuse component has also been reexamined to provide a more physically based model for biological materials such as skin and leaves [115].

2.6   The Rendering Equation

The reflectance equation makes it possible to compute the reflected light distribution from the incident light distribution and the BRDF of the material. The important remaining task is to specify, or preferably to compute, the incident light distribution. This is typically referred to as the *illumination model*.

The first and easiest case to consider is one with no occlusion and direct illumination from simple light sources. In this case there is typically a small number of point or distant lights, and it can be assumed that all light arrives at the surface; that is, there is no shadowing. Since this model does not consider the environment as a whole and only depends on the individual properties of the light sources and the surface being shaded, it is often called a *local* illumination model. Shadows can be added by testing whether a point on the surface is visible to the light source. This is what is done in a ray tracer, but it requires access to the entire environment and is therefore an example of a *global* illumination model.

The second and considerably more difficult case is indirect illumination. In this case light may come from any surface in the environment, and it is very important to consider shadowing.

In the following sections, the interreflection of light between surfaces will be taken into account, and the *rendering equation* is derived from the reflectance equation. The *radiosity equation*, a simplified form of the rendering equation, that results by assuming all surfaces are Lambertian reflectors is also derived.

2.6.1 Local or Direct Illumination

It is easy to incorporate direct lighting from point light sources into the previous reflection models. Recall the reflectance equation

$$L_r(\vec{\omega}_r) = \int_{\Omega_i} f_r(\vec{\omega}_i \to \vec{\omega}_r) \, L_i(\vec{\omega}_i) \, \cos \theta_i \, d\omega_i \qquad (2.39)$$

Recall also that the irradiance from a single point light source was derived,

$$E = \frac{\Phi}{4\pi} \frac{\cos \theta}{|\mathbf{x} - \mathbf{x}_s|^2} \qquad (2.40)$$

If the direction to the light source is given by $\vec{\omega}_s$, then the radiance from a point light source can be expressed with a delta function.

$$L_i(\vec{\omega}_i) = \frac{\Phi}{4\pi \, |\mathbf{x} - \mathbf{x}_s|^2} \, \delta(\cos \theta_i - \cos \theta_s) \, \delta(\phi_i - \phi_s) \qquad (2.41)$$

Substituting equation 2.41 into the reflectance equation yields

$$
\begin{aligned}
L_r(\vec{\omega}_r) &= \int f_r(\vec{\omega}_i \to \vec{\omega}_r) \, L_i(\vec{\omega}_i) \, \cos \theta_i \, d\omega_i \\
&= \frac{\Phi}{4\pi |\mathbf{x} - \mathbf{x}_s|^2} f_r(\vec{\omega}_r, \vec{\omega}_s) \, \cos \theta_s
\end{aligned}
\qquad (2.42)
$$

If there are n light sources, then the hemispherical integral collapses to a sum over the n sources. This is the lighting model used by 3D graphics workstations.

It is easy to extend this model to light sources with arbitrary directional distributions, as well as distant light sources. The above formulae are changed to use the radiant intensity in the direction of the surface. In principle, linear and area light sources can also be used, although this involves integrating the reflectance function over the range of possible directions incident from the light source. Nishita and Nakamae [175] and Amanatides [7] discuss this possibility.

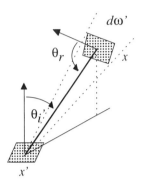

Figure 2.15: *Two point transport geometry.*

2.6.2   Global or Indirect Illumination

The first step in using a global illumination model is to relate the illumination on one surface to the reflected light distribution from another surface. This requires that the spatial dependence of radiance is made explicit and that occlusion is considered.

Using the fact that radiance is invariant along a ray, the incident radiance at $\mathbf{x}'$ due to the radiance from $\mathbf{x}$ is

$$L_i(\mathbf{x}', \vec{\omega}_i') = L_o(\mathbf{x}, \vec{\omega}_o) V(\mathbf{x}, \mathbf{x}') \tag{2.43}$$

where $\vec{\omega}_i$ is a direction vector from $\mathbf{x}'$ to $\mathbf{x}$, and $\vec{\omega}_o$ is in the opposite direction.

$$\vec{\omega}_i = -\vec{\omega}_o = \frac{\mathbf{x} - \mathbf{x}'}{|\mathbf{x} - \mathbf{x}'|} \tag{2.44}$$

The function $V(\mathbf{x}, \mathbf{x}')$ is a visibility function. It is 1, if $\mathbf{x}$ and $\mathbf{x}'$ are mutually visible; otherwise it is 0.

Returning to the reflectance equation, the next step is to switch the hemispherical integral over all incident directions to an area integral over all the other surfaces in the environment. This is easily done by relating the solid angle subtended by the source to its projected surface area.

$$d\omega_i' = \frac{\cos \theta_o \, dA}{|\mathbf{x} - \mathbf{x}'|^2} \tag{2.45}$$

Dotting this to form the projected solid angle results in

$$d\omega_i' \cos \theta_o \, dA = G(\mathbf{x}, \mathbf{x}') \, dA \tag{2.46}$$

where

$$G(\mathbf{x}, \mathbf{x}') = G(\mathbf{x}', \mathbf{x}) = \frac{\cos \theta'_i \cos \theta_o}{|\mathbf{x} - \mathbf{x}'|^2} \qquad (2.47)$$

Substituting $G(\mathbf{x}, \mathbf{x}')$ into the reflectance equation leads to the following integral equation over the surfaces, S:

$$L(\mathbf{x}', \vec{\omega}') = \int_S f_r(\mathbf{x}) \, L(\mathbf{x}, \vec{\omega}) \, G(\mathbf{x}, \mathbf{x}') \, V(\mathbf{x}, \mathbf{x}') \, dA \qquad (2.48)$$

Since this equation only involves outgoing radiances and directions, the subscripts denoting incoming and outgoing directions can safely be dropped (except from f_r).

Equation 2.48 was first introduced to the computer graphics literature by Kajiya [135], who appropriately named it the *rendering equation*. Actually, his notation (and development) is slightly different than that used in equation 2.48. He introduced a new intensity quantity, $I(\mathbf{x} \rightarrow \mathbf{x}')$—the *two point transport intensity* from $\mathbf{x}$ to $\mathbf{x}'$ (see Figure 2.15). This intensity quantity is a function of surface position only and does not involve solid angles. The two point transport intensity is defined by the following equation:

$$d\Phi = I(\mathbf{x} \rightarrow \mathbf{x}') \, dA \, dA' = L(\mathbf{x}, \vec{\omega}) \, G(\mathbf{x}, \mathbf{x}') \, dA \, dA' \qquad (2.49)$$

This is the flux flowing in the beam connecting dA to dA'. Equation 2.48 can be put in this form by multiplying both sides by $G(\mathbf{x}', \mathbf{x}'') \, dA' \, dA''$ which leads to the following equation:

$$I(\mathbf{x}' \rightarrow \mathbf{x}'') = G(\mathbf{x}', \mathbf{x}'') \int_S f_r(\mathbf{x} \rightarrow \mathbf{x}' \rightarrow \mathbf{x}'') \, V(\mathbf{x}, \mathbf{x}') I(\mathbf{x} \rightarrow \mathbf{x}') \, dA \qquad (2.50)$$

Equation 2.50 defines the amount of light flowing from $\mathbf{x}$ to $\mathbf{x}'$ and reflected to $\mathbf{x}''$. Thus, it is sometimes referred to as the multipoint transport equation (see Figure 2.16). The quantity

$$f_r(\mathbf{x} \rightarrow \mathbf{x}' \rightarrow \mathbf{x}'') = f_r(\mathbf{x}', \vec{\omega}'_i \rightarrow \vec{\omega}'_r) \qquad (2.51)$$

is just a reparameterization of the BRDF.

There is one final step required to arrive at the full rendering equation, and that is to account for all modes of light transport at a surface. In an environment consisting only of opaque surfaces, the only other source of light is due to emission from the surface.

$$L(\mathbf{x}', \vec{\omega}') = L_e(\mathbf{x}', \vec{\omega}') + \int_S f_r(\mathbf{x}) \, L(\mathbf{x}, \vec{\omega}) \, G(\mathbf{x}, \mathbf{x}') \, V(\mathbf{x}, \mathbf{x}') \, dA \qquad (2.52)$$

where L_e is the two point intensity of emitted light.

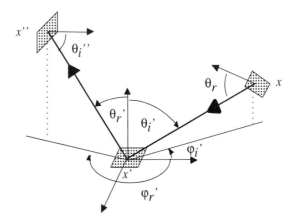

Figure 2.16: *Three point transport geometry.*

2.6.3 The Radiosity Equation

Finally, the rendering equation can be simplified given the *radiosity assumption*. In radiosity, it is assumed that all surfaces in the environment are Lambertian diffuse reflectors. Thus, the BRDF is independent of the incoming and outgoing directions and can be taken out from under the integral.

$$
\begin{aligned}
L(\mathbf{x'} \to \mathbf{x''}) &= L_e(\mathbf{x'} \to \mathbf{x''}) + f_r(\mathbf{x'}) \int_S L(\mathbf{x} \to \mathbf{x'})\, G(\mathbf{x}, \mathbf{x'})\, V(\mathbf{x}, \mathbf{x'})\, dA \\
&= L_e(\mathbf{x'} \to \mathbf{x''}) + \tfrac{\rho(\mathbf{x'})}{\pi} \int_S L(\mathbf{x} \to \mathbf{x'})\, G(\mathbf{x}, \mathbf{x'})\, V(\mathbf{x}, \mathbf{x'})\, dA
\end{aligned}
\tag{2.53}
$$

More importantly, the outgoing radiance from a Lambertian surface is the same in all directions and in fact equals the radiosity B divided by π. This leads to even more dramatic simplifications.[4]

$$
B(\mathbf{x}) = E(\mathbf{x}) + \rho(\mathbf{x}) \int_S B(\mathbf{x'}) \frac{G(\mathbf{x}, \mathbf{x'})\, V(\mathbf{x}, \mathbf{x'})}{\pi} \, dA'
\tag{2.54}
$$

The rendering equation expresses the conservation of light energy at all points in space. The key feature of such an integral equation is that the quantity to be computed—in this case, the radiance or radiosity—appears on the left-hand side as well as under an integral on the right-hand side. For this reason, integral equations are notoriously difficult to solve. They very rarely have closed-form analytic solutions, and numerical methods must be used.

---

[4]Note the switch in notation: E is the energy per unit area emitted by the surface, or $\frac{L_e}{\pi}$. In addition, for clarity in the following chapters, the geometric term G($\mathbf{x}$,$\mathbf{x}$') will absorb the visibility term and the π in the denominator.

Chapter 3

Discretizing the Radiosity Equation

3.1 The Radiosity Equation

The radiosity equation was derived at the end of Chapter 2 from the rendering equation under the assumption that all surfaces (and light sources) exhibit Lambertian diffuse reflection (emission). Repeating the radiosity equation 2.54:

$$B(\mathbf{x}) = E(\mathbf{x}) + \rho(\mathbf{x}) \int_S B(\mathbf{x}') \, G(\mathbf{x}, \mathbf{x}') \, dA' \tag{3.1}$$

where the geometric term, $G(\mathbf{x}, \mathbf{x}')$, now includes the visibility term, $V(\mathbf{x}, \mathbf{x}')$, and division by π. (A complete table of the mathematical terms used in this chapter is provided in Tables 3.1 and 3.2.)

The radiosity, $B(\mathbf{x})$, describes an arbitrary *scalar* function across the surfaces (i.e., the radiosity function defines a single value at each location on a surface).[1] The potential complexity of the radiosity function is suggested by Figure 3.1, where the radiosity function across a partially shadowed polygon is plotted as a surface. The radiosity function is piecewise smooth, that is, it is continuous in all derivatives within regions bounded by discontinuities in value or derivatives. These characteristics will be discussed in much greater detail in chapters 6 and 8.

The dimension of the *function space* of the radiosity function, $B(\mathbf{x})$, is infinite (for a discussion of function spaces, refer to the box on page 45). This means that solving the radiosity equation for a point $\mathbf{x}$ on a surface does not

---

[1] A full solution to the radiosity problem must also take into account the distribution of energy across the visible spectrum (i.e., the *color* of the light). Assuming that the wavelength of light is not changed by interaction with surfaces (i.e., ignoring *fluorescence*), independent radiosity equations differing only in the reflectivities, ρ, can be formed and solved for each of a small number of wavelengths or color bands. The selection of these sample wavelengths and the reconstruction of colors suitable for display are discussed in Chapter 9. Elsewhere in the book, the radiosity problem will be discussed in terms of an achromatic (i.e., black, gray, white) world.

S	surfaces, the domain of the radiosity (and other) functions
n	the number of basis functions or nodes
i, j	indices into vectors and arrays
$\mathbf{x}, \mathbf{x}'$	two points in the domain S, e.g., (x, y, z), (x', y', z')
$\mathbf{x}_i$	a specific point in S, the location of the ith $node$
A, A_i	area, area of element i
dA	a differential area at $\mathbf{x}$, i.e., $dx\, dy$
$B(\mathbf{x})$	radiosity function
$\mathbf{B}$	column vector of values, $(B_1, B_2, ..., B_i, ..., B_n)^T$
$\hat{B}(\mathbf{x})$	approximate radiosity function
$E(\mathbf{x})$	emission function
$\mathbf{E}$	column vector of values, $(E_1, E_2, ..., E_i, ..., E_n)^T$
$\rho(\mathbf{x})$	diffuse reflectivity
ρ_i	diffuse reflectivity at $\mathbf{x}_i$ or of element i
$\varepsilon(\mathbf{x})$	error function
$r(\mathbf{x})$	residual function
$\mathbf{K}$	matrix of interaction coefficients

Table 3.1: *Table of Terms*

determine the radiosity at an immediately neighboring location. As a result, a full and exact solution to the radiosity equation requires either finding the exact functional form of the radiosity across each surface or computing radiosity values for an infinite number of surface points.

The first step in constructing a practical global illumination algorithm is thus to reformulate the problem as one that can be solved for a finite set of unknown values, which can then be used to construct an *approximate* solution. This is the topic of the present chapter, in which the finite element method will be used to derive a linear system of equations that can be solved for discrete unknowns. These unknowns then define an approximation to the radiosity function.

3.2   Making Image Synthesis Tractable

A great deal of research has been conducted on solving integral equations such as the radiosity equation. A good source for this work is [69]. The finite element approach used in radiosity methods is one of two distinct approaches that have been taken in image synthesis to solving the global illumination problem.

One basic approach is the use of Monte Carlo or quasi-Monte Carlo ray

K_{ij}	ij^{th} term of $\mathbf{K}$
$\mathbf{F}$	matrix of form factors
$\mathbf{M}$	matrix of basis interactions, often the identity, $\mathbf{I}$
$\mathbf{P}$	diagonal matrix of element reflectivities
$N_i(\mathbf{x})$	the ith basis function
$N_i(\mathbf{x}_j)$	the ith basis function evaluated at $\mathbf{x}_j$
$G(\mathbf{x}, \mathbf{x}')$	function of geometric relationship between $\mathbf{x}$ and $\mathbf{x}'$
G_{ij}	geometric relationship between points in elements i and j
$G_{i\omega}$	geometric function of a point and a direction
$V(\mathbf{x}, \mathbf{x}')$	visibility relationship between $\mathbf{x}$ and $\mathbf{x}_i$
V_{ij}	visibility relationship between points in elements i and j
θ	angle between normal at $\mathbf{x}$ and vector from $\mathbf{x}$ to $\mathbf{x}'$
θ'	angle between normal at $\mathbf{x}'$ and vector from $\mathbf{x}'$ to $\mathbf{x}$
Ω	the hemispherical solid angle around the surface normal
r	$|\mathbf{x} - \mathbf{x}'|$, the distance from $\mathbf{x}$ to $\mathbf{x}'$
δ_{ij}	Kronecker delta, 1 if $i = j$, 0 otherwise
u, v	parametric coordinates

Table 3.2: *Table of Terms (cont.)*

tracing to solve the rendering equation for locations and directions determined by the view specification. This approach solves the rendering equation for only those surface locations that are visible in the image and for only those directions that lead back to the eye. If interreflection is limited to the ideal (mirror) specular component and light sources are limited to point lights, Monte Carlo evaluation of the rendering equation is essentially equivalent to classical ray tracing. Ray tracing and Monte Carlo methods for image synthesis have been extensively investigated [64, 135, 198, 215]. Basic Monte Carlo integration will be discussed in Chapter 4.

Because the solution is limited by the view, ray tracing is often said to provide a *view-dependent* solution, although this is somewhat misleading in that it implies that the radiance itself is dependent on the view, which is not the case. The term *view-dependent* refers only to the use of the view to limit the set of locations and directions for which the radiance is computed. When a new view is specified, previously computed radiances are still valid but are often no longer relevant, and the rendering equation must be solved for a new set of locations and directions.

The radiosity method is based on the other basic approach to solving the

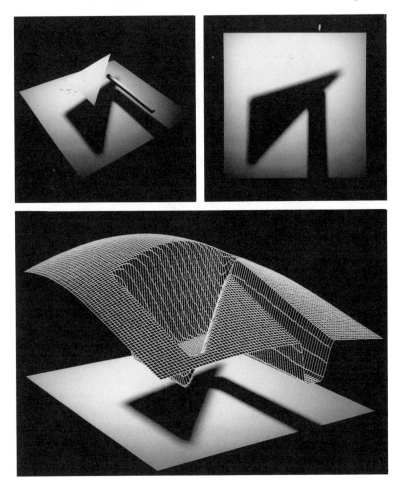

Figure 3.1*: An image; the shadow on the floor; and the radiosity function across the floor plotted as a surface.*

global illumination problem, which is to compute and store an approximation of the radiance function across the surfaces of the scene in object space, often in the form of radiance values at discrete locations in the environment. During a final rendering step, the shading of visible surfaces is derived from this approximation as needed. Because the view is not used to limit the scope of the solution, a change in the view does not require recomputing the solution, and this approach is often referred to as *view-independent*. Figure 3.2 shows both approaches. Combinations of view-dependent and view-independent approaches are also possible, and examples will be discussed in Chapters 9 and 10.

Function Spaces

A *function space* defines a set of possible functions. For example, the radiosity function is in the space of $\mathcal{L}^2$ functions over some finite domain S (e.g., the surfaces). The $\mathcal{L}^2$ function space is defined to contain all functions $f(x)$ such that

$$\int_S |f(x)|^2 \, dx < \infty$$

In other words, the function is finite everywhere in the domain (except possibly in infinitesimal regions). Another function space would be the space of all functions that are piecewise constant over integer intervals between 0 and 100. This function space can be defined as a linear sum of box basis functions:

$$\hat{f}(x) = \sum_{i=0}^{99} f_i \, N_i(x)$$

where the basis $N_i(x) = 1$ for $i < x \le i + 1$, and 0 elsewhere. The coefficients, f_i, describe the height of the function (step) in the ith interval.

The *dimension* of a function space is the number of discrete values required to describe the function fully. Thus the dimension of the $\mathcal{L}^2$ function space is infinite since the function can take on any form. In contrast, the piecewise constant function space above is a *finite function space* since exactly 100 numbers (the coefficients f_i) fully define the function.

Since any function in the piecewise constant function space is also in $\mathcal{L}^2$, this finite function space is a *subspace* of $\mathcal{L}^2$.

The *projection* (or more precisely the orthogonal projection) of a general function $f(x)$ into the subspace (or basis) defined by basis functions $N_i(x)$ involves selecting the *coefficients* or *weights*, f_i, so as to minimize the l_2 norm (see section 6.1) of the difference between the original function, $f(x)$, and $\hat{f}(x)$, (i.e., min $\| f(x) - \sum_i f_i N_i(x) \|_2$).

Computing and storing an object space approximation is particularly straightforward in the case of the radiosity equation, since for Lambertian diffuse reflection the radiance is independent of direction and is simply a constant multiple of the scalar radiosity value at any given point on a surface. This means that the approximation needs to define only a single value for each surface location. The *radiosity method* was the first application of this approach to image synthesis.

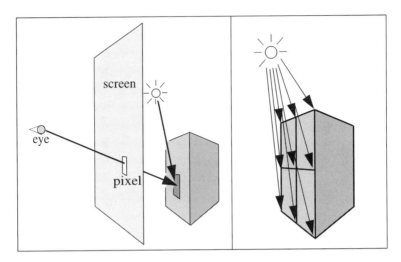

Figure 3.2: *View-dependent and view-independent approaches to computing global illumination.*

3.3 The Radiosity Approach

As shown by Heckbert and Winget [125], the radiosity method as developed in the field of radiative heat transfer can be viewed as a simple finite element formulation.[2] Finite element methods represent a complicated function by subdividing the domain into elements over which the function is approximated by a linear sum of simple *basis functions*, also sometimes called *shape functions* [38, 273]. The contribution of each basis function to the approximation is determined by values computed at a finite number of locations, or *nodes*. These nodal values become the unknowns in a linear system of equations, which can be solved using a variety of techniques.

The basic steps to formulating and solving a generic radiosity problem are outlined here (corresponding to the flow diagram in Figure 3.3):

1. Subdivide the surfaces into *elements*.

2. Select locations or *nodes* on the elements at which to determine discrete radiosity values. These will ultimately become the finite set of unknowns in the linear system of equations.

---

[2]In the case of the radiosity function, whose domain is the surfaces of the environment but where the interaction occurs across the space between surfaces, *boundary element methods* are specifically relevant. The basic approximation method in finite and boundary element methods is the same.

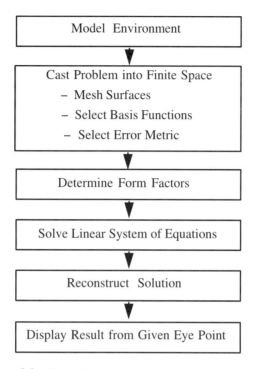

Figure 3.3: *Flow chart of traditional radiosity program.*

3. Assume a simple functional form for the variation of radiosity across an element. This is accomplished by associating a *basis function* with each node. The basis functions are typically simple polynomials with *local support* (i.e., zero everywhere except in the neighborhood of the associated node). When weighted by the nodal radiosity values, the basis functions for a particular element sum to define an approximate radiosity at each point on the element.

4. Select a finite error metric to minimize by *projecting* a *residual function* onto a set of basis functions. This approximates the error as a finite sum, thus casting the infinite dimension problem into a finite set of linear equations.

5. Compute the coefficients of the linear system. These coefficients are primarily based on the geometric relationships that determine the transport of light between elements. The geometric relationships are called *form factors*.

6. Solve the resulting system of equations for the unknown nodal radiosity values.

7. Reconstruct the approximate radiosity solution as the linear sum of the basis functions weighted by the resulting nodal values from step 6.

8. Render an image, deriving shading values from the radiosity approximation as needed for the particular view. The approximation used during the solution may be modified during this stage to meet the particular requirements of rendering.

Note that this is a generic radiosity method; many of the enhancements to the radiosity method that will be discussed in later chapters of this book complicate this simple flow by looping back to repeat earlier steps. It should also be noted that steps 3 and 4, in particular, are stages in formulating the basic solution approach and should not be interpreted as steps that might be explicitly performed by an algorithm.

The goal of the first four steps in the previous outline is to derive a linear system of equations that can be solved for a finite number of discrete unknowns. The remainder of this chapter will expand the explanantion of these steps to provide techniques for obtaining this system of equations.

3.4   Approximating Radiosity across a Surface

The heart of the finite element method is the approximation of a complicated function by a linear sum of a finite number, n, of simpler *basis* functions, $N_i(\mathbf{x})$, each of which is nonzero over a limited region of the function domain. The domain of the function (the surfaces, in the case of radiosity) is subdivided into a *mesh* of elements, each of which has one or more nodes located at points, $\mathbf{x}_i$, inside or on the element boundary. The mesh of elements and nodes organizes the basis functions.

Each node is associated with a basis function. Each basis function, although defined over the full domain of the original unknown function, is chosen to have a zero value everywhere except over a small region of the domain. This *support* of the basis function is confined to the elements adjacent to the node (a node on an element boundary may be adjacent to two or more elements). This limited support implies that the coefficient of single basis will only effect a small range of the overall function. The approximation within an element is thus determined by summing only the few basis functions whose support overlaps the element, with the contribution of each basis function weighted by a coefficient value, B_i, at the associated node. The radiosity function, $B(\mathbf{x})$, is thus approximated by

$\hat{B}(\mathbf{x})$, where

$$B(\mathbf{x}) \approx \hat{B}(\mathbf{x}) = \sum_{i=1}^{n} B_i N_i(\mathbf{x}) \tag{3.2}$$

Evaluating $\hat{B}(\mathbf{x})$ at a particular point $\mathbf{x}_j$ involves summing only those basis functions with their support over the point.

There are many possible basis functions. Low-order polynomials are the most common, including constant, linear, quadratic, and cubic functions. The constant (or "box") basis, which is often used in radiosity, is defined by

$$N_i(\mathbf{x}) = \begin{cases} 0 & \text{if } \mathbf{x} \text{ is outside element} \\ 1 & \text{if } \mathbf{x} \text{ is inside element} \end{cases} \tag{3.3}$$

The number and placement of nodes within elements will depend on the order of the polynomial. In the case of constant elements, defined by constant basis functions, a single node located in the center of the element is commonly used.

The radiosity function across linear elements is defined by nodes and associated basis functions at the boundaries or corners (in two dimensions) of the element. A simple example of function approximation using linear bases is shown in Figure 3.4 for a function of a single variable. In this example, a *linear* basis function is associated with each node, and the nodes are located at element boundaries. The linear (or "hat") basis function in one dimension is defined by

$$N_i(x) = \begin{cases} \frac{x - x_{i-1}}{x_i - x_{i-1}} & \text{for } x_{i-1} < x < x_i \\ \frac{x_{i+1} - x}{x_{i+1} - x_i} & \text{for } x_i < x < x_{i+1} \\ 0 & \text{otherwise} \end{cases} \tag{3.4}$$

In Figure 3.4 the nodal values, B_i, are determined by simply evaluating the function to be approximated at the node locations. In general, the function to be approximated is not known, thus the coefficient values are computed to minimize an error estimate or provide an overall best fit according to some criterion.

The generalization of finite element approximations to functions defined over a two-dimensional domain, such as the radiosity function, is straightforward (see Figure 3.5). The elements are typically simple shapes, usually triangles and/or convex quadrilaterals. Nodes for constant, linear, and quadratic elements are shown in Figure 3.6. The approximation of a function for a single, two-dimensional element using constant and linear basis functions is shown in Figure 3.7. Note that the tensor product of the two one dimensional linear basis functions results in a bilinear basis in two dimensions and is thus curved along the diagonals.

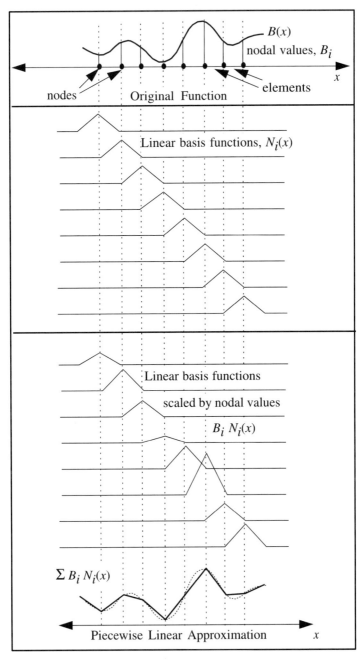

Figure 3.4: *Finite element approximation of a function using linear basis functions.*

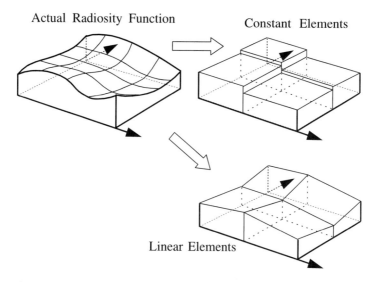

Figure 3.5: *Finite element approximation of the radiosity function.*

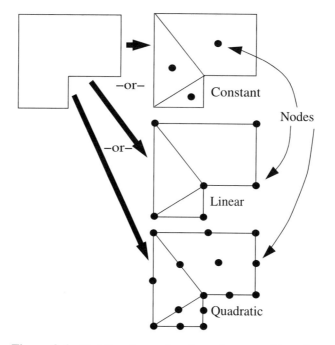

Figure 3.6: *Dividing the surface into elements with nodes.*

In two dimensions, the linear basis function, $N_i(\mathbf{x})$, has the properties:

$$N_i(\mathbf{x}) = \begin{cases} 1 & \text{at node } i \\ 0...1 & \text{within adjacent elements} \\ 0 & \text{at all other node points} \\ 0 & \text{outside adjacent elements} \end{cases} \qquad (3.5)$$

This definition ensures that the basis function associated with a particular node is zero outside of the elements adjacent to the node, as well as at any other nodes within those elements.

The variation of the linear basis function from a value of 1 at the node to 0 across the element depends on the parametric mapping of a generic basis defined on a *standard element* to the triangular or quadrilateral elements. In the case of triangles, barycentric coordinates are often used to define the 2D linear basis. In the case of quadrilaterals a tensor product of two one-dimensional linear basis functions defines one quarter of a bilinear basis within each element. For example, the value of the hat function is determined by the interpolation, $N_i(\mathbf{x}) = (1-u)(1-v)$, where (u, v) is the $(0,0)$ to $(1,1)$ parametric coordinate of the point $\mathbf{x}$ within the element with node i at the parametric origin (see Figure 3.9). Parametric mappings are discussed briefly in section 3.8 and in more detail in most finite element texts [273].

Elements constructed using other types of basis functions are also possible. For example, cubic *Hermite* elements provide continuity of derivatives across element boundaries by using basis functions that interpolate function derivatives at the nodes as well as values. Given the radiosity values and their parametric derivatives at the four corners of a quadrilateral, one can derive a bicubic variation of radiosity across the element. Hybrid sets of basis functions with constant, linear, and higher-order functions can also be employed. Other polynomial bases (e.g., Jacobi polynomial sets [270]) and non-polynomial functions are other possible choices. For a given approximation accuracy, there is typically a tradeoff between the number of elements required and the complexity of the basis functions.

To date, radiosity implementations have used constant basis functions almost exclusively. Linear functions have been explored in one dimension by Heckbert [122]. Max and Allison [163] have implemented radiosity using linear elements. Lischinski *et al.* [154] have used quadratic elements in a radiosity solution. For radiosity, as will be discussed at length in Chapter 9, elements of linear or higher order have more commonly been used during the rendering stage [203].

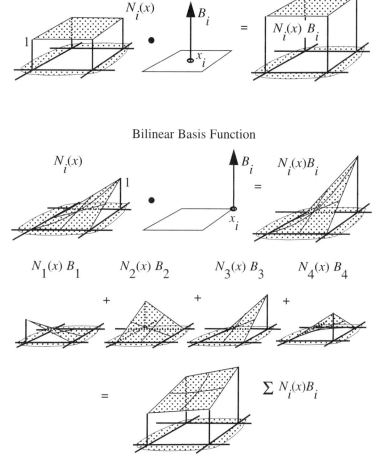

Figure 3.7: *Basis functions.*

3.5 Error Metrics

A set of discrete elements, with a total of n nodal values at n nodal points, $\mathbf{x}_i$, and n basis functions, N_i, defines a *finite dimension function space* (see box on page 45). This finite function space has n degrees of freedom, the n nodal values, B_i, thus $\hat{B}(\mathbf{x})$ is everywhere defined by the finite set of the n coefficients, B_i.

Ideally, one would like the approximate radiosity solution $\hat{B}(\mathbf{x})$ to agree with the actual solution $B(\mathbf{x})$ everywhere. This is not possible in general since $\hat{B}(\mathbf{x})$ is restricted to the finite subspace of functions representable as the linear sum of the selected basis functions. Given the choice of basis functions, the goal is then to find the nodal values that generate a solution *minimizing* the error according to some measure or *metric*.

The actual error, $\varepsilon(\mathbf{x})$, is the difference between the approximate and exact solutions, that is,

$$\varepsilon(\mathbf{x}) = B(\mathbf{x}) - \hat{B}(\mathbf{x}) \tag{3.6}$$

Unfortunately, it is impossible to determine $\varepsilon(\mathbf{x})$ directly since the exact solution is not known.

An alternative characterization of the error is provided by the residual. If $\hat{B}$ is substituted for both occurrences of B in the original radiosity equation

$$\hat{B}(\mathbf{x}) = E(\mathbf{x}) + \rho(\mathbf{x}) \int_S \hat{B}(\mathbf{x}') G(\mathbf{x}, \mathbf{x}') \, dA' \tag{3.7}$$

then the *residual* function is given by the difference of the left and right hand sides

$$r(\mathbf{x}) = \hat{B}(\mathbf{x}) - E(\mathbf{x}) - \rho(\mathbf{x}) \int_S \hat{B}(\mathbf{x}') G(\mathbf{x}, \mathbf{x}') \, dA' \tag{3.8}$$

An exact solution will make $r(\mathbf{x})$ zero everywhere, but this is unobtainable since, as we have seen, $\hat{B}$ is restricted to the subspace of functions realizable using the basis functions. Although $\hat{B}$ is restricted to a finite function space, the residual, r, is not. However, a similar approach to that taken in approximating B can be taken to project the residual into a finite function space. In this way, rather than seek a solution technique that makes $r(\mathbf{x})$ zero everywhere, the goal will instead be to minimize $r(\mathbf{x})$ according to a *finite dimensional* error metric.

The general approach is to choose n independent *weighting functions*, $W_i(\mathbf{x})$, each having local support, much like the earlier basis functions. The *norm* or size of the residual is then approximated as a finite sum:[3]

$$|r(\mathbf{x})| = \sum_{i=1}^{n} | < r(\mathbf{x}), W_i(\mathbf{x}) > | \tag{3.9}$$

This residual norm can be driven to zero by finding radiosity values such that each of the n terms $< r(\mathbf{x}), W_i(\mathbf{x}) >$ is equal to zero. As will be derived below,

---

[3]The notation $< f(x), g(x) >$ indicates the *inner product* of the two functions. The *inner product* of two functions is analogous to the dot product of two vectors and is defined to be

$$< f(x), g(x) > = \int_S f(x) \, g(x) \, dx$$

If $< f(x), g(x) > = 0$, then $f(x)$ and $g(x)$ are *orthogonal*.

setting each of these terms to zero results in a linear equation. The set of n such linear equations (one for each weighting function) of the n nodal values, B_i, can be solved simultaneously as discussed in Chapter 5.

This approach defines a general class of methods called *weighted residual methods*. Two different choices for the weighting functions $W_i(\mathbf{x})$ lead to two contrasting formulations, *point collocation* and the *Galerkin method*, which will be discussed in the following sections.

3.5.1 Point Collocation

The simplest set of weighting functions are *delta* functions:

$$W_i(\mathbf{x}) = \delta(\mathbf{x} - \mathbf{x}_i) \qquad (3.10)$$

which are zero unless $\mathbf{x}$ is coincident with the node at $\mathbf{x}_i$.

Using these weighting functions, the norm of the residual defined by equations 3.8 and 3.9 is minimized (i.e., zero) when $r(\mathbf{x})$ is exactly zero at all the node points, x_i (i.e., $r(\mathbf{x}_i) = 0$, $\forall i$). This clearly differs from requiring $r(\mathbf{x})$ to be zero everywhere, since $r(\mathbf{x})$ is free to vary away from zero in between the nodes. However, as the number of nodes increases this difference diminishes. In general, the points at which the residual function is minimized are selected to be located at the nodes used in approximating the radiosity function. This technique is known as *point collocation*.

If there are n nodes, there is now a finite number of conditions that must be met. These are captured by the n simultaneous linear equations, one for each node i located at location $\mathbf{x}_i$:

$$\hat{B}(\mathbf{x}_i) - E(\mathbf{x}_i) - \rho(\mathbf{x}_i) \int_S \hat{B}(\mathbf{x}') \, G(\mathbf{x}_i, \mathbf{x}') \, dA' = 0, \, \forall i \qquad (3.11)$$

Note that the only change from equation 3.8 to equation 3.11 is that equation 3.11 is defined only at the n node locations, x_i, as opposed to the entire surface domain, S. Expanding $\hat{B}$ using equation 3.2 gives

$$\sum_{j=1}^{n} B_j \, N_j(\mathbf{x}_i) - E(\mathbf{x}_i) - \rho(\mathbf{x}_i) \int_S \sum_{j=1}^{n} B_j \, N_j(\mathbf{x}') \, G(\mathbf{x}_i, \mathbf{x}') \, dA' = 0 \quad (3.12)$$

Grouping terms and factoring B_j, which is independent of $\mathbf{x}'$, out of the integral leaves

$$\left[\sum_{j=1}^{n} B_j \left[N_j(\mathbf{x}_i) - \rho(\mathbf{x}_i) \int_S N_j(\mathbf{x}') \, G(\mathbf{x}_i, \mathbf{x}') \, dA' \right] \right] - E(\mathbf{x}_i) = 0 \quad (3.13)$$

Equation 3.13 can be restated simply as the set of n linear equations

$$\sum_{j=1}^{n} B_j K_{ij} - E(\mathbf{x}_i) = 0 \tag{3.14}$$

or in matrix/vector form as

$$\mathbf{K}\mathbf{B} = \mathbf{E} \tag{3.15}$$

The coefficients K_{ij} are given by

$$K_{ij} = N_j(\mathbf{x}_i) - \rho(\mathbf{x}_i) \int_S N_j(\mathbf{x}') G(\mathbf{x}_i, \mathbf{x}') \, dA' \tag{3.16}$$

These coefficients are independent of the nodal radiosities and are defined solely by the geometry and material properties of the environment. The evaluation of these coefficients will be the topic of the following chapter. However, it should be noted here that for any particular term, K_{ij}, the integral only needs to be evaluated over the nonzero support of the jth basis function. Also, the term $N_j(\mathbf{x}_i)$ is simply the Kronecker delta δ_{ij}, (i.e., one if $i = j$ and zero otherwise), for constant and linear basis functions with local support limited to adjacent elements. Equation 3.14 completes the objective of deriving a linear system of equations that can be solved for the unknown nodal radiosities, B_i.

3.5.2   Galerkin Form of Weighted Residuals

The point collocation formulation defines the error metric to be zero when the approximate residual is zero at the node points only. An alternative approach to deriving a linear system of radiosity equations defines the approximate residual to be zero when a set of *weighted integrals* of the residual are zero.

The weighting functions in this case are selected to have local support much like the basis functions used to approximate the radiosity function. In this case the *weighted residual method* seeks a solution for which there is a weighted "average" zero residual over each small region of the domain. If n weighting functions, $W_i(\mathbf{x})$, are defined, a solution is found if

$$< W_i(\mathbf{x}), r(\mathbf{x}) > = \int_S W_i(\mathbf{x}) \, r(\mathbf{x}) \, dA = 0, \, \forall i \tag{3.17}$$

or expanding $r(\mathbf{x})$ above with equation 3.8

$$0 = \int_S W_i(\mathbf{x}) \hat{B}(\mathbf{x}) dA -$$

$$\int_S W_i(\mathbf{x}) E(\mathbf{x}) \, dA - \int_S W_i(\mathbf{x}) \, \rho(\mathbf{x}) \int_S \hat{B}(\mathbf{x}') \, G(\mathbf{x}, \mathbf{x}') \, dA' \, dA \tag{3.18}$$

The *Galerkin* formulation selects the same basis functions used to approximate the radiosity function as the weighting functions, (i.e., $W_i(\mathbf{x}) = N_i(\mathbf{x})$), thus, equation 3.18 becomes,

$$0 = \int_S N_i(\mathbf{x})\hat{B}(\mathbf{x})\,dA -$$

$$\int_S N_i(\mathbf{x})E(\mathbf{x})\,dA - \int_S N_i(\mathbf{x})\,\rho(\mathbf{x})\int_S \hat{B}(\mathbf{x}')\,G(\mathbf{x},\mathbf{x}')\,dA'\,dA \quad (3.19)$$

Finally, expanding $\hat{B}$ and grouping terms as before results in:

$$\left[\sum_{j=1}^{n} B_j \left[\int_S N_i(\mathbf{x})N_j(\mathbf{x})\,dA - \int_S N_i(\mathbf{x})\rho(\mathbf{x})\int_S N_j(\mathbf{x}')\,G(\mathbf{x},\mathbf{x}')\,dA'\,dA\right]\right]$$

$$- \int_S E(\mathbf{x})N_i(\mathbf{x})\,dA = 0 \quad (3.20)$$

The unknowns, B_j, have been isolated in this expression. There are n such expressions, one for each node i and, as with point collocation, the linear system of equations can be expressed as the matrix equation

$$\mathbf{K}\,\mathbf{B} = \mathbf{E} \quad (3.21)$$

The entries of $\mathbf{K}$ are given by

$$K_{ij} = \int_S N_i(\mathbf{x})N_j(\mathbf{x})\,dA - \int_S N_i(\mathbf{x})\rho(\mathbf{x})\int_S N_j(\mathbf{x}')\,G(\mathbf{x},\mathbf{x}')\,dA'\,dA \quad (3.22)$$

and the entries in $\mathbf{E}$ by

$$E_i = \int_S E(\mathbf{x})N_i(\mathbf{x})\,dA \quad (3.23)$$

The Galerkin method has been explored for one-dimensional "flatland" radiosity by Heckbert [122, 123].

3.6 Constant Element Radiosities

The previous two sections have taken two different approaches to achieving the same basic objective, a linear system of equations for the discrete nodal values. However, the relationship of these equations to the physical problem of global illumination may still be somewhat obscure. The complexity in the above formulations is reduced if constant basis functions are used, with the reflectivity and emission of each element assumed to be constant. This set of assumptions has been made in most radiosity implementations to date and provides the clearest physical intuition.

For constant basis functions, N_i, the Galerkin formulation can be rewritten by performing the integration for each term in equation 3.20. First, using the fact that the box basis functions have values of only 1 and 0, and do not overlap with one another,

$$\int_S N_i(\mathbf{x}) N_j(\mathbf{x})\, dA = \left\{ \begin{array}{ll} A_i & \text{if } i = j \\ 0 & \text{otherwise} \end{array} \right\} = \delta_{ij} A_i \qquad (3.24)$$

where δ_{ij} is the Kronecker delta, and A_i is the area of element i. Note that the integration only has to be performed across elements i and j since the corresponding basis functions are zero elsewhere. Likewise,

$$\int_S E(\mathbf{x}) N_i(\mathbf{x})\, dA = E_i A_i \qquad (3.25)$$

where E_i is the area average emission value for element i.

Finally, since the basis functions have unit value within the element, the basis functions themselves can be dropped and it is possible to integrate explicitly over element areas. Thus, assuming the reflectivity $\rho(\mathbf{x})$ is a constant ρ_i over A_i,

$$\int_S N_i(\mathbf{x}) \rho(\mathbf{x}) \int_S N_j(\mathbf{x}') G(\mathbf{x}, \mathbf{x}')\, dA'\, dA = \rho_i \int_{A_i} \int_{A_j} G(\mathbf{x}, \mathbf{x}')\, dA_j\, dA_i$$
$$(3.26)$$

Making these substitutions into equation 3.20 results in, for all i:

$$\left[\sum_{j=1}^{n} B_j \left[\delta_{ij} A_i - \rho_i \int_{A_i} \int_{A_j} G(\mathbf{x}, \mathbf{x}')\, dA_j\, dA_i \right] \right] - E_i A_i = 0 \qquad (3.27)$$

Dividing through by A_i and moving the emission term to the right side gives

$$\sum_{j=1}^{n} B_j \left[\delta_{ij} - \rho_i \frac{1}{A_i} \int_{A_i} \int_{A_j} G(\mathbf{x}, \mathbf{x}')\, dA_j\, dA_i \right] = E_i \qquad (3.28)$$

or

$$\left[\sum_{j=1}^{n} B_j \left[\delta_{ij} - \rho_i F_{ij} \right] \right] = E_i \qquad (3.29)$$

where F_{ij}, called the *form factor*, is given by

$$F_{ij} = \frac{1}{A_i} \int_{A_i} \int_{A_j} G(\mathbf{x}, \mathbf{x}') \, dA_j \, dA_i \qquad (3.30)$$

The form factor represents the fraction of energy that leaves element i and arrives directly at element j. Evaluating the form factor is the topic of Chapter 4.

As in previous formulations, the system of equations can be represented by the matrix equation $\mathbf{K B} = \mathbf{E}$. As evident in equation 3.29, the entries in $\mathbf{K}$ are given by

$$K_{ij} = \delta_{ij} - \rho_i F_{ij} \qquad (3.31)$$

Rearranging equation 3.29 gives the *classical radiosity equation*:

$$B_i = E_i + \rho_i \sum_{j=1}^{n} B_j F_{ij} \qquad (3.32)$$

A more physically intuitive form is obtained by first reinserting the area terms, A_i:

$$B_i A_i = E_i A_i + \rho_i \sum_{j=1}^{n} B_j F_{ij} A_i \qquad (3.33)$$

and then using the reciprocity relationship between form factors,

$$F_{ji} A_j = F_{ij} A_i \qquad (3.34)$$

to obtain

$$B_i A_i = E_i A_i + \rho_i \sum_{j=1}^{n} B_j F_{ji} A_j \qquad (3.35)$$

A physical interpretation of equation 3.35 is that the total power, $B_i A_i$ leaving an element depends on any light that it emits directly plus light that is reflected. This reflected light depends, in turn, on the light leaving every element in the environment, since some fraction of the light leaving every other surface may arrive at the surface in question and be reflected back into the environment. This fraction depends on the geometric relationship between the elements and on the element reflectivities.

A radiosity equation of the form of equation 3.32 exists for each element. The system of equations can be expanded into matrix form:

$$\begin{bmatrix} 1 - \rho_1 F_{1,1} & \cdot & \cdot & -\rho_1 F_{1,n} \\ -\rho_2 F_{2,1} & \cdot & \cdot & -\rho_2 F_{2,n} \\ \cdot & & & \\ \cdot & & & \\ -\rho_{n-1} F_{n-1,1} & & & \cdot \\ -\rho_n F_{n,1} & \cdot & \cdot & 1 - \rho_n F_{n,n} \end{bmatrix} \begin{bmatrix} B_1 \\ B_2 \\ \cdot \\ \cdot \\ B_{n-1} \\ B_n \end{bmatrix} = \begin{bmatrix} E_1 \\ E_2 \\ \cdot \\ \cdot \\ E_{n-1} \\ E_n \end{bmatrix} \qquad (3.36)$$

Solving this linear system is the topic of Chapter 5. The radiosity formulation for constant elements that has just been derived will be used for most of the remainder of the book.

3.7 Higher-Order Basis Functions

The use of linear or higher-order basis (and residual weighting) functions does not affect the basic formulation of the last section. A similar set of linear equations results, but the physical interpretation is slightly altered. As described, the form factor, F_{ij}, from constant basis functions represents the fraction of energy leaving element i that arrives directly at element j. Generalizing to any basis functions, F_{ij} represents the weighted effect of the energy leaving the region under the support of one basis function on the energy of the region under the support of another basis function (see Figure 3.8). The differential interaction between two differential areas is similar to that with constant bases, except in this case it is weighted by the local values of the two basis functions at each end of the interaction. Although the physical intuition is somewhat less direct, this is still essentially a geometric term.

The general $\mathbf{K}$ matrix can be expressed as the difference of two matrices, $\mathbf{M} - \mathbf{PF}$. For constant basis functions, the $\mathbf{M}$ matrix is simply the identity matrix and the $\mathbf{F}$ matrix is the form factor matrix ($\mathbf{P}$ is a diagonal matrix of element reflectivities ρ). M_{ij} captures the inner product of the two basis functions, N_i and N_j:

$$M_{ij} = < N_i(\mathbf{x}), N_j(\mathbf{x}) > = \int_S N_i(\mathbf{x}) N_j(\mathbf{x}) \, dA \qquad (3.37)$$

For orthonormal bases, this results in an identity since the inner products will be zero unless they are the same function. Put differently, the terms in $\mathbf{M}$ are zero unless the basis functions overlap as, for example, for linear functions associated with nodes belonging to the same element. Thus, the $\mathbf{M}$ matrix is sparse. The nonzero "area" terms, in the case of constant bases, are divided out and disappear in the "classical" radiosity formulation.

In general, however, it is not possible to divide through by the area terms as with the constant basis functions. Instead, one must be satisfied with the general form

$$\mathbf{K} = \mathbf{M} - \mathbf{PF} \qquad (3.38)$$

with $\mathbf{M}$ from equation 3.37, and the unnormalized

$$F_{ij} = \int_S N_i(\mathbf{x}) \int_S N_j(\mathbf{x}') \, G(\mathbf{x}, \mathbf{x}') \, dA' \, dA \qquad (3.39)$$

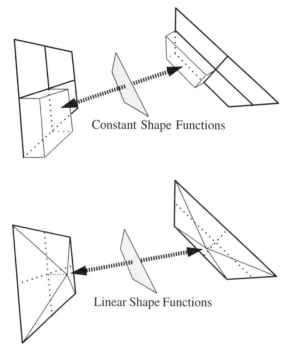

Constant Shape Functions

Linear Shape Functions

Figure 3.8: *Form factors between basis functions.*

3.8 Parametric Mapping to a Master Element

3.8.1 Master Elements

The complexity of handling many different types of surfaces and basis functions can be ameliorated to a great extent by developing a bookkeeping scheme based on the use of generic *master elements*. This topic is only briefly described here. The specific derivations of and the use of master elements is described in great detail in most finite element books such as [23, 273].

The radiosity function has been defined over the domain of the two-dimensional surfaces embedded in three dimensional space. The basis functions are defined in terms of the shape and size of the elements over which they have non-zero support. Thus, each basis function is unique in terms of its location, size and shape. One would like to be able to perform certain computations independent of the specific element under consideration. For this reason, it is useful to develop the notion of a small set of standard *master elements* and associated basis functions to which all elements can be *mapped*. Generic methods

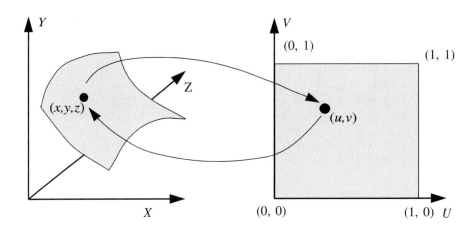

Figure 3.9: *Parametric mapping.*

for interpolation, integration of form factors, and other operations can then be developed to act on the standard elements in their local setting and the results transferred to the specific element in the global environment. This eliminates a great deal of awkwardness that may be associated with working directly in the more general global setting of planes and curved surfaces in three-dimensional space.

Although many master element shapes are possible, most applications use triangles and quadrilaterals. The original elements may or may not be planar; however, it is important that there is an invertible mapping from the world space coordinates to the two-dimensional (u, v) parametric coordinates of the master element (see Figure 3.9). Typically, the master element coordinates are defined over the unit 0 to 1 interval or the two unit -1 to 1 interval.

In the case of planar elements, the (u, v) coordinates are typically derived by establishing a coordinate system on the plane of the element. Surface patches that are already defined in terms of parametric coordinates may require a further scaling to the master element coordinate system.

It is also important to be able to determine the transformation of differential areas to the parameterized space. This requires careful attention in the case of parametrically defined polygons and curved surface patches.

3.8.2 Isoparametric Mapping

The above discussion has not relied on the actual form of the mapping functions other than to specify that they should be *one to one* and *invertible*. (In practice this means that polygonal elements must be *convex*.) Although many mapping functions are possible, commonly the basis functions themselves are used as the mapping functions. This is called an *isoparametric* mapping.

In this case, both the radiosity function and the geometry are mapped in the same way. For linear basis functions, the one-to-one mapping requirement will permit the use of triangles and *convex* quadrilaterals in parametric space. Quadratic basis functions will permit three- and four-sided elements bounded by quadratic curves to be mapped to square master elements. A full set of element types and mapping functions can be found in most finite element texts such as [273]. In the case of constant basis functions a *superparametric* mapping is often employed using barycentric and bilinear functions to map triangles and quadrilaterals to equilateral triangular and square master elements.

The example of linear bases and a square master element ranging from (0,0) to (1,1) results in four mapping functions for the four corner nodes,

$$N_{0,0}(u, v) = \tfrac{1}{4}(1 - u)(1 - v)$$

$$N_{1,0}(u, v) = \tfrac{1}{4}(v)(1 - v)$$

$$N_{1,1}(u, v) = \tfrac{1}{4}(v)(v)$$

$$N_{0,1}(u, v) = \tfrac{1}{4}(u)(v)$$

(3.40)

These mapping functions can then be used to find the world coordinates corresponding to a parametric location inside a master element, thus defining the shape of the element in world coordinates. If the world coordinates of the four corners of a quadrilateral element are (in counter-clockwise order) $\mathbf{x}_1, \mathbf{x}_2, \mathbf{x}_3$, and $\mathbf{x}_4$, then

$$\mathbf{x}(u, v) = \sum_{i=1}^{4} N_i(u, v)\mathbf{x}_i \qquad (3.41)$$

The inverse of this mapping function is described in section 9.2.1 in the context of interpolating radiosity values. In a similar fashion, curved element geometries can be defined with higher order basis functions.

3.9 Summary

This chapter has provided a mathematical framework for approximately solving the radiosity integral through the solution of a system of linear equations. Given this framework, many practical questions remain to be explored. What is a good element subdivision and how can it be obtained automatically? How are the coefficients of the $\mathbf{K}$ matrix to be computed numerically and how is the accuracy of that computation to be controlled? What matrix techniques are appropriate to solving this system of equations? How is the resulting solution applied to the rendering of an actual image? Efficiency and accuracy will be primary concerns throughout the discussion of these and other questions in the following chapters.

Chapter 4

The Form Factor

I. The Form Factor Integral

As shown in Chapter 3, the solution of the radiosity integral equation using point collocation or Galerkin methods leads to a system of linear equations of the form

$$\mathbf{K} \mathbf{B} = \mathbf{E} \qquad (4.1)$$

Evaluating the terms of $\mathbf{K}$ is the major computational bottleneck of the radiosity method. This chapter will address the computation of the entries in $\mathbf{K}$, comparing algorithms according to their efficiency and accuracy. Chapter 7 addresses another approach to increased efficiency, that is, limiting the number of entries in the operator that are actually computed.

The matrix $\mathbf{K}$ is defined as the difference of matrices:

$$\mathbf{K} = \mathbf{M} - \mathbf{P}\mathbf{F} \qquad (4.2)$$

where $\mathbf{M}$ and $\mathbf{P}$ are diagonal in structure and defined by the selected basis functions and element reflectivities, respectively. The *form factors* (entries in $\mathbf{F}$) make up the most important component of $\mathbf{K}$. They are central to the radiosity method and to understanding the propagation of light within an environment. Simply put, the form factor represents the geometric relationship between two surface areas, although, depending on the selection of basis functions, the form factor will take on more and less intuitive meanings. In the common case of constant basis functions, the form factor represents the fraction of light leaving one element that arrives directly at another. Thus, in the case where one element is a light source, the form factor itself represents the direct illumination of the other element per unit of emissive power from the light. *The form factor is purely a function of geometry.* It does not depend on the reflective or emissive characteristics of the surfaces. It does depend on the distance and orientation of the two elements, as well as the visibility relationship between them.

The computation of each form factor and thus each K_{ij} involves evaluating an integral of a geometric kernel over the areas of support of two basis functions.[1] Integrals of this type can sometimes be solved in a closed form, and this will be the case for special geometric arrangements of the elements. These special-case analytic formulae will be discussed; however, in general, there will be no closed form solution for this integral. Thus the bulk of the chapter will explore a variety of numerical algorithms designed specifically for this problem.

4.1   The Coefficients of K

As described in Chapter 3, the matrix **K** results from the projection of the radiosity function onto a selected basis set followed by the projection of the linear integral operator itself (or the residual) onto a basis.[2] The matrix **K** consists of the difference of two matrices, $\mathbf{M} - \mathbf{PF}$, where **M** accounts for the overlap (inner product) of neighboring basis functions, **P** is a diagonal matrix of surface reflectivities, and **F** is a matrix of form factors.

The coefficients of the matrix **F** represent the weighted direct influence of the radiosity of a region under the support of one basis function to the radiosity of another such region. Repeating from the previous chapter, the coefficients of **F** are given by

$$F_{ij} = \int_S N_i(\mathbf{x}) \int_S N_j(\mathbf{x}') G(\mathbf{x}, \mathbf{x}') \, dA' \, dA, \qquad (4.3)$$

where $N_i(\mathbf{x})$ and $N_j(\mathbf{x}')$ are the basis functions evaluated at $\mathbf{x}$ and $\mathbf{x}'$ and $G(\mathbf{x}, \mathbf{x}')$ incorporates the geometric and visibility relationship between the two regions as it affects radiant energy transport.

In the case of constant basis functions, $N_i(\mathbf{x})$ and $N_j(\mathbf{x}')$ are both equal to 1 over the finite areas of the corresponding elements. In this case, the **M** matrix is simply a diagonal matrix of element areas. Thus, each equation in the system can be divided by the area of the corresponding element. Then **M** is simply the identity and

$$F_{ij} = \frac{1}{A_i} \int_{A_i} \int_{A_j} G_{ij} \, dA_j \, dA_i \qquad (4.4)$$

where the geometric kernel is now denoted using the shorthand G_{ij}. In this case, the coefficients F_{ij} take on a particularly intuitive physical meaning: F_{ij} is the fraction of light leaving element i that arrives directly at element j. The F_{ij} in

---

[1] One basis may be a point as in the case of point collocation.
[2] The same basis set is used in Galerkin methods.

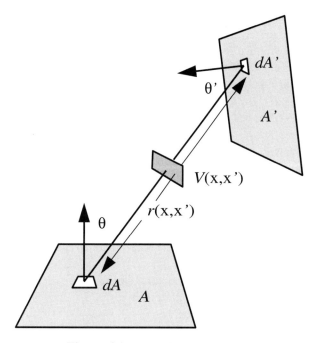

Figure 4.1: *Form factor geometry.*

this case are commonly called *form factors*.[3] We will use the term form factor for both constant and higher order bases, although the physical interpretation is somewhat less straightforward in the more general case.

The form factor is purely a function of the geometric relationship between elements and thus does not depend on the reflectivity (color) of surfaces. This is a potential advantage of the radiosity method, since it allows surface attributes to be changed without repeating the expensive form factor computation.

4.2 The Differential Form Factor

The geometric kernel in equation 4.3, $G(\mathbf{x}, \mathbf{x}')$, was derived in Chapter 2. It corresponds to the form factor between differential areas dA and dA' and is given by

$$dF_{dA \to dA'} = \frac{\cos \theta}{\pi} \, d\omega' = \frac{\cos \theta \, \cos \theta'}{\pi \, r(\mathbf{x}, \mathbf{x}')^2} \, dA' \qquad (4.5)$$

---

[3]*Form factor* has emerged as the common term in image synthesis. In the field of heat transfer, the terms *configuration factor* and *shape factor* also appear, among others.

where $r = |\mathbf{x} - \mathbf{x}'|^2$ is the distance between $\mathbf{x}$ and $\mathbf{x}'$, θ is the angle between the normal to the surface at $\mathbf{x}$ and the direction from $\mathbf{x}$ to $\mathbf{x}'$, θ' is angle between the normal to the surface at $\mathbf{x}'$ and the direction from $\mathbf{x}'$ to $\mathbf{x}$, and $d\omega'$ is the differential solid angle subtended by dA' from dA. The geometry for these terms is shown in Figure 4.1.

The fraction of light leaving dA that arrives at dA' is proportional to the solid angle $d\omega'$ subtended by dA' as viewed from dA. The form factor thus depends inversely on the square of the distance between the areas and on the cosine of the angle θ'. The form factor also drops off as dA' moves toward the horizon of dA, according to the cosine of the angle between the normal at dA and the line from dA to dA'. This follows from the definition of Lambertian diffuse reflectivity, which dictates that the energy per unit solid angle leaving dA in a certain direction is constant per unit *projected area*. The π in the denominator originates with the transformation from radiance to radiosity (see section 2.4.4), and acts to normalize the form factor to integrate to unity over the hemisphere.

The differential form factor is a smooth function, in the sense that the cosine and $1/r^2$ factors are continuous in all derivatives as dA' moves about over the domain. However, a singularity occurs as $r \to 0$ when the two differential areas meet at some point ($\mathbf{x} = \mathbf{x}'$). This can cause practical difficulties in evaluating the form factor between elements that intersect or share a common edge.

Equation 4.5 does not account for occlusion due to surfaces positioned between the two differential areas, which block the direct transfer of light. Determining occlusion is often the most computationally demanding aspect of the form factor computation since determining the visibility between two points may require testing all surfaces in the environment. Also, because changes in visibility can cause perceptually important discontinuities in the radiosity function, visibility must often be determined to a high accuracy.

Occlusion is accounted for formally by adding a visibility term, $V(\mathbf{x}, \mathbf{x}')$, to equation 4.5. $V(\mathbf{x}, \mathbf{x}')$ takes the value 1 if dA is visible from dA', and 0 otherwise. With the incorporation of occlusion, the complete differential form factor equation becomes

$$F_{dA \to dA'} = G(\mathbf{x}, \mathbf{x}') \, dA' = \frac{\cos\theta \, \cos\theta'}{\pi \, r^2} V(\mathbf{x}, \mathbf{x}') \, dA' \qquad (4.6)$$

where $G(\mathbf{x}, \mathbf{x}')$ captures all the geometric terms.

Finally, it is useful to note that the differential form factor from one differential area to another, $F_{dA \to dA'}$, is equal to the reverse form factor, $F_{dA' \to dA}$. This is known as the *reciprocity* relationship. The reciprocity relationship for form factors follows from the Helmholtz reciprocity principle discussed in Chapter 2.

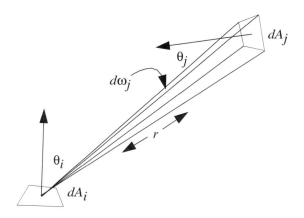

Figure 4.2: *Differential solid angle.*

4.3 Three Formulations of the Form Factor

The full form factor integral for constant bases, equation 4.4, involves performing an integration over the support of two basis functions (i.e., the two element areas). Three different formulations of this form factor integral between elements can be derived. Each is used in the algorithms that will be described in the following sections.

The first formulation results from inserting the differential form factor (equation 4.6) into the form factor integral, equation 4.4. Thus, the element-to-element form factor is the *double area* integral, with geometric kernel, G_{ij},

$$F_{ij} = \frac{1}{A_i} \int_{A_i} \int_{A_j} \frac{\cos\theta_i \, \cos\theta_j}{\pi \, r^2} V_{ij} \, dA_j \, dA_i \qquad (4.7)$$

where V_{ij} is the visibility term between differential areas dA_i and dA_j.

The second formulation results from replacing the inner integration over area with an equivalent integration over the hemisphere around dA_i. The differential solid angle (see Figure 4.2) $d\omega_j$ from dA_i to dA_j is

$$d\omega_j = \frac{\cos\theta_j}{r^2} \, dA_j \qquad (4.8)$$

Thus, the inner integral of equation 4.7 can be rewritten over the hemisphere of directions, Ω, and over dA_i, resulting in the *area–hemisphere* integral,

$$F_{ij} = \frac{1}{A_i} \int_{A_i} \int_{\Omega} \frac{\cos\theta_i}{\pi} V_{ij} \, d\omega_j \, dA_i \qquad (4.9)$$

where V_{ij} is now 1 if element j is visible from dA_i in *direction* $d\vec{\omega}_j$. The new geometric kernel, $V_{ij}\cos\theta_i/\pi$, will be denoted $G_{i\omega}$. This alternate form of the integral will be used in some algorithms to compute the form factors from dA_i to *all* elements at once.

If the elements are assumed to be fully visible to one another, a third variation of the form factor integral can be derived by applying Stokes' theorem to convert the double area integral into a double *contour* integral [143, 222]. The result (not derived here) is

$$F_{ij} = \frac{1}{2\pi A_i} \oint_{C_i} \oint_{C_j} \ln r \, dx_i \, dx_j + \ln r \, dy_i \, dy_j + \ln r \, dz_i \, dz_j \qquad (4.10)$$

where C_i and C_j are the boundaries of elements i and j. This third form of the integral will also be used by some algorithms when visibility can be determined a priori.

4.4   Computing the Form Factor

Both closed form analytic and numerical methods have been applied to solving the form factor integral.[4]

---

[4]An excerpt from Schröder and Hanrahan [206]: "The history of computing the amount of light impinging on a diffusely reflecting surface from some light source is very long. A closed form expression for the form factor between a differential surface element and a polygon had already been found by Lambert in 1760 [143]. Lambert proceeded to derive the form factor for a number of special configurations among them the form factor between two rectangles sharing a common edge with an angle of 90 degrees between them. He writes about the latter derivation:

> Although this task appears very simple its solution is considerably more knotted than one would expect. For it would be very easy to write down the differential expression of fourth order, which one would need to integrate four fold; but the highly laborious computation would fill even the most patient with disgust and drive them away from the task. The only simplification which I was able to achieve was to reduce the expression to a second order differential, using [the formula for differential surface element to polygon form factor (equation 4.15)], with which I was able to perform the computation.

Lambert also formulates the reciprocity principle in his theorem 16 and uses form factor algebra to compute unknown factors from known ones. The first use of Stokes' theorem [224] to solve for the form factor between two arbitrary surfaces can be found in a book by Herman in 1900 [126]. Through two applications of Stokes' theorem he reduces the form factor between two arbitrary surfaces to a double contour integral. He uses this result to give the form factor for two parallel quadrilaterals in an exercise. A similar derivation can be found in an article by Fock in 1924 [83]. Fock proceeds by applying the formulation to elliptical disks for which he derives a closed form solution. In 1936 Moon [169], aware of Fock's work, derives closed form solutions for a number

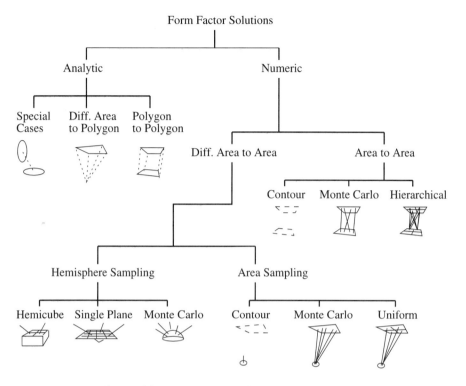

Figure 4.3: *A taxonomy of form factor algorithms.*

A taxonomy of form factor computation methods is shown in Figure 4.3. The discussion of these methods will begin with an examination of closed form (analytic) solutions. Although there is no closed form solution to the general form factor integral, if the two elements are assumed (or can be determined) to be fully visible to each other, there are some useful analytic formulae.

---

of specialized configurations. In the same year, Gershun [93] puts various photometric quantities on a vector calculus footing and gives an especially elegant derivation of the double contour integration using differential forms. Sparrow [221] in 1963 used the double contour form to derive closed form solutions for the case of parallel disks and parallel quadrilaterals. However, none of these sources, or any since, that we are aware of, has given a closed form solution of the form factor between two general polygons."

II. Closed Form Solutions for the Form Factor

4.5   Formulae for Simple Shapes

Analytic formulae for specialized geometries can be found in the appendices of
most radiative heat transfer texts [131, 155, 216, 222]. The formulae given in
Figure 4.4 for opposing and perpendicular rectangles are typical. Although the
geometries are simple and visibility is not an issue, the analytic formulae are far
from straightforward.

Analytic formulae are often used in conjunction with *form factor algebra*,
which allows the form factors for the union or difference of simple areas to be
computed from the form factors to the individual areas. As shown in Figure 4.5,
the form factor from element i to element j plus the form factor from element i
to element k must be equal to the form factor from element i to a new element
made up of the union of j and k. Similarly, the form factor from the union of
j and k to element i is the area average of the two individual elements. Thus,
if an element shape can be decomposed into simple shapes for which analytic
form factors are known, the form factor algebra can be used to determine the
full form factor.

Closed form formulae are also available for a differential area to various
finite geometries. An example is shown in Figure 4.6 for a parallel, axially
aligned disk. The differential area to finite area form factor arises naturally in
point collocation, where the radiosity equation is evaluated at element nodes. It
is also used in some numeric algorithms, since the outer integral in equations
4.7 and 4.9 can be performed numerically by evaluating the inner integral at one
or more locations on region i and averaging the result.

4.6   Differential Area to Convex Polygon

The analytic formula for the form factor from a differential area to a polygon is
particularly useful, since polygonal models are often encountered in image synthesis [19, 130, 143, 175]. The geometry for this formula is given in Figure 4.7.
The form factor is computed as a sum around the perimeter of the polygon:

$$F_{dA_i \to A_j} \;=\; \frac{1}{2\pi} \sum_{i=1}^{n} \beta_i \, \cos \alpha_i \tag{4.15}$$

or equivalently,

$$F_{dA_i \to A_j} \;=\; \frac{1}{2\pi} \sum_{i=1}^{n} \beta_i \, N_i \bullet \overline{(R_i \times R_{(i+1)\%n})} \tag{4.16}$$

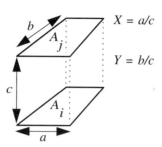

$$F_{ij} = \frac{2}{\pi XY} \left\{ \ln \left[\frac{(1+X^2)(1+Y^2)}{1+X^2+Y^2} \right]^{1/2} \right.$$

$$\left. + Y\sqrt{1+X^2}\ \tan^{-1}\left(\frac{Y}{\sqrt{1+X^2}}\right) - X\tan^{-1}X - Y\tan^{-1}Y \right\} \tag{4.11}$$

$$F_{ij} = \frac{1}{\pi W} \left(W\tan^{-1}\frac{1}{W} + H\tan^{-1}\frac{1}{H} - \sqrt{H^2+W^2}\ \tan^{-1}\frac{1}{\sqrt{H^2+W^2}} \right.$$

$$\left. + \frac{1}{4}\ln\left\{ \frac{(1+W^2)(1+H^2)}{1+W^2+H^2} \left[\frac{W^2(1+W^2+H^2)}{(1+W^2)(W^2+H^2)} \right]^{W^2} \left[\frac{H^2(1+W^2+H^2)}{(1+H^2)(H^2+W^2)} \right]^{H^2} \right\} \right) \tag{4.12}$$

Figure 4.4: *Analytic form factors between rectangles.*

where n is the number of sides on the polygon, β_i is the angle between R_i and $R_{(i+1)\%n}$ in radians, α_i is the angle between the plane of differential area dA_i and the triangle formed by dA_i and the ith edge of the polygon, and N_i is the unit normal to dA_i.

This formula does not take into account occlusion. However, in conjunction with the appropriate visibility algorithm, the form factor algebra can be used to compute an exact result. In an algorithm by Nishita and Nakamae [175], the form factor to the original polygon is first computed, ignoring occlusion.

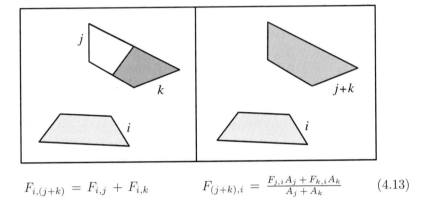

$$F_{i,(j+k)} = F_{i,j} + F_{i,k} \qquad F_{(j+k),i} = \frac{F_{j,i}A_j + F_{k,i}A_k}{A_j + A_k} \qquad (4.13)$$

Figure 4.5: *Form factor algebra.*

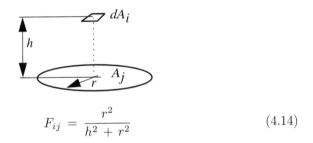

$$F_{ij} = \frac{r^2}{h^2 + r^2} \qquad (4.14)$$

Figure 4.6: *Analytic form factor from point to disk.*

Other polygons in the scene are clipped against this polygon (as viewed from the differential area) and against each other. The form factor to each of the clipped polygons is computed and subtracted from the unoccluded form factor, giving the form factor to the visible portion of the original polygon.

4.7   General Polygon to Polygon

Schröder and Hanrahan give a closed form solution for general polygon-to-polygon form factors, ignoring occlusion [206]. The formulation is non-elementary, as it is based on the *dilogarithm* [151] arising in the integration of the contour integral form of the form factor, equation 4.10. The specifics of the closed form solution are not repeated here as they involve a long series of complex terms.

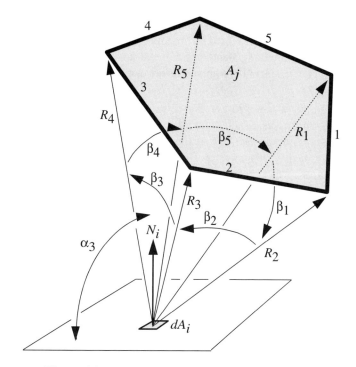

Figure 4.7: *Differential area to polygon form factor.*

III. Numerical Solutions for the Form Factor

Closed form analytic formulae do not lend themselves to the direct evaluation of form factors between complex shapes or where occlusion is a factor. For more general situations, numerical approaches are required to approximate the form factor.

Numerical methods of evaluating integrals (known as *quadrature* methods) generally involve sampling the kernel at various points and approximating the integral as a weighted sum of the kernel evaluated at the sample points. In general, the more sample points selected, the more accurate the approximation. However, *the cost of approximating the integral is directly related to the number of kernel evaluations required* (each of which generally requires a visibility calculation). Thus, the goal in developing a numerical algorithm (or *quadrature rule*) to solve the form factor integral is to get the most accuracy with the fewest (and/or cheapest) kernel evaluations.

There are a number of choices to make in designing a quadrature rule for form factor evaluation. First, in the case of constant basis functions, one can choose to evaluate any of the different formulations of the form factor integral given in section 4.3. The area–area form (equation 4.7) and the area–hemisphere form (equation 4.9) are equivalent, and the contour form (equation 4.10) is also a suitable choice if one can determine a priori that the elements are fully visible to one another.

In addition, there is not just a single form factor to be evaluated, but rather a matrix of form factors. Each entry of a row (or column) of the form factor matrix shares a common element as the domain of integration, thus one may take advantage of this *coherence* by simultaneously solving for a complete row and/or column of form factors.

Finally, one is free to a great extent to choose where to sample the kernel and how to weight the samples so long as it can be shown that as the number of samples increases, the weighted sum converges to the true solution.

After a brief discussion of the general topic of numerical integration, the chapter will proceed with a description of a variety of numerical algorithms that have been developed for form factor evaluation. Other surveys of form factor algorithms such as [78, 187] provide additional insights. The approaches are broadly classified according to which form of the form factor integral they use, how the sample points are selected and weighted, and in what order the form factors are evaluated (e.g., one at a time or a row at a time).

4.8   Numerical Integration in General

Generically, quadrature rules approximate some integral H with kernel $h(x)$ over the domain X as a weighted sum $\hat{H}$:

$$H = \int_X h(x)\, dx \approx \hat{H} = \sum_{k=1}^{n} w_k\, h(x_k) \qquad (4.17)$$

One is free to use any information available about $h(x)$ in choosing the quadrature points, x_k.

Normally, one would like to make n as small as possible to limit the cost incurred in the evaluation of the $h(x_k)$, without compromising accuracy. The simplest methods, like the trapezoidal rule or Simpson's rule, sample the domain at evenly spaced intervals, evaluate the kernel at these points, and sum the results weighted by the size of the interval. Clearly, as the number of samples increases, and the size of the intervals decreases, the approximation approaches the true integral.

4.8.1 Gaussian Quadrature

Simple methods like the trapezoidal rule ignore any knowledge of the integrand. A more efficient selection of quadrature points and weights can be made given the available knowledge about the nature of the integrand $h(x)$. For example, if one knows $h(x)$ is constant across the limits of the integral, then one quadrature point anywhere is sufficient and the weight is simply the difference of the upper and lower limits of integration (in our case, the area of the elements). In general, the smoother the integrand, the fewer quadrature points required to approximate the integral to within some given error.

In one dimension, Gaussian quadrature methods [185] can be used to evaluate exactly integrals of polynomials up to order $2n + 1$ with n carefully selected points and proper weights. The theory behind this observation is quite elegant [226]. The specific quadrature points and associated weights are tabulated and can be found in most numerical methods books or can be computed through recurrence relationships. Extensions to multiple dimensions as in the form factor problem are possible but can be difficult due to the exponential growth in the number of quadrature points required with respect to dimension.

4.8.2 Quadrature Points and the Form Factor Integral

In the double area integral form of the form factor (equation 4.7), the quadrature *point* is now defined in the four-dimensional space, $\mathbf{R}^2 \times \mathbf{R}^2$, of the combined elements.[5] In other words, a quadrature point represents the selection of a pair of 2D points, $\mathbf{x}$ and $\mathbf{x}'$, in elements i and j at which to evaluate the integrand. Similarly, in the area–hemisphere form (equation 4.9), a quadrature point is in the space $\mathbf{R}^2 \times \mathbf{S}^2$, that is, a point $(\mathbf{x}, \vec{\omega})$ is in the combined space of an element area and the hemisphere of directions above that point.

4.8.3 Monte Carlo Methods

Monte Carlo methods are a family of quadrature methods of very general applicability, often used for difficult equations where other methods are impractical or unavailable. Monte Carlo techniques use random numbers to select sample locations in the domain of integration at which to evaluate the integrand.[6] The integral is then taken to be a weighted average of the kernel evaluation at sample points. The weights associated with each sample evaluation depend on how

---

[5]$\mathbf{R}$ is the space of the real number line and $\mathbf{S}$ is the space of directions on a circle. Thus $\mathbf{R}^2$ corresponds to a plane and $\mathbf{S}^2$ corresponds to the surface of a sphere.

[6]*Quasi-random* distributions, such as the Poisson disk, may also be used. The samples in a quasi-random distribution are not completely independent, but have statistical properties that allow them to be used in place of random samples. See, for example, discussions by Shirley in [212].

the samples are selected. If, for example, samples are evenly distributed in the domain, then the weights are simply $\frac{A}{n}$ for n samples with A the size of the domain of integration.

One would like, however, to make as few evaluations of the integrand as possible to reach an answer with some level of confidence of being within some error bound. This process can be enhanced by taking advantage of whatever knowledge one has of the integrand. For example, if the integral H to be evaluated has a kernel $h(x)$ that can be factored, $h(x) = f(x) \cdot g(x)$, where $g(x)$ is a simple known positive function ($g(x) > 0$ for $x \in X$), then the integral can be written

$$H = \int_X f(x)\,g(x)\,dx \tag{4.18}$$

In this case, one would like to find a distribution of samples x_k in X that mimics the known function, $g(x)$. This method of selecting samples is called *importance sampling*, since more samples are taken where $g(x)$ is large (important) and fewer are taken where $g(x)$ is small. More formally,

$$H = \int_X f(x)\,g(x)\,dx = \int_X f(x)\,G\,p(x)\,dx \tag{4.19}$$

where

$$G = \int_X g(x)\,dx \quad \text{and} \quad p(x) = \frac{g(x)}{G} \tag{4.20}$$

$p(x)$ is essentially a normalized $g(x)$ (i.e., $\int_{-\infty}^{\infty} p(x) = 1$) and is thus a *probability density function*. The *cumulative density function* $P(x)$ can be defined as

$$P(x) = \int_{-\infty}^{x} p(x)\,dx \tag{4.21}$$

Loosely speaking, if $p(x)$ represents the odds of picking x, then $P(x)$ represents the odds of picking some number less than or equal to x. If the inverse of the function $P(x)$ is $P^{-1}(x)$, then the Monte Carlo evaluation for the approximation $\hat{H} \approx H$ is simply

---

$\hat{H} = 0$;

for ($k = 1$ to n) {   for n samples
　　choose ξ ;   randomly in the interval from 0 to 1
　　$x = P^{-1}(\xi)$; x will be chosen with probability $p(x)$
　　$\hat{H} = \hat{H} + f(x)$;   sum the sample values of $f(x)$
}
$\hat{H} = \hat{H} * \frac{G}{n}$;   normalize by G and divide by n samples

---

This type of *importance sampling* will be used, for example, to distribute samples according to the cosine in the form factor integral to reduce the number of expensive visibility evaluations. Explicit inverses for $P(x)$ may be difficult to derive, in which case analog procedures, or precomputed lookup tables may be useful. Malley's method, discussed in section 4.9.5, is an example of this approach.

Monte Carlo integration in general is a broad topic, to which numerous textbooks and articles are devoted. Monte Carlo integration for image synthesis is discussed in greater detail in [71, 135, 147, 215]

4.9 Evaluating the Inner Integral

The area–area and the area–hemisphere forms of the double integral both share the same outer integral over element i. Thus, one can separate the question of evaluating the full integral into two parts: first, the evaluation of the inner integral from some dA_i, and second, the selection of one or more sample points on element i at which to evaluate the inner integral. If points on element i are chosen with an even distribution then the full integral is the average of the inner integral evaluations.

In fact, many implementations use only one representative point on element i, in essence making the following assumption (valid also for the area–area form):

$$F_{ij} = \frac{1}{A_i} \int_{A_i} \int_{\Omega} G_{i\omega} \, d\omega \, dA_i \approx \int_{\Omega} G_{i\omega} \, d\omega \quad \text{at sample point } x_i \qquad (4.22)$$

This assumes that the inner integral is constant across element i, which may be reasonable when the distance (squared) is much greater than the area of element j. However, changes in visibility between elements i and j also affect the validity of this approximation. Whether or not this assumption is used, or the inner integral is evaluated at many sample points in element i, one is left with the problem of evaluating the inner integral. This will be the topic of the following sections.

4.9.1 Hemisphere Sampling Algorithms

The use of the hemispherical integral provides a direct basis for evaluating the form factor from a differential area, dA_i, to *all* elements simultaneously. The geometric kernel, $G_{i\omega}$, is given by

$$G_{i\omega} = \frac{\cos \theta_i}{\pi} V_{ij} \qquad (4.23)$$

The visibility term, V_{ij}, which is 1 if element j is visible in direction $d\vec{\omega}$, is the computationally expensive part of the kernel evaluation. Determining the visibility of an element j in a particular direction involves intersecting a ray emanating from dA_i with element j and with all surfaces that may block the ray.

Since form factors from element i to all elements are needed eventually, there is a clear advantage in performing the visibility calculation once and simply summing a differential form factor into F_{ik}, where element k is the element "seen" in direction $d\vec{\omega}$ from dA_i. Thus, *a single integration over the hemisphere results in a full row of differential area-to-element form factors.* Given this observation, the question is how to sample the hemisphere of directions above dA_i, and how to perform the visibility calculations in the chosen directions.

Hemisphere sampling approaches can be principally differentiated by the hidden surface algorithm they use. Certain algorithms provide efficiency by exploiting coherence in the geometry of visible surfaces, while others provide flexibility for stochastic, adaptive or nonuniform sampling. A geometric analog to the differential area-to-area form factor equation is given first to provide some useful intuition for the algorithms that follow.

4.9.2 Nusselt Analog

The Nusselt analog provides a geometric analog to the differential area-to-area form factor equation 4.7 (ignoring the visibility factor). An imaginary unit hemisphere is centered on the differential area, as in Figure 4.8. The element is projected radially onto the hemisphere and then orthogonally down from the hemisphere onto its base. The fraction of the base area covered by this projection is equal to the form factor.

Why does this work? The area of the projection of the element on the unit hemisphere is equal to the solid angle subtended by the element, by definition of the solid angle, and thus accounts for the factor $\cos\theta_j/r^2$. The projection down onto the base accounts for the $\cos\theta_i$ term, and the π in the denominator is the area of a unit circle.

In heat transfer applications, form factors have sometimes been computed for complex shapes by evaluating the Nusselt analog photographically, using a fisheye lens that effectively performs the same double projection. The area covered by the object in the resulting photograph is measured manually to obtain the form factor.

4.9.3 The Hemicube

The Nusselt analog illustrates the fact that elements covering the same projected area on the hemisphere will have the same form factor, since they occupy the

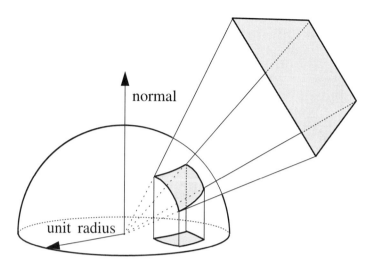

Figure 4.8: *Nusselt analog. The form factor from the differential area dA_i to element A_j is proportional to the area of the double projection onto the base of the hemisphere.*

same solid angle. Likewise, if an element is projected radially onto any inter-mediate surface, as in Figure 4.9, the form factor for the projection will be the same as for the element itself. This observation forms the basis for the *hemicube* form factor algorithm, in which elements are projected onto the planar faces of a half cube instead of onto a hemisphere [62].

A hemicube is placed around a differential area (see Figure 4.10), with the hemicube faces subdivided into small grid cells. Each grid cell defines a direction and a solid angle. A *delta form factor*, ΔF, is computed for each cell based on its size and orientation (see Figure 4.11). For this purpose, it is convenient to consider a unit hemicube (i.e., with a height of 1, and a top face 2×2 units), although the size of the hemicube is arbitrary, since it is the solid angles subtended by the grid cells that are of interest. The delta form factors are precomputed and stored in a lookup table. Only one eighth of the delta form factors need be stored, due to symmetry (one eighth of the top face and half of one side face).

Each face of the hemicube defines a perspective projection, with the eye point located at the differential area and a $90°$ viewing frustum.[7] The form factor to an element is then approximated by projecting the element onto the

---

[7]The sides of the hemicube actually define the top half of a $90°$ frustum since the bottom half falls below the horizon.

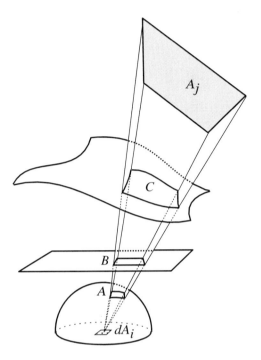

Figure 4.9: *Areas with same form factor. Areas A, B, and C, have the same form factor as A_j from dA_i.*

faces of the hemicube and summing the delta form factors of the grid cells covered by the projection. The visibility problem of determining the closest surface for a regular grid of cells is, of course, a familiar one in computer graphics, since it is essential to producing a raster image. The hemicube uses the Z-buffer algorithm [84], which is simple and efficient, and has the additional advantage of wide availability in hardware graphics accelerators.

The only difference between rendering onto the hemicube and normal image rendering is that in addition to a Z depth, an ID for the visible element is stored at each grid cell, instead of a color (the result is often called an *item buffer* after [260]). The distances are initialized to infinite and the identifiers to NONE. Each element in the environment is projected onto the face of the hemicube one at a time. If the distance to the element through each grid cell is less than what is already recorded, the new smaller distance is recorded as well as the identifier for the element. When all elements have been processed, each grid cell will contain an identifier of the closest element. The grid cells are traversed and the delta form factor for each cell is added to the form factor for the element whose

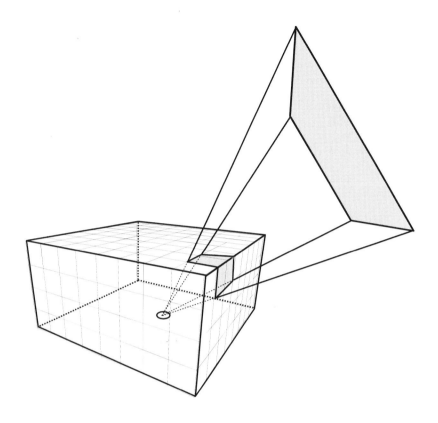

Figure 4.10: *The hemicube.*

ID is stored with that cell. The form factor to element j is thus

$$F_{i,j} = \sum_{q \in j} \Delta F_q \qquad (4.26)$$

where q represents delta grid cells covered by element j. Pseudocode is supplied in Figures 4.12 and 4.13. Hall [114] also provides a detailed pseudocode for the hemicube algorithm.

The hemicube algorithm defines a specific form of quadrature for evaluating the inner form factor integral, $F_{dA_i,j}$. The directions on the hemisphere are predetermined by the orientation and resolution of the grid imposed on the hemicube. The weights associated with each quadrature point are precisely the delta form factors, ΔF, described above. The ΔF, in turn, have been evaluated

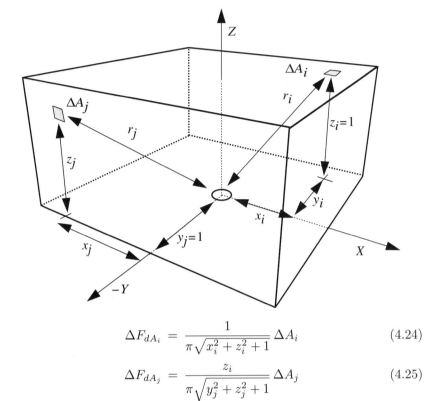

$$\Delta F_{dA_i} = \frac{1}{\pi\sqrt{x_i^2 + z_i^2 + 1}} \Delta A_i \qquad (4.24)$$

$$\Delta F_{dA_j} = \frac{z_i}{\pi\sqrt{y_j^2 + z_j^2 + 1}} \Delta A_j \qquad (4.25)$$

Figure 4.11: *Delta form factors.*

by a one-point quadrature from the center of the hemicube to the hemicube pixel centers.

The efficiency of the hemicube derives from the incremental nature of the Z-buffer algorithm, which exploits coherency in the projected geometry. However, the inflexibility of the Z-buffer is also the source of many of the hemicube's disadvantages.

The hemicube divides the domain of integration, the hemisphere, into discrete, regularly spaced solid angles. When projected elements cover only a few of the grid cells, aliasing can occur. The result is often a plaid-like variation in shading as the hemicube subdivision beats against the element discretization (see Figure 4.14). Very small elements may fall between grid cells and be missed entirely. This is a particular problem for small, high-energy elements like light emitters. Increasing the hemicube resolution can reduce the problem, but this

/* Preprocess: determine delta form factors, given a resolution of the
hemicube. Note: resolution may vary for sides and top of hemicube. Also
Note: symmetry can be used to minimize the storage and computation of
delta form factors. */

/* Top */

```
    dx = dy = 2.0/res;
    x = dx/2.0;
    dA = 4.0/(res²);
    for ( i = 1 to res ) {
        y = dy/2.0;
        for ( j = 1 to res ) {
            ΔF[i][j] = 1.0/(π * (x² + y² + 1.0)²);
            y = y + dy;
        }
        x = x + dx;
    }
```

/* Side, Note: keep track of ordering for scan conversion below */

```
    dx = dz = 2.0/res;
    x = dx/2.0;
    dA = 4.0/(res²);
    for ( i = 1 to res/2 ) {
        z = dz/2.0; /* Note: z goes from bottom to top */
        for ( j = 1 to res ) {
            ΔF[i][j] = z/(π * (x² + z² + 1.0)²);
            z = z + dz;
        }
    x = x + dx;
    }
```

Figure 4.12: *Pseudocode for hemicube form factor calculation.*

is an inefficient solution, since it increases the effort applied to all elements,
irrespective of their contribution.[8]

Because scan conversion requires a uniform grid, the hemisphere subdivision
imposed by the hemicube is also inefficient. From an importance sampling point
of view, the hemisphere should be subdivided so that every grid cell has the same
delta form factor, to distribute the computational effort evenly. Because it uses a

---

[8]Typical hemicube resolutions for images in [62, 246] range from 32 by 32 to 1024
by 1024 on the top hemicube face.

```
/* For each element, determine form factor to each other element */
    for ( i = 1 to num_elements ) {
            initialize F_{ij} = 0 for all j ;
            initialize all hemicube grid cells to NULL element ID ;
            initialize all hemicube grid cells to large Z value ;
            place eye at center (sample point on element i) ;
    /* scan convert and Z-buffer element projections */
            for ( top and each side of hemicube ) {
                Align view direction with top or side;
                for ( j = 1 to num_elements ) {
                    Project element_j onto hemicube ;
                    for ( each grid cell covered )
                            if ( Z distance < recorded Z ) grid cell ID = j ;
                }
                for ( j = 1 to num_elements )
                    F_{ij} = F_{ij} + ∑ ΔF of grid cells with ID = j ;
            }
    }
```

Figure **4.13**: *Pseudocode for hemicube form factor calculation (cont.).*

uniform grid, the hemicube spends as much time determining form factors close to the horizon as it does near the normal direction.

Max [162] has investigated variations of the hemicube in which the resolution of the top and sides are allowed to differ, the cubical shape can become rectangular, and the sizes of the grid cells are allowed to vary with position. By assuming a statistical distribution of the elements being projected, he derives *optimal* resolutions, shapes, and grid cell spacings to reduce quadrature errors. For example, a top face resolution about 40% higher than for the sides, and a side height of approximately 70% of the width provides are found to minimize the error for a given number of grid cells.

The advantage of the hemicube is that it determines form factors to all elements from a single point. This can also be a liability if only one form factor is required. In addition, computing the full area–hemisphere form factor requires repeating the hemicube[9] at a sufficient number of sample points on element i to ensure the desired accuracy for elements that are relatively close together.

---

[9]Rotating the hemicube for each selected sample point is useful for eliminating aliasing artifacts.

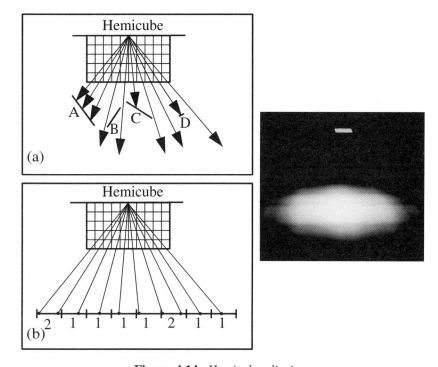

Figure 4.14: *Hemicube aliasing.*

Increasing accuracy in this way will be inefficient, since element i will be close to only a fraction of the other elements in the environment, and the effort of the extra hemicube evaluations will be wasted for elements that are distant from i.

In spite of these limitations, the hemicube can be a useful and efficient means of computing form factors, as long as its limitations are taken into account. Baum *et al.* [19] provide an extensive discussion of the inaccuracies introduced by the hemicube, along with useful error estimates. Comparing results for the hemicube to analytic results for a variety of geometries, Baum *et al.* find that elements must be separated by at least five element diameters for the relative error in the form factor to drop below 2.5 percent. This result will naturally depend on the particular geometries and hemicube parameters, but it provides a useful rule of thumb.

A cube is, of course, not the only solid constructed of planar faces, and other shapes might be used similarly to the hemicube in constructing faces for projection and scan conversion. For example, Beran-Koehn and Pavicic [24, 25] describe an algorithm similar to the hemicube based on a cubic tetrahedron. Spencer [223] describes the use of a regularly subdivided hemisphere.

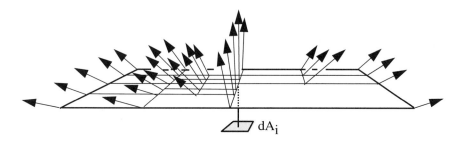

Figure 4.15: *Single plane method.*

4.9.4 Single-Plane Method

The *single-plane* form factor algorithm developed by Sillion [218] partially addresses the inflexibility of the hemicube by replacing the Z-buffer with an adaptive hidden surface algorithm based on Warnock [255]. Sillion's algorithm projects elements onto a single plane above the differential area dA_i. Warnock's [84] algorithm is used to subdivide the image plane adaptively into *windows* for which the element visibility can be determined trivially. Sillion's algorithm is able to subdivide coarsely for large elements and finely for small elements, and thus avoids some of the sampling problems of the hemicube. The delta form factors associated with regions on the projection plane can be precomputed, similarly to delta form factors for the hemicube.

Sillion's algorithm can also compute form factors that take into account specular surfaces. Rays are cast through the corners of the region if the visible element is specular and traced recursively until a diffuse element is encountered (see Figure 4.15).

A single plane algorithm similar to Sillion's is described by Recker [191], who uses a Z-buffer for the hidden surface removal. Both Sillion and Recker note that the single plane will miss elements near the horizon. However, these elements will typically contribute very little to the overall radiosity, due to the cosine dependence of the form factor. Of course, there is no reason, in principle, why a Warnock-style hidden surface algorithm could not be applied to the full hemicube.

Single plane algorithms are based on projection, like the hemicube, and thus compute form factors from a single point. The single plane thus has the same problems as the hemicube for computing full area–hemisphere form factors.

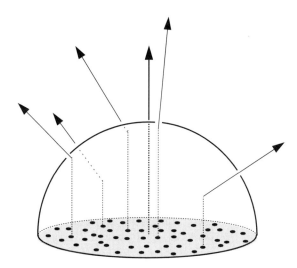

Figure 4.16: *Malley's method.*

4.9.5 Monte Carlo Ray Tracing

Ray tracing (as opposed to scan conversion and the Z-buffer) provides an extremely flexible basis for evaluating the visibility term in the numerical integration of the form factor equation. Because rays are cast independently they can be shot to and from any distribution of points on the elements or directions in the hemisphere. Nonuniform and adaptive sampling can be used to distribute computational effort evenly. Rays can also be distributed stochastically, which can render the effects of inadequate sampling less noticeable by converting aliasing to noise.

In addition, ray tracing handles a wide variety of surface types, including curved surfaces, and a number of efficiency schemes to accelerate ray intersections exist. A disadvantage of ray tracing is that the expense per quadrature point will generally be higher since coherency from ray to ray is more difficult to exploit than in scan conversion algorithms.

Ray casting provides an excellent basis for Monte Carlo integration of the form factor equation over the hemisphere. In equation 4.9, the kernel contains the factor $\cos \theta_i$. Thus importance sampling can be performed by selecting directions over the hemisphere with a sample density proportional to the cosine. In this way, more effort will be expended where the form factor is largest. Since the density of rays is then proportional to the differential form factor, each sample will carry equal weight.

Malley describes a straightforward method for generating a set of sample

directions with the desired distribution [157]. Malley's method is essentially a
Monte Carlo evaluation of the Nusselt analog (see Figure 4.8) run in reverse. He
begins by generating a set of random points uniformly distributed in the circle[10]
under the hemisphere (see Figure 4.16). [11] To determine a direction to shoot
a ray, one of these points is projected vertically to intersect the hemisphere.
The ray is then directed radially out from the center of the hemisphere through
this projected point. Rays are shot in this manner for every sample point in the
circle. The number of times each element in the scene is hit by a ray is recorded.
The form factor is then given by the number of rays that hit a given element
divided by the total number of rays shot. Referring back to Nusselt's analog,
the total number of rays shot is an estimate of the area of the circle covered by
the double projection. The fraction of the total rays that hit a given element thus
approximates the area of the projection of the element on the hemisphere base,
relative to the total area of the base. This fraction is equal to the form factor.
Maxwell also describes the computation of form factors with ray tracing [164].

4.9.6   Area Sampling Algorithms

The hemisphere sampling algorithms described in the previous sections are most
efficient when form factors to all elements from a single point must be computed
at once. Certain solution techniques (e.g., the progressive radiosity algorithm
described in the next chapter) require form factors between only a single pair of
elements at a time, thus the full hemisphere methods are inefficient. In this case,
the area–area formulation (equation 4.7) is a more efficient basis for algorithm
development.

For convenience, the equation for the form factor from a differential area i
to a finite element j is repeated

$$F_{dA_i \rightarrow A_j} = \int_{A_j} \frac{\cos \theta_i \, \cos \theta_j}{\pi \, r^2} \, V_{ij} \, dA_j. \tag{4.27}$$

The integration can be performed by evaluating the kernel at randomly distributed points for a Monte Carlo solution. Wang's discussion of Monte Carlo
sampling of spherical and triangular luminaires in [248] contains much practical
information that can be applied to form factor integration.

---

[10] A random set of points in a circle can be derived by generating two random numbers
between 0 and 1 to locate a point in the square surrounding the circle. If the point is in
the circle, use it; if not discard it. Independently generating a random angle and radius
will not result in a uniform distribution of points.

[11] These points are only used to determine a direction, not to select a point to start a
ray. For an area-to-area computation, the ray origin can also be stochastically distributed
over the area of the element.

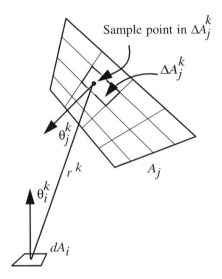

Figure 4.17: *Numerical integration of form factor from differential area to finite area.*

Alternatively, the integration can be performed by subdividing the area uniformly. Wallace *et al.* subdivide A_j into a set of m smaller areas ΔA_j^k and select a sample point at the center of each subarea (see Figure 4.17). The form factor then becomes

$$F_{dA_i - A_j} = \sum_{k=1}^{m} \frac{\cos \theta_i^k \cos \theta_j^k}{\pi (r^k)^2} V(dA_i, \Delta A_j^k) \Delta A_j^k \qquad (4.28)$$

The equation is evaluated by shooting a ray from dA_i to each delta area to determine the visibility, $V(dA_i, \Delta A_j^k)$. The contributions of those delta areas that are visible is then summed.

Equation 4.28 assumes that the subareas are reasonable approximations to differential areas, which is the case only if $\Delta A_j^k << r^2$. Otherwise, ΔA_j^k should be treated as a finite area. For example, each term of the summation could evaluate the exact polygon form factor formula for the particular subarea, as discussed in Tampieri in [230].

A less expensive alternative is to approximate ΔA_j^k by a finite disk of the same area, as suggested by Wallace *et al.* [247]. The analytic formula for a point-to-disk form factor can then be substituted into the summation of Equation 4.28. The form factor from a differential area to a directly opposing disk of area ΔA_j

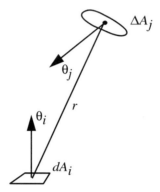

Figure 4.18: *Configuration for approximation of the form factor from a differential area to arbitrarily oriented disk.*

is

$$F_{dA_i \to \Delta A_j} = \frac{\Delta A_j}{\pi r^2 + \Delta A_j} \qquad (4.29)$$

The effect of element orientation can be approximated by including the cosines of the angle between the normal at each surface and the direction between the source and the receiver (see Figure 4.18):

$$F_{dA_i \to \Delta A_j} = \frac{\Delta A_j \cos \theta_i \cos \theta_j}{\pi r^2 + \Delta A_j} \qquad (4.30)$$

The form factor from a differential area to an element j approximated by a set of m disks of area A_j/m is thus

$$F_{dA_i \to A_j} = A_j \sum_{k=1}^{m} \frac{\cos \theta_i^k \cos \theta_j^k}{\pi r^2 + \frac{A_j}{m}} V(dA_i, \Delta A_j) \qquad (4.31)$$

The reciprocity relationship can also be used to approximate the form factor from a finite area to a differential area through the ratio of the areas:

$$F_{A_j \to dA_i} = F_{A_j \to dA_i} \frac{dA_i}{A_j} = \frac{\cos \theta_i \cos \theta_j}{\pi r^2 + A_j} dA_i \qquad (4.32)$$

The disk approximation breaks down when the distance from the disk to the receiver is small relative to the size of the delta area, and visible artifacts may result, as shown in Figure 4.19(a). An additional difficulty with uniform subdivision of the element is that since a single ray is cast to each of the source subdivisions, the element is essentially treated as several point lights as far

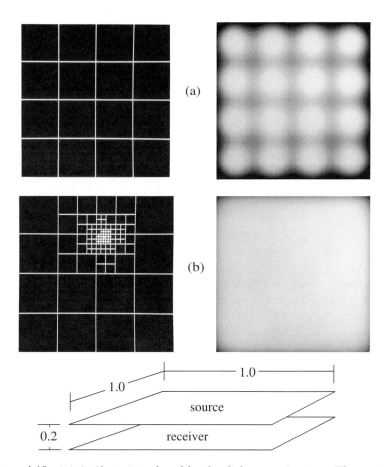

Figure 4.19: *(a) Artifacts introduced by the disk approximation. The receiving surface consists of 30 by 30 elements. (b) Adaptive subdivision of the source element for a typical node on the receiving element.*

as visibility is concerned. As a result, the shadow boundary may appear as a number of overlapping, sharp-edged shadows rather than a smoothly shaded penumbra.

Both of these problems can be addressed by adaptively subdividing area A_j. This is performed in a straightforward manner by subdividing the area recursively until the resulting delta areas fulfill some criterion. The criterion may be geometric (e.g., the delta area must be much less than r^2) or based on the energy received from the delta area. The result of adaptive element

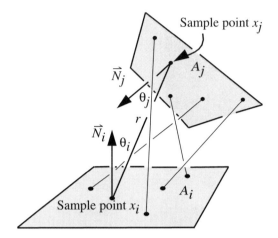

Figure 4.20: *Monte Carlo area-to-area form factor.*

subdivision is shown in Figure 4.19(b). Tampieri [230] provides a detailed practical discussion of this approach, including pseudocode.

4.10   Full Area-to-Area Quadrature

Any of the analytic or numeric differential area-to-area form factor solutions discussed so far can be used to approximate the full area to area form factor. The differential area-to-area form factor is evaluated at one or more points on element A_i and the result averaged. For example, the ray tracing algorithm just described could be performed for several points on A_i. However, since many rays connecting the two surfaces originate at the same points on A_i, this approach samples A_i inefficiently. There are several more effective approaches, including Monte Carlo integration, numerical solution of the contour integral form, and hierarchical subdivision.

4.10.1   Monte Carlo Integration

The double area integral can be approximated more accurately by distributing the endpoints of the rays over A_i as well as A_j. In a Monte Carlo approach ray endpoints on both elements would be distributed randomly, or according to some quasi-random distribution like the Poisson disk. Pseudocode is for a simple area-to-area Monte Carlo form factor algorithm is given in Figure 4.21 (the geometry is shown in Figure 4.20).

$F_{ij} = 0$
for $k = 1$ to n
    randomly select point $\mathbf{x}_i$ on element i or use stratified sample
    randomly select point $\mathbf{x}_j$ on element j or use stratified sample
    determine visibility between $\mathbf{x}_i$ and $\mathbf{x}_j$
    if visible
        compute $r^2 = (\mathbf{x}_i - \mathbf{x}_j)^2$
        compute $\cos\theta_i = \vec{r_{ij}} \bullet \vec{N_i}$
        compute $\cos\theta_j = \vec{r_{ji}} \bullet \vec{N_j}$
        compute $\Delta F = \frac{\cos\theta_i \cos\theta_j}{\pi r^2 + \frac{A_j}{n}}$
        if($\Delta F > 0$) $F_{ij} = F_{ij} + \Delta F$
    end if
end for
$F_{ij} = F_{ij} * A_j$

where $\vec{r_{ij}}$ is the normalized vector from $\mathbf{x}_i$ to $\mathbf{x}_j$, and $\vec{N_i}$ is the unit normal to element i at point $\mathbf{x}_i$ (and vice versa for switching i and j).

Figure 4.21: *Pseudocode for Monte Carlo area-to-area form factor computation.*

One can do better in terms of fewer rays by sampling the elements nonuniformly and adaptively. An elegant solution for this decision-making process is presented in Chapter 7.

4.11 Contour Integral Formulation

In the earliest work introducing the radiosity method to computer graphics, Goral *et al.* [100] used Stokes' theorem to convert the double *area* integral into the double contour integral of equation 4.10.

The contour integrals can be evaluated numerically by "walking" around the contours of the pair of elements, [12] evaluating the kernel at discrete points and summing the values of the kernel at those points [100]. In fact, Goral *et al.* use a three-point quadratic Gaussian quadrature (nine-point in 2D) along

---

[12]Nishita and Nakamae point out that the contour integration approach can be used to compute a single form factor to objects constructed of multiple non-coplanar surfaces. The form factor computed for the contour of the composite object as viewed from the differential area is equal to the sum of the form factors to each of the component surfaces, since it is the solid angle subtended by the surfaces of the object that determines their contribution to the form factor. This is a valuable observation that has not yet been taken advantage of in radiosity implementations for image synthesis.

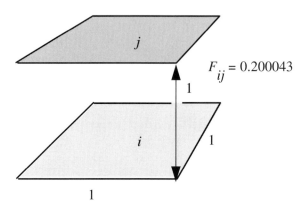

$$F_{ij} = 0.200043$$

Figure 4.22: *Simple test environment.*

the boundaries. Care must be taken when the boundaries are shared between elements, as $\ln(r)$ is undefined as $r \to 0$.

Equation 4.10 does not account for occlusion. If only the inner contour integral is to be evaluated (in computing a differential area-to-area form factor), occlusion can be accounted for using a polygon clipping approach such as Nishita and Nakamae's [175].

4.12   A Simple Test Environment

To provide a concrete illustration of some of the issues discussed in this chapter, three numerical form factor algorithms have been tested on the simple two-polygon environment shown in Figure 4.22. Results are shown in Figure 4.23. The two polygons are parallel unit squares one unit distance apart. The analytic form factor between them is approximately 0.1998.

Tests were run using the hemicube method, Malley's method for randomly selecting directions, and the area–area Monte Carlo method. In each case, two tests were run, (Test 1) from the center point only of element i, and (Test 2) from a set of randomly selected points in element i. A series of 1000 runs was made of each. The mean, standard deviation (box height in graph) and minimum and maximum values (vertical lines) are displayed in the graphs.[13] The horizontal axis is given in terms of the resolution of the hemicube, the number of random directions that fell in element j in Malley's method and the number of sample points in element j in the Monte Carlo method. In Test 2, the same number

---

[13]The hemicube method from the center of element i (Test 1) has no deviation since it is a deterministic algorithm.

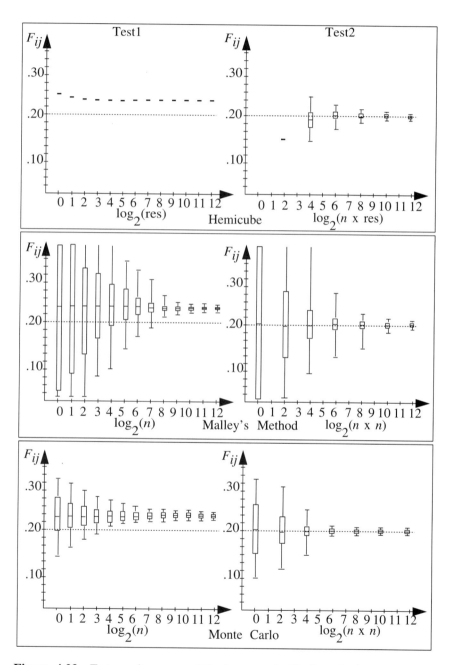

Figure 4.23: *Test results on parallel elements. In Test1, only the center point was chosen on element i and n points on element j. In Test 2 n points are chosen on both elements. res is the resolution of the hemicube in both tests.*

was chosen for sample points in element i and the horizontal axis represents the product of the number of sample points and directions.

All of the methods converged reasonably well in this case as the sampling density (resolution, in the case of the hemicube) increased. Note that the form factor from the center of element i to element j is approximately 0.2395, and thus the solution always converged to about 20% over the actual value for Test 1. Also, note the single point on the graph for the hemicube with resolution 2 performed at 2 random points chosen on element i. Because of the low resolution and the fixed orientation of the hemicube with respect to the environment coordinate frame, the form factor happens always to be the same, no matter where the hemicube is position on element i. This extreme case highlights the problems due to the regular sampling enforced by the hemicube that are encountered as the resolution becomes small relative to the projected area of the elements.

4.13   Nonconstant Basis Functions

The discussion so far has been limited to evaluating form factors where constant basis functions are used. This has been the dominant approximation used in radiosity implementations to date. In this section we briefly introduce the computation of form factors for higher order elements. However, this remains largely an area for future development.

Recall from the last chapter that the coefficients of the linear operator $\mathbf{K}$ are given by

$$K_{ij} = M_{ij} - \rho_i F_{ij} \qquad (4.33)$$

For orthonormal (e.g., constant) bases, the M matrix is simply the identity after division by "area" terms. In the more general case, it represents the inner product of the ith and jth basis functions:

$$M_{ij} = \int_S N_i(\mathbf{x})\, N_j(\mathbf{x})\, dA \qquad (4.34)$$

The integral will be nonzero only where the support of the two basis functions overlaps. This integral can generally be evaluated analytically since the basis functions are chosen to be simple polynomials.

Slightly reorganizing equation 4.3, the F_{ij} are given by

$$F_{ij} = \int_{A_i} \int_{A_j} N_i(\mathbf{x})\, N_j(\mathbf{x}')\, G(\mathbf{x}, \mathbf{x}')\, dA'\, dA \qquad (4.35)$$

The interpretation of the coefficients F_{ij} is slightly less intuitive in this general case. The integral is still over the support (A_i, A_j) of the two basis functions as before. The only difference is the inclusion of the basis functions in the integrand. The form factor now represents the exchange of energy between regions under the support of the basis functions, weighted by the local values of basis functions.

4.13.1 The Hemicube for General Form Factors

Many numeric form factor algorithms can be generalized in a straightforward manner to higher order basis functions. Wallace's ray casting algorithm, for example, could evaluate the basis functions at each delta area and weight the delta form factor accordingly. This is essentially the approach used by Tampieri and Lischinski in [231].

Max and Allison [163] describe a hemicube algorithm for linear elements that makes clever use of graphics hardware. Performing a hemicube for higher order elements requires that the delta form factor for each grid cell be weighted by the value of each basis function that is nonzero at the point on element j seen through that particular grid cell.

Max and Allison use the Gouraud shading hardware in a graphics accelerator to interpolate the basis function for triangular elements. Each of the three vertices is given the maximum value for one of the r, g, b color channels. The faces of the hemicube are set up as perspective views and the elements passed as polygons to the hardware. The Gouraud shading hardware will then interpolate the vertex colors to the hemicube grid cells. The value of each color channel gives the value of the respective basis functions at that grid cell.

Noting that the three basis functions for a triangular element sum to 1.0 everywhere on the element interior, Max and Allison actually store colors for only two vertices. The value of the third basis function can be obtained at any grid cell using the identity $N_3(\mathbf{x}) = 1.0 - N_1(\mathbf{x}) - N_2(\mathbf{x})$. This frees up a color channel, which when combined with the alpha channel provides room for a 16-bit element ID.

4.13.2 Monte Carlo for General Form Factors

The Monte Carlo algorithm described earlier in section 4.10.1 for evaluating the area-to-area form factor can also be generalized to higher order elements. The algorithm is basically unchanged, except that each sample point on A_i and A_j now contributes to the form factor for each of the nonzero basis functions at that point, with the contribution weighted by the value of the basis function. A single ray between two sample points $\mathbf{x}$ and $\mathbf{x}'$ can be used to contribute to more than one F_{ij} if the basis functions overlap. For example, with linear, quadrilateral elements, a single ray will typically result in 16 (4 i bases $\times$ 4 j bases) nonzero

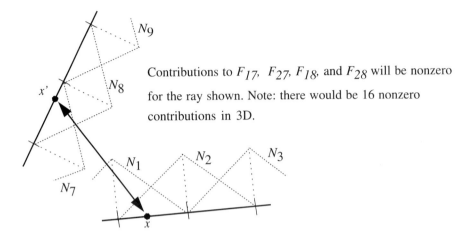

Contributions to F_{17}, F_{27}, F_{18}, and F_{28} will be nonzero for the ray shown. Note: there would be 16 nonzero contributions in 3D.

Figure 4.24: *Monte Carlo for form factors with general basis functions.*

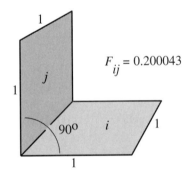

Figure 4.25: *Simple test environment with a singularity.*

contributions to the **K** matrix (see Figure 4.24). The same samples can also be used to evaluate the M_{ij} numerically if desired.

4.13.3   Singularities in the Integrand

Although most of the algorithms described above will provide reasonable evaluations of the form factor for most cases, they can suffer serious inadequacies in the presence of singularities in the kernel. The singularity in the integrand for equations 4.7 and 4.10 occurs when the two differential areas meet (i.e., $r \rightarrow 0$).

Potential difficulties are illustrated by an experimental comparison in which three variations of numerical form factor algorithms were tested as before, but this time on two unit squares at right angles with a shared edge (see Figure 4.25). The test environment thus contains no transitions in visibility but does have a region (along the shared edge) at which the kernel of the area–area integrand becomes singular.

Results are shown in Figure 4.26. Although in all the algorithms the mean tends toward an accurate answer, any single invocation of the Monte Carlo method can return an extremely inaccurate answer due to the singularity. The standard deviation is much less in the hemicube and Malley's method since the area–hemisphere method removes the singularity analytically before the numerical evaluation.

There are a number of other ways to deal with the singularities. If the singularities in the kernel are guaranteed to occur only on the edges of the elements (e.g., where a wall meets the floor), and the basis set is chosen to have zeros of multiplicity 2 at its edges, then the singularity will disappear when weighted by the basis function under the integral. One example of such a basis is provided by the Jacobi polynomial set on the element parameterized by u and v ranging from -1 to 1:

$$N(u, v) = (1 - u^2)^2(1 - v^2)^2 \qquad (4.36)$$

Although the numerator goes to zero *as fast* as the denominator, this of course does not prevent a divide by zero in practice. One would need explicitly to check for this condition. This option is not pursued further here. Details of this approach can be found in [270].

Another solution is to move the quadrature point away from the singularity by a small amount. In other words, if r is below some threshold, the quadrature points are moved away from the intersection of the elements where the singularity occurs. Care must be taken that the movement is *inward* on the elements. Since there is no analytic justification for moving the points inward, the accuracy of the results will not converge to zero with large numbers of samples, but the possible large errors incurred from hitting the singularity will be avoided. Hybrid methods that handle singular regions analytically coupled with numerical methods for the rest of the integral are also possible but have not been extensively explored.

In point collocation, nodes on concave corners, such as on the floor where it intersects the wall, will result in a form factor of zero for the intersecting surface. In the case of a projection algorithm like the hemicube, this is because the intersecting surface passes through the eye point and thus projects as a line [163]. The form factor will be zero for other algorithms, since the cosine of the angle with respect to the intersecting surface is zero. If that surface reflects a significant amount of energy, a visible dark streak along the receiving surface near the intersection may result. Moving the node inward may help in these

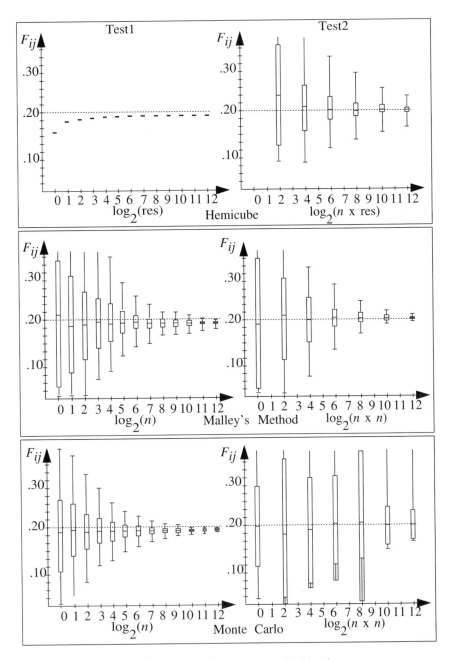

Figure 4.26: *Test results on perpendicular elements.*

cases. The hierarchical subdivision algorithms discussed in Chapter 7 provide a more systematic approach to this problem.

4.14 Acceleration Techniques

The form factor computation is expensive and is repeated many times during the radiosity solution. It has thus been a natural target for acceleration. Improved algorithms and hardware assistance have both been applied, particularly to the visibility problem. In the following sections we will survey methods for speeding up the hemicube and ray-tracing-based form factor algorithms. (A discussion of coarser grained parallel algorithms will be held off until Chapter 5.)

4.14.1 Hemicube Acceleration

Visibility Preprocessing

Performing a single hemicube consists essentially of determining the surfaces visible from a particular point of view. During the radiosity solution this visibility calculation is repeated over and over for potentially thousands of different viewpoints. Since the geometry of the scene does not change during this process, radiosity is a natural candidate for visibility preprocessing.

In a visibility preprocess, the surfaces of the scene are organized by a spatial data structure that allows the visibility from any particular viewpoint to be quickly determined. Visibility preprocessing has a long history in computer graphics; the need to render a fixed geometry from many different viewpoints is often encountered in interactive simulation or "walk-through" and "fly-through" applications. Algorithms date back to Schumaker's *list priority* method [208] and include octree [72] and BSP-based [87] visibility algorithms.

Wang and Davis [249] build an octree as a visibility preprocess for radiosity. As space is split recursively into octants, surfaces are subdivided into elements by clipping them against the octant boundaries. As a result, when the preprocess is complete each element will fall into one and only one octree cell. For a particular hemicube, the goal is to traverse the octree cells in front-to-back order with respect to the hemicube location. The elements can then be painted onto the hemicube faces in front-to-back order, which eliminates the need to compute and store the z-depth.

For a particular viewpoint, a visibility priority can be established for the eight children of a given octant. The subdivision of the octant determines eight subspaces. The priority ordering of the eight children is determined by which of these subspaces the viewpoint falls into. Each of the children is visited according to the priority ordering and traversed recursively in the same fashion. The leaves of the octree are thus visited in front-to-back order with respect to the viewpoint.

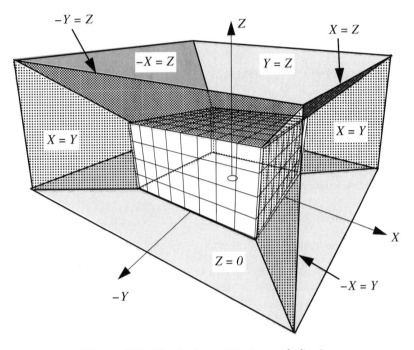

Figure 4.27: *Hemicube positioning and clipping.*

If more than one element is contained in a single leaf cell, the priority of these must be established by some other means.

View Coherence

Although a hemicube requires projecting the scene onto five different image planes, the five planes are obviously far from arbitrarily related. The hemicube determines five orthogonal 90-degree view frustums. If the five planes are positioned to face in the $+X$, $-X$, $+Y$, $-Y$, and $+Z$ directions (see Figure 4.27), the coherence that arises from this arrangement provides several opportunities for optimization.

Vilaplana and Pueyo [245] observe that once the elements have been transformed to the view coordinates of the front face of the hemicube, they can be rapidly transformed for the other faces simply by swapping coordinates and changing signs appropriately. Given a coordinate x, y, z in the top face's view, the transformations are

$$
\begin{array}{llll}
Left & : & (x',y',z') = (y,z,x) \\
Right & : & (x',y',z') = (-y,z,x) \\
Front & : & (x',y',z') = (x,z,-y) \\
Back & : & (x',y',z') = (-x,z,y)
\end{array}
\tag{4.37}
$$

Vilaplana and Pueyo also suggest a way of accelerating the clipping that must be performed against each of the five view frustums. The top view frustum shares a clipping plane with each of the four side view frustums, and each of the side frustums shares planes with two other side frustums. Vilaplana and Pueyo describe a modified Sutherland-Hodgman clipping algorithm in which each edge of each element is clipped against all five frustums in one pass (as well as against the sixth horizon plane determined by the base of the hemicube). Vertices are transformed into the view coordinates for the top face. Each vertex of an element is then classified in turn by testing against the six clipping planes. The vertices, including those created by clipping edges, are added to lists maintained for each frustum. Following clipping, the vertices for each frustum are transformed as above, projected onto the corresponding hemicube face, and scan-converted as usual.

Hardware Z-Buffering

One inspiration for the original hemicube algorithm was the availability of hardware depth-buffers to do the visibility determination. The basic approach to using graphics acceleration is to specify a view for each face of the hemicube and pass the elements down the hardware pipeline for scan-conversion and Z-buffering. Instead of a color, an item ID is stored at each pixel, which identifies the visible element. The ID can be generated by assigning each element a color corresponding to its ID. The colors can then be read back from the frame buffer and decoded, with the contribution due to the delta form factor at each pixel computed in software as usual. This approach has been implemented by Baum *et al.* [21] and others. Bu [39] also describes a hardware implementation for fast form factor computation.

A similar approach is used by Recker *et al.* [191]. Instead of the hemicube, Recker uses a single plane method, which requires that each element be projected, clipped and scan converted once rather than five times.

An interesting hardware alternative to the hemicube has been proposed by Fuchs *et al.* [88] for the *Pixel Planes* 5 graphics engine. This algorithm computes Nusselt's analog directly, taking advantage of the ability of *Pixel Planes* 5 to evaluate a quadratic expression at every pixel. Their estimated time to compute form factors to 100,000 elements is 1 second.

4.14.2 Ray Tracing Acceleration

One advantage of ray tracing for computing form factors is the wealth of acceleration algorithms and data structures that are available. Bounding box hierarchies, voxel grids, and octrees are all applicable to ray tracing for radiosity.[14]

The rays used for form factor computations are generally *shadow* rays. Thus they need only determine whether occlusion occurs or not, as opposed to determining the closest intersection along the ray. There are several specialized tricks for accelerating shadow ray testing that are worthwhile looking at for radiosity implementations [111]. Perhaps the simplest, *shadow caching*, is always to test the ray against the most recently encountered occluding object, on the assumption that an extended object will tend to intersect a number of neighboring rays.

Directional acceleration schemes are particularly well suited to radiosity. These take advantage of the coherence between rays leaving a particular region of space in a particular set of closely related directions [11]. As has been seen, computing the form factor from one element to another may require shooting many rays between the two elements. These rays tend to have similar origins and directions.

The *shaft-culling* algorithm described by Haines and Wallace [112] and by Zhang [271] is intended to exploit this coherence. Haines and Wallace organizes the objects of the scene into a bounding box hierarchy. Rays can always be tested for an intersection by traversing this hierarchy starting at the root node. Intuitively, however, if many rays are to be shot between two limited regions, such as two elements, it is worth some effort to create a short *candidate list* of objects for testing. Candidate objects are those that lie in the region of space joining the starting and ending areas.

Haines and Wallace first construct a volume, or *shaft*, using planes to join the bounding boxes of the objects or elements that define the endpoints of the rays. The bounding boxes are constrained to be orthogonal to the world coordinate axes. This allows a number of geometric and algebraic simplifications in the construction of the shaft. An example is shown in Figure 4.28.

Once the shaft is created, it is tested against the bounding box hierarchy. A box that is entirely contained within the shaft is added to the candidate list. A box that partly intersects the shaft is usually opened up, and its sons tested against the shaft recursively, in a depth-first manner. In some cases it may be better to add the box on the candidate list without opening it up. A box that is entirely outside the shaft is *culled*, and traversal of that branch of the tree is ended. The final result is a candidate list of bounding boxes and objects.

---

[14]The best introduction to this topic is Arvo and Kirk's *Survey of Ray Tracing Acceleration Techniques* in [97].

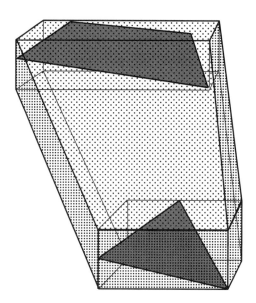

Figure 4.28: *Shaft culling: first an axis aligned bounding box in constructed around each polygon. Then a convex hull (or shaft) is constructed between pairs of bounding boxes.*

Shaft culling is potentially useful for occlusion algorithms other than ray tracing. For example, the polygon contour clipping algorithm of Nishita and Nakamae [175] could be accelerated using shaft culling to produce a candidate list of polygons for clipping.

Marks *et al.* [160] describe an algorithm related to shaft culling in which the object is to rapidly cull away empty portions of the volume connecting two elements. The volume is subdivided recursively, with recursion stopping when a volume becomes empty. After a certain subdivision limit is exceeded, the remaining volumes are tested for occlusion using rays.

Teller and Hanrahan investigate incremental visibility algorithms that rapidly preprocess the environment and categorize pairs of surfaces as fully visible to one another, fully blocked, or partially blocked [232]. They also maintain a candidate list of blocking surfaces between each pair. This preprocessed information then greatly accelerates visibility calculations during form factor computation.

Chapter 5

Radiosity Matrix Solutions

In Chapter 3, techniques were described for approximating the radiosity integral equation (3.1) by a system of linear equations. Depending on whether *point collocation* or *Galerkin* techniques are used, a system of linear equations is obtained (equations 3.13 or 3.20) which when solved provide the nodal values that determine an approximate radiosity function. In either case the linear equations can be summarized by

$$\mathbf{K}\,\mathbf{B} \;=\; \mathbf{E} \tag{5.1}$$

where $\mathbf{K}$ is a matrix of interactions, $\mathbf{B}$ is a vector of nodal radiosity values, and $\mathbf{E}$ is a vector of emission terms. The $\mathbf{K}$ matrix can be broken down into the difference of a (almost) diagonal matrix and a matrix of coefficients scaled by reflectivity terms,[1] ρ:

$$[\mathbf{M} - \mathbf{PF}]\,\mathbf{B} \;=\; \mathbf{E} \tag{5.2}$$

If the radiosity function is approximated using constant basis functions, area terms can be divided out, and $\mathbf{M}$ is simply the identity I. Thus $\mathbf{K}$ looks like

$$\begin{bmatrix} 1 - \rho_1 F_{1,1} & -\rho_1 F_{1,2} & -\rho_1 F_{1,3} & \cdot & \cdot & -\rho_1 F_{1,n} \\ -\rho_2 F_{2,1} & 1 - \rho_2 F_{2,2} & -\rho_2 F_{2,3} & \cdot & \cdot & -\rho_2 F_{2,n} \\ \cdot & & & & & \cdot \\ \cdot & & & & & \cdot \\ -\rho_{n-1} F_{n-1,1} & & & & & \cdot \\ -\rho_n F_{n,1} & \cdot & & \cdot & \cdot & 1 - \rho_n F_{n,n} \end{bmatrix} \tag{5.3}$$

The previous chapter concentrated on ways to evaluate the entries of $\mathbf{F}$, the form factors. This chapter focuses on how to solve the linear system given $\mathbf{K}$

---

[1] As noted in Chapter 3, the reflectivity, ρ, must be specified for each of the wavelengths or color bands of interest. In most applications for image synthesis, 3 or 4 wavelengths are sufficient. Thus, there will be 3 or 4 $\mathbf{K}$ matrices, one for each wavelength. The form factors discussed in Chapter 4 are only dependent on geometry and are thus valid across the visible spectrum. The radiosity problem will continue to be addressed as a monochrome one, with the understanding that the algorithms described are applicable at each wavelength individually.

and **E**. The characteristics of **K** are examined first followed by a description of applicable techniques from the numerical methods literature on solutions of linear systems. Finally these methods are applied to the radiosity problem.

5.1   Qualities of the Matrix

The following points describe qualities of the matrix **K** that are relevant to the selection of specific numerical algorithms:

- *Size:* In general, the matrix will be square and of size n by n, where n is the number of basis functions (i.e., the unknown coefficients B_i) that make up the approximation of the radiosity function. In Chapter 7 *hierarchical* methods are examined in which rectangular matrices will appear.

- *Sparsity:* As for most systems resulting from integral equations of a form like the radiosity equation, the matrix will typically be more full than sparse. The ijth position of the matrix will be zero only when the reflectivity of a surface is zero (i.e., the surface is black) or the supports of the ith and jth bases are completely invisible to one another (e.g., for constant bases, when element i cannot *see* element j). The bases can be invisible to one another either because of occlusion or because they face away from one other. Only an environment resembling the inside of an empty sphere (i.e., one in which every element can see every other element) will result in a completely full matrix. For a complex environment, the matrix will be fairly sparse, since many elements will be invisible to each other. In fact, if the environment consists of two separate rooms with no means for light to travel between them, the matrix will be block diagonal, meaning that, intuitively, it can be divided into two independent subproblems.

- *Symmetry:* A matrix **A** is symmetric if elements $a_{ij} = a_{ji}$ for all i, j. **K** is not symmetric in its current form. However a simple transformation can produce an equivalent system in which the matrix is symmetric. If each row i is multiplied by the area of the ith element, then the **F** matrix is made symmetric, due to the reciprocity of form factors (i.e., $F_{ij}A_i = F_{ji}A_j$). **K** can also be premultiplied by the inverse of the reflectivities to complete the symmetry, but zero-valued reflectivities (as in the case of light sources) will be a problem. Thus, although there is a type of symmetry in the physical process which is manifest in the matrix, it will not be relied on explicitly in the solution methods discussed in this chapter.

- *Diagonal Dominance:*   A matrix is said to be diagonally dominant if the absolute value of the sum of the off-diagonal terms in each row is less than or equal to the absolute value of the diagonal term itself:

$$\sum_{\substack{j=1 \\ j \neq i}}^{n} |K_{ij}| \leq |K_{ii}|, \forall i \tag{5.4}$$

This is strictly true for the radiosity problem with constant basis functions. This can be seen by examining the matrix equation 5.3, in which the diagonal terms are all equal to one. The sum of the form factors in any row is by definition equal to unity, and in any physically realistic system the reflectivity terms will be less than one. Thus, the off-diagonal terms must sum to less than the diagonal term. The matrix will also be diagonally dominant for general basis functions with local support.

The diagonal dominance of $\mathbf{K}$ ensures that particular iterative solution methods such as Gauss-Seidel (described in section 5.3.2) will converge. However, the diagonal dominance of rows should not be confused with the diagonal dominance of columns, which does not characterize the current form of $\mathbf{K}$. This distinction will arise in the discussion of Southwell's method, described in section 5.3.3.

- *Spectral Radius:* The spectral radius of a matrix is a particular type of *norm* that describes the size of its largest eigenvalue. The detailed definition of these terms is beyond the scope of this text. The spectral radius is an indicator of the speed with which iterative methods will converge. Intuitively, one can see that as the reflectivity values approach unity (i.e., perfect reflectors), the system will require more iterations to converge. Physically speaking the light will reflect about the environment more before being absorbed. Mathematically, the spectral radius is approaching one.

If $\mathbf{PF}$ has a norm less than one, then $\mathbf{K} = [\mathbf{I} - \mathbf{PF}]$ is invertible, and the Neumann series of successive multiplications of $\mathbf{PF}$ will converge to the inverse.

$$\text{If } \| \mathbf{PF} \| < 1 \text{ then } \mathbf{K}^{-1} = [\mathbf{I} - \mathbf{PF}]^{-1} = \sum_{a=0}^{\infty} (\mathbf{PF})^{a} \tag{5.5}$$

This property is also important for iterative methods such as Jacobi iteration, which in essence mimics the Neumann series.

- *Condition:* The condition number of a matrix describes how sensitive the solution is to small perturbations in the input (as in the case the emission terms). In general, the matrix arising in radiosity applications is *well conditioned*, indicating that most solution methods are applicable.

5.2   Linear System Solution Methods

Of the great variety of algorithms that have been developed to solve linear systems, the following sections will concentrate on methods that have proven useful for the radiosity problem. Each of the basic algorithms will be described, followed by a discussion of its behavior in the context of the radiosity problem. More general surveys and more theoretical treatments are widely available in numerical methods texts [138, 185, 226].

5.2.1   Direct Methods

Direct methods for solving linear systems are perhaps most familiar but are not well suited to large systems of equations. Such methods, like Gaussian elimination and its variants, can be applied to systems such as the radiosity problem, but they exhibit a computational complexity related to the cube of the number of equations, $O(n^3)$. Thus, these methods are prohibitively expensive except when applied to small problems, or when the system of equations is sparse. For image synthesis the system of equations is liable to be quite large and relatively full. Thus, iterative solution methods are the focus of the ensuing discussion.

5.2.2   Iterative Methods

In contrast to direct methods, iterative methods begin with a guess for the solution and proceed by performing (preferably) inexpensive operations that move the guess to a better guess. The solution is said to have been found, or *converged*, when there is some confidence that the current guess is very close to the actual solution. Given the linear system

$$\mathbf{K}\,\mathbf{B} = \mathbf{E} \tag{5.6}$$

containing the unknown vector, $\mathbf{B}$, and an initial guess, $\mathbf{B}^{(0)}$, the error, $\mathbf{e}^{(0)}$, is defined to be equal to the difference between the actual answer $\mathbf{B}$ and the current guess

$$\mathbf{e}^{(0)} = \mathbf{B} - \mathbf{B}^{(0)} \tag{5.7}$$

Since the real answer $\mathbf{B}$ is not known, $\mathbf{e}$ cannot be measured directly. However, one can define a *residual*, $r^{(0)}$, where

$$\mathbf{r}^{(0)} = \mathbf{K}\,\mathbf{B}^{(0)} - \mathbf{E} \tag{5.8}$$

Clearly, if the residual is zero, then the solution guess is correct and the error is zero as well. In contrast to the error, the residual is a quantity that can be directly measured.

After each iteration [2] of the solution process, the most recent guess and residual, ($\mathbf{B}^{(k)}$ and $\mathbf{r}^{(k)}$), are replaced by a more accurate guess and residual, ($\mathbf{B}^{(k+1)}$ and $\mathbf{r}^{(k+1)}$).

The initial guess, $\mathbf{B}^{(0)}$, can influence the rate of convergence. In general, an initial guess that is closer to the final solution will require fewer iterations. If there is no information available upon which to base an initial guess, $B^{(0)}$ can simply be a vector of zeros. For the radiosity problem the light source radiosities are given a priori by $\mathbf{E}$, and a better initial guess is $\mathbf{B}^{(0)} = \mathbf{E}$ since light sources typically have zero reflection.

5.3   Relaxation Methods

The types of iterative algorithms explored below are called *relaxation* methods. The idea is that at each step of the algorithm one element of the residual vector will be set to zero. In other words, one of the $B_i^{(k)}$ will be chosen to change in such a way that $r_i^{(k+1)} = 0$. Of course the other $r_j^{(k)}$, $j \neq i$ may increase, but hopefully an improvement has been made on the whole. The input to each step may be the approximate solution $B^{(k)}$ (and perhaps part of the new guess $B^{(k+1)}$) and one or all of the current residuals, in addition to the matrix $\mathbf{K}$ and vector $\mathbf{E}$.

5.3.1   Jacobi Iteration

Perhaps the simplest iterative scheme is to update each element $B_i^{(k)}$ of the solution vector by solving for that variable using the current guess $B^{(k)}$. Thus n steps (one iteration) can be performed simultaneously (one for each i). Solving for a single B_i, beginning with the ith row from the matrix equation 5.3

$$\sum_j K_{ij} Bj = E_i \qquad (5.9)$$

moving all but the ith term to the right hand side

$$K_{ii} B_i = E_i - \sum_{j \neq i} K_{ij} B_j \qquad (5.10)$$

---

[2]Superscripts (e.g., $B^{(k)}$) will be used to indicate a complete *iteration* of the iterative solution process. A superscript of zero indicates the state prior to the first iteration. An iteration is distinguished from a *step*, which refers to the processing of one entry in $\mathbf{B}$ during a particular iteration. A complete iteration will usually involve n steps. Subscripts will be used to indicate position in the vector when necessary.

and dividing by K_{ii} results in a new value for B_i for iteration $k + 1$

$$B_i^{(k+1)} = E_i - \sum_{j \neq i} K_{ij} \frac{B_j^{(k)}}{K_{ii}} \tag{5.11}$$

With the definition of the residual vector (equation 5.8), this can be simplified to adding the residual divided by the diagonal to the previous guess,

$$B_i^{(k+1)} = B_i^{(k)} + \frac{r_i^{(k)}}{K_{ii}} \tag{5.12}$$

Thus *if the residual vector is known* [3] the full iteration (all n steps) can be performed in linear time, $O(n)$. Although each step in isolation would relax one element of the residual if the old solution were still valid, none other than the first element of B dealt with would actually result in zeroing out the corresponding residual. Thus this is not, strictly speaking, a relaxation method. As with all iterative methods, the guess is changing at the same time as it is used to make new guesses. It is this recursive nature of iterative methods that makes them very sensitive to the characteristics of the system outlined above.

A close look at the Jacobi algorithm reveals its essential similarity to the Neumann series described in section 5.1. Thus, it can be said with confidence that this simple algorithm will converge to the correct solution in the case of the radiosity problem.

5.3.2   Gauss-Seidel Iteration

Gauss-Seidel iteration is a slight variation of the Jacobi method. It provides a true relaxation method and will usually improve the speed with which the solution converges. At each step during an iteration, the Gauss-Seidel method uses the most up-to-date version of the solution vector, rather than the solution vector computed by the previous iteration. Thus, at each of the n steps of an iteration, the new entry of **B** is computed using the values $B^{(k+1)}$ computed by previous steps of the current iteration. Otherwise, values computed during the previous iteration $B_{(k)}$ are used. Thus, to relax r_i, set

$$B_i^{(k+1)} = E_i - \sum_{j=1}^{i-1} K_{ij} \frac{B_j^{(k+1)}}{K_{ii}} - \sum_{j=i+1}^{n} K_{ij} \frac{B_j^{(k)}}{K_{ii}} \tag{5.13}$$

---

[3] Although Jacobi iteration is not often used on its own since more efficient methods are known, it will become clear in later sections how one can take advantage of the known residual vector to increase the power of other algorithms.

```
1    for ( all i ) B_i = starting guess ;
2    while ( not converged ) {
3      for ( each i )
4        B_i = E_i - ∑_{j=1,j≠i}^{n} (B_j K_{ij})/K_{ii} ;
5    }
6    output B ;
```

Figure 5.1: *Pseudocode for Gauss-Seidel iterative solver.*

Performing the step for a single entry of $\mathbf{B}$ requires taking the dot product of the current guess, $\mathbf{B}^{(k),(k+1)}$, with a row of the matrix, and thus requires $O(n)$ operations. Consequently, a full iteration consisting of n steps is $O(n^2)$. Alternatively, since

$$r_i^{(k)} = E_i - \sum_{j=0}^{n} K_{ij} B_j^{(k)} \tag{5.14}$$

if all the residuals are updated after *each step*, one can set

$$B_i^{(k+1)} = B_i^{(k)} + \frac{r_i^{(k)}}{K_{ii}} \tag{5.15}$$

In this case the cost of a step is reduced to $O(1)$, but the residual update will be $O(n)$ for each step and a full iteration is again $O(n^2)$. Essentially, these operations are equivalent to the operations in equation 5.12.

The Gauss-Seidel Algorithm

If the i's are relaxed in order, the Gauss-Seidel algorithm in Figure 5.1 results. One iteration of the algorithm involves relaxing each residual in turn. Gauss-Seidel iteration can be shown to be absolutely convergent for diagonally dominant systems such as the one arising in the constant radiosity formulation. A variant of this algorithm has been shown to work well for the radiosity problem [62]. Convergence criteria are typically specified by a maximum residual, $\|\mathbf{r}\|_\infty$, or a maximum change in the solution, $\|\mathbf{B}^{k+1} - \mathbf{B}^k\|_\infty$, where the notation $\|f(x)\|_\infty$ refers to the l_∞ norm (see box page 133).

Gathering: A Physical Interpretation of Gauss-Seidel

Examining a single step in the Gauss-Seidel algorithm (line 4), a single nodal radiosity value, B_i, has been selected to update by summing contributions from

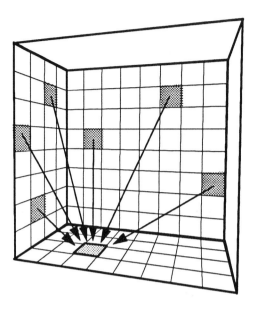

Figure 5.2: *Gathering: a Gauss-Seidel step.*

all other radiosity values weighted by the reflectivities and form factors in the ith row of **K**. Assuming constant elements, each term of summation in line 5 can be expanded using the **K** matrix (equation 5.3) entries and taking advantage of the fact that $K_{ii} = 1$ if elements cannot "see" themselves. Thus

$$\Delta B_i = \rho_i \, B_j \, F_{ij} \qquad (5.16)$$

This term represents the contribution made by element j to the radiosity of element i. Thus the complete step is equivalent to *gathering* the light from all other elements[4] to arrive at a new estimate for B_i (see Figure 5.2). Note that a single step involves one *row* of **K** and updates a *single* radiosity value.

5.3.3   Southwell Iteration

A variation of the Gauss-Seidel method provides an alternative algorithm with a slightly different physical interpretation. In the less well known *Southwell* iteration [90], rather than relax each residual in turn, the row i with the largest residual, $Max(\mathbf{r})$, will always be selected.

---

[4]Strictly speaking, gathering is from the energy under the other basis functions, but for constant bases one can speak of gathering from elements.

Thus a single *step*,[5] p, of the Southwell algorithm is

$$\text{For } i, \text{ such that } r_i = Max(\mathbf{r}) : B_i = E_i - \sum_{j \neq i} \frac{B_j K_{ij}}{K_{ii}} \qquad (5.17)$$

It would seem that Southwell would require $O(n^2)$ operations to compute all the r_i's before picking the greatest one. (The computation of each r_i above involves computing the dot product of $\mathbf{B}^{(p)}$ with the row $\mathbf{K}_i$.) Fortunately, if at some step p, $\mathbf{r}^{(p)}$ is known for a given $\mathbf{B}^{(p)}$, the next approximation can be made if the changes $\Delta \mathbf{B}^{(p)}$ are known. Thus,

$$\mathbf{B}^{(p+1)} = \mathbf{B}^{(p)} + \Delta \mathbf{B}^{(p)} \qquad (5.18)$$

and the updated residual can be computed as:

$$\mathbf{r}^{(p+1)} = \mathbf{E} - \mathbf{K}(\mathbf{B}^{(p)} + \Delta \mathbf{B}^{(p)}) = \mathbf{r}^{(p)} - \mathbf{K} \, \Delta \mathbf{B}^{(p)} \qquad (5.19)$$

since

$$\mathbf{r}^{(p)} = \mathbf{E} - \mathbf{K} \mathbf{B}^{(p)} \qquad (5.20)$$

However, in this case all the $\Delta \mathbf{B}^{(p)}$ are zero except ΔB_i. Therefore,

$$r_j^{(p+1)} = r_j^{(p)} - \frac{K_{ji}}{K_{ii}} * r_i^{(p)}, \; \forall j \qquad (5.21)$$

and expanding $\mathbf{K}$ for the case of constant elements,

$$r_j^{(p+1)} = r_j^{(p)} + \rho_j F_{ji} * r_i^{(p)}, \; \forall j \qquad (5.22)$$

Updating $\mathbf{r}$ thus takes only $O(n)$ steps involving multiplying a scalar by a *column* of the matrix, $\mathbf{K}$.

The final requirement is to compute $\mathbf{r}^{(0)}$ easily at the start of the algorithm. Simply choosing $\mathbf{B}^{(0)}$ to be $\mathbf{0}$ (the zero vector) gives

$$\mathbf{r}^{(0)} = \mathbf{E} - \mathbf{K} \mathbf{B}^{(0)} = \mathbf{E} \qquad (5.23)$$

The Southwell Algorithm

The Southwell relaxation method follows the pseudocode in Figure 5.3. As in the Gauss-Seidel algorithm, each *step* is $O(n)$. It is more difficult to characterize the cost of an entire iteration since some elements may be revisited many times before another is operated on. As will be seen below, a close approximation to the final answer can often be achieved in a small number of steps, resulting in a linear overall solution time.

---

[5]It is impossible to write down a single iteration, since it is possible that one residual will be relaxed many times before another is ever touched. The superscript p is used to indicate the *step* number in this section rather than the iteration number as in other sections

```
1      for ( all i ) {
2          B_i = 0 ;
3          r_i = E_i ;
4      }
5      while ( not converged ) {
6          pick i, such that |r_i| is largest ;
7          B_i = B_i + r_i/K_ii ;
8          temp = r_i ;
9          for ( all j ) r_j = r_j − K_ji/K_ii * temp ;
10     }
11     output B ;
```

Figure 5.3: *Pseudocode for Southwell relaxation.*

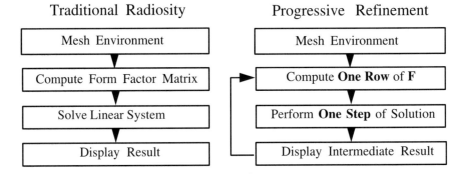

Figure 5.4: *Traditional radiosity versus progressive refinement.*

Shooting: A Physical Interpretation of Southwell Iteration

Each step of the Southwell algorithm does two things. It updates one element of the radiosity vector, B_i, and updates *all* of the residuals. If constant bases are used, the physical interpretation of **B** is the vector of nodal radiosity values and thus the radiosity of each element. What is the physical interpretation of the residuals, **r**? The residuals are the *unshot* radiosity of each element. In other words, the residuals represent the radiosity that has been received as illumination by the elements but has not yet been "reflected" or *shot* back out to contribute further to the illumination of the environment.

It is clear from equation 5.22 that each step takes one residual and adds fractions of it to each of the others. The specific fractions are the ith column of

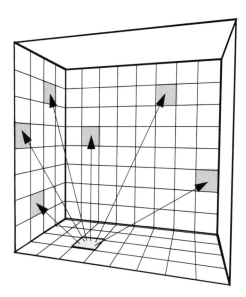

Figure 5.5: *Shooting: a progressive radiosity step.*

K. Rewriting equation 5.22 using the reciprocity principle,

$$r_j^{(p+1)} = r_j^{(p)} + \rho_j F_{ji} r_i^{(p)} = r_j^{(p)} + \rho_j F_{ij} \frac{A_i}{A_j} r_i^{(p)} \qquad (5.24)$$

or rearranging,

$$r_j^{(p+1)} A_j = r_j^{(p)} A_j + \rho_j F_{ij} r_i^{(p)} A_i \quad \text{for each residual } r_j \qquad (5.25)$$

shows that the total *unshot energy* (radiosity × area), is reduced in each step since both the ρ and the sum of the F_{ij}'s are less than one.

Progressive Refinement

Cohen *et al.* [59] describe a slightly different form of Southwell's algorithm, called *progressive refinement* or *progressive radiosity*. The goal of progressive refinement is to display results after each *step* of an iterative process, in order to provide immediate feedback. The requirement is thus not only to provide an algorithm that converges quickly, but one that makes as much progress at the beginning of the algorithm as possible. In progressive refinement the flow of the traditional radiosity approach becomes an iterative repetition of the steps of

```
1     for ( all i ) {
2         B_i = E_i ;
3         ΔB_i = E_i ;
4     }
5     while ( not converged ) {
6         pick i, such that ΔB_i * A_i is largest ;
7         for ( every element j ) {
8             Δrad = ΔB_i * ρ_j F_ji ;
9             ΔB_j = ΔB_j + Δrad ;
10            B_j = B_j + Δrad ;
11        }
12        ΔB_i = 0 ;
13        display the image using B_i as the intensity of element i ;
14    }
```

Figure 5.6: *Pseudocode for progressive refinement.*

computing form factors, performing steps of the solution and displaying inter-mediate results (see Figure 5.4). For constant elements, the progressive radiosity algorithm follows the pseudocode in Figure 5.6.

The previous algorithm has the following physical interpretation. All elements i have a value B_i, which is the radiosity calculated so far for that element, and ΔB_i, which is the portion of that element's radiosity that has yet to be "shot". During one iteration, the element with the greatest unshot radiosity is chosen and its radiosity is shot (see Figure 5.5) through the environment. As a result of the shot, the other elements, j, may receive some new radiosity, Δrad. This Δrad is added to B_j. Δrad is also added to ΔB_j since this newly received radiosity is unshot. As a result of the shooting, element i has no unshot radiosity, so $\Delta B_i = 0$.

In this algorithm one shooting step (lines 7–11 in Figure 5.6) updates all the other elements. Energy is shot from the element that currently has the most unshot radiosity. One shooting step takes O(n) operations and can be viewed as multiplying the scalar B_i by a column of the form factor matrix. Cohen *et al.* [59] show that in many cases only a small fraction of n shooting steps is required to approximate a solution closely.

At first glance Southwell and progressive refinement seem to be quite different. Southwell updates only one entry in **B**, while progressive refinement updates them all at each step. However, recognizing **B** in the progressive refinement algorithm to be the sum of **B** and **r** of the Southwell algorithm, the two

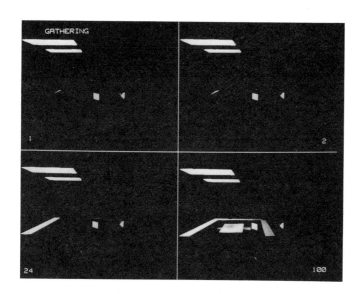

Gauss-Seidel after 1, 2, 24, and 100 Steps

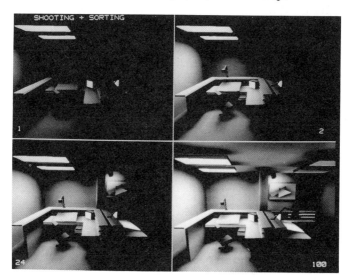

Progressive Refinement after 1, 2, 24, and 100 Steps

Figure 5.7: *Gauss-Seidel versus progressive radiosity.*

algorithms are in fact almost identical. There is one other difference: progressive refinement selects the largest *energy* to shoot (i.e., the largest $r_i A_i$) rather than simply the largest residual. The use of the sum of the *already shot* radiosity and the *unshot* residual to be the current answer can be explained as a hybrid of Southwell and Jacobi iteration. This sum is exactly equivalent to the Southwell algorithm followed by one full iteration of Jacobi iteration before display.

It should be clear why this algorithm should converge faster than a Gauss-Seidel algorithm, particularly in the early steps (see Figure 5.7). The Southwell and progressive refinement algorithms make very good guesses about which element of the residual vector to relax to get the greatest reduction in the residual as a whole. Particularly at the start of the iterations, all the unshot energy resides in the light sources (i.e., only a few emission terms are nonzero) thus there a only a few nonzero residuals. As the light interreflects about an environment, the unshot energy (i.e., residuals) becomes more evenly spread out and thus the advantage of selecting the largest to process is reduced as the algorithm progresses. A full analysis and proof of convergence properties of these algorithms for the radiosity problem can be found in Gortler *et al.* [101].

5.3.4 Ambient Energy and Overrelaxation

Ambient Term

In Cohen *et al.* [59] an additional term, similar to the *ambient* illumination term commonly used in ray tracing, is added to the radiosity approximation, for the purpose of display only. The ambient term is a crude approximation that accounts for the reflected illumination not yet accounted for in the solution. The ambient term models the unknown illumination arriving from unknown directions as a constant illumination from all directions.

At each step of the progressive refinement solution, there is a known amount of energy that has not yet been distributed or *shot*. The average unshot radiosity, $\overline{\Delta B}$, is simply the sum of the entries in the residual vector weighted by the fraction of the total area[6] of the element corresponding to each entry.

$$\overline{\Delta B} = \frac{\sum r_i A_i}{\sum A_i} \qquad (5.26)$$

Each time some of this unshot radiosity is processed in a step of the progressive refinement algorithm, some of that energy is absorbed, but some of it is returned to the unshot quantities of other elements (or basis functions). On average, without knowing in advance where the unshot energy will arrive, one can estimate

---

[6] In the case of nonconstant basis functions, the *area* is the integral of the basis function dotted with itself.

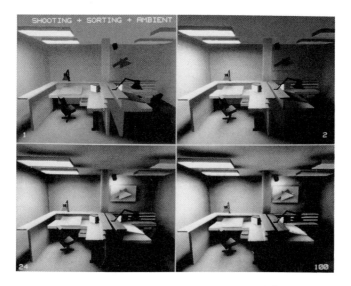

Displayed Image after 1, 2, 24, and 100 Steps

Figure 5.8: *Progressive radiosity with ambient addition.*

that some fraction of the energy will be reflected. This fraction is represented by $\bar{\rho}$, where

$$\bar{\rho} = \frac{\sum \rho_i A_i}{\sum A_i} \tag{5.27}$$

Of course, in the same way that some of the shot energy is reflected, some of the reflected energy will be rereflected and so on. The total reflection, R_{total}, can be represented by the infinite sum

$$R_{\text{total}} = 1 + \bar{\rho} + \bar{\rho}^2 + \bar{\rho}^3 + \dots = \frac{1}{1 - \bar{\rho}} \tag{5.28}$$

Finally, the product of the average unshot radiosity, $\overline{\Delta B}$, and the total reflection gives us an estimate for the *ambient radiosity*, B_{ambient}:

$$B_{\text{ambient}} = \overline{\Delta B} \, R_{\text{total}} \tag{5.29}$$

Each element i will reflect its own fraction ρ_i of this quantity. Thus for display purposes only (see Figure 5.8),

$$B_i^{\text{display}} = B_i + \rho_i B_{\text{ambient}} \tag{5.30}$$

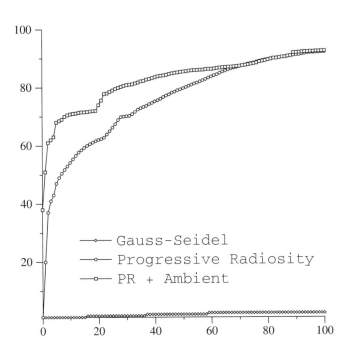

Figure 5.9: *Convergence versus number of steps for three algorithms.*

Adding the ambient term brings the displayed image much closer to the converged solution very early in the process. Figure 5.9 shows a plot of the convergence for the images in Figures 5.7 and 5.8 of the Gauss-Seidel, progressive refinement, and progressive refinement plus ambient versus *number of steps* (not iterations). The vertical axis is in terms of area weighted RMS error:

$$\sqrt{\frac{\sum (B_i^* - B_i^p)^2 A_i}{\sum A_i}} \times 100 \qquad (5.31)$$

where p is the step number, and $\mathbf{B}^*$ is the result of a converged solution.

It should be noted that as each step of the progressive refinement algorithm proceeds, the total unshot energy is reduced and thus the *ambient* term is also reduced and the displayed and actual radiosity values converge.

Overrelaxation

The ambient term described in the previous section is a crude representation of the energy that has not yet been *shot*. It improves the displayed image, but does not speed up convergence of the actual solution. *Overrelaxation* techniques provide a more systematic attempt to acknowledge the energy unaccounted for so far, by "pushing" the solution farther ahead at each step than the current solution vector indicates.

Overrelaxation techniques are similar to the relaxation methods previously described with one exception. When relaxing a particular residual, the change in the solution vector is increased by a factor ω (or equivalently the residual is considered to have been larger than it actually is). Equation 5.12 becomes

$$B_i^{(k+1)} = B_i^{(k)} + \omega \frac{r_i^{(k)}}{K_{ii}} \qquad (5.32)$$

and the ith residual being relaxed is now not set to zero, but rather,

$$r_i^{(k+1)} = (1 - \omega) r_i^{(k)} \qquad (5.33)$$

Overrelaxation involves a value for ω greater than 1, while underrelaxation involves a value between 0 and 1. In cases where Gauss-Seidel methods converge, overrelaxation will often increase the convergence rate. (Underrelaxation is sometimes useful for unstable systems.) The best value for ω will depend on the behavior of the particular problem being solved and is usually determined experimentally. For radiosity algorithms, overrelaxation with ω equal to about 1.2 has been found to give good results [58].

In the context of the progressive refinement method, overrelaxation can be thought of as *overshooting*. Feda [82] discusses a heuristic for overshooting in the progressive refinement algorithm which works well if certain restrictions are placed on the overshot amount to avoid divergence.

Gortler *et al.* [101] propose an analytic approach that simulates the known interreflection between the shooting element and all others while maintaining a linear complexity at each step. In each step all the selected element's residual is relaxed as well as the portion of the residual from all other elements to the selected element. The method is called a *super–shoot–gather*, since in essence light is shot from the element to all other elements, and then gathered back to the shooting element, thus taking further advantage of the form factors that have been computed for the shooting step. This form of overrelaxation was found to be particularly useful in "bright" environments (i.e., environments with a high average reflectivity). This should be no surprise since it is the secondary, tertiary, etc., reflections that are captured by the overshooting.

Other Solution Methods

The above sections do not completely enumerate all methods for solving linear systems. Methods applicable to the radiosity problem have been addressed to the exclusion of others. However, a class of applicable methods based on a *divide and conquer* paradigm remains to be described. This approach will be discussed in Chapter 7, where hierarchical solution methods are outlined.

5.4 Dynamic Environments

All the discussion of the radiosity method in previous chapters has assumed that the environment is unchanging, that is, the geometry, lighting, and material properties are static. Although this is acceptable for some applications, many other applications of image synthesis require the ability to change or move objects. Of course, the solution can always be restarted from scratch after each change, but this requires throwing away potentially valuable information, particularly if the change is small.

5.4.1 Lighting Changes

Changes in the emission terms for the light sources are the simplest type of change to include. The form factors are purely a function of geometry, thus the most computationally expensive part of the radiosity algorithm is not affected by changes in the lighting. Thus the $\mathbf{K}$ matrix is unchanged and modifications to $\mathbf{E}$ require at most a new solution to the linear system of equations, $\mathbf{K}\,\mathbf{B} = \mathbf{E}$. If the changes to $\mathbf{E}$ are small, then the old solution is a good approximation to the new one and should be used as the starting guess for the iterative methods discussed above. For example, one might begin with the old solution and shoot out the additional light from a light source that has changed. This also includes the possibility of shooting *negative* light from lights that have been turned down.

If the application calls for many lighting changes in an otherwise static environment, a separate solution can be run for each light source with a unit emission [5]. Since the radiosity equation is linear, the independent solutions can then be scaled and summed to provide any possible setting for the lights with no extra matrix solutions.

$$\mathbf{B} = \sum_{L=1}^{NumLights} E_L\,\mathbf{B}_L \qquad (5.34)$$

where E_L = the emission of Lth light source, and $\mathbf{B}_L$ = the radiosity solution vector computed using the emission vector set to 1 for Lth light source and 0 elsewhere.

This provides a very rapid means of changing between lighting settings. Dorsey [73] has gone one step further in her opera lighting design system by prerendering multiple images of complex scenes from a fixed viewpoint, differing only by the light emissions (color plates 53, 54 and the back cover). By

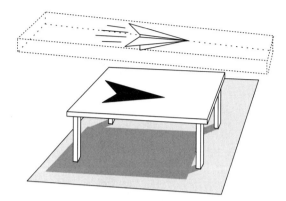

Figure 5.10: *A dynamic environment with bounding box around all positions of moving object.*

scaling and summing the images themselves, different lighting conditions can be set at interactive rates. (More details of the rendering step and this application can be found in Chapters 9 and 11). If the cost of inverting $\mathbf{K}$ is undertaken, then the radiosities $\mathbf{B}$ due to any emission vector $\mathbf{E}$ can be solved by a simple matrix–vector multiplication, $\mathbf{K}^{-1}\,\mathbf{E} = \mathbf{B}$.

5.4.2 Reflectivity Changes

Changes in the reflectivity of surfaces in the environment also do not require new form factor computations. Again, at most this will require modifying the rows of $\mathbf{K}$ based on the new ρ values and performing a new solution of the linear equations. However, a new solution accounting for changes in a single, or a few, surfaces can be found more quickly by starting from the original solution [51]. New unshot energy $\Delta B_j A_j$ (possibly negative) can be shot from the surfaces that have changed, where

$$\Delta B_j = \frac{\rho_j^{new} - \rho_j^{old}}{\rho_j^{old}}\, B_j \qquad (5.35)$$

Clearly, this will not work in the case of surfaces that were originally defined as black (i.e., $\rho_j^{old} = 0$).

5.4.3 Changes in Geometry

Changes in the geometry present the most challenging problem for rapidly determining new solutions. Any individual change in the shape or position of a

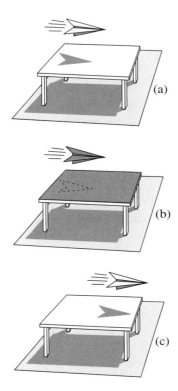

Figure 5.11: *A dynamic environment: (a) initial solution, (b) after shooting negative energy to table top, (c) after shooting positive energy with airplane in new position.*

single object, or the addition (or removal) of a new object, has the potential to change any entry in **K**. However, if it is assumed that only small changes are made, there are a number of acceleration methods that have been described and demonstrated.

Baum *et al.* [20] describe a method that can be used when all changes in the positions of any objects are known in advance of any form factor computation. In this case, a bounding object can be constructed for each dynamic object. The bounding box contains the volume swept by the object as it moves along the path (see the airplane in Figure 5.10). During form factor computation, form factors are marked if their visibility is affected by the composite bounding box. Thus, at subsequent points in time only marked form factors need to be recomputed before a new solution is performed.

Chen [51] and George *et al.* [91] do not assume a priori knowledge of ob-

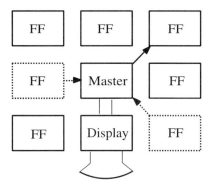

Figure 5.12: *A parallel radiosity implementation. One master processor controls the overall flow of the computation and performs the row or columnwise vector multiply for the solution. A display processor constantly updates the display based on the partial solutions. The remaining processors (two are idle) compute rows (columns) of form factors and report the results to the master processor. This coarse grained approach assumes each processor has a full geometric description of the environment.*

ject motion, addition, or deletion. As in the methods for changes in lighting or material reflectance, they start with an existing solution for an environment (see Figure 5.11) and compute a new solution after some small change, for example moving the position of a chair. The new solution proceeds by identifying the affected form factors (e.g., between the light and the table top in Figure 5.11). Negative energy is shot to "undo" the affected interactions. The dynamic object is then moved to its new position, and positive energy is shot. The unbalanced positive and negative energy are then propagated as before. Both Chen and George *et al.* provide many implementation details concerning the rapid identification of affected form factors, the optimal ordering for the new shooting sequences, and other issues.

5.5 Parallel Implementations

Radiosity solutions for complex environments continue to be slow. Beyond improvements in the radiosity algorithms themselves, one is left with the possibility of speeding up the solutions with the use of parallel hardware. A number of implementations have been described that parallelize various portions of the solution process.

The different implementations range from the use of built-in pipelined hardware in graphics workstations [21], to course grained systems developed on networked workstations [186, 191], to transputer arrays [46, 107, 188] to the thousands of processors on SIMD machines such as the CM2 [77] and MasPar [240]. Other reports describe theoretical analyses of possible algorithms [244].

Methods can be grouped according to where and how they exploit the natural parallelism in the algorithms. The computation of form factors is the primary bottleneck in the radiosity algorithm, and it is on that step that most implementations have concentrated. In [46, 50, 81, 107, 190] several full *rows* of form factors are computed in parallel. Each processor performs a single hemicube or other form factor quadrature and reports the results to another processor which uses the results for the next step in an iterative solution (see Figure 5.12). An additional processor may be devoted to displaying the current state of the radiosity solution. In a finer grained approach, individual form factors are parceled out to processors in [21, 95]. There are also many implementations of parallel ray tracing which can be used at an even finer level within a single form factor computation. Drucker and Schröder [77] exploit parallelism at many levels in their implementation on the Connection Machine.

Each of the reports offers insights into the many subtleties that arise when using and implementing parallel strategies. The reader is encouraged to seek out these references for a fuller understanding of the algorithms and reports of experiments on a variety of environments.

Chapter 6

Domain Subdivision

As described in Chapter 3, the approximation of the radiosity function, $B(\mathbf{x})$, is a fundamental step in the discretization of the radiosity equation. The approximation, $\hat{B}(\mathbf{x})$, is defined by the linear combination of n basis functions, $N_i(\mathbf{x})$:

$$B(\mathbf{x}) \approx \hat{B}(\mathbf{x}) = \sum_{i=1}^{n} B_i N_i(\mathbf{x}) \qquad (6.1)$$

The basis functions define a finite subspace of functions from which the approximation $\hat{B}(\mathbf{x})$ is realized by choosing the coefficients, B_i.

In a finite element approximation, each of the basis functions, $N_i(\mathbf{x})$, has *local support*; in other words, each is nonzero over a limited range of the function domain. A basis function is associated with a single node and has a value of zero outside of elements adjacent to the node.

As discussed in Chapter 3, each type of basis function is defined with respect to a generic element, such as the unit square. The generic basis functions are then mapped to the actual model geometry according to the subdivision of the surfaces into elements. Thus, the form of any *particular* basis function is tied to the placement and size of one or a few elements. The total set of basis functions defining the approximation is thus determined by the *mesh* of elements and nodes.

The next three chapters will describe strategies and algorithms for subdividing the domain of the radiosity function into finite elements, with the goal of producing an efficient and accurate radiosity solution. The accuracy of the approximation, $\hat{B}(x)$, is influenced by the size, shape and orientation of the elements, as well as by the polynomial order of the basis functions. An optimal mesh uses as few elements as possible to achieve a desired accuracy, which generally means distributing errors in the approximation as evenly as possible among the elements.

To achieve a high quality mesh, it is first necessary to be able to measure the accuracy of the approximation produced by a particular subdivision and choice of basis functions. It is also important to understand how various characteristics of the mesh affect accuracy. This knowledge can then be used to develop strategies for producing a good mesh. These basic issues will be discussed in the present chapter. More sophisticated *hierarchical* mesh refinement methods will be discussed in Chapter 7. The actual mechanics of subdividing geometry will then be treated in Chapter 8.

6.1   Error Metrics

6.1.1   True Error

The true error in the approximate radiosity function at location **x** is the difference between the actual function and the approximate function at **x**:

$$\varepsilon(x) = B(x) - \hat{B}(x) \tag{6.5}$$

Of course, equation 6.5 cannot be evaluated directly, since $B(\mathbf{x})$ is not known. Instead, $\varepsilon(\mathbf{x})$ must be estimated. Several error estimators are described in the following sections. Particular implementations of these approaches for radiosity will be described in section 6.3.3.

6.1.2   Local Estimate of Approximation Error

The mesh and associated basis functions determine a subspace of possible functions. Higher-order basis functions increase the space of realizable functions, allowing a closer approximation to the actual function. Thus, one approach to estimating the error is to compare the original approximation

$$\hat{B}(\mathbf{x}) = \sum_{i=1}^{n} B_i \, N_i(\mathbf{x}) \tag{6.6}$$

where the basis functions, $N_i(\mathbf{x})$, are of order k, to a higher order approximation

$$\tilde{B}(\mathbf{x}) = \sum_{i=1}^{n} B_i \, \tilde{N}_i(\mathbf{x}) \tag{6.7}$$

where the new basis functions, $\tilde{N}_i(\mathbf{x})$, are of order $k+1$ or greater. For example, if $\hat{B}(\mathbf{x})$ is constructed using linear basis functions, the error can be estimated by comparing $\hat{B}(\mathbf{x})$ to an approximation $\tilde{B}(\mathbf{x})$ constructed using a quadratic or cubic basis. The error estimate $\hat{\varepsilon}(\mathbf{x})$ is then given by

$$\hat{\varepsilon}(\mathbf{x}) = \hat{B}(\mathbf{x}) - \tilde{B}(\mathbf{x}) \tag{6.8}$$

Function Norms and Error Metrics

A function norm is a measure of the "magnitude" of a function, analogous to a vector norm or an absolute value for a scalar. The L_p function norms are given by

$$L_p(\phi) = \| \phi \|_p = \left[\int_\Phi | \phi(x) |^P \, dx \right]^{1/p} \tag{6.2}$$

where ϕ is a function defined over domain Φ.

When used to characterize the error of an approximation, $\phi(\mathbf{x})$ is simply the difference between the desired and approximate solution: $\phi(x) = \varepsilon(x) = f(x) - \hat{f}(x)$. The norm can be computed over a limited region to characterize *local* error or over the entire domain of the function to measure *global* error.

The most commonly used norms are the L_1, L_2, or L_∞ norms, the cases where p equals 1, 2 or ∞ for equation 6.2. The L_1 norm of the approximation error, ε, is simply the area between the true function curve and the approximate function curve (in the case of a function of two variables, the volume between the function surfaces). The L_2 norm of ε is similar but gives more weight to large errors. The L_∞ norm of ε is simply the maximum value of the error in the region.

As with other integral values, function norms are usually evaluated as a finite sum. A discrete form of the L_p norm is given by

$$L_p(\phi) = \left[\sum_i | \phi(x_i) |^P \, \Delta x \right]^{1/p} \tag{6.3}$$

Note that if the discrete L_2 norm is used as a local measure of mesh element error, merely subdividing an element will produce elements with a smaller local error, even if the global error is unaffected, since the Δx are related to the element size. The root mean square (RMS) error is a useful alternative in this case. The RMS error is related to the L_2 norm and is given by

$$\epsilon_{RMS} = \sqrt{\frac{\sum_i (f(x_i) - \hat{f}(x_i))^2 \, W_i}{\sum_i W_i}} \tag{6.4}$$

where the W_i are weights assigned to each sample point. Typically each weight is the area of the domain represented by the sample point, in which case the RMS error is an area average of the L_2 norm.

For a more detailed discussion of function norms, and of functional approximation in general, see, for example, [180].

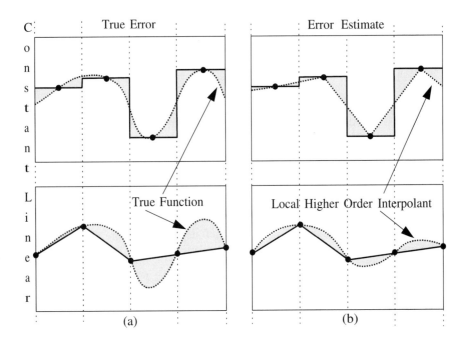

Figure 6.1: *Error measures: true versus approximate error.*

Figure 6.1(a) shows approximations of a function $f(x)$ using piecewise constant and piecewise linear basis functions. The shaded areas between $f(x)$ and the approximation curves represent the approximation error. Figure 6.1(b) shows two plots depicting the estimation of this error by the difference between the original approximation and a higher-order approximation constructed using the same nodal values. In the upper plot the error in a constant element approximation is estimated by comparing it to linear interpolation. In the lower plot, linear and quadratic interpolation are compared.

This estimate of the error is typically evaluated over a local region of the domain, for example, over an element when deciding whether it should be replaced by several smaller elements. A single value characterizing the magnitude of the error function can be obtained using a *function norm*, such as one of the L_p norms (see the box on page 133 for a discussion of function norms).

6.1.3   Residual of the Approximate Solution

The residual of the approximate solution provides another approach to characterizing $\varepsilon(x)$. The residual $r(\mathbf{x})$ is obtained by substituting $\hat{B}(\mathbf{x})$ for $B(\mathbf{x})$ in the original radiosity integral equation:

$$r(\mathbf{x}) = \hat{B}(\mathbf{x}) - E(\mathbf{x}) - \int_S \rho(\mathbf{x}) \, G(\mathbf{x}, \mathbf{x}') \, \hat{B}(\mathbf{x}') \, dA' \qquad (6.9)$$

Clearly, if the residual is zero everywhere, then $\hat{B}(\mathbf{x})$ is an exact solution to the integral equation and the actual error is also zero. Otherwise, the residual function is not identical to the actual error function. Strictly speaking, the residual provides a global rather than local error estimate; a high residual in a certain local region does not necessarily mean that $\hat{B}(x)$ is a poor approximation over that particular region. The residual in that region may be due to inaccuracies elsewhere in the domain. However, in practice the residual is often a useful indicator of local error introduced by the approximation. The residual is expensive to compute because of the integration and is normally evaluated only at selected points.

6.1.4 Error Based on the Behavior of the Kernel

As discussed in Chapter 3, the kernel $\hat{B}(\mathbf{x}') \, G(\mathbf{x}, \mathbf{x}')$ of the radiosity integral equation is also approximated by projecting it onto the selected basis functions. Thus the error can also be characterized by examining the behavior of the kernel function itself rather than the radiosity approximation. For example, while computing the form factors one might recognize large local variations in the geometric kernel, $G(\mathbf{x}, \mathbf{x}')$, across certain pairs of elements. These gradients might result from surfaces that are in close proximity or from shadow edges or penumbra.

The geometric term, $G(\mathbf{x}, \mathbf{x}')$, is a function of two points, typically on two different elements. When it is determined that the basis functions cannot capture the local variation of the geometric kernel itself, a decision can be made to subdivide one or both of the elements in order to reduce the error introduced by the mesh. This topic will be explored in much greater detail in Chapter 7 in the context of hierarchical subdivision methods.

6.1.5 Image Based Error Metrics

The error metrics discussed in the previous sections are based on quantities computed in the same domain as the radiosities, that is, the surfaces. However, the final product of an image synthesis algorithm is actually an image comprised of a finite number of pixels. If an image for a known viewpoint is the goal of the global illumination solution, then an error metric that incorporates view information can provide a valuable means of limiting and focusing computational effort.

Given a particular set of viewing parameters, the accuracy of the approximation for the visible surfaces is clearly the most critical, or the most *important*. The importance of other surfaces depends on their contribution to the illumination of the visible surfaces. Smits *et al.* [220] incorporate a quantity measuring importance in this sense into an image-based error metric. Much like radiosity, importance depends on surface geometry and reflectivity. It is propagated back from the eye point into the environment, much as radiosity is propagated forward from the light sources. Smits' formulation and algorithm are described in detail in Chapter 7.

6.1.6   Perceptually Based Error Metrics

The development of quantitative error metrics for radiosity [116, 120] is a crucial step toward reliable algorithms. However, for image synthesis applications, it is important to keep in mind that computing $B(x)$ is not the ultimate goal. For image synthesis, computing the radiosity, or radiance, is just one step in the process of generating a visual experience.

As outlined in Chapter 1 and discussed in detail in Chapter 9, the display and perception of an image involve converting the radiance or radiosity to screen values and finally to brightness as perceived by the eye and brain. These transformations are nonlinear and highly complex. As a result, certain errors may degrade perceived image quality to a greater or lesser degree than an error measure based on photometric or radiometric quantities alone would indicate.

A perceptually based error metric would perhaps be based on the subjective quantity of perceived brightness rather than radiosity. Low-order derivatives might be incorporated into the metric to account for the sensitivity of the eye to contrast. In the absence of such a metric, current attempts to incorporate perception into the image synthesis process are largely heuristic or ad hoc. [1] Perceptually based error metrics for image synthesis remain an important research topic.

6.2   Mesh Characteristics and Accuracy

An important goal when creating a mesh is to produce an approximation of the required accuracy as inexpensively as possible. This requires understanding how various characteristics of the mesh affect the accuracy of the approximation. These characteristics can be classified into four broad categories: mesh density, element order, element shape and discontinuity representation. Before discussing each of these in more detail, a concrete example will be presented

---

[1] For exceptions and valuable discussions of this issue, see [238] and [250]. Subjective brightness and image display are discussed at length in Chapter 9.

Figure 6.2: *A radiosity image computed using a uniform mesh.*

(see Figures 6.2 through 6.4) to illustrate the related issues of mesh quality, approximation error and visual quality.

6.2.1 An Example

The images in this series compare a radiosity solution to a "correct" reference image. The model is a simple *L*-shaped room illuminated by a single, diffusely emitting area light.

The image in Figure 6.2 shows a radiosity solution on a uniform mesh of linear elements performed using point collocation and rendered with Gouraud interpolation. The solution was performed for direct illumination only (i.e., interreflected light was ignored). The form factors to the light source were computed at each mesh node by shooting 256 rays to randomly selected points on the light polygon.

The reference image (see Figure 6.3(a)) was computed by similarly evaluating the form factor to the light at the surface point visible at the center of each image pixel. Since the contribution of the light source has been evaluated similarly in both the radiosity and reference images, the difference between the two images is essentially due to the approximation created by the element mesh.

Numerous artifacts introduced by the approximation are evident, including blocky shadows (letter A of Figure 6.3(b)), missing features (letter B), Mach

(a) *Reference image.*

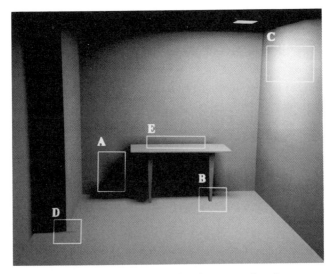

(b) *Artifacts introduced by the approximation.*

Figure 6.3*:*

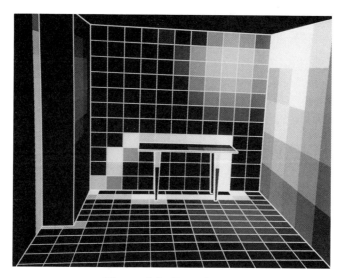

Figure 6.4: *Error image.*

bands (letter C), inappropriate shading discontinuities (letter D), and unresolved discontinuities (letter E).

Figure 6.4 is a visualization of the RMS error (defined in the box on *function norms* on page 133) for each element. The error was computed by evaluating the radiosity at 16 interior points across each element and comparing this to the approximate value. The comparison shows absolute as opposed to relative error. As apparent in this image, the error in the approximation is very unevenly distributed over the mesh. Computational effort has been applied fairly equally over the domain of the approximation, with very unequal contributions to the resulting accuracy.

The example shown in these images will be referred to throughout this chapter, to illustrate the discussion of meshing strategies. That discussion will begin with the description of basic mesh characteristics in the following sections.

6.2.2 Mesh Density

Mesh *density* is determined by the size of the elements into which the domain is subdivided. The density of the element mesh determines the number of degrees of freedom available to the approximation. More elements provide more degrees of freedom, which allows the approximation to follow the actual function more closely and increases the degree to which small features like shadows can be resolved.

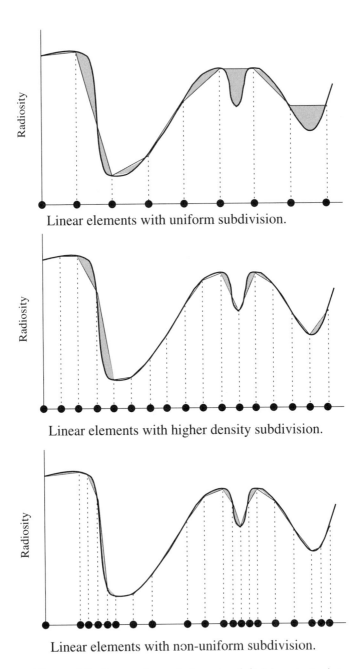

Figure 6.5: *Comparison of element subdivision strategies.*

Figure 6.6: *A radiosity solution with the mesh density increased four times over the mesh used in Figure 6.2.*

To illustrate, a one-dimensional function is approximated in Figure 6.5 using a variety of subdivisions. In the coarsest subdivision (the topmost plot in Figure 6.5) the approximation follows the actual radiosity function closely where it is almost linear, but diverges where the function changes slope quickly. Smaller features of the function are missing entirely when they fall between nodes.

Evaluating the function at smaller intervals increases the accuracy of the approximation, as shown in the second plot of Figure 6.5. However, the errors remain unevenly distributed, meaning that the extra effort has been applied inefficiently. Ideally, the domain should be subdivided more finely only where it will improve the accuracy significantly, as in the third plot of Figure 6.5.

Similar observations apply to approximating the radiosity function. In the example image (see Figure 6.2), inadequate mesh density results in elements that are too large to capture shading detail accurately. This is particularly evident in the "staircase" shadows cast by the table (letter A in Figure 6.3(b)), where the size of the shading feature (the penumbra) is much smaller than the separation between nodes.

Just as in the one-dimensional case, uniformly increasing the mesh density improves the overall accuracy. The image in Figure 6.6 was produced using a uniform mesh with four times as many elements as used in Figure 6.2. The

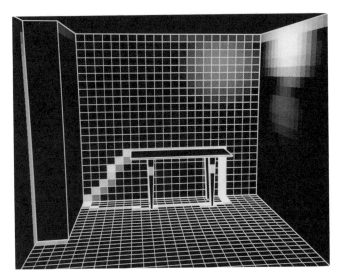

Figure 6.7: *RMS error for the elements in Figure 6.6.*

quality is better and some of the artifacts are almost eliminated. However, the corresponding error image in Figure 6.7 shows that the extra effort has been applied inefficiently, with many elements subdivided where the error was already negligible. This effort would have been better expended in further reducing the error in the remaining problem areas, such as along the shadow boundaries.

6.2.3 Element Order and Continuity

Element order (i.e., the order of the basis functions defined over the element) also has a direct effect on accuracy. Higher-order elements interpolate the function using higher-order polynomials and use more information about the behavior of the function, either by evaluating both values and derivatives at the nodes or by evaluating the function at additional nodes. Thus, higher-order elements can follow the local variations in a function more closely than the same number of lower-order elements. However, higher-order elements are generally more expensive to evaluate. Thus, one approach is to use higher-order elements only where the error is high and the extra effort is justified.

The type of basis functions used also affects the degree of continuity in the approximation at element boundaries. Continuity of value and of lower-order derivatives ($C^0, C^1, C^2, ...$) is important because the human visual system is

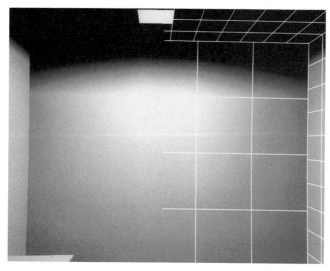

Figure 6.8: *Mach bands caused by first-derivative discontinuities at element boundaries.*

highly sensitive to relative spatial variation in luminance and its derivatives.[2]

For example, the bright streaks along the wall in the example image (see the closeup in Figure 6.8) correspond to discontinuities in the first derivative of the radiosity approximation, which occur at the boundaries of linear elements. The eye accentuates first derivative discontinuities, resulting in the perceptual phenomenon known as Mach bands [189]. Although Mach bands can occur naturally, they are distracting when they are incorrectly introduced by the approximation.

Since interpolation within elements is a linear sum of polynomials, the approximation is smooth (C^∞) on element interiors. However, continuity at element boundaries is not guaranteed. For *Lagrange* elements interpolation inside or on the boundary of the element depends only on the function values at the nodes belonging to that element. Because interpolation along boundaries uses only nodes on the boundary, linear and higher order Lagrange elements guarantee C^0 continuity at element boundaries. (Constant elements are discontinuous

---

[2]The notation C^k indicates that a function is continuous in all derivatives up to and including k. C^0 thus indicates that a function is continuous in *value* (i.e., there are no sudden jumps in value), C^1 that the function is continuous in *slope* (i.e., there are no kinks), and C^∞ that the function is *smooth* (i.e., continuous in all derivatives).

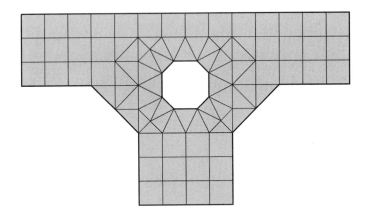

Figure 6.9: *A combination of rectangular and triangular elements used to fill a complicated geometry.*

in value at element boundaries). *Hermite* elements can provide a higher degree of continuity with fewer nodes by interpolating nodal derivatives as well as values. C^1 continuity, for example, requires interpolating the gradient at boundary nodes.

For radiosity, providing continuity greater than C^0 is motivated primarily by perceptual issues. Thus, elements with this property, such as the Clough-Tocher element used by Salesin *et al.* [203], have been applied mainly to the rendering stage. These will be discussed in detail in Chapter 9.

6.2.4   Element Shape

Elements should provide well-behaved, easily evaluated basis functions. For this reason, standard element shapes consist of simple geometries, typically triangles and rectangles. These standard shapes can be mixed to subdivide a complicated geometry more efficiently (see Figure 6.9) or to provide a transition between regions of differing mesh density (see Figure 6.10).

Isoparametric elements allow the standard shapes to be mapped to more general geometries, using the basis functions to interpolate geometric location as well as the radiosity values (see section 3.8). The bilinear quadrilateral element is a common example. Higher order isoparametric elements can be mapped to curved geometries. The parametric mapping must be invertible, which places some restrictions on the element shape. Concavities and extra vertices are normally to be avoided.

If Gouraud shading is to be used for rendering, a number of special problems relating to element shape must be avoided. For example, Gouraud interpolation

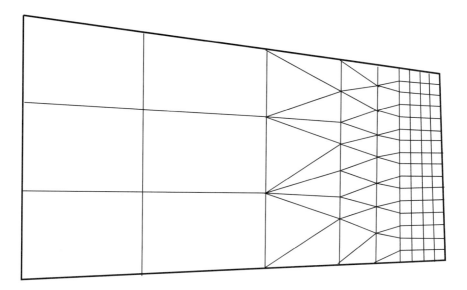

Figure 6.10: *Use of triangular elements to provide transition between regions of high and low mesh density.*

over a concave element can generate discontinuities in value, as shown in Figure 6.11. The problems relating to element shape and Gouraud interpolation will be discussed in Chapter 9.

Aspect Ratio

Element shape affects the efficiency with which the mesh samples the radiosity function [18]. To make the most efficient use of a given number of nodes, the nodes should be evenly distributed over the domain of the function (assuming that the behavior of the function is unknown). A distribution of nodes that is denser in one direction than in another is inefficient, since if elements are subdivided far enough to make sampling adequate in the sparse direction, sampling in the denser direction will be greater than necessary. Poor element shape can also affect the accuracy or efficiency of numerical integration of the form factors.

A reasonably uniform distribution of nodes can be obtained by requiring elements to have as high an *aspect ratio* as possible. The aspect ratio is defined as the ratio of the radius of the largest circle that will fit completely inside the element to the radius of the smallest circle that will fit completely outside the element (see Figure 6.12) [18]. This ratio should be as close to 1 as possible.

However, if the behavior of the function is known, anisotropic sampling

Figure 6.11: *A concave element, with a discontinuity introduced by Gouraud shading (closeup of letter D in Figure 6.3 (b)).*

may be more efficient than a uniform distribution, since the function changes more slowly in the direction orthogonal to the gradient and thus fewer samples are required along that direction. Elements with a lower aspect ratio may be more efficient in this case, if oriented correctly.

In a review of surface triangulation techniques, Schumaker [207] provides an excellent example of the effect of element orientation. A function surface is first approximated by triangulating regularly spaced nodes. However, the approximation is more accurate when the nodes are connected to form triangles with "poor" aspect ratios (see Figure 6.13). Schumaker discusses how approximation accuracy can be incorporated into the quality metric used by the triangulation algorithm. The approximation of a surface in 3-space is analogous to the approximation of the radiosity function and the surface approximation literature is thus a fruitful source for meshing algorithms.

Form factor algorithms may make assumptions that are violated by elements with poor aspect ratios. For example, in the adaptive ray casting algorithm described by Wallace *et al.* [247], (see Chapter 4), elements or pieces of elements (delta-areas) are approximated as disks. The accuracy of the disk approximation decreases with decreasing element aspect ratio.

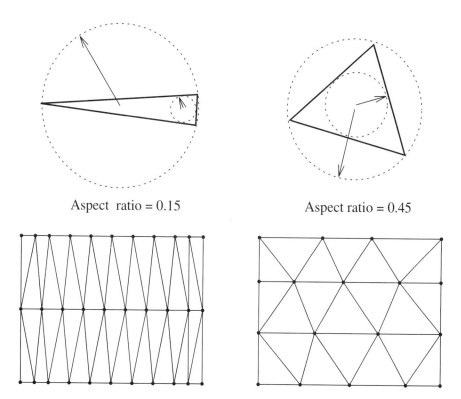

Aspect ratio = 0.15   Aspect ratio = 0.45

Figure 6.12: *The effect of aspect ratio on sampling density. A low aspect ratio tends to produce an anisotropic sampling density.*

Mesh Grading

A nonuniform, or *graded*, mesh may be required to distribute the error evenly in the approximation. In a *well-graded* mesh, element size and shape vary smoothly in the transition between regions of higher and lower density (see Figure 6.14). Abrupt changes in size or shape will often cause visible irregularities in shading, since neighboring elements will approximate the function with slightly different results. Because of the eye's sensitivity to contrast, such differences may be visible even when the error for both elements is within tolerance.

Mesh Conformance

It is important that adjacent elements *conform* across shared boundaries, as shown in Figure 6.15. Discontinuities in value created by nonconforming elements can cause distinctive image artifacts. Conforming elements share nodes

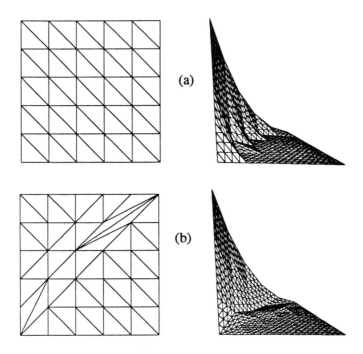

Figure 6.13: *(a) A surface approximation based on a regular subdivision. (b) The same surface approximated using elements with poor aspect ratios but oriented so as to provide a better approximation, (after Schumaker, 1993).*

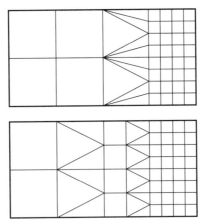

Figure 6.14: *The top mesh shows a poorly graded transition between regions of high and low mesh density. The bottom well-graded mesh provides a smoother transition.*

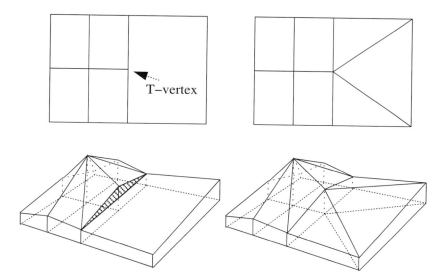

Figure 6.15: *Conforming versus nonconforming elements.*

along boundaries, thus ensuring C^0 continuity at the boundaries. In practice, this means that *T-vertices* (defined in Figure 6.15) must be avoided. Conformance is not an issue for constant elements, which are often used during the radiosity solution, but it is critical for rendering, where linear or higher-order elements are normally used.

6.2.5 Discontinuities

If light sources have a constant emission value (or are C^∞) across the surface and if changes in visibility are ignored, then the radiosity function $B(\mathbf{x})$ across a receiving surface will be continuous in all derivatives (i.e., it will also be C^∞). This is evident from the form factor kernel, $G(\mathbf{x}, \mathbf{x}')$, which itself is C^∞ except where the visibility term $V(\mathbf{x}, \mathbf{x}')$ changes from one to zero, and at singularities where $\mathbf{x}$ and $\mathbf{x}'$ meet and the denominator goes to 0.

If changes in visibility (i.e., shadows) are included, the radiosity function can contain discontinuities of any order [121]. Discontinuities in value and in the first and second derivatives are the most important, since these often provide visual cues to three-dimensional shape, proximity, and other geometric relationships. Much of the "image processing" performed by the eye involves enhancing such discontinuities and, as a result, the failure to reproduce discontinuities correctly can degrade image quality dramatically.

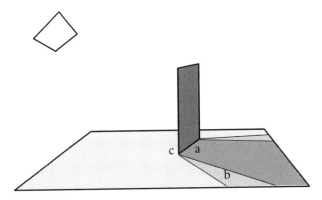

Figure 6.16: *Shadows can cause 0th, 1st, 2nd, and higher-order discontinuities in the radiosity function across a surface.*

Value Discontinuities

Discontinuities in the value of the radiosity function occur where one surface touches another, as at letter *a* of Figure 6.16. In Figure 6.17 the actual radiosity function is discontinuous in value where the wall passes below the table top. The shading should thus change abruptly from light to dark at the boundary defined by the intersection of the wall and the table. Unfortunately, the boundary falls across the interior of elements on the wall. Instead of resolving the discontinuity, interpolation creates a smooth transition and the shadow on the wall appears to leak upwards from below the table top.

Incorrectly resolved value discontinuities can also cause "light leaks," in which interpolation across one or more discontinuities causes light to appear where shadow is expected. In Figure 6.18, for example, elements on the floor pass beneath the wall dividing the room. The resulting light leak gives the incorrect impression of a gap between the wall and the floor. The problem is compounded when these elements incorrectly contribute illumination to the room on the left, which is totally cut off from the room containing the light source.

Derivative Discontinuities

Discontinuities in the first or second derivative occur at penumbra and umbra boundaries (letter *b* of Figure 6.16), as well as within the penumbra. When mesh elements span these discontinuities, interpolation often produces an inaccurate and irregular shadow boundary. The staircase shadows in Figure 6.2 are an example.

Figure 6.17: *Failure to resolve a discontinuity in value. This is a closeup of the radiosity solution shown in Figure 6.2.*

Figure 6.18: *A light leak caused by failure to resolve discontinuities in value where the dividing wall touches the floor. The dividing wall completely separates the left side of the room from the right side, which contains the light source.*

Singularities in the first derivative can also occur, as at letter c of Figure 6.16 where the penumbra collapses to a single point. Tracing along the line of intersection between the two objects, an instantaneous transition from light to dark is encountered at the corner point. The first derivative is infinite at that point, although the function is continuous away from the boundary.

The correct resolution of discontinuities requires that they fall along element boundaries, since the approximation is always C^∞ on element interiors. Thus, discontinuity boundaries must either be determined before meshing or the mesh must adapt dynamically to place element edges along the discontinuities. Since discontinuities may be of various orders, interpolation schemes that can enforce the appropriate degree of continuity at a particular element boundary are also required. Techniques for finding and reconstructing discontinuities will be discussed in detail in Chapter 8.

Continuity at Geometric Boundaries

Discontinuities in value occur naturally at boundaries where the surface normal is discontinuous, such as where the edge of the floor meets a wall. Such discontinuities are normally resolved automatically, since surfaces are meshed independently.

A problem can occur, however, if the boundaries of the primitives generated by a geometric modeler do not correspond to discontinuities in the surface normal. For example, curved surfaces will often be represented by collections of independent polygonal facets. If the facets are meshed independently, adjacent elements will often be nonconforming across facet boundaries, and shading discontinuities will result, as shown in Figure 6.19. It is easiest to maintain conformance in this case if the connectivity of the facets is determined prior to meshing and the surface is meshed as a single unit (see Figure 6.20). This approach is used by Baum *et al.* [18] for the special case of coplanar facets. Better yet, the radiosity implementation should allow the user to enter the faceted surfaces as a topologically connected primitive such as a polyhedron.

6.3   Automatic Meshing Algorithms

With a better understanding of how various mesh attributes affect the accuracy of the solution, it is now possible to discuss automatic meshing strategies. A taxonomy of automatic meshing algorithms is shown in Figure 6.21.[3]

---

[3]Although user intervention can be helpful in constructing a mesh, the discussion in this chapter will be limited to *automatic* mesh generation. Meshes for engineering applications are still often constructed with some interactive help, but good results require an experienced user who understands the underlying principles of the analysis. In image

Figure 6.19: *The polygonal facets representing the curved surface in this image were meshed independently. The resulting elements are nonconforming at the facet boundaries, causing shading discontinuities.*

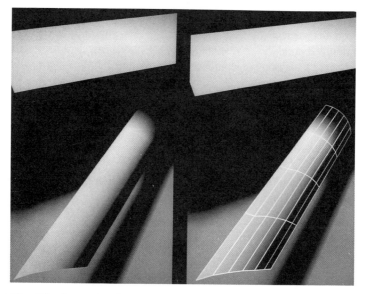

Figure 6.20: *The facets in this image were connected topologically prior to meshing, and the surface was meshed as a unit.*

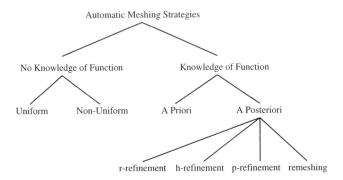

Figure 6.21: *A taxonomy of automatic meshing strategies.*

Meshing algorithms can be broadly classified according to whether or not they use information about the behavior of the function to be approximated. Although obtaining an optimal mesh normally requires such knowledge, in practice some degree of meshing without it is almost always necessary. Meshing in this case generally means subdividing as uniformly as possible (although subdividing complex geometries may require a nonuniform mesh). Algorithms for producing a uniform mesh are described in Chapter 8.

Meshing techniques that use knowledge of the function can be characterized as either a priori or a posteriori [211]. A priori methods specify all or part of the mesh before the solution is performed. Discontinuity meshing, in which discontinuity boundaries associated with occlusion are determined prior to the solution based on purely geometric considerations, is an a priori method. A priori algorithms, including discontinuity meshing, are discussed in Chapter 8.

A posteriori algorithms determine or refine the mesh after the solution has been at least partially completed. An initial approximation is obtained using a uniform or other mesh determined a priori. The mesh is then refined in regions where the local error is high, using information provided by the initial approximation of the function, such as the gradient, to guide decisions about element size, shape, and orientation. A posteriori meshing strategies are the subject of the remainder of this chapter.

6.3.1 A Posteriori Meshing

A posteriori meshing algorithms common to finite element analysis can be categorized as follows [211]:

---

synthesis the analysis of illumination is typically not the user's primary task, and the detailed specification of a mesh is intrusive and often beyond the user's expertise.

- *r-refinement*: reposition nodes

- *h-refinement*: subdivide existing elements

- *p-refinement*: increase polynomial order of existing elements

- *remeshing*: replace existing mesh with new mesh

Each of these approaches addresses one or more of the basic mesh characteristics discussed earlier: mesh density, basis function order, and element shape. Radiosity algorithms have so far relied almost exclusively on h-refinement. However, the other approaches will also be briefly described here, partly to indicate possible directions for radiosity research. See Figure 6.22 for illustrations of these approaches.

R-refinement

In r-refinement the nodes of the initial mesh are moved or *relocated* during multiple passes of mesh relaxation. At each pass, each node of the mesh is moved in a direction that tends to equalize the error of the elements that share the node. (See section 8.4 for a basic algorithmic approach to moving the vertices.) The function is then reevaluated at the new node locations. Relaxation can continue until the error is evenly distributed among the elements.

R-refinement has the advantage that the mesh topology is not altered by the refinement, which may simplify algorithms. It generates an efficient mesh, in that it minimizes the approximation error for a given number of elements and nodes. On the other hand, r-refinement cannot guarantee that a given error tolerance will be achieved. Since the number of elements is fixed, once the error is evenly distributed it can't be lowered further. Also, care must be taken during relocation not to move nodes across element boundaries. It may furthermore be difficult to maintain good element shape near fixed boundaries.

H-refinement

In h-refinement, the local error is decreased by increasing the density of the mesh; elements with a high error are subdivided into smaller elements. (The "h" refers to the symbol commonly used to characterize element size in finite element analysis.) The function is then evaluated at the new nodes. Since new nodes are added, the approximation error can be made as small as desired (although this may not always be practical). Elements and nodes can also be removed in regions where the approximation error is lower than necessary. In some h-refinement algorithms, refinement does not require reevaluation of the function at existing nodes.

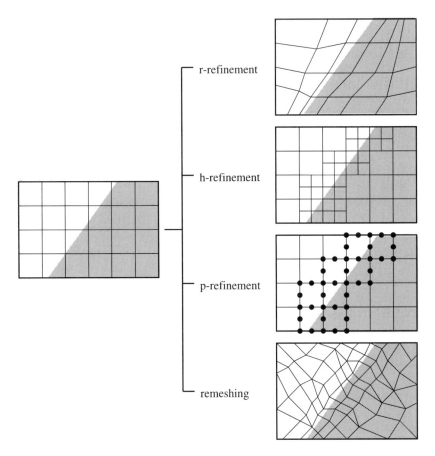

r-refinement

h-refinement

p-refinement

remeshing

Figure 6.22: *Basic a posteriori meshing strategies.*

However, the inability to move existing nodes restricts the ability of h-refinement to reduce error by adjusting element shape or orientation. As a result, h-refinement can be inefficient, in that more elements than necessary may be needed to reach a desired accuracy. Special handling is required to maintain continuity between elements subdivided to different levels of refinement. H-refinement algorithms must also pay careful attention to mesh grading. Radiosity implementations have relied almost exclusively on a variety of h-refinement algorithms. These are expanded on in section 6.3.2. Babuska *et al.* [15] provide a valuable source for h-refinement and p-refinement approaches used in engineering applications.

P-refinement

In p-refinement, the approximation error is reduced by increasing the order of the basis functions for certain elements. (The symbol "p" refers to the polynomial order of the basis functions.) New nodes are added to the affected elements, but the element shape and the mesh topology are not otherwise changed. In contrast to h-refinement, the number of elements in the mesh is not increased, which limits computational costs in some ways. However, the function must be evaluated at additional nodes, and the higher-order basis functions can be more expensive to compute. As with h-refinement, the ability to change element shape or orientation is restricted. Care must also be taken to maintain continuity between adjacent elements having basis functions of different orders.

Remeshing

Remeshing algorithms modify both the node locations and mesh topology; in essence the existing mesh is completely replaced. This allows complete flexibility of element shape and orientation, as well as the ability to decrease arbitrarily the approximation error. Following remeshing, the function must be reevaluated at the nodes of the new mesh.

Hybrid Methods

Hybrid refinement methods can be constructed by combining the above basic approaches. For example, r-refinement works best when it begins with a mesh that is reasonably well refined, since relaxation cannot reduce the local error beyond the minimum achievable with the initial number of nodes. A potentially useful hybrid strategy might thus use h-refinement to achieve a reasonable initial sampling density and r-refinement to more evenly distribute the approximation error.

6.3.2 Adaptive Subdivision: H-refinement for Radiosity

Almost all a posteriori meshing algorithms for radiosity have used h-refinement. This approach, commonly called adaptive subdivision in radiosity applications, follows the basic outline of an a posteriori method: a solution is computed on a uniform initial mesh, and the mesh is then refined by subdividing elements that exceed some error tolerance.

Figure 6.23 illustrates the improvement provided by adaptive subdivision over the uniform mesh approximation shown at the beginning of the chapter in Figure 6.2. The image quality is improved compared to that provided by the high uniform mesh resolution of Figure 6.6, while using the same number of

Figure 6.23: *Adaptive subdivision. Compare to Figure 6.2.*

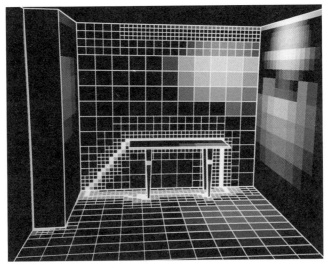

Figure 6.24: *Error image for adaptive subdivision. Compare to Figures 6.4 and 6.7.*

```
Adaptive_Subdivision( error_tolerance ) {
    Create initial mesh of constant elements ;
    Compute form factors ;
    Solve linear system ;
    do until ( all elements within error tolerance
                    or minimum element size reached ) {
        Evaluate accuracy by comparing adjacent element radiosities ;
        Subdivide elements that exceed user-supplied error tolerance ;
        for ( each new element ) {
            Compute form factors from new element to all other elements ;
            Compute radiosity of new element based on old radiosity values ;
        }
    }
}
```

Figure 6.25: *Adaptive subdivision pseudocode.*

elements. The corresponding error image is shown in Figure 6.24. Note that even with adaptive subdivision, the error remains high for elements lying along the shadow boundary.

Cohen *et al.* [61] first applied adaptive subdivision to radiosity meshing, using the algorithm outlined in the pseudocode in Figure 6.25. For clarity, this outline ignores the hierarchical nature of the adaptive subdivision algorithm, which will be discussed in detail in the following chapter. For now, note only that new nodes created by adaptive subdivision have their radiosities computed using the approximation $\hat{B}(x)$ obtained during the initial solution. As a result, it is not necessary to recompute radiosities for existing nodes when an element is subdivided.

Many variations of this basic approach have been developed differing primarily in how they estimate error, and how elements are subdivided. The following sections will survey adaptive subdivision algorithms and how they have addressed these two issues.

6.3.3 Error Estimation for Adaptive Subdivision

Heuristic and Low-Order Subdivision Criteria

Many algorithms subdivide according to a discrete approximation to one or more of the error norms described in section 6.1. For example, Cohen *et al.*

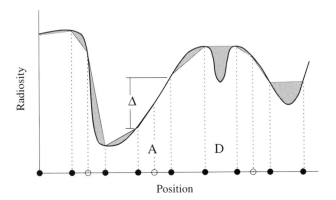

Figure 6.26: *Cohen's subdivision criterion based on the difference between nodal values results in the subdivision of element A, although linear interpolation provides a good approximation in this case. (Added nodes due to the subdivision are indicated by hollow circles.) The local minimum at D is also missed.*

[61] compare the radiosities of an element and its neighbors . If these differ in value by more than a user-specified tolerance, the element is subdivided. For the constant elements, this is essentially equivalent to estimating the local error by comparing the piecewise constant approximation to linear interpolation through the same nodes and nodal values.

For rendering, however, Cohen uses linear interpolation. With respect to linear interpolation, this subdivision criterion is better characterized as a heuristic designed to produce smaller elements in regions where the radiosity is highly variable. This heuristic usually produces acceptable results, although it tends to oversubdivide where the gradient is high but constant. Since linear interpolation is a reasonable approximation for this case, subdividing has little effect on the error (see Figure 6.26.)

This heuristic may also fail to identify elements that should be subdivided. In Figure 6.26 the nodes bounding an element containing a local minimum (letter D in the figure) happen to have almost the same value. The heuristic fails in this case, since the nodal values alone do not provide enough information about the behavior of the function on the element interior. This difficulty is common to all types of error estimators and algorithms make efforts of varying sophistication to characterize the function between nodes.

For example, Vedel and Puech [242] use the gradient at the nodes as well as the function value. Elements are subdivided if the gradients at the element nodes vary by more than a certain tolerance (see Figure 6.27). This criterion avoids subdividing elements unnecessarily where the gradient is high but constant (letter

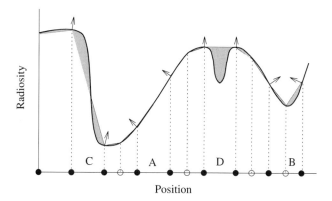

Figure 6.27: *Gradient-based subdivision criterion. Nodes added due to adaptive subdivision are indicated by hollow circles.*

A of Figure 6.27). It may also detect a local minimum within an element whose nodal values happen to be similar (letter B of Figure 6.27). However, the criterion is not foolproof. Letter C of Figure 6.27 shows a situation that might occur when a penumbra falls entirely within an element. The gradients at the nodes spanning the element happen to be equal and the element is not subdivided.

A more stringent criterion can be constructed that uses both the nodal values and gradients. An algorithm based on this approach might first compare gradients at the nodes. If the gradients vary by too much, the element is subdivided. Otherwise, the gradient at the nodes is compared to the slope of the plane determined by the nodal values. If they are inconsistent, the element is subdivided. This criterion correctly identifies the element at letter C in Figure 6.27, although it does not identify the case indicated by the letter D.

Higher-Order Subdivision Criteria

Vedel and Puech describe a test-bed system that estimates local error based on a higher-order (bicubic) interpolant over rectangular elements [242]. The local error estimate is provided by the L_2 norm of the difference between bilinear and bicubic interpolation over an element (see Figure 6.28). This integral is evaluated in closed form as a function of the radiosities and gradients at the element nodes.

In comparing the higher-order error estimate to value- and gradient-based criteria for several simple cases, Vedel and Puech find the bicubic interpolation estimate to be the most accurate of the three when the radiosity is slowly varying. However, it fails to identify elements across which the radiosity is

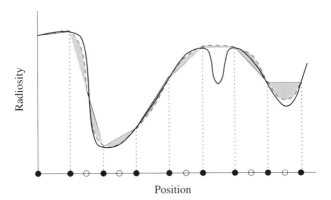

Figure 6.28: *Estimation of error by comparing linear and cubic interpolation. The gray area represents the estimated error. Nodes that will be added due to adaptive subdivision are indicated by hollow circles.*

changing very rapidly, for example, where the element contains a sharp shadow boundary. In this case, the simple comparison of values does better, although as expected, it tends to oversubdivide in other regions. Vedel and Puech conclude that the complexity of the bicubic method is not justified, and they suggest simply comparing both radiosities and gradients.

Estimation Using the Residual

All of the methods described so far ultimately fail at some point because the nodes can never be relied on to completely characterize the behavior of the function elsewhere in the element. A local minimum or maximum can fall entirely within an element without affecting the function or its derivatives at the nodes, as is the case for the local minimum at letter D in Figure 6.26. Small shadows are often missed for this reason, with one common result being the appearance of floating furniture in radiosity images (see the artifact labeled B in Figure 6.3(b).)

In such cases, the only solution is to evaluate the function inside the element. One approach is to evaluate the radiosity equation at one or more points within the element and compare the results to the interpolated values. This is equivalent to estimating the residual, (described in section 6.1.3.)

Lischinski *et al.* [153] have used this technique for one-dimensional elements in a "flatland" radiosity implementation. In [154] they generalize this approach to two-dimensional elements by evaluating the radiosity at the centroid of the element and comparing it to the interpolated value at the same location (see

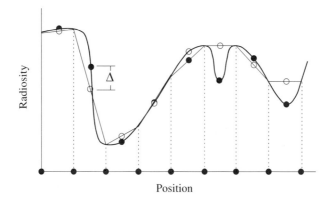

Figure 6.29: *Estimation of error by computing the residual at element centers. The hollow circles represent interpolated values and the solid circles the computed value. The residual is the difference between the two.*

Figure 6.29). The error at the centroid is assumed to be the maximum error for the element. This approach can thus be viewed as estimating the L^∞ norm. This technique is independent of the interpolation order (quadratic interpolation was used by Lischinski *et al.*).

Of course, evaluating the error at the centroid is not guaranteed to catch every case. In Lischinski's implementation, mesh boundaries corresponding to discontinuities in the radiosity function or its derivatives are specified a priori. Thus, a posteriori adaptive subdivision is required to refine the mesh only within regions over which the radiosity function is relatively smooth and well behaved, in which case checking the error at the centroid will generally produce good results.

Campbell [42] describes a more systematic approach to determining the behavior of the function on the interior. This is particularly useful when the radiosity function cannot be assumed to be smooth. Campbell's criterion for subdivision uses the difference between the maximum and minimum radiosities over the entire element, not just at the nodes. Elements that require subdivision are split perpendicularly to the line connecting the maximum and minimum points. Thus, Campbell's algorithm depends on a systematic search for the extrema, which is achieved using standard optimization techniques.

Since Campbell's algorithm computes shadow boundaries a priori, it can identify fully lit regions and treat them differently from penumbra regions, which are more complex. For fully lit regions Campbell computes the gradient at the nodes analytically by differentiating the point–polygon form factor equation. This allows the use of optimization techniques that take advantage of gradient information to accelerate the search. In addition, for a fully lit region there can be only one local maximum on the interior of the element due to a given constant diffuse source.

For regions within the penumbra the gradient cannot be computed analytically and no assumptions can be made about the number of local extrema. In this case global optimization is performed using the *Multistart* method. A grid is laid over the region and the function is evaluated at a random point inside each grid cell. Cells whose neighbors are either all greater or all lesser in value than the cell itself provide the starting point for local optimization.

None of the error criteria that have been described in these sections can guarantee that small features will be found. This is one advantage of discontinuity meshing (discussed in Chapter 8), which locates critical shading boundaries a priori based on the model geometry. Within regions bounded by discontinuities, the radiosity function is reasonably well behaved, and simple error estimators are more reliable.

Computing the Gradient

A number of error estimators require the gradient of the radiosity at the nodes. Campbell points out that the analytic expression for the form factor between a differential area and a constant, unoccluded polygonal element is continuous and differentiable [42]. The expression can thus be symbolically differentiated to provide an analytic formula for the gradient at unoccluded nodes. However, the gradient is difficult or impossible to compute analytically in the presence of occlusion and is actually undefined at certain discontinuity boundaries.

Numerical differencing can also be used to compute partial derivatives. If the nodes fall on a regular grid, a first-order estimate of the partial derivative along grid lines can be made by comparing a nodal value with that of its neighbors. This estimate can be computed using forward or backward differencing, given by

$$\frac{\Delta B}{\Delta \mathbf{x}} = \frac{B(\mathbf{x}_i) - B(\mathbf{x}_{i-1})}{\mathbf{x}_i - \mathbf{x}_{i-1}} \tag{6.10}$$

where $\mathbf{x}_i$ and $\mathbf{x}_{i-1}$ are neighboring nodes. Central differencing can also be used, given by

$$\frac{\Delta B}{\Delta \mathbf{x}} = \frac{B(\mathbf{x}_{i+1}) - B(\mathbf{x}_{i-1})}{\mathbf{x}_{i+1} - \mathbf{x}_{i-1}} \tag{6.11}$$

If the mesh is irregular, the tangent plane at the node can be estimated using a least-squares fit of a plane to the values at the node and its immediate neighbors. (The contouring literature is a good source for techniques of this kind [257].) The accuracy of these techniques depends on the spacing between nodes.

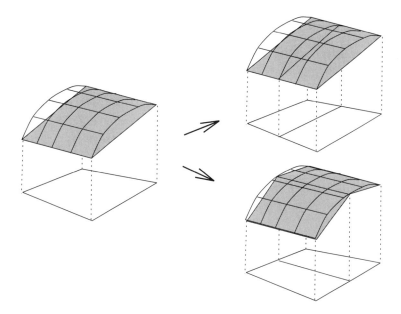

Figure 6.30: *Two different subdivisions of the same element. The upper right subdivision does not reduce the overall error of the approximation.*

Another option is to perform extra function evaluations at points in the neighborhood of the node. For example, Salesin *et al.* [203] use quadratic triangular elements having nodes at the midpoint of each edge. To compute the gradient, a quadratic curve is fit to the values of the three nodes along each edge. The tangents of the two parabolas intersecting a given corner node determine a tangent plane at the node, and thus the gradient. This technique is described in more detail in section 9.2.2.

Ward describes a technique useful for methods that compute the irradiance at a point by sampling the visible surfaces over the entire hemisphere above the point, as in the hemicube [253]. The method was developed in the context of Ward's *Radiance* lighting simulation system, which does not use radiosity. However, a full-matrix (gathering) radiosity solution using the hemicube or similar method for computing form factors is equally amenable to Ward's technique, although as yet no radiosity implementations have taken advantage of it.

6.3.4 Deciding How to Subdivide

Identifying elements that require subdivision is only the first step. The goal in identifying elements for subdivision is to reduce the local error for those elements, but the actual reduction in error will depend on *how* the elements are subdivided. For example, in Figure 6.30, two ways of subdividing an element are compared. In one case, the error is reduced significantly, while in the other it is not reduced at all.

Subdividing intelligently requires some estimate of the behavior of the function inside the element. Campbell's optimization approach, described in the previous section, is one of the few algorithms that attempts to obtain and use this information. Campbell searches for the maximum and minimum points on the interior of the element. The element is then subdivided on a boundary perpendicular to the line connecting the maximum and minimum points. The flexibility required to subdivide in this way places demands on the actual subdivision algorithm. Campbell chooses a BSP-tree based approach for this reason.

Airey [5] and Sturzlinger [227] note a useful technique for the special case of subdividing rectangles into triangles. The edge created to split the rectangle should connect the nodes with the most similar radiosities, since this produces the greatest reduction in the variation between the nodes of each of the resulting elements. Schumaker [207] discusses a generalization of this approach in which the behavior of the approximation is incorporated into the quality metric used during triangulation of the set of nodes. This more general approach has not yet been applied to radiosity, however.

In the absence of knowledge about the function behavior, the best that can be done is to subdivide uniformly. This is the approach taken by most existing adaptive subdivision algorithms. The resulting subdivision will depend on the particular subdivision algorithm. One common approach is to subdivide elements into four similarly shaped elements, generating a quadtree subdivision hierarchy. If the elements are triangles, another approach is to subdivide elements by inserting nodes and adding new edges. These and a wide variety of other subdivision algorithms are surveyed in Chapter 8, with some discussion of how they can be applied to adaptive subdivision.

Chapter 7

Hierarchical Methods

The meshing strategies surveyed in the previous chapter are designed to reduce the computational cost of the radiosity solution by minimizing the number of elements in the mesh. The solution cost depends strongly on the number of elements, since solving the discrete radiosity equation requires computing an interaction between every pair of elements. Thus, the cost of the radiosity solution appears to be inherently $O(n^2)$ in the number of elements. Each of these $O(n^2)$ relationships involves evaluating the form factor integral (the subject of Chapter 4) and is thus expensive to compute. Hence, the goal of the meshing strategies outlined in the previous chapter is to minimize the number of elements while maintaining accuracy.

The subject of this chapter is an alternative approach to reducing the computational cost of the radiosity algorithm. This approach keeps the same number of elements, instead attempting to reduce the number of individual relationships, or form factors, that have to be computed. For example, two groups of elements separated widely in space might reasonably have the total interaction between all pairs of individual elements represented by a single number computed once for the entire group. Attaining this goal involves developing a *hierarchical* subdivision of the surfaces and an associated hierarchy of interactions. The hierarchy will provide a framework for deriving interactions between groups of elements, which will result in computing many fewer than $O(n^2)$ interactions. In fact, it will turn out that only $O(n)$ form factors are required to represent the linear operator **K** to within a desired error tolerance.

This chapter is divided into three major sections. The first two sections describe hierarchical subdivision techniques that minimize the number of form factors to be computed by grouping elements together. The first section assumes that constant basis functions have been selected to approximate the radiosity function. The section begins with a description of a two-level, patch-element hierarchy and continues with the generalization of the basic hierarchical approach, resulting in an $O(n)$ algorithm. The second section then describes an alternate way of approaching the same goal, in which the hierarchical algorithms are derived in terms of hierarchical basis functions. One such class of basis func-

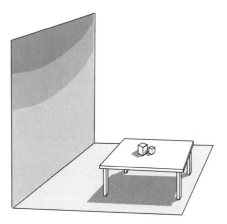

Figure 7.1: *Room with desk and wall.*

tions, known as wavelets, will be used to represent the kernel of the radiosity function at variable levels of detail. This formulation will provide a framework for incorporating higher order basis functions into hierarchical algorithms.

The third section of the chapter introduces an *adjoint* to the radiosity equation that allows the *importance* of a particular element to the final image to be determined. The combined radiosity equation and its adjoint will provide yet another means to reduce greatly the computational complexity for complex environments, in the case where only one, or a few, views are required.

I. Hierarchical Subdivision

7.1   A Physical Example

The basic physical intuition behind hierarchical solution methods is straightforward. Imagine a room containing a table on which are placed several small objects (see Figure 7.1). Light reflected from the table top contributes some illumination to the wall. Intuitively, however, the shading of the wall does not depend significantly on the small details of the illumination leaving the table top. If the objects on the table are rearranged so that the shadows on the table are slightly altered, the shading of the wall does not change significantly.

Representing the contribution of the table top to the wall by a single average value will give a similar result to computing individual contributions from many small elements on the table top. This is because ideal diffuse reflection effectively averages the light arriving over an incoming solid angle. If the solid angle is not too great, as is the case when a source is far away relative to its size from a receiver, it is reasonable to average the source radiosity before the integration step.[1] For radiosity, this means replacing several form factors with a single form factor.

On the other hand, when the table top is eventually rendered in an image, its shading must capture all the details of the light and shadows falling on it. These details will be lost if the effect of illumination arriving at the table is averaged over a large area rather than computed in detail for smaller regions. Thus, the radiosity of a particular surface or group of surfaces will have to be represented at at least two levels of detail: coarsely when the surface acts as a source of illumination and more finely when it acts as a receiver. There is no inherent limitation to two levels, and these notions will be extended in a later section to a generalized hierarchical representation.

7.2   Two-Level Hierarchy

The first hierarchical algorithm for radiosity was developed by Cohen *et al.* [61]. It provides two levels of hierarchy and is based directly on the above-noted distinction between sources and receivers. Surfaces are subdivided coarsely into *patches* to represent the surface when it acts as a source of illumination to other surfaces. The same surfaces, when receiving illumination, are represented by a finer subdivision of the patches into *elements*. Images are rendered using the element mesh. The element mesh can be subdivided adaptively as more information about the illumination of the surface becomes known to achieve an appropriate element size, but the patch subdivision is specified a priori by the user. The algorithm assumes constant basis functions.

The steps in the two-level hierarchical algorithm are as follows (corresponding to the numbers in Figure 7.2):

1. Divide the surfaces into m patches and n smaller elements ($m << n$), where each patch is composed exactly of the union of some subset of the elements. The patches will act as the sources or "shooters" and the elements will act as the receivers or "gatherers." The patches are indexed by i or j and the elements by q.

2. Compute the $m \times n$ form factors from each element to each patch. A single entry from element q to patch j would be F_{qj}.

3. Compute the $m \times m$ form factors between pairs of patches directly from the element-to-patch form factors by summing the form factors for the

---

[1]A similar observation enables the use of a local reflection model to approximate the complex interactions of light with the microscopic geometry of a surface.

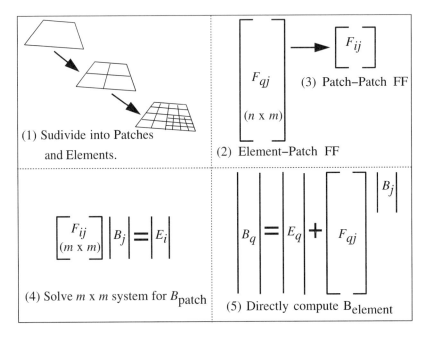

Figure 7.2: *Two-level hierarchical algorithm.*

elements q belonging to patch i, weighted by the areas of the elements:

$$F_{ij} = \sum_{q \in i} F_{qj} \frac{A_q}{A_i} \tag{7.1}$$

4. Solve the $m \times m$ system of equations using Gauss-Seidel to get the patch radiosities:

$$B_i = E_i + \rho_i \sum_{j=1}^{m} B_j F_{ij} \tag{7.2}$$

5. Back solve for the element radiosities. This is accomplished by plugging the element-to-patch form factors computed in step 2 and the patch radiosities, B_j, from step 4, into the radiosity equation expressing the element radiosity as the sum of contributions from each patch:

$$B_q = E_q + \rho_q \sum_{j=1}^{m} B_j F_{qj} \tag{7.3}$$

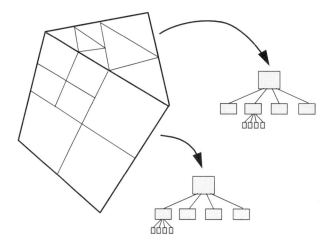

Figure 7.3: *Quadtree surface subdivision.*

6. If the difference in radiosity between neighboring elements is too high, elements can be further subdivided. New patch-to-element form factors are computed ONLY for the new elements, and the new element radiosities can be computed directly from the original patch radiosities without solving a new system (i.e., the original m patches are intact). This last step can be repeated adaptively as needed.

In practice, recursive adaptive subdivision is achieved by constructing a *quadtree*[2] of elements. If the original surfaces are initially divided into quadrilaterals and triangles (see Figure 7.3), there is a simple operation that splits each simple shape along each of its parametric midpoints, resulting in four new smaller elements. The mechanics are discussed in greater detail in Chapter 8.

Following the solution, the radiosity function is approximated by the n elements. However, the solution has required computing only $m \times n$ form factors, where m is much less than n.

7.3 The K Matrix

In Chapter 3 the discrete radiosity system was derived, resulting in the system of linear equations $\mathbf{KB} = \mathbf{E}$, where the operator $\mathbf{K}$ is a matrix that represents the interrelationships between nodes in the finite element approximation. It will

---

[2]A quadtree is the two-dimensional analog to a binary tree (i.e., each node in the tree has four *children* and one parent).

be useful in what follows to understand the relationship between the physical intuition developed in section 7.1 and structure in the **K** matrix.

In the two-level hierarchy of the previous section, grouping elements together into patches allows every element to compute only a single form factor to each patch (rather than to each element), effectively reducing the number of entries to be computed in the matrix **K**. The two-level hierarchy assumes that, in effect, a number of form factors on the same row of **K** are closely related. In particular, the form factors from a single element to all the elements of a particular patch are treated as a constant scaled by the individual element areas. Conversely, using the reciprocity principle, the form factors from all elements of a single patch to *any other* element are assumed to be identical.

To understand better why this assumption is often valid, it is easiest to use a contrived example in a two-dimensional "flatland." In flatland, "surfaces" are lines in a plane. Flatland was introduced to radiosity investigation by Heckbert [122].

Imagine a model consisting of two perpendicular line segments that touch at one end, as depicted in Figure 7.4(a). In this two-dimensional world the kernel function $G(\mathbf{x}, \mathbf{x}')$ (see Chapter 3) of the integral operator depends on the cosine of the angles between the line connecting the points $\mathbf{x}$ and $\mathbf{x}'$ and the surface normals at those points, and inversely on the distance, r, between the points (as opposed to the distance squared in three dimensions). It also depends on visibility, although this is not an issue in this particular example. Also, aside from the singularity at the corner where the surfaces meet, G is *smooth*.

Clearly the value of G is smaller and varies less quickly in cases where $\mathbf{x}$ and $\mathbf{x}'$ are distant from each other, since the $1/r$ and cosine terms are then less sensitive to small changes in $\mathbf{x}$ or $\mathbf{x}'$. This will be reflected in the values of the corresponding entries in the matrix **K**.

The **K** matrix for this model is shown in Figure 7.4(b).[3] The surfaces (line segments) have been divided into eight elements each. There are a row and a column corresponding to each element of the two surfaces, resulting in a 16 by 16 matrix. In this particular model, the upper left and lower right quadrants of the matrix will be identically zero, except for the ones on the diagonal, since the entries in these quadrants represent interactions between elements on the same surface. The interactions between elements on two different surfaces are represented by the upper right and lower left quadrants, enlarged in Figure 7.4(c).

This example has been set up intentionally so that neighboring entries in the upper right quadrant represent interactions that are closely related in a physical sense. For example, entries in the upper right-hand corner of the quadrant represent interactions between elements that are at the far ends of the two surfaces

---

[3]Constant basis functions will be assumed for the discussion of **K** in the following sections. However, the ideas are equally applicable to higher order bases.

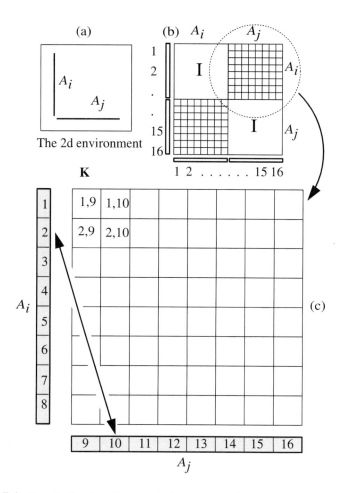

Figure 7.4: *Two flatland surfaces and the upper right quadrant of* **K**. *The value of the entry* 2, 10 *represents the transport of light from element* 10 *to element* 2.

and that are thus widely separated. According to the behavior of the function G just described, these entries will be smaller and change less rapidly than those in the lower left-hand corner of the quadrant, which represent elements that are closer together. This is demonstrated very clearly in Figure 7.5, which is a visualization of the upper right quadrant of a 32 by 32 matrix for the same model.

Returning to the 16 by 16 example, the entries $K_{2,9}$ and $K_{2,10}$, which neighbor each other on row 2, represent the effect of elements 9 and 10 on

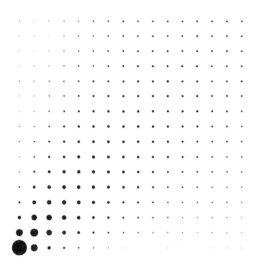

Figure 7.5: *Value of entries in the upper right quadrant of the operator* **K**. *The values are indicated by the area of the circles.*

element 2. If the values of these two entries are almost the same, a single value could be computed and simply used twice. In essence, a single larger element composed of elements 9 and 10 would be used as a source of light for element 2.

Why not just eliminate the two smaller elements entirely by joining them together into a single larger element? This would be reasonable for this particular interaction. However, it may be that in another row the form factors to elements 9 and 10 are quite different, and thus it is important to keep the effects of elements 9 and 10 distinct for those interactions! For example, looking at Figure 7.5, the difference between the entries of the first two columns is clearly much more significant in the bottom row than in the top row.

Similarly, two neighboring entries in a single column may be very similar, indicating that the element corresponding to that column makes a similar contribution to the two receiving elements. In this case, a single larger receiving element would provide sufficient accuracy. Finally, a whole *block* of the matrix may be identical, indicating that the effect of a group of source elements on a group of receiving elements could be treated as a single interaction.

This discussion has ignored visibility, which may decrease or increase the coherence between neighboring entries in the matrix. If some polygon fully or partially obscures the visibility between two other polygons, a series of zeros will occur in the matrix. Rapidly changing partial visibility may also result in a portion of the operator that was very coherent becoming less coherent.

In the matrix for a complex three-dimensional model, neighboring entries are by no means guaranteed to represent "neighboring" physical situations. Nevertheless, the basic principle remains the same: there will be entries throughout the matrix that do represent related physical neighborhoods and that can be grouped along rows, columns, or in blocks to reduce the computation required to formulate the matrix.

Returning now to the two-level, patch-element hierarchy, it is clear that this approach has the user make an a priori guess at which entries along rows of the matrix can be grouped together. This initial grouping is the patch level subdivision. Elements are only grouped together (into patches) in so far as they act as source of illumination for other elements. This reduces the n by n matrix to an m by n matrix of source patches and receiving elements.

The limitations of the two-level algorithm are also clear. First, the grouping of elements into patches is fixed. The same grouping is applied to every row of the matrix whether or not the grouped entries would actually be similar in that row. Thus, even the elements of two surfaces that happen to be quite close together will be treated as a single patch, although this is not justified. The ability to group elements into larger or smaller groups depending on the interaction is important to maintaining accuracy.

Returning to the example of the wall and the table, in a two-level hierarchy the entire table top might be a patch and act as a source for all elements. This might satisfactorily account for the effect of the table on the wall, but would be inadequate to represent the effect of the table on the objects resting on it. A more detailed representation of the illumination provided by the table is necessary in this case.

A second limitation is that entries that are similar within a column cannot be grouped together. This corresponds to the distinction between sources and receivers in the two-level algorithm. This distinction is justified only in terms of maintaining a special, highly refined approximation for rendering purposes. For the purposes of the solution process itself, the inability to group receivers removes a potential source of efficiency.

Finally, the two-level algorithm requires that the user perform the patch subdivision. Since the user does not have access to detailed quantitative data characterizing the interactions being grouped, this is clearly inadequate. An error metric that can be used to evaluate interactions for possible grouping is required, as well as an algorithm for automatically constructing the hierarchy.

These limitations are all addressed in the next section, which describes a general algorithm for constructing multilevel hierarchies of interactions.

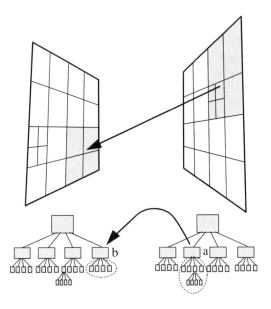

Figure 7.6: *Hierarchical quadtrees and interactions.*

7.4 Multilevel Hierarchy

Hanrahan *et al.* [116] have generalized the notion of subdivision hierarchy to multiple levels, allowing both receivers and sources to be treated at the appropriate level of detail. A basic hierarchical subdivision is diagramed in Figure 7.6, in which two surfaces have been recursively subdivided into a hierarchy of elements and groups of elements. The recursive subdivision of each surface results in a *quadtree* of nodes, each of which represents some portion of the surface. As in the two-level hierarchy, the leaf nodes are the elements, with nodes higher in the quadtrees representing groups of elements.

In the multilevel hierarchy, energy can be shot from *any node* to any other node at any level in the hierarchical subdivision (not only to the leaves as before). One such interaction is indicated by the arrow in Figure 7.6, where energy from a group of seven elements (a) is transported to a group of four elements (b). If energy is shot to a node at a level above the leaves, the nodes below (down to the leaves) will *inherit* the energy received above. This operation will be explained in more detail below. It will be shown that this approach leads to fewer total shooting (gathering) operations. The key result will be that only $O(n)$ interactions (form factors) are required to meet a given error tolerance, where n is the number of leaves of the quadtrees (i.e., the number of elements). Thus, while the two-level hierarchy reduced the number of form factors to $O(n \times m)$, the general hierarchical algorithm is $O(n)$.

7.4.1 N-Body Problem

Hanrahan *et al.* [116] gained their inspiration by relating the radiosity problem to the *N-body problem*, which addresses the gravitational interactions within a collection of n particles.

If each of n particles exerts a force on all the other $n - 1$ particles, there will be $O(n^2)$ interactions between pairs of particles to account for. Fast algorithms have been developed [9] by recognizing that the force due to a group of particles beyond some distance from another particle can be approximated with a single interaction. Likewise, pairs of such groups, where the whole groups are separated by some distance, can be considered with a single interaction. For example, two widely separated galaxies each represent very large groups of particles, but the gravitational interaction between them can be approximated by the interaction of two particles, each representing the combined mass of the stars in the corresponding galaxy. This insight has been refined to develop fast N-body algorithms by Esselink [79], Barnes and Hut [16], and Greengard and Rokhlin [106].

7.4.2 Radiosity and the N-Body Problem

The radiosity problem is similar to the N-body problem in that the interactions (form factors) drop off according to $1/r^2$. The interactions can also be summed as with the form factor algebra. On the other hand, the radiosity problem often starts with large areas to subdivide rather than small particles to group together (although see the discussion of clustering in section 11.3.5). There is also no analog to occlusion in the N-body problem (i.e., the gravitational force between two particles is not affected by intervening particles). Nevertheless, the basic structure of the hierarchical algorithm remains valid.

7.4.3 Hierarchical Refinement

In contrast to previously discussed algorithms, the multilevel hierarchical algorithm never explicitly builds a matrix. Instead, as the subdivision is performed recursively, *links* are built on-the-fly between nodes of the quadtrees associated with each surface.

A link represents the physical relationship between one set of elements and another set of elements, which determines the potential for energy transport between them. The two sets of elements are the leaves of the subtrees below the nodes at which the links terminate (indicated by the dotted ovals in Figure 7.6).

In other words, each link will represent a subset of form factors from the original n by n matrix, that is, the form factors for *all pairs* of elements in the two subtrees. A link between a pair of nodes at the lowest level connects two individual elements and thus represents a single entry in the matrix. Links at higher levels represent successively larger groups of form factors.

The set of entries in the original n by n matrix, **K**, that are represented by a single link will map to *regions* in the domain of the kernel of the radiosity integral. Remember that the kernel function is four-dimensional in the case of a three-dimensional environment, since it is a function of two two-dimensional points on two surfaces. Thus the local four-dimensional region represented by a link is the cross product of the two two-dimensional regions represented by the sets of elements at either end of the link. Since the sets of form factors encompassed in a single link do not define complete columns of the original matrix as in the two-level hierarchy, or neat rectangular blocks in the three-dimensional model, it is more difficult to visualize or to explicitly construct a matrix representation of the links. Instead, a solution method that relies directly on the link data structure is used.

To determine the links, one could conceivably build the whole n^2 form factor matrix and then search for subsets of the matrix for which all entries are similar in magnitude. These would correspond to potential links between quadtree nodes and could then be grouped together into a single value. This might, in fact, reduce the solution time for iterative matrix solution methods by making the matrix–vector multiplications faster, but would not solve the more important problem of reducing the form factor computation.

Instead, the aim is to develop a method of predicting whether a subset of form factors will be *coherent* (e.g., similar in magnitude) before actually computing the subset of form factors. If the subset is predicted to be coherent, a single representative form factor can be computed for the subset. Such a prediction method will be called an *oracle* in the following discussion.[4]

For this discussion of hierarchical algorithms, we will use two data structures, one for a quadtree node, **Quadnode**, and one for a link between quadtree nodes, **Linknode** (see Figure 7.7). The hierarchical algorithm begins with a basic recursive procedure called **Refine** that subdivides the surfaces into quadtrees and create the links between quadtree nodes (see Figure 7.8). Three functions are required:

1. **Oracle**(p, q, ϵ) returns a decision of whether or not to link two quadtree nodes p and q based on the error that would be incurred if the nodes are linked rather than linking multiple nodes at lower levels below p and/or q. If both p and q are already subdivided as far as possible (i.e., their areas

---

[4]The use of an oracle to determine element subdivision is also discussed in [76].

```
struct Quadnode {
    float                   B_g;        /* gathering radiosity */
    float                   B_s;        /* shooting radiosity */
    float                   E;          /* emission */
    float                   area;
    float                   ρ;
    struct Quadnode**       children;/* pointer to list of four children */
    struct Linknode*        L;          /* first gathering link of node */
};

struct Linknode {
    struct Quadnode*        q;          /* gathering node */
    struct Quadnode*        p;          /* shooting node */
    float                   F_qp;       /* form factor from q to p */
    struct Linknode*        next;       /* next gathering link of node q */
};
```

Figure 7.7: Quadnode *and* Linknode *data structures.*

```
Refine(Quadnode *p, Quadnode *q, float F_ε )
{
    Quadnode which, r;
    if ( Oracle1( p, q, F_ε ) )
        Link( p, q );
    else {
        which = Subdiv( p, q );
        if( which == q )
            for( each child node r of q ) Refine( p, r, F_ε );
        else if ( which == p )
            for( each child node r of p ) Refine( r, q, F_ε );
        else
            Link( p, q );
    }
}
```

Figure 7.8: Refine *pseudocode.*

```
SolveSystem()
{
    Until Converged {
        for ( all surfaces p) GatherRad( p );
        for ( all surfaces p) PushPullRad( p, 0.0 ); }
}
```

Figure 7.9: SolveSystem *pseudocode.*

are below a user-specified minimum area, A_ϵ), then the **Oracle** returns **FALSE**.

2. **Subdiv**(p, q) is called if the **oracle** returns true indicating nodes below p or q should be used. **Subdiv** returns p or q depending on for which it appears using lower level nodes will reduce the error. It may also decide not to choose either node. If the selected quadtree node has not yet been subdivided then **Subdiv** performs this operation.

3. **Link**(p, q) actually builds the link between p and q by computing the form factor between the areas represented at nodes p and q of the quadtrees and stores the form factor in the link data structure.

These three functions and a user-supplied error tolerance, F_ϵ, provide the necessary tools to adaptively perform the quadtree subdivision and build the appropriate links between quadtree nodes. Given two (rectangular or triangular) surfaces p and q, representing the roots of two quadtrees, the algorithm proceeds recursively (see the pseudocode in Figure 7.8).

After each ordered pair of surfaces has been handed to **Refine**, the result is a network of links that create connections between pairs of quadtree nodes. Note that every element-to-element pair will be *covered*. In other words, given two elements (leaves) i and j, there will be exactly one link from i or i's ancestors to j or j's ancestors.

The number of links corresponds to the number of form factor calculations that must be performed. Using an inexpensive form factor estimate for the oracle, Hanrahan *et al.* [116] make a counting argument to show that the number of links required is $O(n)$ rather than $O(n^2)$, where n is the maximum number of elements if all surfaces are fully subdivided. In fact, this may be a conservative estimate; their experience has shown that many fewer than n links are usually created.

```
GatherRad( Quadnode *p )
{
1       Quadnode *q; Link *L;
2
3       p→Bg = 0;
4       for ( each gathering link L of p ) /* gather energy across link */
5           p→Bg += p→ρ * L→Fpq * L→q→Bs ;
6       for each child node r of p
7           GatherRad( r );
}
```

Figure 7.10: GatherRad *pseudocode.*

7.4.4 Solution of the Hierarchical System

Although no explicit matrix has been formed, the set of links created by **Refine** defines a linear system that can be solved for the element radiosities. At each quadtree node, the data structure should contain two radiosity values, B_s (for shooting) and B_g (for gathering). Information must also be available about its emission, area and reflectivity. The solution of the system is performed iteratively by the function **SolveSystem** (see Figure 7.9). Each iteration consists of two steps, performed on each top-level surface (i.e., root of a quadtree):

1. **GatherRad** gathers energy over each incoming link, converting B_s at one end into B_g at the other (line 5 of Figure 7.10).

2. **PushPullRad**, *pushes* the received energy B_g down to the children of each quadtree node, and *pulls* the results back up the quadtrees by area averaging (see Figure 7.11), thus preparing the B_s for the next iteration. On the way recursively down the quadtree, the gathered radiosity of each node is simply added to the nodes below (line 9 of Figure 7.11). The radiosity of an area is not diminished by cutting the area into parts since radiosity has units of power per area, thus the simple summing of radiosity values.

   At the leaves of the quadtree, the sum of the gathered radiosity *pushed* down the tree is added to the leaf node's own gathered radiosity and emitted radiosity and the result transferred to the leaf node's shooting radiosity (line 3 of Figure 7.11). This quantity is returned up the tree (line 14). Since radiosity is in units of power/area, the radiosity *pulled* up the tree is the *average* over a node's children (line 10). For example, if

---

PushPullRad(Quadnode $*p$, float B_{down})
```
{
1    float B_up, B_tmp;
2    if ( p→children == NULL)      /* p is a leaf */
3        B_up = p→E + p→Bg + B_down;
4    else
5    {
6        B_up = 0;
7        for (each child node r of p)
8        {
9            B_tmp = PushPullRad(r, p→Bg + B_down);
10           B_up += B_tmp * (r→area)/(p→area)
11       }
12   }
13   p→Bs = B_up;
14   return B_up;
}
```

Figure 7.11: `PushPullRad` *pseudocode.*

four children all have the same radiosity, their parent node will have the same radiosity, since radiosity is measured in power/area. (By contrast, the *power* for the parent is the sum of the powers of the children).

The two steps in **SolveSystem** are performed iteratively until less than a user-specified maximum change occurs in the radiosity values from one iteration to the next. Thus, it may be advisable to store a copy of B_s before zeroing it out and then run a comparison of the copy and new shooting radiosities. This solution process corresponds to the iterative relaxation methods described in Chapter 5.

7.4.5 The Oracle Function

The **Oracle** function plays a key role in the efficiency of the overall hierarchical algorithm. The job of the oracle is to estimate the error that will be introduced by *linking* two quadtree nodes, rather than creating a series of links at lower levels. In essence, the oracle must answer the equivalent question: "By linking nodes p and q, what is the error introduced if a *constant*[5] value is

---

[5]In fact, the constancy test is the result of the use of constant hierarchical basis

```
float Oracle1( Quadnode *p, Quadnode *q, float Fε )
{
    if ( p→area < Aε and q→area < Aε )
        return( FALSE );
    if ( EstimateFormFactor( p, q ) < Fε )
        return( FALSE );
    else
        return( TRUE );
}
```

Figure 7.12: Oracle1 *pseudocode.*

assigned to all K_{ij} entries in the matrix, where i is a descendant of quadtree node p and j is a descendant of q?" It is not immediately clear how to answer the above question. For example, should the error norm reflect the estimated error in the entries of the matrix (i.e., the form factors) or the error in the final radiosity function? In addition, since the goal is to eliminate evaluations of the form factor, the oracle must be less expensive to evaluate than the form factor.

The Oracle as Form Factor Estimate

In the work reported by Hanrahan *et al.*, the value of the oracle is derived from an estimate of the unoccluded form factor (see Figure 7.12):

$$F_{pq} \approx \frac{\cos \theta}{\pi} \omega_q \qquad (7.4)$$

The estimate is computed at the centers of the areas represented by quadtree nodes p and q. The factor ω_q is the solid angle subtended by a sphere (or disk) surrounding the area of node q (see Figure 7.13).

This provides an upper bound on the error of any single entry in **K**. The rationale is that the form factor estimated by equation 7.4 can only get smaller if the real area q is used, or if there is occlusion, or if a descendant of q with smaller area is selected. In [116] both F_{pq} and F_{qp} are estimated. If either estimate is larger than a given F_ϵ, the element corresponding to the larger is subdivided. When both are below the threshold, a bidirectional link is established. This oracle is efficient and simple to implement, and is reported to work well in experiments by Hanrahan *et al.*

---

functions. This will be generalized in Part II of this chapter.

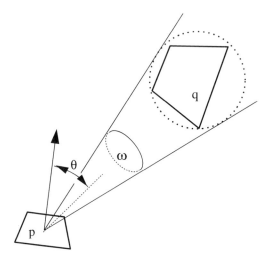

Figure 7.13: *Geometry for simple oracle function that estimates unoccluded form factor.*

Other Oracle Possibilities

The oracle described above establishes a threshold for individual errors in the **K** matrix. Other norms are possible and may offer a better prediction of error. The assumption implicit in creating a link is that the set of entries in the full matrix represented by the link are approximately equal in magnitude. The above test measures the maximum possible form factor value (and thus bounds the individual errors in **K**). However, a better test might be to estimate the potential *variability* in the differential form factor. This would require either an analytic formula for the derivative of the form factor or a multipoint quadrature and the use of finite differences across the two areas at either end of the link. Although this test would be more expensive, it might also lead to less subdivision and fewer total links. In fact, Hanrahan *et al.* perform a variation of this scheme when they take into account knowledge about partial visibility between surfaces in the adaptive algorithm discussed in the next section.

7.4.6   Progressive Refinement of the Hierarchy

The hierarchical algorithm outlined above makes a priori decisions about the level of the hierarchy at which to create the links, then solves the resulting system. Thus, the oracle makes decisions based solely on the geometry of the form factor estimates, independently of how much energy will eventually be transferred across individual links. An adaptive a posteriori version (see Figure 7.14)

```
HierarchicalRad(float BF_ε)
{
    Quadnode *p, *q;
    Link *L;
    int Done = FALSE;
    for ( all surfaces p ) p→B_s = p→E;
    for ( each pair of surfaces p, q )
        Refine( p, q, BF_ε);
    while ( not Done ) {
        Done = TRUE;
        SolveSystem();        /* as in Figure 7.9 */
        for ( all links L )
            /* RefineLink returns FALSE if any subdivision occurs */
            if( RefineLink( L, BF_ε ) == FALSE )
                Done = FALSE;
    }
}
```

Figure 7.14: `HierarchicalRad` *pseudocode.*

of the hierarchical algorithm can make better decisions about the subdivision, thus leading to more efficient performance. The a posteriori algorithm establishes a threshold for the oracle based on the amount of energy transferred across any individual link. The threshold BF_ϵ is based on the radiosity, the element area, *and* the form factor, or $B \cdot F \cdot A$. Since the radiosities, B, are not known a priori, the algorithm proceeds adaptively (see Figures 7.14 and 7.15), using a modified `Oracle2` function (see Figure 7.16).

Using the modified oracle, links are formed only from quadtree nodes from which a significant amount of energy is ready to be "shot." In the first pass, links are formed only at the highest level unless the shooting surface is a light source. As the algorithm progresses and more surfaces receive light to reflect, old links are broken and new links formed at lower levels as necessary. The link structure converges when all links carry approximately the same amount of energy.

An additional enhancement can be made by storing visibility information with the links. When the link is created, the form factor is computed and information describing the visibility between the two elements is recorded (i.e., whether p and q are fully visible, fully occluded, or partially visible to each

```
int RefineLink(Linknode *L, float BF_ε)
{
    int no_subdivision = TRUE;
    Quadnode* p = L→p ;      /* shooter */
    Quadnode* q = L→q ;      /* receiver */

    if ( Oracle2(L, BF_ε ) {
        no_subdivision = FALSE ;
        which = Subdiv( p, q );
        DeleteLink( L );
        if ( which == q )
            for (each child node r of q) Link( p, r );
        else
            for (each child node r of p) Link( r, q );
    }
    return(no_subdivision);
}
```

Figure 7.15: RefineLink *pseudocode.*

```
float Oracle2( Linknode *L, float BF_ε )
{
1       Quadnode* p = L→p ;      /* shooter */
2       Quadnode* q = L→q ;      /* receiver */
3       if ( p→area < A_ε and q→area < A_ε )
4           return( FALSE );
5       if ( p→B_s == 0.0 )
6           return( FALSE );
7       if( (p→B_s * p→Area * L→F_pq) < BF_ε );
8           return( FALSE );
9       else 10 return( TRUE );
}
```

Figure 7.16: Oracle2 *pseudocode.*

Polygons	98	
Potential elements	175964	
Potential interactions	15481576666	
Quadtree Nodes	5674	
Elements	4280	
Interactions	11800	
Totally-invisible	4605	39.0%
Totally-visible	4519	38.3%
Partially-visible	2676	22.7%
Tests		
Refinement tests	14149	
Totally-invisible refines	3901	27.6%
Pre-Totally-invisible refines	0	0.0%
Totally-visible refines	5414	38.3%
Pre-Totally-visible refines	4128	29.2%
Partially-visible refines	4834	34.2%
Partial visibility tests	10021	
Ray tests	53187	
Visibility tests	3545	
Ray tests	56720	

Table 7.1: *Statistics for color plates 18–22 (after Hanrahan et al.).*

other). Clearly, the fully occluded case will not benefit from further subdivision. The fully visible case can have a more relaxed threshold set than the partially visible case, for which one might expect larger fluctuations in the form factor kernel across the portions of the surfaces represented by p and q.

7.4.7   Experimental Results

Reports of experiments [116] using the `HierarchicalRad` algorithm are very encouraging (see Table 7.1). Color plates 18–21 show the links formed during the progressive refinement process. The multiple images are provided in order to show the links at the various levels of the hierarchy. Links are also color-coded by visibility (dark blue: fully occluded, white: fully visible, green: partially occluded). Color plate 22 shows a final image with texture mapping added (see Chapter 10 for a discussion of texture mapping). The statistics in Table 7.1 provide numerical evidence of the algorithm's ability to produce an image with a very limited number of interactions, (e.g., only about 12 thousand out of a potential 15 billion interactions are created).

II. Hierarchical Basis Functions and Wavelets

7.5   Hierarchical Basis Functions

The hierarchical methods just described can alternatively be characterized in terms of *hierarchical basis functions*. This view also provides a framework for

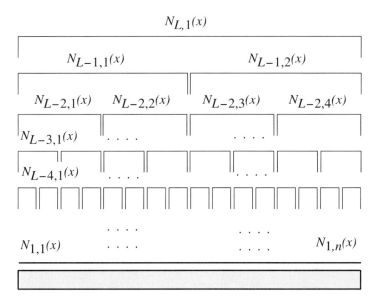

Figure 7.17: *Hierarchical basis set used by Hanrahan et al.*

developing other hierarchical basis functions as well as some understanding of the properties that lead to efficient algorithms. The basis functions discussed in previous chapters all have the property that their support is limited to the elements adjacent to the node at which the basis function is situated. Hierarchical basis functions will be developed by relaxing this restriction.

As an example of a hierarchical basis set, Figure 7.17 shows a binary tree of hierarchical box bases in one dimension. The basis set can be constructed either *top-down* or *bottom-up*. In the top-down approach, a single box basis, $N_{L,1}$, at the top level, L, is subdivided in half, producing two basis functions, $N_{L-1,1}$ and $N_{L-1,2}$, with the same combined support in the domain. These are in turn subdivided recursively until a preset minimum level is reached. The bottom-up approach simply reverses this process, beginning with the lowest level of box bases, $N_{1,1}$ to $N_{1,n}$, and recursively grouping two bases into a new, wider basis one level up. In the radiosity context, a binary tree (in 2D) or quadtree (in 3D) of bases would be constructed *for each surface*.

Figure 7.18 shows a one dimensional function approximated by a set of basis functions at each level of the hierarchy. The coefficients of each basis function represent the average radiosity over the support of the basis. These coefficients would be, for example, the B_s terms after applying the **PushPullRad** function in Figure 7.11.

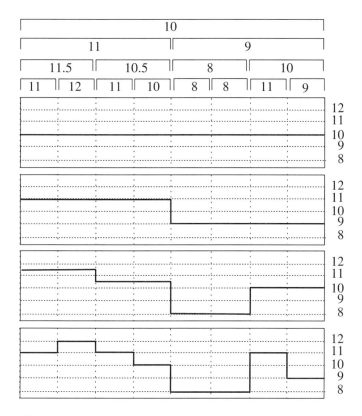

Figure 7.18: *Function represented at each level of hierarchy.*

The hierarchical basis set is *redundant* in the sense that any function representable at one level of the hierarchy can also be represented one level below (with two coefficients having values identical to the higher level coefficient). The reverse is not the case, however. Thus, the use of hierarchical systems does not lead to an increase in the size of the function space *spanned* by the bases. In particular, the multilevel hierarchical system described in the previous sections spans the same piecewise constant space of functions as a nonhierarchical set of box functions consisting of only the lowest level of the hierarchy. Thus, the use of a hierarchical system itself cannot produce an approximation $\hat{B}$ with a better fit to the actual function B. Instead, the use of hierarchy leads to sparser linear operators (i.e., fewer form factors) and thus more efficient algorithms.

The hierarchical set of basis functions, being redundant, would at first appear to be less efficient since there are more bases to represent the same space of functions. The hierarchical system, however, gains its efficiency from the fact that, unlike the nonhierarchical formulations, *not all pairs of basis functions require interaction terms (form factors)*. For example, using the subscripting shown in Figure 7.17 and a superscript to represent the surface at the root of the tree, $N_{3,4}^p$ would be the fourth basis function on the third level, for the L level quadtree associated with surface p. In the nonhierarchical formulations $\mathbf{K}$ has entries for every pair $(1, j)$ of elements (represented as the lowest leaves in the hierarchical system, with the basis functions at level 1). In contrast, in a hierarchical system, if a *link* is established between nodes of the quadtrees on surfaces p and q, for example, between $N_{3,4}^p$ and $N_{5,1}^q$, then no more links can be made from $N_{3,4}^p$ (or any of its children on levels 1 and 2) to $N_{5,1}^p$ (or any of its children on levels 4 and below). Thus, this single link represents all pairings of leaves in the quadtree below $N_{3,4}^p$ and $N_{5,1}^q$. In total, the single form factor on the link from $N_{3,4}^p$ to $N_{5,1}^q$ will represent $2^{(3-1)} \times 2^{(5-1)} = 64$ form factors at the lowest level of the binary trees in two dimensions, and $4^{(3-1)} \times 4^{(5-1)} = 4096$ form factors for the quadtrees in three dimensions!

7.6 Wavelets

A growing body of theory and applications is associated with the *wavelet* family of bases [27, 185]. It is beyond the scope of this book to provide a full discussion of wavelet theory. However, a short introduction will make it possible to cast the hierarchical radiosity formulation in terms of a simple example from the family of wavelets. The intention is to introduce some of the basic ideas necessary to extending hierarchical methods to new basis sets. These new basis sets have properties that allow them to better approximate the radiosity function and may possibly provide even sparser representations of the integral operator. Details can be found in [102].

7.6.1 Haar Basis

Building a wavelet basis begins with two functions, $\Phi(\mathbf{x})$ (called the *smooth* function), and $\Psi(\mathbf{x})$ (called the *detail* function). An example from a simple wavelet basis known as the Haar basis is shown in the center of Figure 7.19. By examining the two box basis functions, N_1 and N_2, and the smooth and detail Haar functions, it can be seen that the two sets both span the same space of functions. In other words, a linear combination of either the two boxes or the two Haar bases can represent any piecewise constant function, $F(x)$, over the two intervals. An example is shown at the bottom of the figure. The coefficient of the Φ function will represent the *average* over its nonzero range, and the coefficient of the Ψ function represents the *difference* from the average.

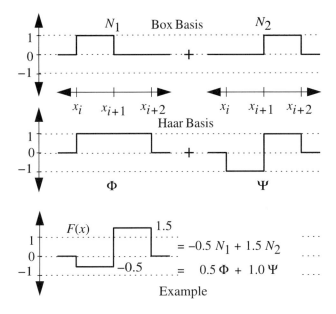

Figure 7.19: *Two consecutive box basis functions are equivalent to the Ψ and Φ functions of the Haar basis.*

Given the above observation, a set of n (where n is a power of 2) box basis functions can be replaced with a hierarchy constructed from the Haar Φ and Ψ functions (see Figure 7.20) using a bottom-up approach. Beginning with eight box basis functions, we can replace these by four sets of Φ and Ψ functions as shown in the first row of Figure 7.20. The resulting four Φ and four Ψ functions are then reordered, grouping each set together. In the second row it can be seen that the four Φ functions are exactly the same in structure as the original box basis functions, but twice as wide. Thus, these four Φ bases can be rewritten as two Φ and two Ψ functions, now twice the width. Once again these can be reordered. Finally, in the bottom row the two new wider Φ functions are rewritten as one Φ and one Ψ function. This results in the *Haar wavelet basis* consisting of one smooth $\Phi_{L,1}$ basis (where L, the top level, equals $\log_2(n)$ for n box bases) at the top level and a *pyramid* of Ψ detail basis functions (see Figure 7.21). Just as any piecewise constant (over unit intervals) function $F(x)$ could be represented by a linear sum of the original box basis functions:

$$F(x) = \sum_{i=1}^{n} f_i N_i(x) \tag{7.5}$$

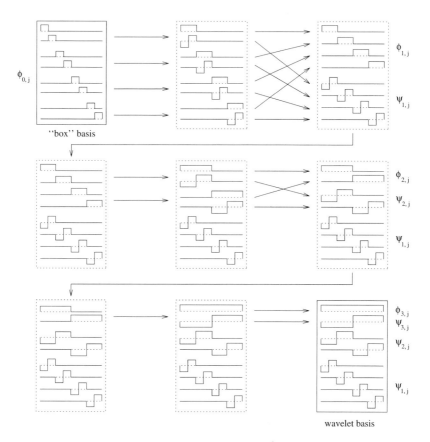

Figure 7.20: *Construction of the hierarchical Haar basis.*

$F(x)$ can also be represented by a linear combination of the Haar wavelet basis functions:

$$F(x) = \phi_{1,L}\Phi_{L,1}(x) + \sum_{i=1}^{L} \sum_{j=1}^{n/2^{(i-1)}} \psi_{i,j}\Psi_{i,j}(x) \qquad (7.6)$$

The coefficients of the box basis functions, f_i, represent the local value of $F(x)$. In the case of the wavelet basis, the coefficient $\phi_{1,L}$ represents the *average* of the function overall, and the $\psi_{i,j}$ represent the local *detail* or variation away from the average in $F(x)$ at each level i. This immediately points to the key advantage of the wavelet basis. If the function being represented is locally smooth (in this case constant) over a portion of its domain, then the coefficients representing the local detail will be zero (note the third coefficient in the Ψ_{L-2}

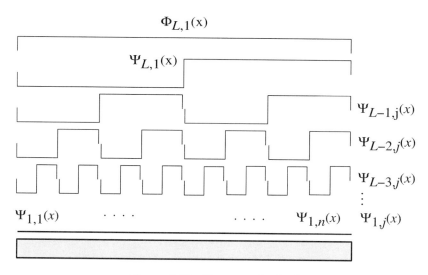

Figure 7.21: *Haar wavelet basis.*

row in Figure 7.22). While the coefficients of the original hierarchical box functions represent local averages, the coefficients of the Haar wavelet bases represent local *differences* and thus are zero in locally constant regions.

The projection of a one-dimensional function into the Haar basis can be thought of as passing a high-pass (Ψ or detail) and low-pass (Φ or smooth) filter over the function. The filters are then applied again recursively on the coefficients obtained in the low-pass filtering operation.

Referring again to the piecewise constant function in Figure 7.22, low and high pass filters are implemented by taking local averages and local differences, respectively. One application of low-pass filtering gives the coefficients 11.5, 10.5, 8.0, and 10.0. High-pass filtering gives the four coefficients, 0.5, -0.5, 0.0 and -1.0, shown in the row labeled Ψ_{L-2}, with the coefficient 0.5, for example, being the difference between the local average, 11.5, and the two segments of the original function, 11.0 and 12.0. The coefficient 0.0 corresponds to a flat region in the function (i.e., no detail). The process then recurses on the coefficients obtained by low-pass filtering, leading to two average values 11.0 and 9.0, and differences of -0.5 and 1.0. Finally, the last filtering pass results in the overall average value of 10.0, which becomes the coefficient of the highest level smooth basis, and a coefficient of -1.0 for the highest level detail basis. The Haar basis thus results in 7 Ψ coefficients and one Φ coefficient. The value of the function $F(x)$ as represented by the basis functions can then be obtained by evaluating equation 7.6 with these coefficients.

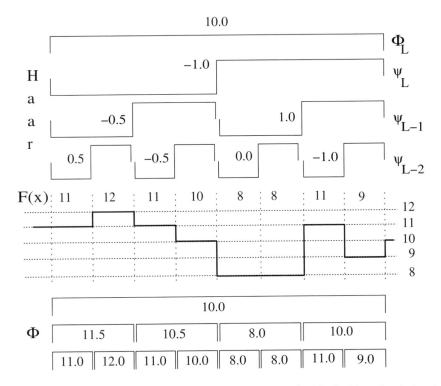

Figure 7.22: *Piecewise constant function represented with the Haar basis (top) and the hierarchical box basis (bottom).*

7.6.2 Vanishing Moments

The purpose of developing the preceding alternate basis for representing piecewise constant functions is to understand how it leads to a sparse representation of a function. In particular, the goal is to find a sparse representation of the radiosity kernel function, and similarly a large number of zeros in the discrete operator, $\mathbf{K}$. Wavelets are finding many uses in data, image, and signal compression for similar reasons.

If it is possible to find a basis set that leads to a sparse representation, and *if one can predict in advance* where the nonzero regions (entries in $\mathbf{K}$) will be, then it will be possible to reduce greatly the number of form factors required. Concepts presented below in one dimension will be extrapolated to apply to the multidimensional kernel of the radiosity problem.

The key concept is that of *vanishing moments*. A function $\Psi(x)$ is said to

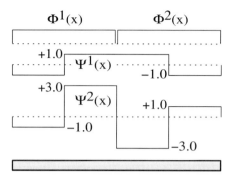

Figure 7.23: *Basis with two vanishing moments in detail functions.*

have M vanishing moments if,

$$\int_{-\infty}^{\infty} \Psi(x)\, x^i \, dx = 0 \quad \text{for } i = 0, ..., M-1 \tag{7.7}$$

For example, a function has one vanishing moment if its integral is zero, since x^0 is a constant. A function has two vanishing moments if when integrated against any linear function the result is zero, and so on for quadratic, cubic, and higher order polynomials. The Haar wavelet detail function has one vanishing moment since any constant function when integrated against it will be zero (i.e., *vanish*). For example, in Figure 7.22 the third coefficient on the Ψ_{L-2} row is zero since the local region of the function is flat.

Figure 7.23 depicts a set of four bases, two smooth and two detail, that also span the same piecewise constant function space [102], but in this case, the detail functions have two vanishing moments (call this the $\mathcal{F}_2$ basis). In other words, any linear function will vanish when integrated against these functions. The price that one must typically pay for more vanishing moments is a wider support, in this case over four intervals rather than the two of the Haar basis. Basis sets can be constructed with varying numbers of vanishing moments and abilities to span higher order function spaces, with associated costs in terms of their support and the difficulty of evaluating integrals in which they appear. Construction of such bases is not pursued here. The reader in encouraged to investigate the expanding literature on wavelets for this purpose.

7.6.3 Vanishing Moments and Sparse Representations

How do vanishing moments in the basis functions lead to sparse representations of functions and integral operators? The answer can be seen in the example of

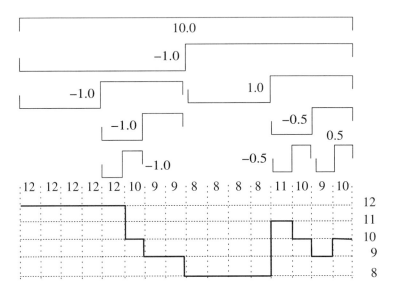

Figure 7.24: *Piecewise constant function represented by 9 hierarchical Haar basis functions versus 16 box bases.*

Figure 7.24. In this specific example, the piecewise constant function can be exactly represented as a weighted sum of 16 individual box bases. Alternatively, it can be represented by a weighted sum of only eight hierarchical Haar detail basis functions plus the average value of the overall function represented by the weight of the single smooth basis function. For areas in which the function is flat (i.e., constant), the projection[6] onto lower-level detail functions vanishes, and thus these basis functions are not necessary. Similarly, projecting onto bases with two vanishing moments will result in zero weights when the function is linear across the support of the basis. In general, functions will not exhibit exactly constant or linear behavior across the support of a basis. However, regions that are *almost* constant (or linear) will result in very small coefficients. In this case, the coefficients (weights) can be set to zero with only a small error in the approximation.

The hierarchical representation of a 2D matrix using the Haar basis is somewhat similar to the hierarchical *mipmap* representation of a texture map [266].

---

[6]The *projection* (more precisely the orthogonal projection) of one function onto a basis is described in Chapter 3. The projection involves finding the coefficient or weight of each basis function so as to minimize the norm of the difference between the original function and the sum of the weighted basis functions.

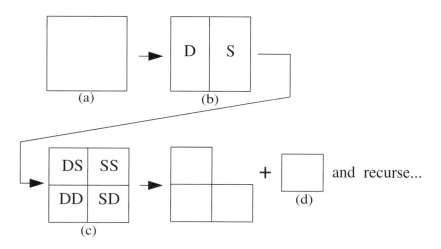

Figure 7.25: *The two-dimensional nonstandard pyramid algorithm (from Gortler et al., 1993). (a) The full n by n matrix. (b) A horizontal high-pass and low-pass filter on each row results in n/2 smooth and n/2 detail coefficients. (c) A vertical pass on this results in n/4 detail–detail coefficients, n/4 detail–smooth coefficients, n/4 smooth–detail, and n/4 smooth–smooth coefficients. (d) The process is recursively applied to the smooth–smooth quadrant.*

To construct a mipmap, a two-dimensional low-pass filter[7] is passed over the original image, giving an image of 1/4 the size. The same filter is applied again on the result recursively, resulting in a pyramid of images. Each successive image moving up the pyramid averages the values from below and thus contains less "detail"; the final image consists of a single value equal to the average value of the original image.

The construction of a representation of a 2D matrix (or image) using the Haar basis begins with the application of low-pass and high-pass filters along the rows and columns of the matrix (see Figure 7.25). For the Haar basis, low-pass filtering consists of averaging together pairs of entries along the row or column and high-pass filtering of taking differences between entries. Each filter is first applied to the matrix in the horizontal direction (along the rows). If there are n entries in a row, the result will be $n/2$ smooth coefficients and $n/2$ detail coefficients. Following the filtering pass, the coefficients resulting from each filter are grouped together (see letter (b) of Figure 7.25), forming a n by n matrix for which the first $n/2$ entries in each row are smooth coefficients,

---

[7]A 2D box filter is equivalent to the tensor product of the one-dimensional smooth Haar basis Φ.

and the last $n/2$ entries are detail coefficients. The filters are then applied in the vertical direction to this matrix and the results are similarly reorganized to give an n by n matrix for which the coefficients in the four quadrants consist of the detail–detail, detail–smooth, smooth–detail, and the smooth–smooth filtering results (see letter (c) of Figure 7.25). This filtering and reorganization process is then repeated recursively on the upper right (smooth–smooth) quadrant.

The final result of this decomposition is a hierarchy of representations of the 2D matrix (in what has been termed a *nonstandard* two-dimensional Haar basis [26]). The differences between this representation and a mipmap are instructive. The levels of a mipmap contain low frequencies (averages) in all levels of the image. The Haar basis also begins at the top with a single average value; however, at each level moving down from the top level the coefficients represent the *variation* of the matrix values from the representation of the previous level. The possibility for efficiency lies in taking advantage of the fact that smooth regions of the matrix result in near zero valued coefficients that can be ignored.

The results of applying the above decomposition process to the **K** matrix are shown in Figures 7.26 and 7.27 for the same "flatland" example (two perpendicular line segments) used in Figure 7.4. The top box in Figure 7.26 shows the 32 by 32 upper right quadrant of a 64 by 64 matrix, with the dot size proportional to the form factor in the original matrix. In the two boxes below, the matrix has been projected into the nonstandard basis (examples are shown for the Haar and $\mathcal{F}_2$ basis). The three quadrants in the lower left of the boxes are the detail–detail, detail–smooth and smooth–detail quadrants following one complete filtering pass (see letter (c) of Figure 7.25). The smooth–smooth quadrant is not shown. Instead, the next three quadrants moving diagonally toward the upper right show the result of the second complete filtering pass applied the missing smooth–smooth quadrant. The recursive application of this process generates the progressively lower detail representations of the matrix, as shown. The four boxes at the bottom of Figure 7.26 show the error in the reconstruction of the matrix (as compared to the original), after discarding (setting to zero) all but the 32 or 64 largest terms.

Figure 7.27 shows a similar example for the case of two parallel line segments. The important thing to note is that only 32 or 64 entries, compared to the original $32 \times 32 = 1024$ matrix coefficients have been used to reconstruct the original matrix while incurring only very small errors. Also, note the reduced error when applying bases with two vanishing moments (the $\mathcal{F}_2$ basis).

7.6.4 A Wavelet Radiosity Algorithm

A full radiosity application differs in two major ways from the above examples. First, the radiosity domain consists of two-dimensional surfaces embedded in

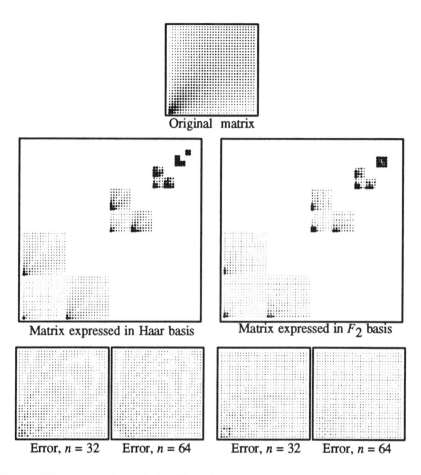

Original matrix

Matrix expressed in Haar basis

Matrix expressed in F_2 basis

Error, $n = 32$ Error, $n = 64$ Error, $n = 32$ Error, $n = 64$

Figure 7.26: *Projecting a flatland kernel (from Gortler et al., 1993). The original matrix shows the kernel function between two perpendicular line segments that meet in a corner discretized into a 32 by 32 grid. Darker entries represent larger kernel values. The kernel values are greatest in the lower left corner, where the two segments meet and $1/r$ goes to infinity. This kernel is projected into both the nonstandard two-dimensional Haar basis and the nonstandard two-dimensional basis with two vanishing moments. In both of these representations many of the 1024 coefficients are small. In both cases, only 32 and 64 of the largest coefficients have been selected to reconstruct an approximate kernel. An error matrix (the difference between actual kernel and approximate kernel) is shown. This demonstrates that a low error can be achieved with very few entries from the projection.*

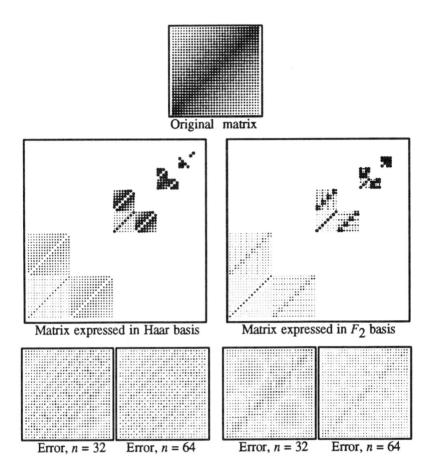

Figure 7.27: *This figure shows the application of the wavelet projection to the flatland configuration of two parallel line segments. The kernel is largest along its diagonal, where points on the two segments lie directly across from each other. Note the greater sparsity provided by the projection into the basis with two vanishing moments.*

three-dimensional space. Thus, the kernel function is four-dimensional, since each basis function is two-dimensional. This does not present any important conceptual problems or changes in the algorithm, but makes illustration in the fashion of Figures 7.26 and 7.27 difficult.

The more important difference is that *the goal is not to compute the full matrix and then decompose it* to find the significant terms, since this entails computing n^2 form factors, where n is the number of elements. Instead, as in the hierarchical algorithms outlined in the previous section, an oracle is relied upon to predict which terms will be significant. The numerical integration of the kernel (form factor computation) is then only performed for the associated pairs of bases that are determined to be significant by the oracle.

The full family of wavelet bases provide options for continuity (e.g., linear, quadratic, and higher order bases) beyond the piecewise constant bases discussed here. They also can exhibit more vanishing moments leading to sparser linear operators. In general, more vanishing moments will require a wider support for the basis functions and higher order continuity leads to higher costs in evaluating the form factor integrals and developing appropriate oracle functions. Further study is required to assess these tradeoffs to develop optimal hierarchical bases for the radiosity application.

Although the section above cannot provide a complete description of the algorithms required to project the integral operator onto the wavelet bases, it is hoped that some understanding of the potential of hierarchical bases has been provided. The reader is directed to the growing body of literature on wavelets and their applications to the solution of integral equations for a detailed study of this new research topic [27, 185].

III. Importance-Based Radiosity

7.7   Importance Meshing

All of the discussion above and in the previous chapters has assumed the goal of generating a *view-independent* solution. Consequently, the error metrics we have described assume all surfaces to be equally important. What if, in contrast, the goal is to create only a single image of the environment from a given viewpoint, or multiple images confined to a small area of an extensive model? This is a common situation in architectural rendering, where models may consist of buildings containing many rooms and floors.

It would be preferable in this case to concentrate the effort on closely approximating the radiosity of surfaces visible in the image. It is still necessary to consider all surfaces, however, since surfaces that are not visible may contribute indirectly to the illumination of visible surfaces.

Making decisions about where and when to subdivide surfaces given the knowledge of a fixed viewpoint for the final image requires an error metric that takes into account the relative importance of a given surface to the image. Developing such a *view-dependent* error metric will lead to more efficient algorithms for this case.

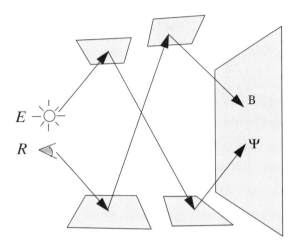

Figure 7.28: *Just as light emission E interreflects about an environment resulting in a radiosity at the surfaces, a* receiver *function R emanating from the eye interreflects among surfaces resulting in the surfaces having varying values of* importance *to the final image.*

7.7.1 The Importance Equation

Smits *et al.* [220] have developed an *importance-driven* approach to radiosity that uses the above ideas. Illumination models such as the radiosity equation capture the transport of photons from the light source to the eye. Ray tracing from the eye typifies a *dual* process in which rays representing photon paths are traced in the reverse direction from that taken by the light. Similarly, just as the radiosity problem can be stated as

$$\mathbf{K}\, B(\mathbf{x}) \;=\; E(\mathbf{x}) \tag{7.8}$$

where $\mathbf{K}$ is a linear operator on the unknown radiosity, B, and E is a *source* term, one can write an *adjoint* equation for the dual process:

$$\mathbf{K}^* \,\Upsilon(\mathbf{x}) \;=\; R(\mathbf{x}) \tag{7.9}$$

In this equation $\mathbf{K}^*$ is again a linear operator, but this time it acts on the unknown *importance*, $\Upsilon(\mathbf{x})$. $R(\mathbf{x})$ is a *receiver* function. The adjoint operator $\mathbf{K}^*$ in this case is simply $\mathbf{K}^T$. In neutron transport theory, a similar adjoint to the transport equation is developed to increase the efficiency of solutions for the flux arriving at a small receiver [68, 152].

Intuitively, one can think of importance as a scalar function over the surfaces, just like radiosity. The value of $\Upsilon(\mathbf{x})$ represents the importance of point $\mathbf{x}$ to

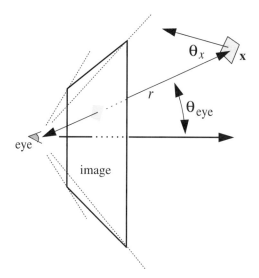

Figure 7.29: *Geometry for initializing receiver function.*

the final image, given a receiver (or eye) position. The receiver function $R(\mathbf{x})$ acts much like the light sources in the radiosity equation. It can be thought of as resulting from a spotlight at the eye location emanating importance in the view direction.

The receiver function can be initialized by assigning each point a value related to the point's visible projected size in the image; thus areas not seen in the image have a zero receiver value. More formally,

$$R(\mathbf{x}) = \left\{ \begin{array}{ll} \frac{\cos\theta_x}{\cos\theta_{\text{eye}}\, r^2} & \text{if } \mathbf{x} \text{ is visible in the image} \\ 0 & \text{otherwise} \end{array} \right\} = \frac{\cos\theta_x}{\cos\theta_{\text{eye}}\, r^2} V(\text{eye}, \mathbf{x})$$

(7.10)

where the terms are shown in Figure 7.29. In the discrete function, the receiver value R_i of each element i is proportional to the area of the image covered by the element. If the eye point moves and multiple images are to be rendered from the solution, the receiver function might be nonzero at any point ever visible in the sequence.

Just as light interreflects about an environment, the importance from the eye interreflects among surfaces (see Figure 7.28). Clearly, a point that is visible in the image will have a large importance, but a point on another surface that has a large potential to reflect light to a visible surface will also have a significant importance value.

7.7.2 Importance-Based Error

If the approximate linear operator and radiosity are given by $\hat{\mathbf{K}}$ and $\hat{\mathbf{B}}$, respectively, and the error $\Delta\mathbf{K}$ in the operator is given by

$$\Delta\mathbf{K} = \hat{\mathbf{K}} - \mathbf{K} \tag{7.11}$$

then a view-dependent error norm is provided by

$$\Upsilon(\mathbf{x})\,\Delta\mathbf{K}\,\hat{B}(\mathbf{x}) \tag{7.12}$$

A detailed derivation can be found in [220]. The importance function $\Upsilon(\mathbf{x})$ is unknown, just like the radiosity function $B(\mathbf{x})$. Thus, the best that can be hoped for is to compute an approximation $\hat{\Upsilon}$ in a manner similar to that used to approximate the radiosity function. A more useful importance-based error norm is thus provided by

$$\hat{\Upsilon}(\mathbf{x})\,\Delta\mathbf{K}\,\hat{B}(\mathbf{x}) \tag{7.13}$$

When evaluated at a point, this norm gives a measure of the error approximation, weighted by the importance of the point to the image and by the magnitude of the radiosity at that point.

This leads to an algorithm (see Figure 7.30) in which one simultaneously solves for the approximate radiosity and importance functions, making adaptive subdivision choices based on the importance-based metric of equation 7.13. Clearly, minimizing the error in either the radiosity function or the importance function alone will reduce the overall error. Importance based algorithms gain their efficiency by taking into account both radiosity and importance, concentrating more effort on the radiosity function in regions of high importance, and more effort on the importance function in brightly lit regions (i.e., high radiosity values).

Solving for importance is very similar to solving for radiosity. If the radiosity associated with element i is

$$B_i = E_i + \rho_i \sum_{j=1}^{n} B_j F_{ij} \tag{7.14}$$

then the importance of element i is given by

$$\Upsilon_i = R_i + \sum_{j=1}^{n} \rho_j \Upsilon_j F_{ji} \tag{7.15}$$

Note the switch in the indices of ρ and F.

```
ImportanceDrivenRad( float Fₑ )
{
    float eps;
    for ( all surfaces p )
    {
        p→Bₛ = p→E;
        p→Υₛ = p→R;    /* visible area in image */
        for (all mutually visible pairs of surfaces (q,q))
            { Link(p, q); Link(q, p); }
    }
    /* beginning with large tolerance, reduce it after each iteration */
    for (ε initially large diminishing to a small error threshold )
    {
        SolveDualSystem();
        for (each link L)
            RefineLink(L, ε); /* see Figure 7.15 */
    }
}
```

Figure 7.30: `ImportanceDrivenRad` *pseudocode.*

Color plates 23 and 24 show independent radiosity and importance solutions, respectively. The more interesting image is color plate 25, which shows the combined radiosity and importance solution. The yellow areas with a high combined radiosity and importance are the most critical to the final accuracy of the image.

7.8 Hierarchical Radiosity and Importance

7.8.1 Pseudocode

The importance-based radiosity approach solves simultaneously for two unknown functions, the radiosity function $B(\mathbf{x})$ and the importance $\Upsilon(\mathbf{x})$ (see Figure 7.31). The discrete forms of the two equations after projection onto constant basis functions are $\mathbf{B} = \mathbf{K}\mathbf{E}$ and $\Upsilon = \mathbf{K}^T\mathbf{R}$. The error norm to be minimized is then based on

$$\Upsilon^T \Delta \mathbf{K}\mathbf{B} \tag{7.16}$$

```
SolveDualSystem()
{
    Until Converged
    {
        for (all surfaces p) GatherRadShootImp( p );
        for (all surfaces p) PushPullRad( p, 0.0 );
        for (all surfaces p) PushPullImp( p, 0.0 );
    }
}
```

Figure 7.31: `SolveDualSystem` *pseudocode.*

```
GatherRadShootImp( Quadnode *p )
{
    p→Bg = 0;
    for (each gathering link L of p)
    {
        /* gather energy across link */
        p→Bg += p→ρ * L→F * L→q→Bs ;
        /* shoot importance across link */
        p→Υg += p→ρ * L→F * L→q→Υs ;
    }
    for (each child q of p) GatherRadShootImp( q );
}
```

Figure 7.32: `GatherRadShootImp` *pseudocode.*

where $\Delta\mathbf{K}$ is the matrix of errors in the operator $\mathbf{K}$. Pseudocode for the hierarchical importance-based algorithm is provided in Figures 7.31, 7.32, and 7.33. The input to the algorithm consists, as before, of the geometry and reflectance properties of the surfaces, the light source emissions, and additionally, the *initial importance R* of each surface. This is typically the visible area of the surface in the desired image (or images). The algorithm then recursively solves the dual system, subdividing elements and creating new links until all interactions are within given tolerances for the product of radiosity and importance.

The changes from the basic hierarchical code (described in section 7.4.3)

```
PushPullImp( Quadnode *p, float Υ_down )
{
1      float Υ_up, Υ_tmp;
2      if ( p→ne == NULL)      /* p is a leaf */
3          Υ_up = p→R + p→Υ_g + Υ_down;
4      else
5      {
6          Υ_up = 0;
7          for (each child node r of p)
8          {
9              Υ_tmp = (p→Υ + Υ_down) * (r→area)/(p→area)
10             Υ_up += PushPullImp(r, Υ_tmp);
11         }
12     }
13     p→Υ_s = Υ_up;
14     return Υ_up;
}
```

Figure 7.33: `PushPullImp` *pseudocode.*

are minimal and much of the pseudocode is reused. The following modifications must be made:

- Fields to hold the receiver value R, and the importance Υ must be added to the **Quadnode** structure.

- Importance is *shot* at the same time that energy is *gathered* over the links (see Figure 7.32).

- *Pushing* and *pulling* importance is similar to the same operations for radiosity except that the area averaging is reversed (see Figure 7.33). This is due to the fact that radiosity is energy *per unit area*. Thus, moving up the quadtree is an averaging operation. Importance, in contrast, is proportional to area. Thus, moving one level up the tree requires summing importance (line 10 in **PushPullImp**). Transferring radiosity and importance down one level is just the reverse; radiosity is transferred directly while importance must be parceled out according to the area of the children (line 9) (compare **PushPullImp** in Figure 7.33 to **PushPullRad** in Figure 7.11).

- The `oracle` function must be modified to include multiplying by the current element importance Υ as well as the form factor on the link and the radiosity and area of the element (line 7 in Figure 7.16).

7.8.2   Example Results

Color plates 26–31 show a series of images of the radiosity–importance solution (color plates 26, 28, 30) and the importance-only solution (color plates 27, 29, 31) for a mazelike environment [220]. As the eye point is backed away from the original point from which importance was propagated, it is apparent that the algorithm has concentrated effort on regions that are either visible in the original image or that contribute significantly to the light eventually arriving at the eye. The timings given by Smits *et al.* indicate a performance increase of two to three orders of magnitude for this environment.

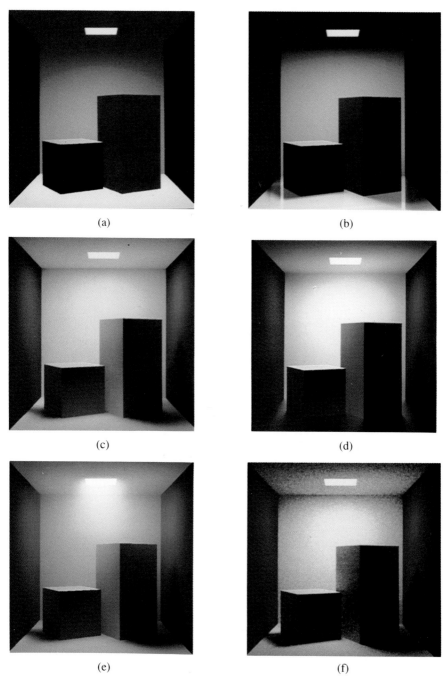

Plate 1. "Six Renderings of Red–Blue Box" (see Chapter 1). (a) Local, (b) Ray Trace, (c) Radiosity, (d) Radiosity + Glossy, (e) Radiosity + Fog, (f) Monte Carlo. *Courtesy of Michael Cohen, Holly Rushmeier, and Ben Trumbore, Program of Computer Graphics, Cornell University.*

Plate 2. A sculpture by John Ferren entitled "Construction in Wood, A Daylight Experiment." Front faces of the panels are white. The color is caused by daylight reflected from rear-facing colored surfaces. *Courtesy of Cindy Goral, Program of Computer Graphics, Cornell University.*

Plate 3. A ray traced image of the above sculpture. All the panels appear white since a standard ray tracer cannot simulate the inter-reflection of light between diffuse surfaces. *Courtesy of Cindy Goral, Program of Computer Graphics, Cornell University.*

Plate 4. A radiosity image of the above sculpture. Note the color bleeding from the backs of the boards to the fronts. *Courtesy of Cindy Goral, Program of Computer Graphics, Cornell University.*

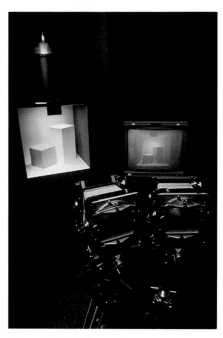

Plate 5. Experimental setup to test accuracy of radiosity method and choice of color spaces. *Courtesy of Gary Meyer, Program of Computer Graphics, Cornell University.*

Plate 7. Upside down view as seen by observer. *Courtesy of Gary Meyer, Program of Computer Graphics, Cornell University.*

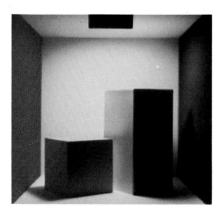

Plate 8. Photograph of real scene taken with portrait camera. (Color adjusted for film and monitor gamuts in Plates 8 and 9.) *Courtesy of Gary Meyer, Program of Computer Graphics, Cornell University.*

Plate 9. Photograph of CRT screen containing radiosity image. *Courtesy of Gary Meyer, Program of Computer Graphics, Cornell University.*

Plate 10. "Magritte Studio." Radiosity with texture mapping of both reflecting surfaces and light sources. *Courtesy of Michael Cohen, Program of Computer Graphics, Cornell University.*

Plate 11. "Computer Room." Shading using direct illumination only. *Courtesy of Tomoyuki Nishita, Fukuyama University.*

Plate 12. "Auditorium." An element mesh in which "T" vertices have been eliminated by triangulation to create conforming elements. *Courtesy of Daniel Baum, Silicon Graphics Corporation.*

Plate 13. "Magritte Studio, Lights Off." Image created using the same form factors as Plate 10. Turning off light requires only resolving the matrix equation with new emission values. *Courtesy of Michael Cohen, Program of Computer Graphics, Cornell University.*

Plate 14. "Computer Room." The same environment as in Plate 11, with radiosity used to compute both direct and indirect illumination. Note the additional illumination on the ceiling. *Courtesy of Tomoyuki Nishita, Fukuyama University.*

Plate 15. The same image as in Plate 12 without displaying the mesh. *Courtesy of Daniel Baum, Silicon Graphics Corporation.*

Plate 16. "Steel Mill." A complex environment shaded using progressive refinement radiosity. *Courtesy of John Wallace and Stuart Feldman, Program of Computer Graphics, Cornell University.*

Plate 17. "Constructivist Museum." The complex interreflection from the ceiling baffles was simulated with the progressive refinement approach. *Courtesy of Shenchang Chen, Stuart Feldman, and Julie O'Brien Dorsey, Program of Computer Graphics, Cornell University.*

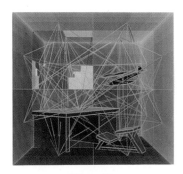

Plate 18.

Plate 19.

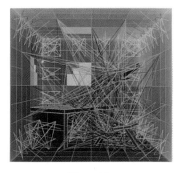

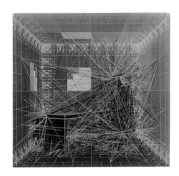

Plate 20.

Plate 21.

A sequence showing the links formed at each level of a hierarchy generated by Hanrahan, Salzman, and Aupperle's algorithm. *Courtesy of Pat Hanrahan, Princeton University.*

Plate 22. Final image with texture mapping. *Courtesy of Pat Hanrahan, Princeton University.*

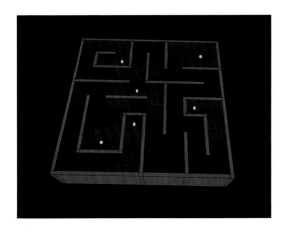

Plate 23. Radiosity solution. *Courtesy of Brian Smits, James Arvo, and David Salesin, Program of Computer Graphics, Cornell University.*

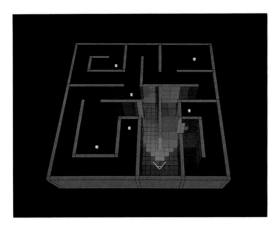

Plate 24. Importance solution. *Courtesy of Brian Smits, James Arvo, and David Salesin, Program of Computer Graphics, Cornell University.*

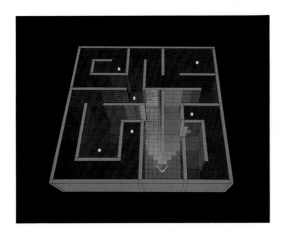

Plate 25. Combined radiosity and importance solutions. *Courtesy of Brian Smits, James Arvo, and David Salesin, Program of Computer Graphics, Cornell University.*

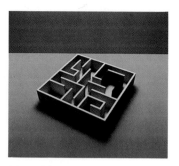

Plate 26. Radiosity/Importance solution with mesh. *Courtesy of Brian Smits, James Arvo, and David Salesin, Program of Computer Graphics, Cornell University.*

Plate 27. Radiosity/Importance solution after reconstruction. *Courtesy of Brian Smits, James Arvo, and David Salesin, Program of Computer Graphics, Cornell University.*

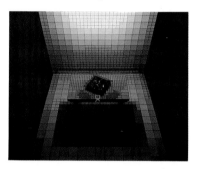

Plate 28. Radiosity solution from further back. *Courtesy of Brian Smits, James Arvo, and David Salesin, Program of Computer Graphics, Cornell University.*

Plate 29. Importance solution. *Courtesy of Brian Smits, James Arvo, and David Salesin, Program of Computer Graphics, Cornell University.*

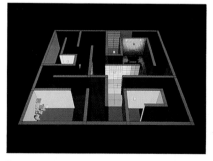

Plate 30. Radiosity from even further back. *Courtesy of Brian Smits, James Arvo, and David Salesin, Program of Computer Graphics, Cornell University.*

Plate 31. Importance from even further back. *Courtesy of Brian Smits, James Arvo, and David Salesin, Program of Computer Graphics, Cornell University.*

Plate 32. Radiosity solution using quadtree based adaptive subdivision. Failure to resolve discontinuities results in the inaccurate representation of shadow boundaries. *Courtesy of Filippo Tampieri and Dani Lischinski, Program of Computer Graphics, Cornell University.*

Plate 33. Radiosity solution of same environment as above, but with the use of discontinuity meshing. *Courtesy of Filippo Tampieri and Dani Lischinski, Program of Computer Graphics, Cornell University.*

Plate 34. Use of discontinuity meshing to create accurate shadow boundaries. *Courtesy of Filippo Tampieri and Dani Lischinski, Program of Computer Graphics, Cornell University.*

Plate 35. Multipass solution after the initial progressive radiosity solution. Total time: approx. 12 minutes. *Courtesy of Shenchang Chen, Apple Computer Corporation.*

Plate 36. Multipass solution: Direct illumination computed with Monte Carlo ray tracing, caustics computed with light ray tracing, combined with indirect component of initial progressive radiosity solution. Total time: approx. 4.5 hours. *Courtesy of Shenchang Chen, Apple Computer Corporation.*

Plate 37. Components of Plate 36. Direct Monte Carlo + Indirect Progressive Refinement Radiosity + Light Ray Tracing. *Courtesy of Shenchang Chen, Apple Computer Corporation.*

Plate 38. Multipass solution after full Monte Carlo solution for both direct and indirect illumination. Total time: approx. 21 hours. *Courtesy of Shenchang Chen, Apple Computer Corporation.*

Plate 39. Components of Plate 38. Direct + Indirect Monte Carlo + Light Ray Tracing. *Courtesy of Shenchang Chen, Apple Computer Corporation.*

Plate 40. A ship's boiler room, with Phong highlights added to a progressive radiosity solution during rendering. *Courtesy of John Wallace, John Lin, and Eric Haines, Hewlett-Packard Corporation.*

Plate 41. Radiosity solution for indirect illumination, with the direct illumination computed at each pixel during rendering. Bump mapping is performed during the per-pixel illumination computation. *Courtesy of Peter Shirley.*

Plate 42. Bidirectional ray tracing. The caustic on the table is caused by light focused through the glass and was computed using light ray tracing. *Courtesy of Peter Shirley.*

Plate 43. Radiosity solution without inclusion of specular to diffuse reflection of light off mirror. *Courtesy of François Sillion, Ecôle Normale Supériuere.*

Plate 44. Radiosity solution with extended form factors to capture light reflected from mirror. *Courtesy of François Sillion, Ecôle Normale Supériuere.*

Plate 45. "Dutch Interior, after Vermeer." A two-pass solution: radiosity plus the reflection frustum algorithm during rendering to compute glossy reflection from floor to eye. *Courtesy of John Wallace, Program of Computer Graphics, Cornell University.*

Plate 46. Computation of glossy and mirror specular reflection using spherical harmonics to approximate directional radiance distribution. *Courtesy of François Sillion, Program of Computer Graphics, Cornell University.*

Plate 47. Main Council chamber in the new Jerusalem City Hall. Designed by A. J. Diamond, Donald Schmitt and Co. Rendered using radiosity software being developed at Lightscape Graphics. *Courtesy of Stuart Feldman, Lightscape Graphics Software.*

Plate 48. Use of zonal method to include a participating medium (smoke) within a radiosity solution. *Courtesy of Holly Rushmeier, Program of Computer Graphics, Cornell University.*

Plate 49. A unified solution for Lambertian diffuse, glossy, and mirror specular reflection using spherical harmonics to approximate radiance distribution. *Courtesy of François Sillion, Program of Computer Graphics, Cornell University.*

Plate 50. The main council chamber in Plate 47. *Courtesy of Stuart Feldman, Lightscape Graphics Software.*

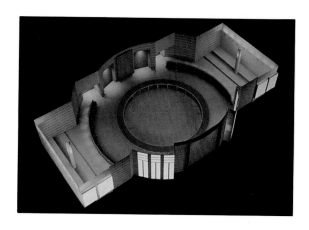

Plate 51. "Gemäldegalerie BERLIN." Image produced using the COPHOS lighting design software under development at Zumtobel Licht GmbH. *Courtesy of Zumtobel Licht GmbH, Austria.*

Plate 52. "Home of the Brain," from a project on Virtual Reality and Telecommunications. *Courtesy of Monika Fleischmann and Wolfgang Strauss, ART+COM, Berlin.*

Plate 53. Scene from the opera "Turandot," rendered with software for stage lighting design. *Courtesy of Julie O'Brien Dorsey; Program of Computer Graphics, Cornell University.*

Plate 54. Scene of Venice from "Tales of Hoffman." *Courtesy of Julie O'Brien Dorsey, Program of Computer Graphics, Cornell University.*

Chapter 8

Meshing

The general strategies for automatic meshing described in the previous chapters determine where and when to subdivide, but not how to subdivide. The actual mechanics of subdividing geometry will be addressed in this chapter.

Basic subdivision techniques are addressed first. These are useful both for producing an initial uniform mesh as well as for further refining a mesh by adaptive subdivision. A priori algorithms for determining mesh boundaries that correspond to discontinuities in the radiosity function will also be discussed.

Meshing algorithms are best constructed on an underlying topological data structure that efficiently represents the adjacencies between nodes, edges and elements. The basic characteristics of such data structures and how they can be applied to meshing will be described.

Finally, several alternatives to meshing have been developed in order to avoid some of the complexities of surface subdivision. These approaches will be examined both for their own sake as well as for the somewhat different light they shed on the overall problem of approximating the radiosity function.

8.1 Basic Subdivision Techniques

A wide variety of subdivision techniques has been developed for finite and boundary element analysis. Surveys have organized these techniques according to a variety of taxonomies [92, 146, 211]. For our purposes, subdivision techniques are broadly classified according to whether or not the mesh topology is predetermined.

Algorithms that use a predetermined topology subdivide by mapping a mesh *template* to the geometry. The template is a predefined subdivision into standard elements, such as a rectangular grid. The essential step of the meshing process consists of determining a mapping between the geometry and the template. The alternative, in which the topology is not predetermined, is to *decompose* the geometry into elements by locating and connecting nodes according to some procedure. As a trivial example, a polygon might be subdivided by connecting its vertices to form triangles.

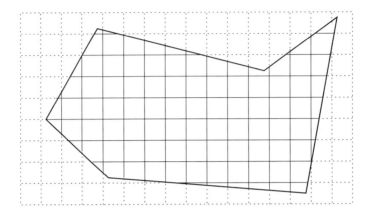

Figure 8.1: *Subdivision using a mesh template.*

Both basic subdivision approaches have been used for radiosity and are described further in the following sections.

8.2   Mesh Template Methods

8.2.1   Grid Superposition

The most direct way of mapping a mesh template to the geometry is simply to superimpose the template on the geometry. The geometry is then split along the grid lines to create the mesh (see Figure 8.1). The chief advantage of this approach is that it generates perfectly regular, well-shaped elements on the interior of the geometry.

Unfortunately, the "cookie-cutter" approach frequently generates unacceptable elements where the template intersects the boundary. Elements are often poorly shaped, with low aspect ratios, concavities or extra vertices. Element shape can be improved by smoothing the mesh (as in section 8.4), but smoothing cannot eliminate extra vertices.

Grid superposition schemes improve on the cookie-cutter approach by providing special handling for elements near the boundary. For example, elements of the template that contain pieces of the boundary may be partially collapsed to eliminate extra vertices.

Baum *et al.* [18] describe an alternative in which the mesh template is used to create only those elements that lie fully inside the boundary. The region between the boundary and the interior elements is then triangulated.[1]

---

[1]This subdivision technique was first described by Rockwood as a means of tesselating

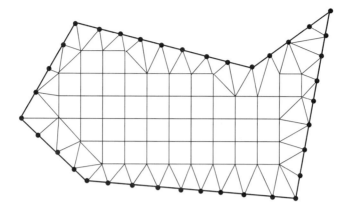

Figure 8.2: *Subdivision using a template for interior elements and triangulation to connect to boundary.*

In the first step of Baum's approach the template is superimposed on the geometry. The grid is traversed and elements are created only where all four corners of the grid square are well inside the boundary. Grid corners that are inside but very close to the boundary are rejected, since they may cause poorly shaped elements during the triangulation step. Next, the boundary is subdivided at regular intervals corresponding to the desired mesh density. Finally, the region between the subdivided boundary and the internal elements is triangulated (see Figure 8.2).

Since the triangulation will link element edges to all boundary vertices, small boundary features are incorporated into standard three-sided elements. However, if the boundary contains features or edges that are much smaller than the target element size, triangulation will often result in poorly shaped elements and a poorly graded mesh (see Figure 8.3).

In general, the graceful incorporation of small boundary features requires a nonuniform mesh. Producing a well-graded, nonuniform mesh requires greater control over element size than is provided by a uniform template. However, template methods can be generalized to produce nonuniform meshes by using an adaptive, variable-size template [211].

8.2.2 Template Mapping

The use of a template is simplified if the template can be mapped to fit the geometry exactly. For example, a rectangular template can be mapped exactly

---

trimmed spline surfaces for display [194].

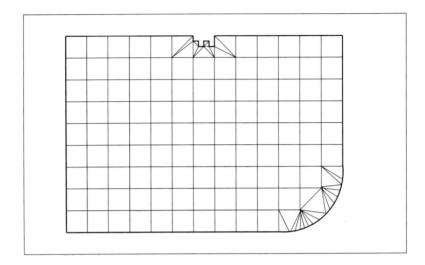

Figure 8.3: *Small features of the geometry may cause poorly shaped elements.*

to fill a convex quadrilateral. The mapping in this case is the same as for the bilinear isoparametric element described in Chapter 5. Once the mapping is obtained, a set of elements corresponding to the template can be turned into an actual mesh simply by transforming the parametric coordinates for each node to geometric coordinates. More general mappings can be used to handle regions with curved boundaries or with more than four sides [235], although these have not been applied to radiosity to date.

Although mapping increases the range of geometries that can be meshed with template subdivision, there are limitations. The mapping may introduce severe distortions, resulting in a nonuniform mesh of poorly shaped elements. In addition, although a conformal mapping does exist between any two simply connected regions with an equal number of vertices, directly mapping geometries with more than four sides can be complicated.

8.2.3 Multiblocking

An alternative when the geometry is too complicated or is concave is to subdivide the geometry into simpler regions or *blocks* first. Templates can then be mapped directly to each of the regions.

Cohen *et al.* [61] use multiblocking with mapped templates in an early radiosity implementation. Surfaces are subdivided into convex quadrilaterals and triangles by connecting vertices of the geometry. These regions are then subdivided into quadrilateral or triangular elements by splitting the edges in half

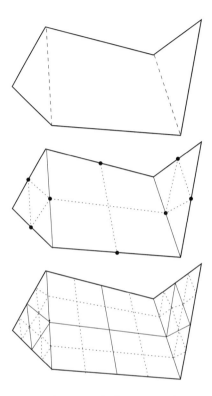

Figure 8.4: *Subdivision with mapped elements. The geometry is first split into simple shapes. In Cohen's algorithm, the boundaries are then bisected and new vertices joined to form elements. Subdivision proceeds recursively as needed.*

and joining them across the interior to create four elements. Finer mesh densities are obtained by continuing the subdivision recursively until the desired element size is reached (see Figure 8.4). Splitting edges at the midpoint guarantees that new elements created on either side of the edge will be conforming.

When the initial blocks are obtained by joining the vertices of the original geometry, the blocks may sometimes have extreme shapes that produce highly distorted mappings. These can be avoided by adding new vertices on the boundary or the interior of the geometry. As noted in [146], however, once such an algorithm is available for the initial subdivision, there is little reason not to use it to produce the entire mesh.

8.2.4   Adaptive Subdivision with Templates

Once the mapping has been established, a mesh produced using a template can be refined during adaptive subdivision by applying the template again to elements requiring further subdivision. In Cohen's quadtree subdivision algorithm, for example, quadtree subdivision is invoked again following the initial solution to refine elements where needed.

As a means of a posteriori mesh refinement, mapped templates (of which the quadtree scheme is the most common example for radiosity) have the disadvantage that the placement of element boundaries is inflexible. New element edges cannot be oriented to distribute the error as evenly as possible. As a result, adaptive subdivision using template mapping may require more elements than necessary to achieve a certain accuracy.

Template mapping approaches, like the quadtree algorithm, also tend to generate nonconforming elements in regions of changing mesh density. For example, when neighboring elements are subdivided to different levels, quadtree subdivision creates T-vertices. If the node at the T-vertex is not shared by the larger neighboring element, a discontinuity in the approximation will be introduced along that edge, since the interpolated value at that point will generally be different from the value computed at the node for the same point (see Figure 8.5). On the other hand, if the node at the T-vertex is shared with the larger element, the large element is no longer well shaped, since it contains 5 nodes, one of which is at the apex of edges forming a 180-degree angle.

Quadtree algorithms have employed several techniques for handling T-vertices. Cohen *et al.* create special nodes at T-vertices, sometimes called *slave* nodes in the finite element literature. The function is not actually evaluated at slave nodes. Instead, the value at a slave node is interpolated (linearly, in this case) from the nodes of the largest element sharing that edge (nodes A and B in Figure 8.6). This allows interpolation on the larger element to ignore the slave nodes without introducing discontinuities.

Baum, *et al.* [18] describe an alternative way of handling T-vertices. Nodes at T-vertices are shared by all elements surrounding the vertex and the function is evaluated at the node. To maintain correct element shape, the larger element is then triangulated to form smaller properly shaped elements (see Figure 8.7). The resulting modified hierarchy is called a *tri–quadtree*.

The extra triangulation in the tri–quadtree is not a permanent part of the mesh. The triangulation of a problem element is used only when needed for linear interpolation. If further adaptive subdivision is required later in the solution, it will be performed on the original element, not the triangulation.

Adaptive subdivision using a quadtree often produces poorly graded meshes. Figure 8.8 shows an example in which a large element is adjacent to a highly

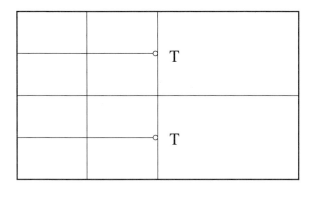

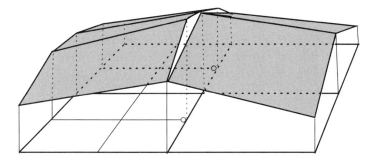

Figure 8.5: *Discontinuity introduced by incorrectly handled T-vertices.*

subdivided region. Triangulation of the large element in this case will produce triangles with a poor aspect ratio. The use of slave nodes may produce a visible artifact along the long edge, due to its close proximity to nodes at which the function is actually evaluated.

Better mesh grading can be achieved by requiring a *balanced* or *restricted* quadtree [18, 211]. Neighboring elements in a restricted quadtree are allowed to differ by only one level of subdivision. A balanced tree can be achieved by checking the neighbors of an element when it is subdivided, and by subdividing those neighbors recursively.[2]

---

[2]Algorithms for performing this and other operations on quadtrees can be found in Samet [204].

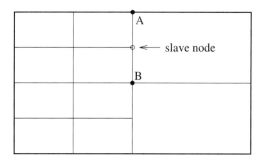

Figure 8.6: *T-vertices treated as slave nodes.*

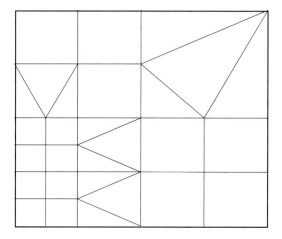

Figure 8.7: *Tri-quadtree used to eliminate t-vertices.*

8.3 Decomposition Methods

Mapped template methods are efficient and produce well shaped elements for simple geometries. However, their limited flexibility is a drawback when subdividing more complicated geometries and during a posteriori mesh refinement.

Subdivision methods that decompose the geometry into elements piece by piece provide greater flexibility. There are two basic approaches to this decomposition: the nodes and elements can be produced at the same time using a single procedure or the nodes can be produced first and then connected to form edges in an independent step.

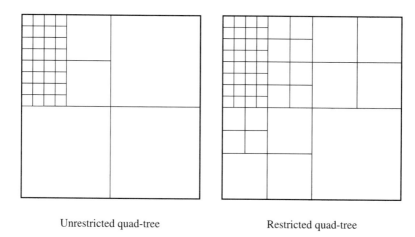

Unrestricted quad-tree   Restricted quad-tree

Figure 8.8: *Use of restricted quadtree to improve mesh grading.*

8.3.1 Nodes–Elements–Together Decomposition

In this approach, the geometry is subdivided by creating nodes and joining them with edges to generate new elements one by one. Subdivision can be performed recursively, first subdividing the entire geometry into initial elements, then splitting those elements again until the desired element size is reached. During subdivision, new nodes can be positioned according to criterion selected to produce a mesh with certain density or smoothness properties. Chew [53] and Watson [256] describe incremental Delaunay triangulation algorithms of this type. Alternatively, subdivision may proceed from the boundary inward, splitting off triangles one by one until the entire geometry is meshed.

8.3.2 Decomposition by Recursive Splitting

Campbell and Fussell [43] subdivide surfaces by recursive splitting using a two-dimensional binary space partition (BSP) tree. The BSP-tree allows arbitrary orientation of element edges (see Figure 8.9). Elements are created by splitting larger regions along an arbitrary edge. The ability to incorporate arbitrarily oriented edges allows Campbell and Fussel to include previously determined discontinuity boundaries into the mesh.

Campbell and Fussell also use the flexibility of BSP subdivision advantageously during adaptive subdivision. The edge used to split an element is oriented to minimize the variation in radiosity over the new elements. Using optimization techniques, Campbell and Fussell locate the global maximum and minimum for the element and subdivide halfway between the two extreme points

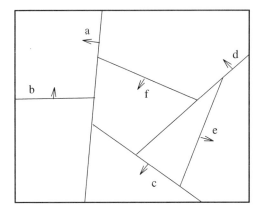
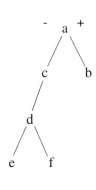

Figure 8.9: *Hierarchical surface subdivision using a BSP tree (after Campbell, 1990).*

along an edge perpendicular to the line joining the extrema.

Although the BSP-tree is more flexible than the quadtree, it is also more difficult to maintain conforming elements with the BSP-tree. T-vertices occur frequently, since neighboring elements are split along edges that are not likely to meet at a common node. Campbell and Fussell treat T-vertices as slave nodes. They also recommend a final clean-up pass following adaptive subdivision, during which the tree is balanced by subdividing elements with highly subdivided neighbors and those with a poor aspect ratio.

Lischinski and Tampieri [154], who also use a BSP-tree to represent surface subdivision, avoid the clean-up pass by simultaneously maintaining a data structure representing the mesh topology. Nodes of the BSP-tree point to edges in a winged-edge data structure. T-vertices can then be eliminated using a simple triangulation pass.

8.3.3 Decomposition by Advancing Front

In contrast to recursive splitting, decomposition may also proceed from the boundary inward, splitting off finished elements one at a time. This is sometimes called the *advancing front* method, because the forward boundary of the meshed region is progressively advanced into the unmeshed region until the entire geometry is subdivided [92]. Algorithms of this type are distinguished by the technique with which the front is advanced. For example, the front may be searched to locate the smallest angle, which is then incorporated into a new triangular element and split off from the unmeshed region (see Figure 8.10). The advancing front method is also known as *paving* when it is used to subdivide

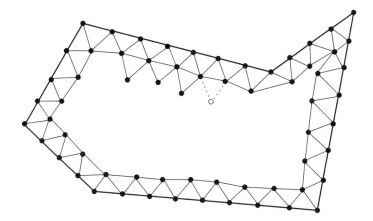

Figure 8.10: *A intermediate stage of an advancing front algorithm.*

into quadrilateral elements.

The advancing front method allows control over element quality, since quality criteria can be explicitly incorporated into the rules according to which elements are split off from the front. However, this approach can run into difficulties for complicated geometries. For example, backtracking may be required to undo decisions, resulting in fronts for which no good candidates are available for splitting. The advancing front technique has not yet been applied to radiosity meshing.

8.3.4 Nodes-First Decomposition

In a *nodes-first* method, decomposition is accomplished by first positioning the nodes and then connecting them to form edges. Because nodes are placed and connected in independent steps, the procedures for each task can be chosen independently from a greater range of possibilities. This leads to greater overall flexibility. Nodes can be placed anywhere, with nonuniform density if desired, either to handle small features of the geometry, or to address some anticipated behavior of the function. All the nodes may be laid out before any edges are created or the subdivision may proceed recursively by creating some nodes and linking them, then creating more nodes within the resulting elements, and so on. Figure 8.11 shows an example in which nodes are generated by superimposing a grid over the geometry and placing a node more or less randomly in each grid cell.

The nodes are usually connected by triangulation. Delaunay triangulation[3]

---

[3]A Delaunay triangulation connects a given set of points so that the circle circum-

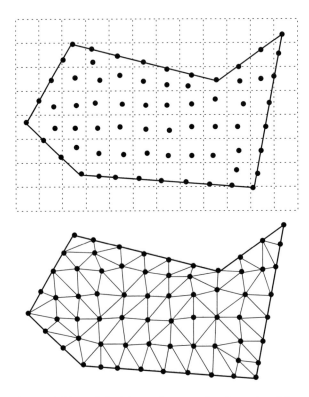

Figure 8.11: *Subdivision using a* nodes-first *algorithm.*

is commonly used since it guarantees triangles that are as well shaped as possible (according to a certain criterion) for a given set of nodes. Delaunay triangulations are often also constructed incrementally, positioning new nodes in relationship to existing elements in order to achieve elements with desired shape or density. Algorithms for connecting nodes into quadrilaterals are less common.

For radiosity applications, Heckbert [121] has incorporated a triangulation approach into an a priori discontinuity meshing scheme. Critical element bound-

---

scribing any triangle contains only the points belonging to that triangle (except in the case where four or more points are cocircular). A Delaunay triangulation also minimizes the smallest angle of its triangles over all possible triangulations of the set of points and thus avoids thin slivers as far as possible. A further, not inconsequential, advantage of Delaunay triangulations is that they are a generally useful construct for computational geometry and algorithms for producing them have thus received great attention. The standard computational geometry text by Preparata and Shamos [184] provides a detailed discussion. The article by Schumaker [207] provides a short overview and a discussion of practical issues.

aries corresponding to discontinuities in the radiosity function are placed first. The remainder of the mesh is determined by placing and connecting nodes using a *constrained* Delaunay triangulation, which preserves existing edges [53] (Heckbert uses an algorithm based on [33]). The flexibility of decomposition by triangulation is particularly useful when dealing with the complex region boundaries often created by discontinuity meshing. Lischinski *et al.* [154] have also used triangulation to incorporate discontinuity edges.

Sturzlinger [227] employs a variation on the nodes-first approach designed specifically for a radiosity implementation in which constant elements are used during the solution and linear interpolation is used during rendering. The initial mesh is created by first positioning nodes according to a uniform grid. Constant elements consisting of the Voronoi polygonalization of the nodes are used during the solution. Prior to rendering, the same nodes are triangulated to provide elements suitable for linear interpolation. The Voronoi diagram is the straight-line dual of the Delaunay triangulation, which makes conversion between the Voronoi mesh and the triangular mesh easy and convenient. Sturzlinger also uses incremental refinement of the Voronoi polygonalization to implement adaptive subdivision.

8.4 Mesh Smoothing

The quality of the subdivision produced by both template and decomposition methods can often be improved by *smoothing* the mesh. Mesh smoothing consists of several passes of relaxation during which nodes are repositioned to improve element shape and grading. In each relaxation pass each node is typically relocated to the centroid, P, of the n adjacent nodes located at P_i using a formula like the following:

$$P = \frac{1}{n} \sum_{i=1}^{n} P_i \qquad (8.1)$$

Not all nodes are equally free to move. Nodes along fixed boundaries can move only along the boundary. Fixed boundaries include the original edges of the geometry and mesh boundaries that may have been added a priori, such as discontinuity boundaries. Nodes at the intersection of fixed boundaries are not free to move at all.

Mesh smoothing is a useful tool because it relieves the subdivision algorithms of some responsibility for element shape. The subdivision algorithm is then free to concentrate on creating a correct topology. For radiosity, mesh smoothing has been employed by Heckbert [121] as a final step following triangulation.

Mesh relaxation can also be used for a posteriori mesh refinement (the r-refinement method described in Chapter 6) by incorporating local element error into the relocation method. For example, the following relocation formula moves the node P according to the area weighted errors of the n elements adjacent to the node:

$$P = \frac{\sum_{i=1}^{n} x_i \, e_i \, A_i}{\sum_{i=1}^{n} A_i} \tag{8.2}$$

where n is the number of elements adjacent to P, x_i is the centroid of adjacent element i, e_i is the approximation error for element i, and A_i is the area of element i. This formula will tend to move the node in a direction that equalizes the error among the elements adjacent to the node.

8.5   Discontinuity Meshing

The radiosity function is piecewise smooth (C^∞) within regions bounded by discontinuities of various orders. The failure to resolve these discontinuities correctly can result in highly visible artifacts, as demonstrated in Chapter 6.

A posteriori refinement is not very effective at reducing error in the neighborhood of discontinuities. Since the basis functions are continuous, discontinuities can only be introduced into the approximation along element boundaries. Reducing error in the neighborhood of a discontinuity requires either a relatively high mesh density, which is expensive, or exact alignment of element edges with the discontinuity, which is difficult to achieve using an a posteriori algorithm.

However, it is possible to determine the location of discontinuity boundaries a priori. Discontinuities in the radiosity function correspond to transitions in occlusion between source and receiving surfaces. These are purely geometric in nature and can be determined before radiosities are computed.

8.5.1   Discontinuities in Value

A discontinuity in the value of the radiosity function occurs when one surface touches another (see Figure 8.12).[4] The discontinuity is caused by the abrupt transition from complete visibility to complete occlusion that is encountered in crossing the line of contact between the surfaces. The locations of these value discontinuities can be identified by determining the geometric intersections of all surfaces, as described by Baum, *et al.* [18]. Although conceptually straightforward, the intersection computation requires careful handling to avoid numerical difficulties. *Isect*, the program used by Baum to resolve surface intersections,

---

[4]Value discontinuities also occur at the boundaries of shadows cast by point light sources. Point lights are discussed in the context of the radiosity method in Chapter 10.

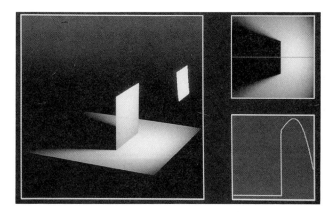

Figure 8.12: *A discontinuity in value. The plot to the lower right shows the radiosity of the surface as a function of position along the horizontal line overlayed on the upper right image.*

was designed to compute the intersection of solid model boundary representations robustly [209].

Once boundaries have been identified, they can be inserted into the representation of the polygon as specially flagged edges. The insertion of new edges is easier if polygons are represented by a robust topological data structure, like the winged-edge data structure (topological data structures are discussed in section 8.6). When the polygon is meshed, the discontinuity edges become element boundaries. Correct reconstruction of the discontinuity requires that adjacent elements do not share nodes along such boundaries.

In a point collocation radiosity method, in which form factors are evaluated at the nodes, occlusion testing must be handled carefully along value discontinuities. As shown in Figure 8.13, the geometric location of a node on such a boundary is not sufficient in itself to determine its occlusion with respect to the intersecting surface. Such nodes actually represent the behavior of the radiosity function in the limit moving towards the boundary from the left or the right. Any purely numerical shadow algorithm, such as the Z-buffer or ray tracing, will return the same answer for nodes with the same location (in most cases it will ignore occlusion by the intersecting surface).

One solution is to move the node temporarily away from the boundary by a small amount in the appropriate direction. It is also possible to determine the occlusion with respect to the intersecting surface topologically. If the source and the element to which the node belongs are on opposite sides of the plane of the intersecting surface, the node is in shadow. If they are on the same side, the

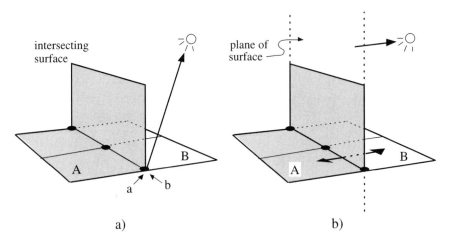

Figure 8.13: *Occlusion testing at a discontinuity in value. a) A numerical shadow test will return the same value for nodes* a *and* b, *since they have the same geometric location. b) Occlusion with respect to the* intersecting surface *is determined by whether the corresponding element lies on the same side or the opposite side of the plane from the light source.*

node is in the light (or, at least, not shadowed by the intersecting surface). When the light straddles the plane of the occluder, the test remains straightforward for point sampling form factor algorithms (e.g., ray traced form factors), since it is performed for each point sample. For other algorithms, the light in the straddling case may have to be split temporarily across the plane.

The image in Figure 8.14 shows artifacts typically produced when value discontinuities are ignored. Note also the extra elements generated by adaptive subdivision in an unsuccessful attempt to resolve the discontinuity. Compare this image with Figure 8.15, in which discontinuity boundaries are incorporated into the mesh. The shadow leak on the wall behind the table top is eliminated and no adaptive subdivision is required along the boundary.

8.5.2   First and Second Derivative Discontinuities

Discontinuities in the first and second derivatives of the radiosity function result from qualitative transitions in occlusion between surfaces in a polygonal environment.[5] The image in Figure 8.16 shows the geometry of occlusion for a simple scene. The resulting first and second derivative discontinuities are evident in the

---

[5]Additional discontinuities of arbitrary degree will occur due to interreflection, as Heckbert demonstrates [120], but these are of much lesser visual consequence.

Figure 8.14: *Artifacts due to ignoring a discontinuity in value.*

Figure 8.15: *Discontinuity in value correctly handled.*

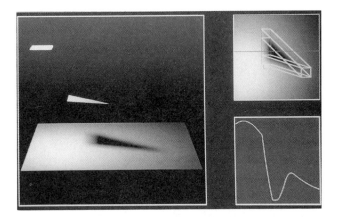

Figure 8.16: *First and second derivative discontinuity boundaries for a polygonal environment. Note the visible discontinuity in the first derivative of the radiosity function plotted in the lower right of the figure. Courtesy of Daniel Lischinski and Filippo Tampieri, Program of Computer Graphics, Cornell University.*

plot of the radiosity function. As apparent in this image, discontinuities define the outer boundary of the shadow penumbra and the boundary of the umbra. Additional discontinuities occur within the penumbra itself.

In a polygonal environment, certain geometric events cause a qualitative transition in the occlusion of an illumination source. The variation in the occlusion of a source undergoes a qualitative transition at certain geometric *events*. Imagine viewing a partially occluded source from a point moving along a receiving surface. As the viewpoint moves, more of the source is revealed (see Figure 8.17). In general, the visibility of the source (and thus the direct energy transfer for a constant source) varies quadratically according to a function determined by the relative orientation of the overlapping edges of the source and the occluding polygon.

Whenever an edge joins or leaves the set of overlapping edges, a new quadratic variation is determined and there is a discontinuity in the first or second derivative. This transition is called a *visual event*. There are two classes of visual events, *Vertex–Edge* (VE or EV) and *Edge–Edge–Edge* (EEE), corresponding to the two possible ways that an edge can leave or join the set of overlapping edges.

A VE event occurs when a vertex of the source crosses an edge of the occluding polygon (first row of Figure 8.17), or conversely when an edge of the source crosses a vertex of the occluder (for convenience this case may be differentiated as an EV event). The event defines a *critical surface*, that is, the

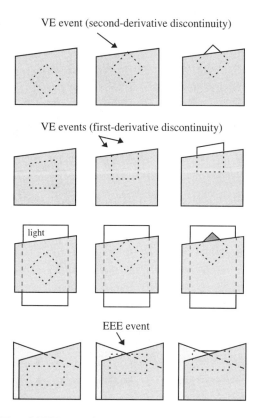

Figure 8.17: *VE and EEE visual events, from a viewpoint looking back toward the occluded light source.*

wedge formed by the vertex and the edge that cause the event. The intersection of this wedge with the scene polygons determines the discontinuity boundaries resulting from this event. The critical surface and its effect on the radiosity function are shown in Figures 8.18 and 8.19.

A discontinuity in the first derivative occurs when an edge of the source and an edge of the occluder are coplanar, as shown in the second row of Figure 8.17. First derivative discontinuities are evident in Figure 8.16.

Visual events can also occur where neither the vertex nor the edge belongs to the source, as shown in row three of Figure 8.17. The visual event involving the two occluding polygons in this case modifies the function describing the change in source visibility, even though the event does not involve any of the source vertices or edges.

The other class of visual events, EEE events, involves transitions caused by

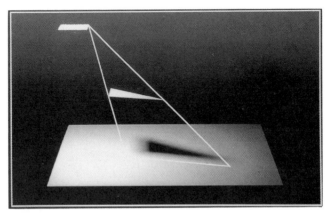

Figure 8.18: *A VE event caused by a source vertex and an occluder edge. Courtesy of Daniel Lischinski and Filippo Tampieri, Program of Computer Graphics, Cornell University.*

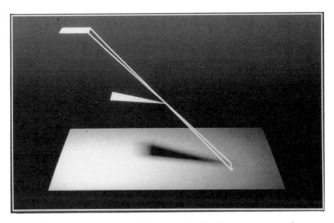

Figure 8.19: *A VE event caused by an occluder vertex and a source edge. Lischinski et al. differentiate these as EV events. Courtesy of Daniel Lischinski and Filippo Tampieri, Program of Computer Graphics, Cornell University.*

overlapping edges of multiple occluders (fourth row of Figure 8.17). The critical surfaces in this case are quadric and the resulting discontinuity boundaries are curves.

The computational challenge in discontinuity meshing is to test the scene polygons against the critical surfaces efficiently and robustly and insert the resulting boundaries into the polygon mesh.

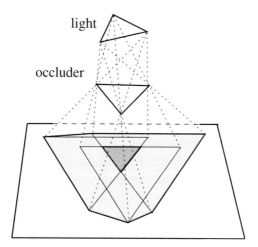

Figure 8.20: *Determining penumbra and umbra volumes using Nishita and Nakamae's algorithm. (After Nishista and Nakamae, 1985).*

8.5.3   Shadow Volume Algorithms

Early algorithms deal only with the subset of events that define the boundaries of the umbra and penumbra. Nishita and Nakamae [175] determine these boundaries by computing shadow volumes formed by an object and each vertex of the light polygon (see Figure 8.20.) The umbra volume for a single occluder is defined by the intersection of the shadow volumes. The penumbra volume is defined by the three-dimensional convex hull containing the shadow volumes. The intersection of the umbra and penumbra volumes with surfaces defines the penumbra and umbra boundaries. This approach ignores discontinuities within the penumbra.

Campbell [42] also resolves only the outer penumbra and umbra boundaries. Like Nishita and Nakamae, Campbell constructs umbra and penumbra volumes for each source–occluder pair. However, he avoids computing a three-dimensional convex hull by constructing the volumes directly from critical surfaces.

Campbell's algorithm assumes convex source and occluder polygons. For each edge of the occluder, or *blocker*, there exists a critical surface formed with respect to each vertex of the source. The minimum blocker extremal plane is defined to be the critical surface that forms the minimum angle with respect to the plane of the blocker (see Figure 8.21). A minimum blocker extremal plane exists for each occluder edge. Likewise, there is a minimum *source* extremal plane for each edge of the source. The penumbra volume consists of the intersection

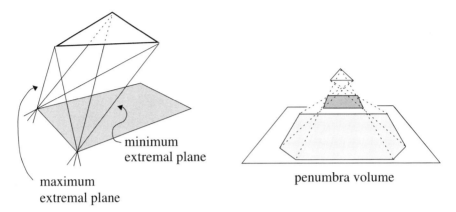

Figure 8.21: *The minimum and maximum extremal planes and the penumbra volume created using the minimum blocker and source extremal planes. (After Campbell, 1991).*

of the negative halfspaces of all of the minimum blocker and source extremal planes (see Figure 8.20). The umbra volume is constructed similarly, using the *maximum* blocker extremal planes.

The resulting umbra and penumbra volumes are stored as BSP-trees. These volumes are then merged with a BSP-tree representing the unified penumbra and umbra volumes for the entire scene to provide an efficient means of testing polygons against the volumes. Chin and Feiner [54] first describe the use of a BSP-tree to represent merged shadow volumes, but for point lights only. The merging of occlusion and umbra volumes for area lights requires more general methods, for which Campbell uses algorithms developed by Naylor [171]. Later work by Chin [55] describes a similar generalization of the BSP-tree shadow volume technique to area lights.

After constructing the shadow volumes, Campbell's algorithm tests each polygon in the scene against the shadow BSP-tree. Polygons are split where they cross planes defining shadow volumes, thus effectively inserting the discontinuity edges. Campbell's approach allows all regions to be classified as totally in shadow, totally in light, or partially occluded. Shadow testing can be eliminated for the subsequent computation of form factors for nodes within regions classified as totally in the light or totally in shadow. Figure 8.22 shows an example of a mesh produced by Campbell's shadow algorithm.

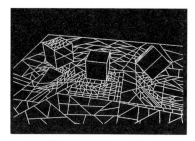

Figure 8.22: *A mesh produced by Campbell's penumbra volume algorithm. Courtesy of A. T. Campbell III, University of Texas.*

8.5.4   Critical Surface Algorithms

Heckbert [121] and Lischinski *et al.* [154] have independently developed similar algorithms that compute discontinuity boundaries due to VE (and EV) events involving the vertices or edges of source polygons. For a given source polygon, the wedge for each VE event is formed and intersected with the scene polygons. These intersections determine discontinuity edges, which are then inserted into the mesh data structure for the polygon.

For the intersection step, Heckbert tests the wedge against every polygon in the scene (see Figure 8.23). Each intersection forms a two-dimensional span on the wedge surface. A two-dimensional hidden span algorithm determines the visibility of the spans with respect to the wedge vertex. The visible portions of the spans correspond to discontinuity boundaries. These are accumulated for each polygon. Following the intersection step, a line-sweep algorithm is performed on each polygon to connect the discontinuity edges at coincident endpoints, split overlapping edges where necessary, and assemble the result into a connected winged-edge representation. The steps of this algorithm are diagramed in Figure 8.23. Heckbert performs discontinuity meshing for emitters only, on the assumption that discontinuities due to reflected light contribute very little to error in the approximation.

Lischinski, *et al.* store the scene polygons as a BSP-tree. The construction of the BSP-tree requires additional processing and storage, but has the advantage of allowing the polygons to be visited in front-to-back order when testing for intersections against the wedge. Each intersection of the wedge with a polygon generates a discontinuity edge and clips that portion of the wedge. When the wedge is entirely clipped away, no further polygons need be tested.

Each polygon's mesh is stored as a two-dimensional BSP-tree. As discontinuity edges are generated, they are filtered down the BSP-tree until they reach leaf nodes, at which point the corresponding faces of the meshed polygon are split. Lischinski also maintains a winged-edge representation of the mesh

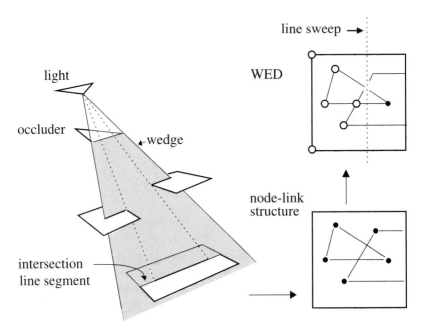

Figure 8.23: *Steps in Heckbert's computation of discontinuity edges.*

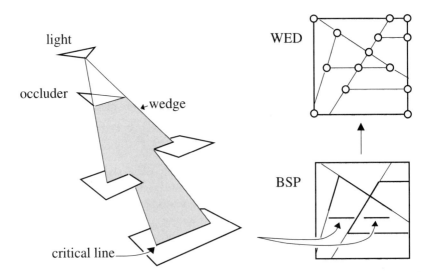

Figure 8.24: *Steps in the method of Lischinski et al. for the computation of discontinuity edges.*

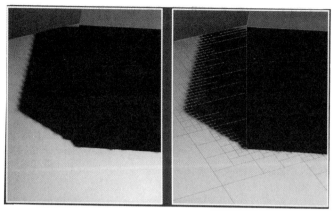

Figure 8.25: *Artifacts resulting from conventional quadtree-based adaptive subdivision. Courtesy of Daniel Lischinski and Filippo Tampieri, Program of Computer Graphics, Cornell University.*

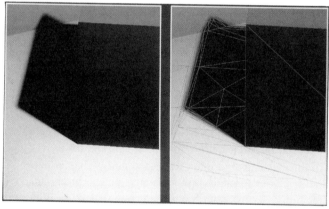

Figure 8.26: *Discontinuity Meshing. Courtesy of Daniel Lischinski and Filippo Tampieri, Program of Computer Graphics, Cornell University.*

topology, with each node of the tree pointing to an edge in the winged-edge data structure. The steps of Lischinski's algorithm are shown in Figure 8.24. Figures 8.25 and 8.26 compare results for conventional quadtree meshing and discontinuity meshing using this algorithm. Color plates 32 and 33 show images computed with and without Lischinski's algorithm.

Heckbert and Lischinski ignore EEE events and VE events involving multiple occluders. Handling EEE events correctly is an involved problem. Algorithms applicable to finding discontinuity boundaries due to EEE events are

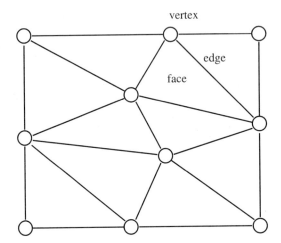

Figure 8.27: *Representation of mesh topology using an embedded graph.*

described by Teller [233] for the case of a sequence of convex holes.

8.6 Topological Data Structures and Operators

The representation of a mesh naturally includes data describing node locations, surface normals, material attributes, and so on. In addition to geometric data, a complete representation also includes the mesh topology, which describes the adjacency between mesh elements, element edges, and nodes.

Many of the meshing algorithms described in this chapter depend on knowledge of adjacency. For example, splitting one element during adaptive subdivision often requires inserting a new node on an edge shared by adjacent elements. Computing a gradient at a node may require visiting adjacent nodes. A data structure that maintains the adjacency, or topology, of these entities explicitly can greatly improve the efficiency and simplicity of the algorithms described in this chapter.

The topology of a mesh can be represented by an *embedded* graph, that is, a graph that has been mapped to a surface. The faces of an embedded graph are the regions of the surface bounded by the graph edges. The graph vertices correspond to mesh nodes, edges correspond to element boundaries and faces correspond to elements (see Figure 8.27). When the meshed surface does not form the closed boundary of a solid, there are no elements adjacent to the outer edges of the mesh and a "pseudo-face" is often assumed in order to maintain topological consistency.

8.6.1 Data Structure Criteria

A variety of data structures for representing the adjacency graph has been developed for solid modeling. Several are described and evaluated by Weiler in [261, 262] and by Mantyla in [158]. The data structures compared by Weiler are *edge-based*; all information required to find adjacent vertices, edges or faces is contained in the edge record. The *winged-edge data structure*, first developed by Baumgart for computer vision [22], may be the most familiar example, but many others have also been devised.

Topological data structures can be compared on the basis of storage and performance. Evaluation of the storage required to represent a given number of edges (or vertices) is straightforward. (A comparison of the storage requirements for several data structures, including the winged-edge, can be found in [6, 261].) However, compactness must be weighed against performance; an extremely succinct data structure may require extra pointer manipulations to extract certain information.

Performance is less straightforward to evaluate. The number of field accesses required for various operations is often used as a measure. Performance also depends on how often operations access different records, since these may reside on different pages in virtual memory. Papers by Ala and Woo contain experiments and discussions that help clarify these issues [6, 268]. However, actual performance will depend strongly on the mix of operations typical of the application. A careful evaluation of data structures would require statistical measurements of the operations performed by the particular application.

To date no such evaluation of topological data structures has been made for radiosity meshing. One reason is undoubtedly that the cost of numerical computation (integration, interpolation, etc.) tends to overwhelm other costs. Storage, on the other hand, is of immediate practical concern. Image synthesis is often a small component of a larger application, such as an architectural or industrial design package, and the additional memory requirements of radiosity are a serious consideration.

8.6.2 The Winged-Edge Data Structure

The winged-edge data structure (WED) will be used to illustrate how a topological data structure can be used to represent a mesh. The winged-edge data structure is fairly compact, provides reasonable performance, and has often been used for radiosity [61, 121, 154].

Figure 8.28 contains a diagram of the basic winged-edge data structure. As the name implies, the basic record is that of an edge. The record points explicitly to the pair of faces that are adjacent to the edge. It also points to the two vertices that are the endpoints of the edge (in order, thus orienting the edge). At each

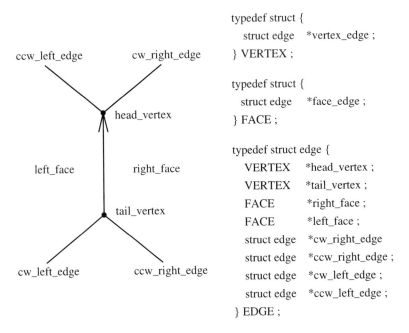

```
typedef struct {
    struct edge   *vertex_edge ;
} VERTEX ;

typedef struct {
    struct edge   *face_edge ;
} FACE ;

typedef struct edge {
    VERTEX      *head_vertex ;
    VERTEX      *tail_vertex ;
    FACE        *right_face ;
    FACE        *left_face ;
    struct edge *cw_right_edge
    struct edge *ccw_right_edge ;
    struct edge *cw_left_edge ;
    struct edge *ccw_left_edge ;
} EDGE ;
```

Figure 8.28: *The winged-edge data structure.*

endpoint, the next edge (or *wing*) around each of the adjacent faces is stored in both the clockwise and counterclockwise directions. The data structures for a face and a vertex need only keep a single pointer to any of the adjacent edges.

Operations on the topology represented by the winged-edge data structure consist of either modifications to the topology or queries about adjacency relationships. Modifications to the topology can be expressed in terms of *Euler* operators [22]. (Good introductions are provided by [117, 158, 159, 267].) Euler operators are so called because they maintain Euler's formula, which expresses the relationship between the number of vertices, edges and faces in a topologically consistent adjacency graph. For a simple polyhedron with no holes this formula is

$$V - E + F = 2 \qquad\qquad (8.3)$$

where V, E, and F are the number of vertices, edges, and faces, respectively.[6]

A complete set of Euler operators provides for all possible modifications to the topology, and guarantees that the topology following any operation will be consistent. In addition, the use of operators simplifies the coding of higher

---

[6]The more general formula is given by $V - E + F = 2 - 2g$, where g is the *genus* of the polyhedron. Generalizations also exist for other dimensions.

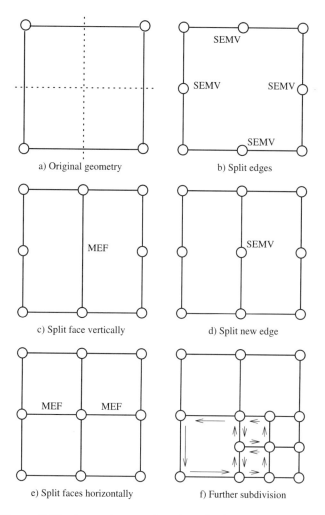

Figure 8.29: *Operations on the winged-edge data structure.*

level meshing operations by encapsulating the manipulation of the underlying data structures.

A complete set of Euler operators requires only five operators and their inverses [159]. Assuming no holes for the purpose of this discussion, these can be reduced to three. The three operators, plus one more included for convenience, are listed here:

1. Make-Vertex-Face (MVF) creates a new graph by creating a single vertex and face.

2. Make-Edge-Vertex (MEV) adds a vertex and connects it to an existing vertex using a new edge.

3. Make-Edge-Face (MEF) connects two existing vertices to create a new edge, which splits an existing face into two faces.

4. Split-Edge-Make-Vertex (SEMV) creates a new vertex and a new edge by splitting an existing edge into two edges.[7]

Figure 8.29 shows how a simple quadtree meshing scheme could be implemented using Euler operators. A graph representing the original geometry is first created using an initial MVF operation, followed by several calls to MEV, and finishing with MEF to close the polygon. (One of the two resulting faces is a "pseudo-face" that represents the exterior region of the graph). The polygon is then split along the vertical and horizontal directions using SEMV to split edges and MEF to split faces by linking vertices with new edges. Finally, one element of the initial mesh is split further, showing how the use of a topologically complete data structure correctly handles the insertion of the new vertex (labeled A in the diagram) along the shared edge.

Once the mesh has been created, higher level algorithms will need to query the topological data structure for adjacency information. For example, various ways of traversing the topology can be thought of as queries: get next face, get next vertex around face, get next edge around vertex, and so on. The implementations are straightforward in most cases, although edge orientation requires special handling. When traversing the boundary of a face in a winged-edge data structure for example, edges may be oriented arbitrarily. Therefore, comparisons are required to determine which endpoint of the edge is the next vertex around the face.

The basic topological data structure can be augmented with extra information to speed up certain queries. Back-pointers might be added to allow direct access to the parent object record from the vertex record. An extra pointer can be added to the vertex record, allowing nodes to be linked into a list that can be traversed directly during the solution, when it is necessary to visit all the nodes of the scene in sequence to compute form factors or to update radiosities.

Finally, certain algorithms require the imposition of a mesh hierarchy. Hierarchical data structures, like quadtrees or BSP-trees, can be maintained in parallel with the topological data structure, with nodes of the tree pointing to faces of the topology.

---

[7]A helpful approach to implementing winged-edge operations is described in [98].

Figure 8.30: *Approximation of the radiosity function using the rex data structure. Each square on the shaded floor corresponds to a cell in the rex. Courtesy of Paul Heckbert, University of California, Berkeley.*

8.7 Alternatives to Meshing

The representation of the radiosity function by a mesh of elements requires the subdivision of the model geometry, which is clearly a complicated process in general. Several investigators have proposed that the representation of shading be decoupled from the geometry as completely as possible to simplify algorithms and data structures.

If nodes are uniformly distributed across the surface, they can be organized as a simple array of sample points. An array of discrete samples representing a continuous function suggests a texture map. Heckbert [119] has proposed texture mapping as an alternative approach to storing and reconstructing an approximation of the radiosity function [119].

In Heckbert's approach the power arriving at a surface is sampled (using Monte Carlo ray tracing) and stored at the pixels of a radiosity texture, or *rex*. The connection between rex pixels and sample locations on the surface is implicit in the mapping between texture coordinates and surface coordinates. The rexes are organized into a quadtree to support adaptive sampling. During rendering, the radiosity can be reconstructed from the rex samples using any one of a wide selection of reconstruction kernels, just as in conventional texture

Figure 8.31: *Use of the rex data structure with a higher sampling rate. Courtesy of Paul Heckbert, University of California, Berkeley.*

mapping. Heckbert uses linear interpolation and averaging to reconstruct the radiosity function in image space.

An image computed using the rex algorithm is shown in Figure 8.30. In Heckbert's implementation, light and eye ray tracing are used to traces paths that include specular reflection or transmission (such as for the lens in this image). A low number of eye and light rays were used to compute the light transport in this image. Statistical variance makes the structure of the rex visible. The image in Figure 8.31 was computed using a higher number of light and eye rays.

The regularity of sampling imposed by rexes reduces the size and complexity of the data structures since no explicit topology is maintained. Rather, adjacency information needed during rendering is implicit in the quadtree.

The rex scheme limits the coupling of shading and geometry to the mapping between texture and surface coordinates. This is a particular advantage for curved surfaces, which are turned into polygonal facets by most meshing algorithms. However, determining an appropriate mapping is not always straightforward. Further, the regularity imposed by the rex does not provide the full sampling flexibility provided by meshing. These limitations are ameliorated in Heckbert's approach by subdividing rexes until they are smaller than a certain size in image space. The difficulties in sampling the shading function adequately are then greatly reduced. For example, if the image resolution is known during sampling, discontinuities need not be determined exactly, since they will never be resolved beyond pixel resolution during rendering.

Vedel [241] uses a sampling data structure similar to the rex. Vedel's algorithm takes advantage of the flexibility of reconstruction from an array samples by computing the radiosity gradient and reconstructing using an elliptical filter oriented perpendicularly to the gradient. The heuristic is that the sample values change most quickly in the direction of the gradient, and the reconstruction kernel should thus give less weight to values in that direction.

A related example of the decoupling shading and geometry is provided by Ward's *Radiance* program [254]. In Ward's algorithm, radiances computed using stochastic eye-ray tracing are cached in a spatial data structure (an octree). Whenever shading is required at a new point, the octree is checked. If values are stored within a close enough neighborhood, the new value is interpolated instead of being computed directly. The spatial data structure is decoupled from the surface geometry and mapping difficulties are avoided, since the world coordinates of any surface point map directly into the spatial data structure without transformation. Ward's algorithm is specifically view-based, but a similar approach might be applied to a view-independent radiosity approach.

Data structures that decouple shading and geometry may prove useful for radiosity, particularly when image information is available to bound the required sampling resolution. Published implementations for radiosity have been limited to simple environments and thus many practical issues related to mapping and sampling complicated geometries remain to be explored.

Chapter 9

Rendering

Once a radiosity solution has been computed, the remaining step is to render an image. During rendering, the model is projected onto the image plane, the visible surfaces are determined, and a color is computed for each pixel. The pixel color is derived from the radiance of the surface location visible at the pixel. The radiance can be determined directly from the approximation of the radiosity function computed during the solution. However, this approximation is often not the best choice for rendering, due primarily to characteristics of the human visual system. Previous chapters have addressed the computation of an *objectively* accurate solution. This chapter will be concerned with the derivation of a *subjectively* accurate image from such a solution.

The first sections of this chapter focus on obtaining an approximation from the radiosity solution that is more suitable for rendering. These include approaches that construct a higher order approximation based on the radiosity solution, as well as methods that partially reevaluate the radiosity equation at image resolution. Hardware-assisted rendering and techniques for rendering texture and bump maps using radiosity are also described.

Section 9.5 examines the question of how to map radiance values resulting from the radiosity analysis to pixel values in such a way as to produce a subjectively accurate image. Typically, allowable pixel values are integers in the 0–255 range for each of the red, green, and blue color channels of the display device. The conversion should compensate as far as possible for the limited range of radiance values and color resolution offered by typical monitors, as well as for perceptual effects.

The radiosity method has thus far been presented for a monochrome (i.e., single color band) solution. This chapter concludes with a description of the issues relating to color perception and the selection of appropriate red, green, and blue pixel values to represent the more general spectra of the visible wavelengths of electromagnetic radiation.

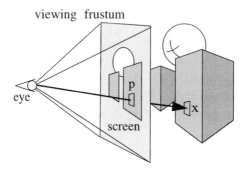

Figure 9.1: *Mapping a pixel location to a position on a surface in the environment.*

9.1   Reconstructing the Radiosity Function

Given an eye location and viewing frustum (see Figure 9.1) a function $\mathbf{x}(\mathbf{p})$ can be constructed to map the center of a pixel ($\mathbf{p} = (p_x, p_y)$) to a point $\mathbf{x}_p$ on a surface in the environment. This mapping is equivalent to tracing a ray from the eye through the pixel until it hits a surface at point $\mathbf{x}_p$. The most straightforward choice for the radiosity at this point is simply the value of the approximate radiosity function $\hat{B}(\mathbf{x}_p)$. This value can be found by evaluating the basis functions that are nonzero at that location and summing the results, weighted by the corresponding nodal values:

$$\hat{B}(\mathbf{x}_p) = \sum_{i=1}^{n} B_i N_i(\mathbf{x}_p) \tag{9.1}$$

Repeating this process for each pixel produces a discrete map (or image) of the approximate radiosity function.[1]

Unfortunately, an approximation that provides sufficient accuracy during the solution may not be adequate for rendering. Visual perception gives certain features more weight and others less, with the result that quantitative accuracy does not translate directly to perceived quality. One consequence is that the constant elements often used during the radiosity solution cannot be used during rendering, since discontinuities in value are immediately perceived as unrealistic

---

[1]This description ignores the issue of correctly sampling the finite solid angle of the pixel as seen from the eye so as to avoid aliasing (jaggies) in the image. *Antialiasing*, the removal of these sampling artifacts, is beyond the scope of this text. For the current discussion, it will simply be assumed that one or more samples have been used to reconstruct a scalar radiosity value per pixel.

Figure 9.2: *A comparison of constant and linear elements for rendering.*

(see Figure 9.2). Because the eye is sensitive to first derivative discontinuities, a C^1 approximation (continuous in the first derivative) may also be desirable.

Elements providing the desired continuity could be used throughout the radiosity solution, but if the solution is otherwise accurate enough, this unnecessarily increases its cost. Instead, most radiosity implementations derive a new approximation with the desired characteristics just prior to rendering. Several methods that take this approach are described in the following sections.

9.2 Interpolation Methods for Rendering

When the original solution approximation $\hat{B}$ is not adequate for rendering, it can be replaced by another approximation using a new set of basis functions and coefficients. The new basis functions are selected for

1. the desired degree of continuity to avoid perceptual artifacts,

2. fidelity to the original approximation,

3. and (if appropriate) suitability for fast rendering using hardware Gouraud shading.

9.2.1 C^0 Interpolation

If linear elements, which provide a C^0 approximation, are used in the solution they can be applied directly for rendering. However, the radiosity solution is often performed with constant elements. In this case, a linear interpolation or approximation must be derived from the constant element solution to produce C^0 shading in the image. A piecewise linear interpolation can be constructed

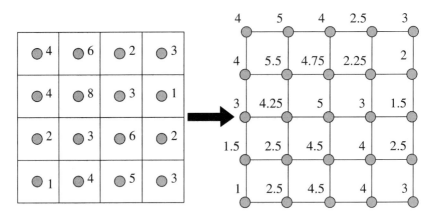

Figure 9.3: *Creating nodes at element corners using nodal averaging.*

by creating linear elements with nodes at the element vertices. The values at these vertices are then derived from the nodes of the original constant elements.

One approach to constructing a C^0 interpolant is to create new nodes at the corners of the existing elements. The radiosity at these nodes can then be obtained by averaging the radiosities of the adjacent elements [62] (see Figure 9.3). Values at nodes on the boundary of the geometry can be extrapolated from interior nodes, although care must be taken not to create negative values. Finally, values in the interior of the elements are linearly (in triangular elements) or bilinearly (in the case of quadrilateral elements) interpolated from the new nodal values at the vertices. Nodal averaging tends to smooth the radiosity function, which can often help mask artifacts. On the other hand, smoothing may eliminate subtle but important shading variations.

Another approach is to create a new element subdivision by connecting the existing nodes at the centers of each original element with edges, thus using the same set of nodes during the solution and rendering stages. For example, to define constant elements for the solution, Sturzlinger [227] computes the Voronoi diagram for the nodes and uses the Voronoi polygons as elements. For linear interpolation during rendering, the corresponding Delaunay triangulation provides elements with nodes at the vertices.

It is also possible to use a modified constant element with nodes located at element corners instead of the center during the solution. Wallace *et al.* [247] use this hybrid of constant and linear elements. During the solution, radiosities are computed directly at the corner nodes. When needed, the constant radiosity value for the element is taken as the average of the nodal values.[2] The nodes

---

[2]For very little extra effort, of course, these elements could be treated as true linear

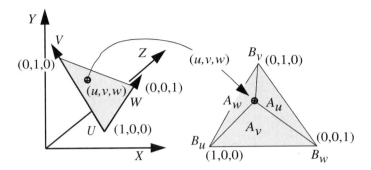

Figure 9.4: *Barycentric interpolation.*

can then be used directly for bilinear interpolation during rendering. However, evaluating the radiosity equation at element vertices has to be handled carefully. Problems may occur where surfaces meet and the kernel of the integral operator becomes singular, such as along the boundary of the floor where it meets a wall.

Bilinear Interpolation

Once values have been obtained at element corners, linear or bilinear interpolation can be used to determine the radiosity at each pixel during rendering. Since interpolation is performed in the parametric coordinates of the element, the parametric coordinates of the point to be shaded are required. Depending on the rendering algorithm, this may require transforming the world coordinates (x, y, z) of the point $\mathbf{x}_p$ to the parametric coordinates of the element.

In the case of a triangle, barycentric coordinates provide a natural parameterization for linear interpolation. If the three vertices of a triangle are labeled U, V, and W, with corresponding barycentric coordinates $(1, 0, 0)$, $(0, 1, 0)$, and $(0, 0, 1)$, then the barycentric coordinate u of a point in the triangle is simply the ratio of the area A_u of the subtriangle opposite the vertex U to the area of the whole triangle (see Figure 9.4):

$$A = A_u + A_v + A_w$$

$$
\begin{aligned}
u &= A_u/A \\
v &= A_v/A \\
w &= A_w/A
\end{aligned}
\tag{9.2}
$$

The radiosity $B(u, v, w)$, is then interpolated from the corner radiosities, B_u,

---

elements during the solution [231].

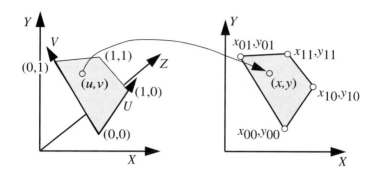

Figure 9.5: *Determining parametric (u, v) coordinates from (x, y, z) world co-ordinates.*

B_v, B_w, using

$$B(u, v, w) = u * B_u + v * B_v + w * B_w \tag{9.3}$$

as shown in Figure 9.4.

For bilinear interpolation on planar quadrilateral elements, the transformation from world coordinates to the parametric coordinates of the element involves solving a quadratic form that is guaranteed to have real roots for convex quadrilaterals. The basic equations are described below. An efficient algorithm is described in detail, along with several practical issues, by Haines [108].

The first step is to project the element and intersection point onto one of the three orthogonal planes XY, XZ, or YZ. For numerical reasons, the plane chosen should be the one corresponding to the largest component of the element normal. For example, if the element normal is (0.10, -0.50, 0.86) then the XY plane is best since the Z component of the normal is largest in absolute value. The projection onto the XY plane then simply involves dropping the Z coordinate of each vertex and the intersection point. (The equations below continue with (x, y) but (x, z) or (y, z) can be substituted in a straightforward manner.)

If the intersection point is (x, y) and the four corner vertices are (x_{00}, y_{00}) for the vertex at $(u, v) = (0, 0)$, (x_{01}, y_{01}) for the vertex where $(u, v) = (0, 1)$, etc., then (see Figure 9.5)

$$\begin{aligned} v &= Z \\ u &= \frac{x - x_{00} + x_{00}Z - x_{01}Z}{-x_{00} + x_{00}Z - x_{01}Z + x_{11}Z + x_{10} - x_{10}Z} \end{aligned} \tag{9.4}$$

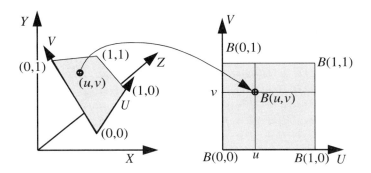

Figure 9.6: *Bilinear interpolation.*

where

$$
\begin{aligned}
Z &= \text{real solution to} \quad aZ^2 + bZ + c = 0 \\
a &= -y_{10}x_{00} + y_{11}x_{00} + y_{10}x_{01} - y_{01}x_{10} - y_{00}x_{11} \\
&\quad + y_{00}x_{10} - y_{11}x_{01} + y_{01}x_{11} \\
b &= 2y_{10}x_{00} + y_{01}x_{10} - 2y_{00}x_{10} + yx_{01} + yx_{10} \\
&\quad - y_{10}x_{01} - yx_{11} - yx_{00} + y_{00}x + y_{11}x - y_{01}x \\
&\quad - y_{10}x + y_{00}x_{11} - y_{11}x_{00} \\
c &= y_{10}x - y_{10}x_{00} - yx_{10} + y_{00}x_{10} - y_{00}x + yx_{00}
\end{aligned} \tag{9.5}
$$

Once the (u, v) parametric coordinates of the point have been obtained, the bilinear interpolation of the radiosities at the corners B_{00}, B_{01}, B_{11}, B_{10} of a quadrilateral element is

$$
B(u, v) = (1 - u)(1 - v)B_{00} + (1 - u)vB_{01} + uvB_{11} + u(1 - v)B_{10} \tag{9.6}
$$

as shown in Figure 9.6.

Gouraud Shading

Since bilinear interpolation is performed in the parametric coordinates of the element, it is independent of the projection of the element onto the image plane. For reasons of computational speed, however, some algorithms perform linear interpolation directly in image space. Gouraud shading, the most common example, is an incremental formulation of linear interpolation designed for hardware scan conversion [103]. During hardware rendering, colors defined at polygon vertices are linearly interpolated along the polygon edges in the screen projection. At each scanline, these values are then interpolated horizontally between the two edges intersecting the scanline (see Figure 9.7).

A hardware graphics accelerator can be used to render a radiosity solution at high speed by passing the mesh elements to the hardware as polygons, with

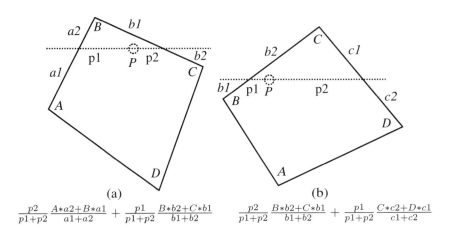

$$\frac{p2}{p1+p2}\frac{A*a2+B*a1}{a1+a2} + \frac{p1}{p1+p2}\frac{B*b2+C*b1}{b1+b2} \qquad \frac{p2}{p1+p2}\frac{B*b2+C*b1}{b1+b2} + \frac{p1}{p1+p2}\frac{C*c2+D*c1}{c1+c2}$$

Figure 9.7: *Gouraud interpolation.*

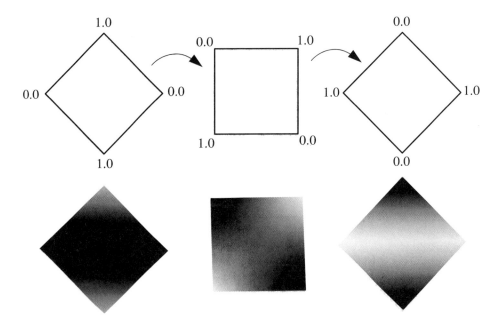

Figure 9.8: *A polygon rendered at three different orientations using Gouraud shading. The numbers indicate the color at the polygon vertices. The polygon is rotated 45 degrees clockwise at each step moving from left to right. Courtesy of Eric Haines, 3D/EYE, Inc.*

the vertex colors determined by the nodal radiosities. Unfortunately, Gouraud shading has limitations that can severely degrade image quality if not taken into account. Since the perspective transformation from *world space* to *image space* is nonaffine, linear interpolation in image space is not equivalent to interpolation in the parametric space of the element.[3] Furthermore, Gouraud shading does not uniquely determine the interpolated value on the polygon interior for a given location. Gouraud shading is dependent on the *orientation* of the polygon on the image plane, and the interpolated shading may change visibly as the view changes. This is particularly obvious in the case shown in Figure 9.7, where for one orientation the value at point P depends on the vertices A, B, and C, and in the other on B, C, and D. Figure 9.8 shows a polygon rendered at three different orientations using Gouraud shading.

Since Gouraud shading interpolates only between the two closest edges spanning the scanline, it also handles concave polygons poorly and will often introduce discontinuities between neighboring scanlines on the polygon interior (see Figure 6.11). A discontinuity at polygon boundaries is also possible if adaptive subdivision is allowed to introduce T-vertices into the mesh. When the view is oriented so that the collinear edges joined at the T-vertex fall along a scanline, interpolation along the next scanline below or above will ignore the T-vertex, and there will usually be a visible discontinuity in shading between the two scanlines.

The limitations of Gouraud shading can be avoided with careful meshing. For example, concave elements and T-vertices can be avoided using methods described in Chapter 8. Baum *et al.* [18], for example, triangulate elements containing T-vertices before rendering and thus avoid the view-dependent discontinuities that can occur in such cases. Gouraud shading is orientation invariant for triangles (except for the effect of the perspective transformation described above), so triangulating all elements before sending them to the hardware will largely eliminate view-dependent interpolation effects.

Since Gouraud shading is a form of linear interpolation it cannot be used directly to render higher order elements if they have been used for the radiosity solution. In such cases, hardware display can be accomplished by recursively tessellating (subdividing) the elements into smaller polygons whose vertex values are determined from the higher order interpolation. The subdivision ends when some flatness criterion is fulfilled. The smaller polygons can then be passed to the hardware for linear interpolation to provide an approximation of the original element.

---

[3]Since the perspective projection is nonlinear, distances across a polygon in the image plane do not map linearly to distances measured on the actual polygon. Some hardware implementations correct for the perspective transformation during interpolation.

Figure 9.9: *A comparison of C^0 and C^1 interpolation. The image on the left was rendered using bilinear interpolation. The image on the right was rendered using a C^1 element constructed from quadratic triangular Bézier patches. Mach bands corresponding to element boundaries are evident on the inside face of the fireplace and along the ceiling panels. Courtesy of Mark Reichert, Program of Computer Graphics, Cornell University.*

9.2.2 C^1 Interpolation

Although linear interpolation is C^0 and is thus an improvement over constant shading, it does not eliminate all perceptual problems. Linear interpolation is still discontinuous in the first derivative at element boundaries, with the result that Mach bands often appear along mesh boundaries (see Figure 6.2). A finer mesh density or higher order interpolation, such as the quadratic interpolation offered by some graphics hardware [139], can reduce or eliminate Mach bands, since it tends to decrease the difference in slope across discontinuities. However, piecewise quadratic or higher order interpolation does not necessarily provide higher than C^0 continuity at boundaries. Elements that provide a C^1 approximation will eliminate Mach bands in most cases without the need for a finer subdivision.

The problem of interpolating or approximating the radiosity function during rendering is analogous to the problem of constructing a surface in three-dimensional space for modeling, where C^1 or C^2 surfaces are desired. The surface modeling literature is thus a valuable source of methods relevant to achieving approximations with particular continuity requirements. In the case of radiosity, the surface to be interpolated is defined by the two parametric coordinates of the geometry, with the third coordinate being the radiosity value (see Figure 3.1).

A surface that is everywhere C^1 can be constructed using quadratic or higher order Bézier patches. A Bézier patch describes a surface that passes through control points on the corners of the patch. Other control points on the boundary and interior determine the tangent to the surface at the patch corners and the shape of the surface on the interior. Max [161] has used cubic triangular Bézier patches in screen space to produce C^1 shading. Interpolation using quadratic triangular Bézier patches has been applied to radiosity by Reichert [192], using a scheme based on Powell and Sabin [183] and Cendes and Wong [45]. The advantages of a C^1 approximation for rendering are demonstrated in Figure 9.9, in which the image on the right was computed using Reichert's approach. Note the Mach bands corresponding to element boundaries in the left-hand image, for which linear elements were used.

Surfaces with the desired continuity can also be constructed using more general B-splines, in which case the surface will generally not pass through the control points (although control points can be computed so as to make the surface pass through a desired set of values.) There are many references on surface construction and continuity [17, 80, 170] that provide fuller explanations of these issues.

Clough-Tocher Interpolation

Salesin *et al.* [203] have applied the Clough-Tocher element [56] to rendering for radiosity. This element is constructed from three cubic triangular Bézier patches and provides a C^1 interpolant at boundaries. Salesin *et al.* have developed algorithms that take advantage of the large number of degrees of freedom in this construction to relax selectively the continuity at boundaries corresponding to actual discontinuities in the radiosity function. When discontinuity boundaries have been identified (at some cost), it is desirable that they not be smoothed over by the interpolation.

The Clough-Tocher construction begins by determining radiosity values and *normals* (cross products of derivatives) to the radiosity surface at the vertices of the triangular elements used during the solution. Salesin *et al.* begin with triangular quadratic elements, which have nodes at the triangle vertices and at the midpoint of each side, but quadratic elements are not essential to the algorithm. The construction ends with each triangle subdivided into three new cubic Bézier triangles. The additional control points introduced in the formulation allow for explicit control of the continuity at element boundaries.

The Clough-Tocher construction proceeds as follows:

- The first step in the algorithm is to determine "normals" to the radiosity function at each element vertex. If linear or constant elements have been used during the solution, this can be accomplished by fitting a plane

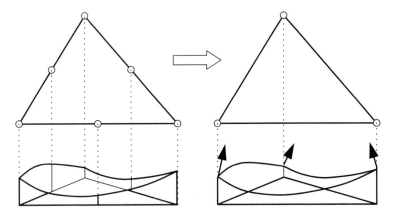

Figure 9.10: *Computing the normal to the radiosity "surface" at the vertices of the Clough-Tocher element.*

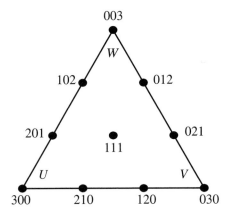

Figure 9.11: *A cubic Bézier patch is defined by 10 control points.*

through adjacent nodes. In the case of the quadratic elements used by Salesin *et al.*, the normals are computed using the values at the vertex and midpoint nodes (see Figure 9.10).

The normals are computed by fitting parabolas along each edge of the triangle through the three nodal values, one for each of the two endpoints and for the midpoint of each edge. The cross product of the tangents of the two parabolas at each vertex provides a normal vector. Since each corner of the triangle may also be a vertex of other adjacent elements, this process is repeated independently for each adjacent element, and the

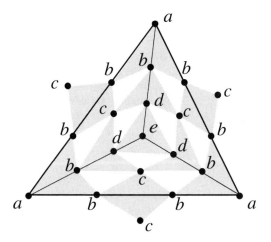

Figure 9.12: *Three Bézier patches are constructed in the subtriangles created by connecting the centroid to the vertices. The control points in each shaded region are constrained to be coplanar to ensure C^1 continuity across element boundaries.*

resulting normals at the vertex are averaged.

- The second step is to construct three cubic Bézier triangular patches within each element. A Bézier patch is defined by 10 control points as shown in Figure 9.11. The value at a point $B(\mathbf{x})$ within the patch is determined by the barycentric coordinates of the point and the values of the 10 control points using,

$$B(\mathbf{x}) = \sum_{\substack{0 \leq i,j,k \leq 3 \\ i+j+k=3}} \frac{3!}{i!j!k!} \beta_u^i \beta_v^j \beta_w^k \, b_{ijk} \qquad (9.7)$$

where $(\beta_u, \beta_v, \beta_w)$ is the barycentric coordinate of the point, and the b_{ijk} are the control point values. The indices ijk for each of the 10 control points are shown in Figure 9.11. Note that the Bézier surface interpolates the values at the triangle vertices. For example, when $(ijk) = (300)$, then $(u, v, w) = (1, 0, 0)$, and $B(\mathbf{x}) = \frac{3!}{3!1!1!} 1 * 1 * 1\, b_{300} = b_{300}$.

The Clough-Tocher construction involves dividing the element into three cubic patches by connecting the element centroid to each vertex (see Figure 9.12). The 10 control points of each subelement provide the degrees of freedom required to ensure continuity across the element boundaries and also make it possible to relax the continuity conditions when an edge represents a shadow or penumbra boundary.

- All four control points in each of the shaded wedges are constrained to be coplanar. These constraints are determined as follows:

  1. The control point values at the original triangle vertices (labeled a in Figure 9.12) are taken directly from the original radiosity values.

  2. The control points adjacent to the original triangle vertices (labeled b in 9.12) are constrained to lie in the plane defined by the adjacent triangle vertex and its normal.

  3. Three of the wedges include one control point from an adjacent element, (labeled c in Figure 9.12) thus ensuring element-to-element continuity. The control points of these wedges are determined by the two control points labeled b computed in step 2, and by the normal to the wedge taken as the average of the normals at the adjacent element vertices (labeled a).

  4. This provides three of the four values for each wedge containing a control point labeled d in the figure. Thus, the values of the d control points are determined by the plane through the three previously determined points (labeled b and c). The value for the center point e is then simply the average of the three points labeled d.

A representative cubic Bézier surface for the Clough-Tocher construction outlined above is shown in Figure 9.13.

The constraints on the control points can be relaxed when a boundary that is C^0 or C^{-1} (discontinuous in value) is indicated. An element edge can be lowered to C^0 by relaxing constraint 3 for the wedge that spans the adjacent elements. If the original vertices of the elements are also to be lowered to C^0, then there is no unique normal at the vertex and a different normal can be used for each adjacent element. Care must be taken to ensure that the control points along the element boundaries still provide C^0 continuity between elements. This is accomplished by adjusting the computed normals of adjacent wedges until their respective components along the element are the same. The continuity of the radiosity function across element boundaries can be further relaxed to create discontinuities in value. In this case, multiple instances of the control points at a single location are created, thus decoupling neighboring elements completely. Pseudocode can be found in [203].

In Figure 9.14 interpolation using linear (a), C^1 quadratic Bézier (b), and Clough-Tocher elements (c) is compared to a reference solution (d). The mesh consists of 58 triangular elements and incorporates discontinuity boundaries. The two C^1 methods eliminate the inappropriate Mach bands apparent in the linear

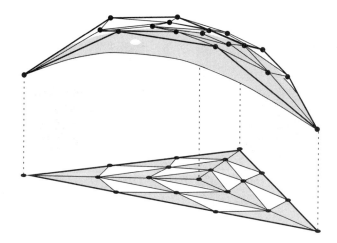

Figure 9.13: *The Clough-Tocher element, showing the control net and the radiosity "surface" produced. The shaded triangles indicate the control nodes that must be kept coplanar to generate a C^1 surface.*

example. However, C^1 quadratic Bézier interpolation also incorrectly eliminates Mach bands corresponding to actual C^0 boundaries along shadow edges. It also tends to overshoot near the discontinuities, causing unexpectedly bright regions.

In the reference solution, the Mach bands along the shadow boundaries fade away at the corners of the shadow. Salesin *et al.* prove that the radiosity at the apex of two noncollinear C^0 boundaries is actually C^1. The Clough-Tocher interpolant reproduces this result. This example is an excellent demonstration of the subtleties involved in reproducing actual shading effects.

Elements that use a Bézier basis, such as the Clough-Toucher element, produce a surface that passes through the nodal values. Reconstruction can also be performed by methods that approximate the surface without actually interpolating the nodal values. For example, Metaxas and Milios [165] use thin-plate splines to reconstruct images from sparse, noisy samples in image space, as might be obtained by Monte Carlo ray tracing. In general, the field of scattered-data interpolation and approximation represents a largely untapped source of potentially useful techniques for radiosity and image synthesis [86].

9.3 Two-Pass Methods

With the exception of the *importance-based* approach discussed in Chapter 7, the radiosity methods described so far have been inherently *view-independent*. Decisions concerning the size and placement of elements have thus not taken into

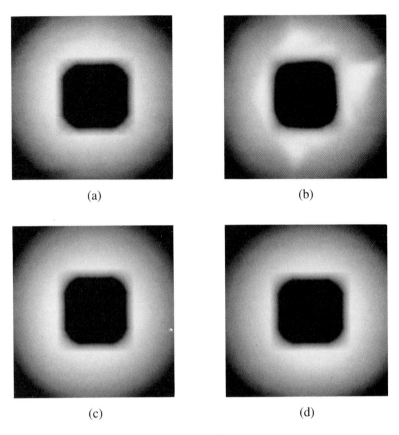

Figure 9.14: *Comparison of linear (a), C^1 quadratic (b), and Clough-Tocher (c) elements to a reference solution (d). Courtesy of David Salesin, Program of Computer Graphics, Cornell University.*

account the projected size of the element in the image. If the mesh resolution is too coarse for a particular view, small features may be absent or incorrectly represented. However, increasing the mesh density during the solution increases the solution cost with no guarantee that the higher resolution will be adequate for any other view.

One approach to ensuring adequate detail is to incorporate view information into the error metric used to guide adaptive meshing. The algorithms of Heckbert [119] and Smits *et al.* [220] take this approach and have been discussed in previous chapters. Discontinuity meshing can also help guarantee that important shadow details are captured.

Another alternative is to evaluate the rendering equation directly at image resolution, using the radiosity solution to provide the approximation of secondary illumination [192, 198]. This is a *two-pass* method, in which the solution to the transport equation is partially performed in a *view-independent* first pass and completed for a particular view in an *image-based* second pass. Two-pass methods are particularly useful in handling non-Lambertian reflection, as will be described in the next chapter, but they are potentially useful whenever some aspect of energy transport contributes a high spatial frequency to the image.

9.3.1 Evaluating the Radiosity Equation per Pixel

The radiosity for the surface seen at a particular pixel, p, is described by the integral radiosity equation,

$$B(\mathbf{x}_p) = E(\mathbf{x}_p) + \rho(\mathbf{x}_p) \int_S B(\mathbf{x}') G(\mathbf{x}_p, \mathbf{x}') \, dA' \qquad (9.8)$$

where $\mathbf{x}_p$ is the point in the environment visible at pixel p.

A radiosity solution provides an approximation $\hat{B}(x)$ that already takes into account multiple reflections between surfaces. In the methods described so far, this approximation has been used during rendering to determine radiances directly by interpolation. An alternative approach is to substitute the approximate radiosity solution $\hat{B}(\mathbf{x}')$ for $B(\mathbf{x}')$ inside the integral on the right-hand side of equation 9.8:

$$B(\mathbf{x}_p) = E(\mathbf{x}_p) + \rho(\mathbf{x}_p) \int_S \hat{B}(\mathbf{x}') G(\mathbf{x}_p, \mathbf{x}') \, dA' \qquad (9.9)$$

Instead of using $\hat{B}(\mathbf{x}')$ directly during rendering, this version of the integral is then evaluated at each pixel. In effect, the final bounce of light rays to the eye is computed at image resolution. This includes evaluating the geometric factor $G(\mathbf{x}_p, \mathbf{x}')$ at each pixel, meaning that shadows are also resolved to image resolution.

The decision to break the solution at this point may seem somewhat arbitrary, but it is a reasonable choice, since higher order reflections tend to contribute progressively less to the pixel variance [135]. High spatial frequencies in the radiance of surfaces that illuminate a diffusely reflecting surface are averaged during integration over the hemisphere of incoming directions. Intuitively, inaccuracies in small, high-contrast features of the radiosity function affect image quality much less dramatically in contributing to the illumination of other surfaces than when they are seen directly.

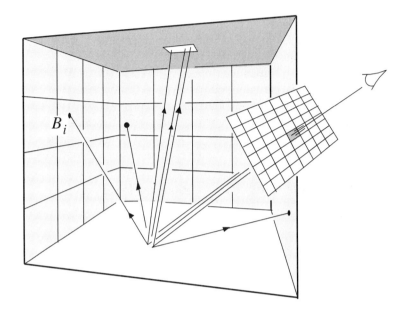

Figure 9.15: *Monte Carlo ray tracing, using the radiosity approximation to determine radiance for secondary rays.*

More generally, the computation of $B(\mathbf{x}_p)$ using equation 9.9 can be restricted to locations in the image where the visible element has been identified during the solution as liable to be inaccurate, according to any of the error metrics discussed in Chapters 6 and 7. In the hierarchical formulation of Chapter 7, one might go a step farther and only reevaluate the integral for specific interactions that involve partial visibility and a large amount of energy.

Evaluating the integral of equation 9.8 at each pixel requires considerable computation since it involves form factor type computations from the point $\mathbf{x}_p$. Most of the form factor algorithms discussed in Chapter 4 are applicable. Several algorithms using this approach are described in the following sections.

Monte Carlo Ray Tracing per Pixel

Rushmeier [198] describes a two-pass approach in which the first pass consists of a constant element radiosity solution. During the rendering pass the rendering equation is evaluated using Monte Carlo path tracing [135], with paths limited to one bounce (see Figure 9.15). Multiple rays are traced from the eye through each pixel into the scene. From the intersection point of each ray, a single ray is traced to a random point on a light source and a second ray is traced in a

Figure 9.16: *An image computed using Monte Carlo path tracing, with the radiosity solution supplying the radiance at secondary ray intersections. Courtesy of Holly E. Rushmeier, Program of Computer Graphics, Cornell University.*

random direction chosen with a probability proportional to the cosine of the angle measured from the normal.

The radiance at the point intersected by the secondary ray is obtained from the radiosity solution. If the secondary ray hits a light source, it must be counted as making a contribution of zero, since the sources are already accounted for by the ray to the light. The final pixel color resulting from n rays through the pixel is then

$$\frac{1}{n} \sum_{i=1}^{n} \rho(\mathbf{x}_i) \left(E(\mathbf{x}_i^L) + \hat{B}(\mathbf{x}_i^j) \right) \tag{9.10}$$

where the ith ray from the eye intersects the environment at $\mathbf{x}_i$, the secondary ray from $\mathbf{x}_i$ to a light intersects the source at $\mathbf{x}_i^L$ and the secondary ray reflected randomly from $\mathbf{x}_i$ intersects the environment at $\mathbf{x}_i^j$.

Rushmeier points out that meshing algorithms can be greatly simplified when the radiosity solution is no longer required to capture shading features like shadows in great detail. As with all Monte Carlo solutions, noisy images will occur if too few sample rays are used. Figure 9.16 shows an image computed using Rushmeier's algorithm.

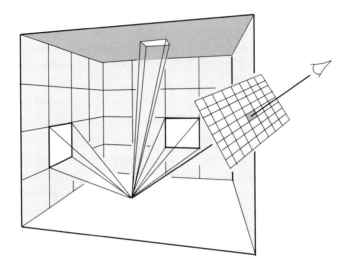

Figure 9.17: *Computing form factors to every element at every pixel to compute the final bounce of the radiosity equation.*

Form Factors per Pixel

In a two-pass method described by Reichert [192], the radiosity at each pixel is computed by evaluating a form factor to every element in the radiosity mesh (see Figure 9.17). This is ultimately less efficient than Rushmeier's Monte Carlo approach, since it computes a contribution from every element, regardless of its contribution to the pixel variance. For the same reason, however, this approach has the advantage of never missing an important source of illumination. Although expensive, it produces images of extremely high quality (see Figure 9.18.)

Reichert notes that although meshing requirements for the radiosity solution are less rigorous when the final bounce is evaluated at image resolution, sampling in image space can exacerbate certain types of errors. For example, the illumination provided by constant elements can cause shading artifacts for nearby receivers (see Figure 9.19 (a)). Similarly, coherent errors introduced by the form factor evaluation used at each pixel may create highly visible patterns in the image, as shown in Figure 9.19 (b), where form factors are computed with point sampling. Monte Carlo integration of the form factor may be preferable in this case since it will produce noise that is less objectionable than coherent errors.

Figure 9.18: *Image computed by evaluating form factors at each pixel to every element. Courtesy of Mark Reichert, Program of Computer Graphics, Cornell University.*

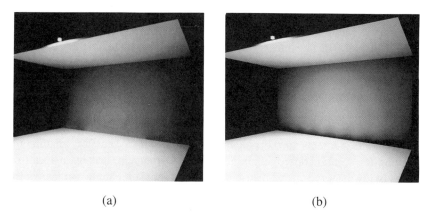

(a)   (b)

Figure 9.19: *(a) Artifacts caused by pixel-by-pixel form factor evaluation in proximity to large discontinuities in $\hat{B}$. The high gradients on the wall near the floor correspond to the boundaries of constant elements on the floor. (b) Artifacts caused by coherent errors in the form factor evaluation. Courtesy of Mark Reichert, Program of Computer Graphics, Cornell University.*

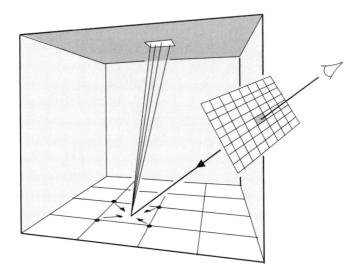

Figure 9.20: *Shooting rays to compute the direct component of illumination during rendering. The indirect component is interpolated from the radiosity solution.*

Direct Illumination per Pixel

It is not necessary in a two-pass method to integrate over all the elements that provide illumination. Typically only a few such elements contribute to high frequencies in the image. Integration can be limited to these elements, with the contribution of the remainder interpolated from the radiosity solution. Shirley [212] describes a two-pass method based on this approach in which only the contribution of direct illumination (illumination from light emitters) is recomputed by integration during rendering. Direct illumination typically arrives from small relatively high energy sources and is thus more likely to produce high gradients in the radiance function, which generally require fine sampling for accurate approximation. Indirect illumination usually arrives from relatively low energy sources distributed over a large solid angle and is thus less likely to create high gradients.

Shirley computes the indirect component of illumination in a first pass consisting of a modified progressive radiosity solution, during which the direct and indirect components are stored separately. In the second pass the direct component of the radiosity function is reevaluated at each image pixel using Monte Carlo sampling of the light emitters (see Figure 9.20). This is added to the indirect component interpolated from the radiosity mesh. An example, which also incorporates bump mapping and specular reflections, is shown in color plate 41.

Kok *al.* [141] describe a generalization of this approach in which illumination due to the most significant secondary reflectors as well as the emitters is recomputed during rendering, based on information gathered during the radiosity pass.

9.3.2 Multi-Pass Methods

Although two-pass methods take advantage of the view to focus computational effort, they have limitations. While two-pass approaches can account for high frequencies across surfaces with respect to the final reflection of light to the eye, they also assume that the global first pass radiosity solution is a sufficiently accurate approximation of the secondary illumination for the particular view. Two-pass methods provide no mechanism for recognizing when this assumption is violated and, when it is, for refining the first-pass solution accordingly. In splitting the solution into separate view-dependent and view-independent passes, two-pass methods explicitly break the connection that would ultimately allow automatic refinement of the solution to achieve an image of a specified accuracy. The importance meshing algorithm of Smits *et al.* [220] addresses this problem directly.

The *multi-pass* method described by Chen *et al.* [52] is a generalization of the two-pass method that offers another approach to overcoming this limitation. In the multi-pass algorithm, the radiosity solution is merely the initial step of a progressive rendering process. Over a sequence of steps the radiosity approximation is eventually replaced by a Monte Carlo solution at each pixel (with specular reflection also accounted for in later passes). The use of multiple steps allows finely tuned heuristics to be used to determine where and when to commit computational resources in creating an increasingly accurate image. However, care must be taken in designing a multi-pass method. In particular:

1. Redundant energy transport must be avoided. Each possible path for light transfer must be accounted for only once. This may require removing part of the radiance computed in an earlier pass before summing in a more accurate estimate. Transport paths are discussed in more detail in the Chapter 10.

2. Heuristics should be *unbiased*. In the limit, as more computational resources are used, the solution should always converge to the true solution. This is often a subtle and difficult aspect to assess.

Color plates 35–39 show the improvement of images with successive passes of Chen's algorithm.

9.4   Incorporating Surface Detail

In the discussion of the radiosity method so far it has been assumed that surface properties such as reflectivity are constant over each surface, or at least over the support of an individual basis function or element. This has allowed the reflectivity term to be moved outside the integral during the computation of the linear integral operator.

Surface detail is often simulated in image synthesis by using a *texture map* to specify the variation over the surface of properties such as reflectivity, transparency, or the surface normal. Techniques for incorporating texture mapping and bump mapping (mapping the surface normal) into radiosity algorithms are described in the next sections.

9.4.1   Texture Mapping

When surface reflectivity is specified by a texture map, the resulting shading typically contains very high spatial frequencies. These are difficult to represent adequately with a finite element approximation. As an alternative, during the radiosity solution the reflectivity ρ of a texture mapped surface can be approximated by the average texture reflectivity (the texture color), $\bar{\rho}$, over the support of a basis function. This is a reasonable assumption in most cases, since high frequency variations in radiance are averaged together during integration.[4]

During rendering, computing the radiosity at a particular point on a texture mapped surface requires knowing the incident energy (irradiance) at that point. This is computed explicitly in the two-pass methods previously discussed, and texture maps are handled trivially in such methods. However, even if the radiosities are interpolated from the solution, it is still possible to extract an approximation of the incident energy.

For elements on a texture mapped surface, the nodal radiosities will have been computed using an average reflectivity, $\bar{\rho}$. When rendering the texture mapped surface, the radiosity $\hat{B}(\mathbf{x}_p)$ at any pixel can be modified to include the reflectivity at $\mathbf{x}_p$ specified by the texture map:

$$\hat{B}(\mathbf{x}_p, \rho(\mathbf{x}_p)) \;=\; \hat{B}(\mathbf{x}_p, \bar{\rho}) \, \frac{\rho(\mathbf{x}_p)}{\bar{\rho}} \tag{9.11}$$

The radiosity is simply multiplied by the texture mapped reflectivity for the pixel over the average reflectivity [61]. This effectively undoes the multiplication of

---

[4]This assumption can be violated when a texture mapped surface containing large scale variations in color is located near another surface. For example, a floor with a black and white tile pattern may produce noticeable shading variations on the wall near the floor due to light reflected from the tiles.

the incident energy by the average reflectivity $\bar{\rho}$ that was performed during the solution and then multiplies the incident energy by the reflectivity $\rho(\mathbf{x}_p)$ specified for that location by the texture map. The paintings in Color Plates 10, 13, 17, and 22 as well as the floor tiles in color plate 45 are texture maps incorporated into the image using this technique.

It is also possible to combine texture mapping with radiosity using hardware accelerators that support texture mapping. This is discussed in section 9.7, where the details of rendering radiosity using hardware graphics accelerators are described.

9.4.2 Bump Mapping

A *bump map* represents variations in the surface normal using an array of values mapped to the surface, analogously to a texture map. Like texture maps, bump maps generally produce shading with high spatial frequencies. Hence, by nature, bump maps are best handled by per-pixel shaders. Two-pass methods handle bump maps in a straightforward manner by using the perturbed normal at each pixel during the view pass when computing the final radiosity. The image by Shirley (color plate 41), includes a bump mapped brick pattern that was added during the rendering pass [213].

It is also possible to support bump mapping when interpolation is used for rendering. During the solution, instead of computing a single radiosity value at each node, the variation of radiosity with surface orientation at the node is sampled by computing independent radiosity values for several surface normals distributed over the hemisphere. During rendering, the perturbed normal at a particular pixel is determined from the bump map. For each of the element nodes, the radiosity corresponding to that orientation is interpolated from the hemisphere sampling, and the radiosity at the pixel is bilinearly interpolated from these nodal values.

Chen [49] implements this algorithm by applying the hemicube gathering approach. A single hemicube is computed at each node. The form factors for each sampled surface orientation are computed from this hemicube by resumming the delta form factors, which are modified from the usual values to correspond to the new surface orientation. Chen samples 16 surface orientations at each node.

9.5 Mapping Radiosities to Pixel Colors

Having finally computed a radiance at every pixel, the remaining rendering step consists of assigning a corresponding frame buffer pixel value, typically an integer in the range of 0 to 255. If color is desired, the radiosity solution will have been computed at several wavelengths, and the mapping will include a transformation to the red–green–blue (RGB) color space of the monitor. The monochrome issues will be addressed first, followed by a short discussion of color.

The ultimate goal is to construct an image that creates the same sensation in the viewer as would be experienced in viewing the real environment. As discussed in the introductory chapter, there are many obstacles to realizing this ideal, most of which are not unique to image synthesis. These include the nonlinear relationship between voltage and luminance in the display device, the restricted range of luminance values available on the display, limited color gamut, the ambient lighting conditions under which the image is viewed, as well as the basic limitations of representing three-dimensional reality as a projection onto a two-dimensional image plane.[5]

9.5.1   Gamma Correction

The first difficulty encountered is that monitors, in general, do not provide a linear relationship between the value specified at a frame buffer pixel (which determines the voltage of the electron gun at that pixel) and the resulting screen radiance. Rather, the radiance, I, is related to voltage, V, by [84],

$$I = kV^\gamma \tag{9.12}$$

The value of γ varies between monitors, but is usually about 2.4 ± 0.2. Thus

$$V = (\frac{I}{k})^{\frac{1}{\gamma}} \tag{9.13}$$

Therefore, assuming that the target radiance is in the available dynamic range of the monitor, a voltage must be selected from the available discrete voltages, V_j, using

$$V_j = round(\frac{I}{k})^{\frac{1}{\gamma}} \tag{9.14}$$

The adjustments for the nonlinear relationship between voltage and radiance through the use of the exponent, $1/\gamma$, is called *gamma correction*.

9.5.2   Real-World Luminance to Pixel Luminance

A more challenging problem is the limited dynamic range of the display device. Luminance values experienced in the real-world range from 10^{-5} cd/meter^2 (star-lit forest floor) to 10^5 cd/meter^2 (sun reflected off snow). In contrast, a typical CRT can display luminances in the range of only 1 to 100 cd/meter^2. It is therefore necessary to map the values produced by the radiosity simulation to the

---

[5]These issues are covered in much greater detail in Hall's monograph [114].

range available on the CRT. The goal is to produce a subjective impression of *brightness* in viewing the image on a CRT that is equivalent to that experienced in viewing the real environment.

One simple approach is to map the luminance values in the radiosity solution linearly to the luminance range of the monitor. Unfortunately, the only thing visible in images produced using a linear mapping will usually be the light source, since its luminance is typically several orders of magnitude greater than that of any reflecting surface. Radiosity implementations often get around this by mapping the highest *reflected* luminance (as opposed to the light sources) to slightly less than the maximum pixel value and set the light sources themselves to the maximum value. The "slightly less" ensures that light sources appear brighter than any reflecting surface.

This mapping is completely arbitrary, and it is thus difficult to judge from the image what the appearance of the real environment might be under equivalent lighting conditions. Tumblin and Rushmeier [238] demonstrate this using the example of a room illuminated by a light emitting with the power of a firefly versus a room illuminated by a light with the same geometry, but with the power of a searchlight. Because of the linearity of the integral operator in the rendering or radiosity equations, scaling each resulting luminance range by the maximum reflected luminance will produce identical images!

What is required is a *tone reproduction operator*, which will transform luminances to frame buffer values in such a way that the perceived brightness of the image equals that experienced by a hypothetical observer viewing a real scene having the same luminances. Tumblin and Rushmeier derive such an operator from simple models of the display and viewing processes. Their work is a good example of how a model of perception might be incorporated into image synthesis.

Figure 9.21 contains a diagram of the processes of perceiving real-world and synthesized scenes. In the real-world, the luminance of the scene, L_{rw}, is received by the eye and converted to a subjective perceived brightness, B_{rw}.[6] This is represented by the real world observer, which transforms luminance to brightness under the conditions of viewing in the real world.

For a simulated scene, the computed luminance (which is assumed to closely approximate the real-world luminance, L_{rw}), is mapped to a frame buffer pixel value, V, (assumed here to be a number ranging from 0.0 to 1.0) by the tone reproduction operator, which is to be derived. The pixel value is then transformed by the display operator to a displayed luminance, L_{disp}. Finally, displayed lu-

---

[6]Luminance measures light energy in terms of the sensitivity of a standard human eye, and is computed by integrating the spectral radiance weighted by the luminous efficiency curve for the eye over the visual spectrum (see Chapter 2). Brightness is a measure of the subjective sensation created by light.

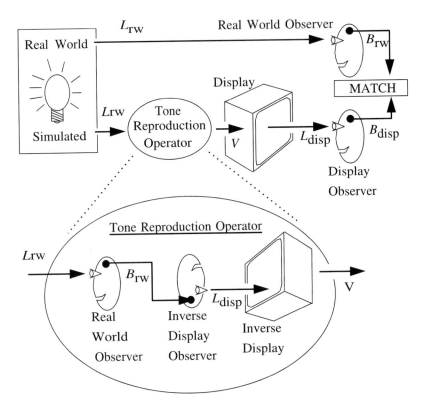

Figure 9.21: *The goal is to match the perception.*

minance is transformed to perceived brightness, B_{disp}, through the process of perception by the observer. This is represented by the display observer, which transforms luminance to brightness under the conditions of viewing a CRT.

The goal is to derive a tone reproduction operator that makes B_{disp} as close to B_{rw} as possible. Such an operator can be constructed using the concatenation of three operators:

1. the real-world observer, (i.e., the perceptual transformation from simulated luminance, L_{rw}, to brightness, B_{rw}),

2. the *inverse* of the display observer, (i.e., the transformation of B_{disp} to L_{disp}), and

3. the *inverse* of the display device operator, (i.e., the transformation from display luminance, L_{disp}, to the required pixel value, V).

Applying these three operators in sequence transforms the simulated luminance to a pixel value that can be sent to the frame buffer. The inverse operators in this sequence effectively undo the subsequent application of the display and observer operators in advance, thus making the net overall transformation from simulated luminance to perceived brightness equivalent to applying only the real world observer. Since the real world observer transforms L_{rw} to B_{rw}, the result is the desired match.

Tumblin and Rushmeier formulate the above real-world and display observer operators using an observer model based on the work of Stevens [225]. Stevens' model expresses the relationship between luminance, L_{in}, and perceived brightness B by

$$\log_{10} B = \alpha(L_w) \log_{10}(L_{in}) + \beta(L_w) \quad (9.15)$$

where α and β account for the observer's adaptation to the overall image luminance, L_w. This equation provides the model for both the real-world observer and the display observer, with different α and β in each case corresponding to the adaptation levels for the different viewing conditions. The α and β parameters are given by

$$\alpha(L_w) = 0.41 \log_{10}(L_w) + 2.92$$
$$\beta(L_w) = -0.41 \left(\log_{10}(L_w)\right)^2 + \left(-2.584 \log_{10} L_w\right) + 2.0208 \quad (9.16)$$

where L_w approximates the average overall luminance of the viewed real world scene in one case and of the synthesized image in the other.

The display operator is expressed in terms of the contrast between a displayed luminance L_{disp} and the maximum displayable luminance L_{dmax}:

$$\frac{L_{disp}}{L_{dmax}} = V^\gamma + \frac{1}{C_{max}} \quad (9.17)$$

where V is the pixel value in the frame buffer, and C_{max} is the *maximum contrast* between onscreen luminances. The γ in V^γ is the gamma term for video display described earlier. The $1/C_{max}$ term accounts for the effect of ambient light falling on the screen on image contrast. The C_{max} term is defined by the ratio of brightest to dimmest pixels, typically a value of about $35 : 1$.

Combining equations 9.15 and 9.17 and inverting them where called for, a single operator is derived that takes a luminance, L_{rw}, to a pixel value, V:

$$V = \left[\frac{L_{rw}^{\alpha_{rw}/\alpha_{disp}}}{L_{dmax}} 10^{(\beta_{rw} - \beta_{disp})/\alpha_{disp}} - \frac{1}{C_{max}}\right]^{1/\gamma} \quad (9.18)$$

This relation maps the results of the global illumination simulation into a "best" choice of pixel values, thus providing the last step in the image synthesis process.

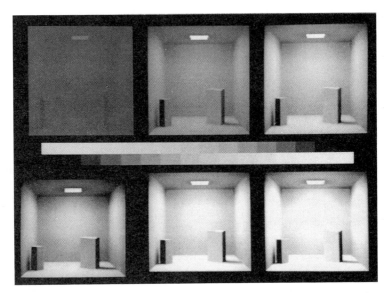

Figure 9.22: *Images produced after accounting for brightnesses and viewer adaptation based on work by Tumblin and Rushmeier. Light source intensities range from 10^{-5} lamberts to 10^3 lamberts in geometrically increasing steps by 100. Coutesy of Jack Tumblin, Georgia Institute of Technology.*

The advantage of using equation 9.18 is demonstrated in Figure 9.22 for a model in which the light source ranges in intensity from 10^{-5} lamberts to 10^3 lamberts in geometrically increasing steps. Linear scaling would generate the lower left image no matter what the light source energy. Using Tumblin and Rushmeier's tone reproduction operator, the sequence successfully (and automatically) reproduces the subjective impression of increasingly bright illumination.

If hardware rendering is used to create the image, it will obviously be impossible to perform a sophisticated mapping to the radiosity at every pixel. Instead, the nodal radiosities will have to be transformed before they are sent to the hardware as polygon vertex colors. The result will differ somewhat from the foregoing, since the pixel values in this case will be obtained by linear interpolation from the mapped values, while the mapping itself is nonlinear.

As Tumblin and Rushmeier point out, the observer model upon which this operator is based simplifies what is in reality a very complex and not completely understood phenomenon. For example, color adaptation is ignored. There is also the question of what adaptation luminance to use in computing the α and β terms. Tumblin and Rushmeier use a single average value over the view or screen, but further research might explore whether or not the adaptation level should be considered constant over the field of view.

However, this work is an important step toward quantifying the perceptual stage of the image synthesis process. The significance of such quantitative models lies in their ultimate incorporation into the error metrics that guide the solution refinement. Current metrics, for example, may force mesh refinement in regions that are bright and washed out in the image, and thus contain little visible detail. The goal of a perceptually based error metric would be to focus computational effort on aspects of the solution only to the extent that they affect image quality.

9.6   Color

The topic of color has been ignored in the previous chapters partly because it is a complex topic in its own right, and partially because it is not integral to the explanation of the radiosity method. Each of the issues addressed in the earlier chapters is valid (with a few provisos[7]), for a full color world as well as a monochrome one. The geometric quantities such as the form factor are independent of material properties like color. The solution process is independent of color in as much as a separate solution can be performed for each wavelength or color band of interest.

A full description of color and color perception cannot be provided here. Instead, interested readers are referred to a number of excellent sources for more detail [156]. Valuable information from researchers in image synthesis can be found in [114, 166].

Questions of immediate interest addressed in this section are,

- What and how many wavelengths or color bands should be used in the radiosity solution?

- Can a single scalar value be used for error criteria, and if so, how is a reasonable achromatic value derived from the color model?

- How can one transform values between color models to finally derive RGB pixel values?

The following sections outline properties of human color perception and how these relate to the selection of *color models*. A color model provides a framework to specify the color of light sources and reflective surfaces. Color

---

[7]One assumption in this process is that light of one wavelength is not reflected at another. With the exception of fluorescent materials, this assumption is not violated. It has also been assumed that light that is absorbed is not reemitted in the visible spectrum. This again is true at "normal" temperatures.

models are used at three stages in the radiosity simulation: (1) as part of the description of the environment to be rendered, (2) during the radiosity solution, and (3) during the creation of the final image on the output device. The same or different color models may be used at each of these stages. Different color models and means to transform values between them are discussed below.

The selection of a color model for the radiosity solution depends on the required accuracy of the color reproduction and available information about the lights and surfaces contained in the input to the simulation. For example, if colors are input in terms of red, green, and blue components, then the simulation can proceed by computing red, green, and blue radiosity values at each node. The results can then be mapped directly to the RGB phosphors on a CRT based on the specific properties of the monitor. However, this simple RGB color model contains inherent limitations that make it difficult or impossible to reproduce exactly the subtleties of color in the real-world. A fuller description of the visible energy (light) at each point requires a specification of the energy at all wavelengths in the visible spectrum. If a full (or sampled) spectrum of the emitted energy of light sources and of the reflectivity of materials is available, methodologies can be developed that lead to more accurate color simulations.

9.6.1   Human Vision and Color

The normal human eye is sensitive to electromagnetic radiation (light) at wavelengths between approximately 380 and 770 nanometers. The familiar rainbow presents the spread of the visible spectrum from the short (blue) to the long (red) wavelengths. Light leaving a surface and entering the eye will generally contain some energy at all wavelengths in the visible spectrum. The relative amounts of energy at each wavelength determine the color we see. For example, equal amounts of energy at all wavelengths produce a sensation of white light.

It might at first seem that producing an accurate color image would require reproducing the complete details of the energy across the visible spectrum, in other words, the amount of energy at each wavelength at each point on the environment's surfaces.

Fortunately for the image synthesis process the human visual system greatly simplifies the problem. Experiments have shown that very different energy spectra can produce identical color sensations. Two different spectra that produce the same sensation are called *metamers*. The reasons for this phenomenon and the way in which this fact can be taken advantage of in the image synthesis process are discussed below.

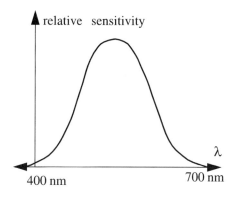

Figure 9.23: *Luminous efficiency function.*

Luminous Efficiency Function

The eye is not equally sensitive to light of different wavelengths even within the visible portion of the electromagnetic spectrum. The *luminous efficiency function* (see Figure 9.23) describes the eye's sensitivity to light of various wavelengths and can be used to convert between *radiance*, which is independent of perceptual phenomena, and the perceptual quantity, *luminance*.[8]

Thus, when working in an achromatic context (black and white), it is best to multiply the energy spectrum by the luminous efficiency function to obtain a scalar luminance value that can be displayed as a gray value or used as a decision variable for element subdivision. As will be discussed below, certain color models contain one channel devoted to carrying achromatic luminance information and are thus a convenient model for image synthesis. Scalar luminance values can also be derived from sampled wavelength-based models by weighting the energy at each sample wavelength by the corresponding value in luminous efficiency function.

Color Sensitivity

Color perception results from receptors in the eye called *cones*. It has been found that normal human eyes have only three types of cones, each with distinct responses to light across the visible spectrum (see Figure 9.24). One type of cone is sensitive primarily to short (S) wavelengths, one to medium (M) wavelengths, and the other to longer (L) wavelengths. Color blindness is believed to be caused

---

[8]The corresponding units of measure from the fields of radiometry and photometry are discussed in Chapter 2.

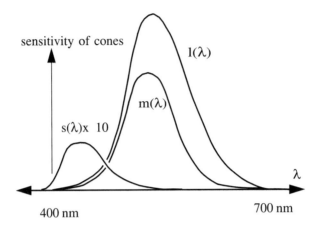

Figure 9.24: *Response of three color cones in eye (after Meyer, 1986).*

by a deficiency in one or more of the three cone types. It is the response of colorblind individuals to color that has provided much of the evidence of the three distinct color cones.

The fact that color perception appears to be a function of only three stimulus values provides the basis for metamerism. If two light spectra, when integrated against the cone response functions, result in the same three values, then the human eye is unable to distinguish between them. This is the root of metamerism and is of great help in image synthesis since it provides a basis to produce a wide range of color sensations by combining only a very few sources. In particular, combinations of light produced by the red, green, and blue phosphors of the typical CRT can recreate most possible color sensations.

9.6.2   Color Matching Functions and the CIE Chromaticity Diagram

Given the above observation, a three dimensional *color space* can be organized. Experiments, as depicted in Figure 9.25, have been conducted in which an observer is shown light from a monochromatic (single wavelength) test source, and is simultaneously shown the combined light from three other monochromatic sources or *primaries* chosen at short, medium, and long (s, m, l) wavelengths. The observer is allowed to adjust the (s, m, l) primaries until there is a match. One can then plot the resulting amounts of the three primaries as the test source wavelength is varied across the visible spectrum resulting in three *color matching functions*, $(s(\lambda), m(\lambda), l(\lambda))$. Although most test sources can be matched by a positive combination of the three adjustable sources, some cannot be matched. In this case, the observer is allowed to move one of the three primaries to the left

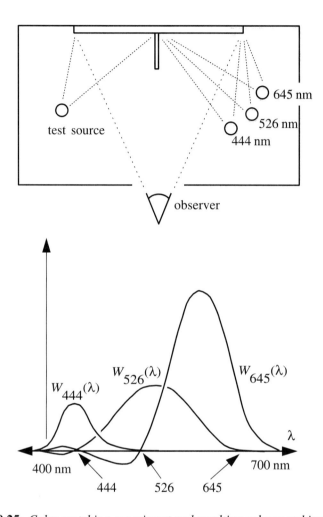

Figure 9.25: *Color matching experiment and resulting color matching functions.*

side and add it to the test source. This quantity is then counted as a "negative" amount of that primary.

The three resulting matching functions now provide all the information required to match not only the monochromatic test sources, but any combination of energy across the spectrum. A general spectrum $E(\lambda)$ can be represented with a linear combination of the primaries (s, m, l) given by

$$E(\lambda) = S * s + M * m + L * l \tag{9.19}$$

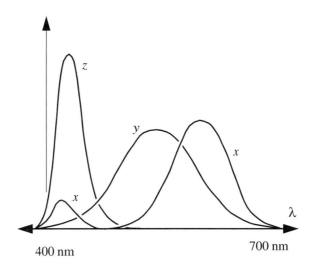

Figure 9.26: *CIE standard observer matching functions.*

where

$$S = \int E(\lambda)\, s(\lambda)\, d\lambda$$

$$M = \int E(\lambda)\, m(\lambda)\, d\lambda \qquad (9.20)$$

$$L = \int E(\lambda)\, l(\lambda)\, d\lambda$$

In fact, the three matching functions can be replaced by any three independent linear combinations of the original three matching functions, resulting in a new *color space* defined by new matching functions. These can be used in exactly the same way as the results of the original matching experiment.

A commonly used set of matching functions was developed in 1931 by the *Commission Internationale de l'Éclairage* (CIE) based on the "standard observer's" matching functions. The CIE functions, $x(\lambda)$, $y(\lambda)$, and $z(\lambda)$, are shown in Figure 9.26. These were chosen such that the XYZ color space contains all possible spectra in the positive octant and $y(\lambda)$ corresponds to the luminous efficiency function.

Figure 9.27 shows the CIE XYZ color space. A *direction* emanating from the origin in this space represents all multiples of a particular linear combination of the three matching functions. Within the limits discussed in section 9.5, the points along a line from the origin will all produce the same color sensation at different brightnesses. The horseshoe-shaped curve indicates the directions in the space corresponding to the set of monochromatic sources (i.e., the rainbow)

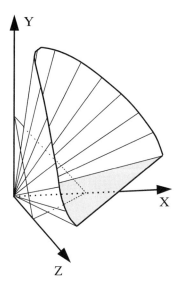

Figure 9.27: *The CIE XYZ color space with cone of realizable color.*

from approximately 400 to 700 nanometers. Any point (X, Y, Z) lying within this *cone of realizable color* represents some linear combination of visible light.[9]

The triangle $(X + Y + Z = 1)$ is also shown. A *chromaticity diagram* can be constructed by projecting the set of points on this triangle onto the XY plane. A point on this projection (x, y) represents a vector $\overline{(X, Y, Z)}$ where

$$x = \frac{X}{X+Y+Z}$$

$$y = \frac{Y}{X+Y+Z}$$

$$(9.21)$$

Figure 9.28 shows this projection including the location of the red, green, and blue phosphors of a typical CRT. All possible colors on a CRT (the monitor's *gamut*) include only linear combinations of the RGB phosphors, which explains why not all colors can be reproduced. In particular, it is impossible to display saturated yellow-green colors on a CRT.

The CRT is also constrained by the dynamic range of the phosphors, as was described earlier. Figure 9.29 shows the CRT's RGB color space and its transformation into the XYZ color space. All possible colors on a CRT thus lie within the skewed cube shown.

---

[9]A point outside the cone of realizable color simply does not exist, as it would require a negative amount of light at some set of wavelengths.

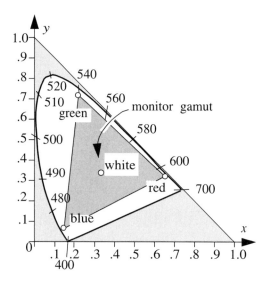

Figure 9.28: *The CIE XYZ chromaticity diagram.*

The transformation between XYZ and RGB spaces depends on the specific phosphors of the monitor in question. Details of how to measure the phosphors can be found in [114]. The NTSC transformation for a generic or *standard* monitor is given by

$$\begin{bmatrix} X \\ Y \\ Z \end{bmatrix} = \begin{bmatrix} 0.67 & 0.21 & 0.14 \\ 0.33 & 0.71 & 0.08 \\ 0.00 & 0.08 & 0.78 \end{bmatrix} \begin{bmatrix} R \\ G \\ B \end{bmatrix} \tag{9.22}$$

The approximate inverse is

$$\begin{bmatrix} R \\ G \\ B \end{bmatrix} = \begin{bmatrix} 1.730 & -0.482 & -0.261 \\ -0.814 & 1.652 & -0.023 \\ 0.083 & -0.169 & 1.284 \end{bmatrix} \begin{bmatrix} X \\ Y \\ Z \end{bmatrix} \tag{9.23}$$

Hall [114] provides an appendix with code for this and other transformations between color spaces.

9.6.3   Color Spaces and Image Synthesis

Given an understanding of color perception and representation, one is left with the question of how handle color in an image synthesis system. The above sections have discussed color in terms of a number of color spaces, including

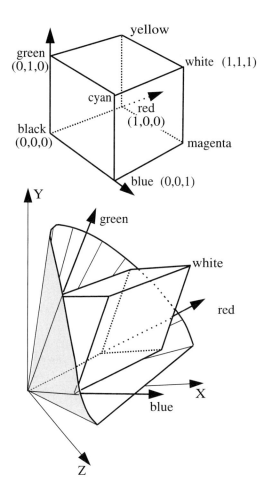

Figure 9.29: *RGB cube and monitor gamut within the CIE XYZ color space.*

- Wavelength: the full visible spectrum includes an infinite number of individual wavelengths. However, a finite number of discrete wavelengths can be used to define a finite dimensional color space.

- RGB: the red, green, and blue phosphor values.

- CIE XYZ: a standard color space based on color matching functions.

Other color spaces exist for a variety of reasons. The YIQ space is designed primarily for television with the Y channel carrying luminance. A color space based on cyan, magenta, and yellow (CMY) is used for printing since inks *subtract* light. Thus, in this context, CMY is complementary to the RGB space. Hue, saturation, and value (HSV) and hue, lightness, and saturation (HLS) spaces are also used for their direct mapping to human subjective descriptions of color. Other color systems have been developed to attempt to create linear color spaces in a perceptual sense through nonlinear transformations of the earlier-mentioned primaries. These additional color spaces will not be discussed here as they are not generally used for image synthesis directly. However, many computer-aided design systems use them. For each color space, a transformation to the XYZ space can be found.

Any of the three color spaces can be used for radiosity computations. The solution step, for example the Gauss-Seidel or Southwell iterations discussed in Chapter 5 or the **PushPull** steps in the hierarchical solutions of Chapter 7, must be repeated for each dimension (or channel) of the selected color space.[10] Independent of the choice of color space, the values should be stored in a floating point format or a large enough integer format to handle many orders of magnitude. The reason for this lies in the nonlinear response of the eye to light. Thus, the transformation to one-byte (0–255) phosphor values should only take place at the final display stage.

Conceptually, using an RGB color space throughout the image synthesis process is simplest and requires no intermediate processing after converting light source and reflection spectra into RGB. In fact, many CAD modeling systems only allow specification of color in terms of RGB. However, this immediately restricts the possible colors for both lights and reflective surfaces to the monitor's gamut. In addition, accounting for differences from monitor to monitor is very difficult to incorporate into such a system.

The limitations of the RGB space would argue for a display independent color space such as the CIE XYZ space. An additional argument for such a system as the CIE XYZ is that the Y channel can be used directly as a measure of luminance and thus provides a simple criteria for error metrics in decisions such as element subdivision. In fact, one might choose to perform all radiosity computations only on the Y channel until element subdivision has completed. The X and Z channels can then be processed based on the final element mesh. However, any three-dimensional coordinate space requires an a priori integration of the reflection and light source emission spectra. This can cause inaccuracies as light from one wavelength will influence another through this prefiltering operation.

---

[10]It is worth repeating that the form factor computations are independent of color and thus only need to be computed once.

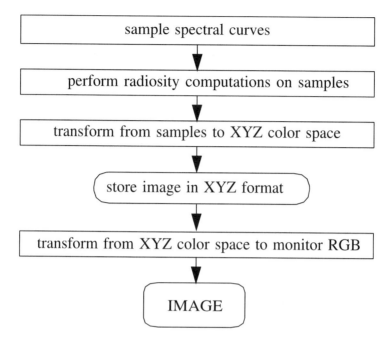

Figure 9.30: *Color computations from reflection–emission spectra to image.*

9.6.4 Direct Use of Spectral Data

Meyer argues for the use of a set of samples at discrete wavelengths as the primary color space [166]. This involves selecting specific wavelengths at which to sample the reflection and emission spectra, performing the radiosity solution at each sample wavelength, and then reconstructing the spectrum or directly converting them to the CIE XYZ (see Figure 9.30). The XYZ to RGB conversion can then be done for display on a particular monitor. The number and wavelengths of the sample of the visible spectrum should be based on perceptual data. The larger the number of sample wavelengths chosen to represent the reflectivity and emission spectra, the closer the approximation. However, since each sample wavelength requires a separate solution step, the larger the number of samples, the higher the computational cost. After a careful study of experimental data (see the experiment outlined in Chapter 11), Meyer concludes that four samples can in most cases provide a good balance of cost and accuracy. In particular, given a choice of only four sample wavelengths—456.4, 490.9, 557.7, and 631.4 nanometers—were shown statistically to produce the most accurate simulations when observers were asked to compare synthesized images of the Macbeth ColorChecker Charts with the real charts. The XYZ components are then found by weighting the energies at each wavelength, as follows:

$$
\begin{bmatrix} X \\ Y \\ Z \end{bmatrix} = \begin{bmatrix} 0.1986 & -0.0569 & 0.4934 & 0.4228 \\ -0.0034 & 0.1856 & 0.6770 & 0.1998 \\ 0.9632 & 0.0931 & 0.0806 & -0.0791 \end{bmatrix} \begin{bmatrix} E_{456.4} \\ E_{490.9} \\ E_{557.7} \\ E_{631.4} \end{bmatrix}
$$
(9.24)

Light sources characterized by spectra with one or more narrow bands will cause problems in systems that rely on discrete wavelength sampling; however, most reflectors exhibit smooth reflection spectra. The details of the derivations and experimentation in Meyer's studies are not repeated here. A set of C code implementations can be found in the appendices of Hall's book [114].

9.7   Hardware Accelerated Rendering

9.7.1   Walkthroughs

If views of the radiosity solution can be rendered quickly enough, an interactive walkthrough of the shaded environment is possible. Airey [5] reports that the sensation of interaction requires at least six frames per second. Thus, radiosity solutions are often rendered using hardware graphics accelerators, in spite of the limitations of Gouraud shading discussed earlier. This section provides a short discussion of some of the practical issues with the use of hardware graphics accelerators for radiosity rendering.

The basic approach is to define a view camera, then pass each element in the mesh to the graphics accelerator as a polygon with a color at each vertex corresponding to the (scaled) nodal radiosity. Light sources are turned off during the rendering, since the radiosity simulation has precomputed the shading. If the use of mesh primitives (e.g., triangular strip, quadrilateral mesh or polyhedron) is supported by the hardware, they can be used instead of individual polygons to speed up rendering further. The basic flow of data to the graphics pipeline is shown in Figure 9.31.

It is straightforward to add specular highlights during hardware rendering. In this case, one or more light sources are turned on, approximating the positions of the light sources used during the solution. Specular colors and the Phong coefficient are defined as appropriate as the elements are passed down the pipeline. Where the original geometry was defined with vertex normals, these should be interpolated to the nodes and passed along with the other vertex data for each element. The diffuse color of all polygons should be set to zero, since the radiosities at each vertex provide the diffuse component. Depending on the hardware shading equation, it may be necessary to turn on the ambient light source so that the vertex colors are included in the shading equation.

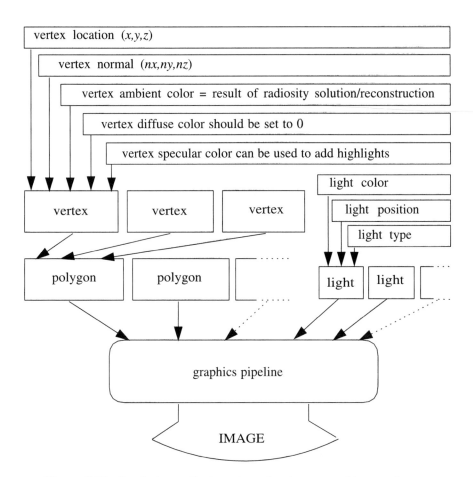

Figure 9.31: *Rendering radiosity using a hardware graphics accelerator.*

9.7.2 Hardware-Supported Texture Mapping

Some hardware graphics accelerators support texture mapping. During rendering, data describing the texture map is passed to the accelerator, followed by the polygons to which it applies. The mapping of the texture to the surface is often specified by supplying a texture coordinate, (u, v), at each polygon vertex. During rendering, the u, v coordinates are interpolated to each scanline pixel (typically using Gouraud interpolation). The u, v coordinate at the pixel is used to look up the color defined by the texture map for that surface location. This color is then incorporated into the hardware shading equation.

Depending on how the texture color is incorporated into the shading equation, it can be possible to apply texture mapping to polygons that have been shaded using radiosity. The goal is to have the shadows and other shading variations computed by radiosity appear on the texture mapped surface. For this to work, the hardware shading equation must multiply the texture color at a pixel by the color interpolated from the polygon vertices. The polygon vertex colors can then be used to represent the *incident* energy at the element nodes, with the texture color representing the reflectivity of the surface. As described in Chapter 2, the incident energy at a node can be obtained by dividing the radiosity at the node by the surface reflectivity used during solution (usually the average color of the texture map). The product of the incident energy and the reflectivity determined from the texture map then gives the reflected energy or radiosity at the pixel.

If u, v texture coordinates are defined at the original polygon vertices, they will have to be interpolated to the element nodes during meshing. During rendering the vertex u, v coordinates and vertex colors corresponding to the incident energy are then passed down to the hardware for each element.

9.7.3   Visibility Preprocessing

Even with hardware acceleration, an adequate frame rate may be unattainable for models containing tens or hundreds of thousands of polygons, particularly after the polygons have been meshed. Models of this size are not uncommon in architectural applications.

Airey [5] proposes an approach to accelerating hardware rendering that is particularly appropriate to building interiors, where only a fraction of the model is potentially visible from any particular room. Airey uses a visibility preprocess to produce candidate sets of the polygons potentially visible from each room. A candidate set includes the polygons inside the room, as well as those visible through *portals* (typically doorways) connecting the room with other rooms. During rendering only the candidate set for the room containing the eye point needs to be passed to the hardware renderer. The preprocess is simplified by allowing the candidate list to overestimate the list of potentially visible polygons, since the hardware renderer makes the ultimate determination of visibility at each pixel. Airey's algorithm uses point sampling to determine the candidate list, and thus may miss candidate polygons.

Teller describes an algorithm that can produce reliable candidate lists in two dimensions [234] and Funkhouser *et al.* [89] discuss the use of this technique to support walkthroughs of a model containing over 400,000 polygons. For the three-dimensional case, Teller [233] gives an efficient algorithm to determine the volume visible to an observer looking through a sequence of transparent convex holes or portals connecting adjacent cells in a spatial subdivision. Only objects inside this volume are potentially visible to the observer. The details of this algorithm are beyond the scope of this book. However, the reader is encouraged to investigate this work as it introduces a number of concepts and techniques of potential value to future research.

In addition to the development of candidate sets for visibility, interactive rates can sometimes be maintained by displaying a lower detail environment. If the mesh is stored hierarchically, a low-resolution version of the mesh can be displayed while the view is changing rapidly, and then replaced with a high-resolution version when the user rests at a certain view [5].

Chapter 10

Extensions

Radiosity demonstrates the potential power of finite element methods for global illumination calculations, at least in the case of environments consisting of Lambertian diffuse reflectors. Given this success, it is natural to ask whether this approach might be generalized to handle a wider variety of global illumination phenomena.

In Chapter 2, the radiosity equation is derived from a general model of light energy transport by restricting the problem in various ways. For example, diffraction, polarization, and fluorescence are ignored, on the assumption that these make only small, specialized contributions to everyday visual experience. Light is assumed to move with infinite speed, so that the system is in a steady state. Scattering and absorption by the transport medium (e.g., the air) are disregarded. Most importantly, the directional dependency of the bidirectional reflectance distribution function (BRDF) is eliminated by limiting the model to Lambertian diffuse reflection.

Although computationally convenient, some of these assumptions are too restrictive for general-purpose image synthesis. This chapter presents approaches to lifting the restrictions to Lambertian diffuse reflection and nonparticipating media. Specialized light emitters, such as point lights, spot lights, and sky or natural light, are also discussed in the context of a radiosity solution.

10.1 Nondiffuse Light Sources

Perhaps the simplest extension to the basic radiosity method is to allow light sources to emit with a non-Lambertian diffuse distribution. The simplicity of this extension derives from the fact that lights are normally predefined. Lights are also typically treated as emitters only (i.e., they do not reflect light). However, difficulties are created by the variety of light sources in common use, each of which requires subtly different handling.

Computer graphics applications use a variety of ad hoc and physically based light sources. These include

- Isotropic Point light: light emanates from a point with equal radiant intensity in all directions. The flux density falls off according to $1/r^2$.

- Parallel light: the light source is at infinity in a particular direction. Thus, the flux density is constant. Direct sunlight can be approximated using a parallel light.

- Spot light: light emanates from a point with a variable intensity that falls off from a maximum as the direction deviates from a given axis.

- General luminaires: light emanates from a point or area according to a general distribution function defined either by a *goniometric diagram* (see Figure 10.1 (d)), often available from lighting manufacturers [3], or by an analytic functional form.

- Sky light: light emanates from a hemisphere representing the sky, possibly accounting for weather conditions and solar position (but not the sun itself).

General light emitters are discussed in the context of a ray tracing algorithm in [243]. General luminaires and/or sky light have been incorporated into radiosity applications in [74, 144, 176].

Although conceptually simple, the inclusion of more general light emitters into a radiosity solution requires some care, particularly with regard to units and normalization. In previous chapters, emission has been specified in units of energy/unit area/unit time (or power/area). Since point and parallel sources have no area, they will require different units. Normalization relates to the problem of defining the total power of a spot (or more general) light independently of the width of the spot beam or the shape of the intensity distribution.

The following discussion will assume constant basis functions, but the basic concepts apply equally to higher order basis functions.

10.1.1   Form Factors to and from Light Sources

With the assumption of Lambertian diffuse area light sources, the rows and columns corresponding to the light source in the approximate integral operator **K** are derived in a similar fashion to entries for reflectors. However, light sources are usually assumed not to be reflecting surfaces. Thus, if the ith element is a light source, the ith row of the matrix, $K_{i,*}$, contains all zeros except for a one on the diagonal (since $\rho_i = 0$). The entries of the ith column, $K_{*,i}$ will, in general, not be zeros. These will be the terms responsible for *shooting* the light to the receiving elements.

Point or parallel sources obscure the intuitive definition of the form factor somewhat, since they have no area. For the same reason, units of power/area have no meaning for point light sources and the *total* power or power per solid angle (power/steradian) must be used instead. Using the reciprocity relationship

$$F_{ij} A_i = F_{ji} A_j \tag{10.1}$$

the total contribution of a light source i to the radiosity of an element j is

$$B_j \text{ due to } i = \rho_j E_i A_i F_{ij}/A_j \tag{10.2}$$

In general, the new light sources will be defined in terms of *power*, which is equivalent to the factor $E_i A_i$, as opposed to the emitted radiosity E_i (power/area). Including such a light source into the matrix formulation requires modifying the row and column corresponding to the source. First, for a light i the ith column of $\mathbf{K}$ must be "divided" by A_i to account for the fact that the light's contribution as represented by those terms will be in units of power rather than radiosity. The corresponding entry B_i in the vector of radiosities is now interpreted in units of power, since it is the power of the light source (i.e., it is "multiplied" by A_i to account for the division in the ith column). The entries K_{ji} of the matrix were originally given by

$$K_{ji} = -\rho_j F_{ji} = -\rho_j F_{ij} \frac{A_i}{A_j} \tag{10.3}$$

Although A_i is undefined in this case, the division can be performed symbolically to obtain the new entry

$$K_{ji} = -\rho_j F_{ij}/A_j \tag{10.4}$$

which is computable, since A_j is not zero.

All entries in row i of the matrix are zero, since the light is not a reflector, except for the diagonal term $1 - \rho_i F_{ii}$. The row is "multiplied" by A_i, leaving a one on the diagonal. This also results in the E_i term now also being in units of power (i.e., $E_i A_i$) as desired.

An alternative to incorporating the light source into the matrix formulation is to handle specialized light sources in a separate step prior to the actual radiosity solution. In this approach, the row and column of the light source is removed, and the contribution due to the light source is computed for every element (or node) in the radiosity system, using the appropriate equation for that source. The resulting element radiosities are then used as the emission (**E**) values for the subsequent solution of the matrix equation.

In the following sections the factors F_{ij} will be derived for the various types of light sources.

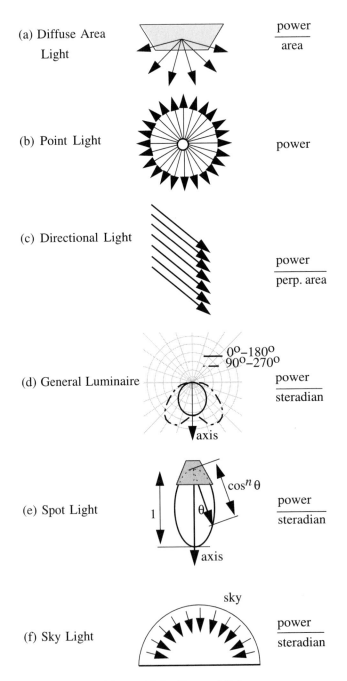

Figure 10.1: *Types of lights.*

10.1.2 Point Lights

The inclusion of an isotropic point source (see Figure 10.1 (b)) emitting with equal radiant intensity in all directions can be accomplished by a shift in units and a modification to the form factor. As discussed in the previous section, the source can be specified in terms of its total power. The fraction of energy leaving the source located at x_i and arriving at some element, j, is then

$$F_{ij} = \int_{A_j} \frac{1}{4\pi} \frac{\cos \theta_j}{r^2} V(\mathbf{x}_j, \mathbf{x}_i) \, dA_j \qquad (10.5)$$

The $1/4\pi$ term converts the total power to power per steradian, and the remainder of the integrand is the visible solid angle subtended by element j.

10.1.3 Parallel Lights

Parallel lights (see Figure 10.1 (c)) can be thought of as a point source at a great distance, or a very large source with light emanating in only a given direction, $\vec{\omega}$. An obvious application is the modeling of direct sunlight. In this case, the appropriate units are power per *perpendicular* area, that is, the amount of power per unit area falling on a surface oriented to the light. In this case, the form factor is simply the visible projected area of element j:

$$F_{ij} = \int_{A_j} \cos \theta_j \, V(-\vec{\omega}, \mathbf{x}_j) \, dA_j \qquad (10.6)$$

where $V(-\vec{\omega}, \mathbf{x}_j)$ is the visibility of the infinite source from a point $\mathbf{x}_j$ on element j in the inverse direction of the light. The function $V(-\vec{\omega}, \mathbf{x}_j)$ equals *one* if a ray from dA_j in direction $-\vec{\omega}$ does not hit anything, and *zero* otherwise.

10.1.4 General Luminaires

A more general lamp or *luminaire* may be a point source or an area source and may have an anisotropic intensity. Often, luminaire manufacturers will supply a *goniometric diagram* that specifies the radiant or luminous intensity (defined in section 2.4.5) of the source in candelas over a range of directions [3]. Standards for such diagrams are prescribed by the IES [4]. The diagram includes the effect of shadowing and reflection by the light fixture. The complete specification of a general point light thus includes the light's position, orientation, and goniometric diagram.

In Figure 10.1 (d) a typical goniometric diagram depicts two perpendicular slices through the intensity distribution in polar coordinates. These coordinates are with respect to a main orientation axis. More complicated goniometric distributions are, unfortunately, difficult to specify and do not have a standard form.

Expressing the goniometric distribution in terms of power per steradian, the goniometric diagram can be reformulated as a *maximum* power per steradian $I_{\max}$ scaled by a polar function ranging from 0 to 1. The polar scaling function $S(\vec{\omega})$ is defined to takes a direction, $\vec{\omega}$, away from the source and returns a value between 0 and 1.

Interpolation is required to obtain a value $S(\vec{\omega})$ from the goniometric diagram for a direction that does not lie on either of the two perpendicular planes defining the distribution. Languénou and Tellier [144] suggest the following method of interpolating smoothly between the given goniometric slices:

1. Project the direction $\vec{\omega}$ onto the two planes. For example, if the main axis is in the $+Z$ direction and the diagram depicts the XZ and YZ slices, then the projection of an arbitrary vector $\vec{\omega} = (x, y, z)$ yields the new vectors, $(x, 0, z)$ and $(0, y, z)$, with angles $\phi_x = \mathrm{atan2}(x, z)$ and $\phi_z = \mathrm{atan2}(y, z)$ off the Z axis.

2. Perform elliptic interpolation:

$$S(\vec{\omega}) \;=\; \sqrt{S_x(\phi_x)\cos^2\phi_x \;+\; S_y(\phi_y)\cos^2\phi_y} \qquad (10.7)$$

3. Finally, divide the result by the maximum, $I_{\max}$.

The form factor from a point light i to an element j can now be derived. Again, the form factor is proportional to the solid angle subtended by j from the point of view of the light and is scaled at each dA_j by $S(\vec{\omega})$:

$$F_{ij} \;=\; \int_{A_j} S(\vec{\omega}) \frac{\cos\theta_j}{r^2} V(\mathbf{x}_i, \mathbf{x}_j)\, dA_j \qquad (10.8)$$

where $\vec{\omega}$ is a vector from the light sources to dA_j.

For general area lights, the goniometric diagram must be converted to luminance by dividing by the projected area of the source. For example if the light intensity, I, is given in terms of *candelas* (cd), then the luminance (cd/m^2) is given by

$$L_e(\theta) \;=\; \frac{1}{\cos\theta} \frac{I}{A_i} \qquad (10.9)$$

In this case, the form factor must be integrated over the area A_i of the light and normalized by dividing by A_i,

$$F_{ij} \;=\; \frac{1}{A_i} \int_{A_i} \int_{A_j} S(\vec{\omega}) \frac{\cos\theta_j}{r^2} V(\mathbf{x}_i, \mathbf{x}_j)\, dA_j \qquad (10.10)$$

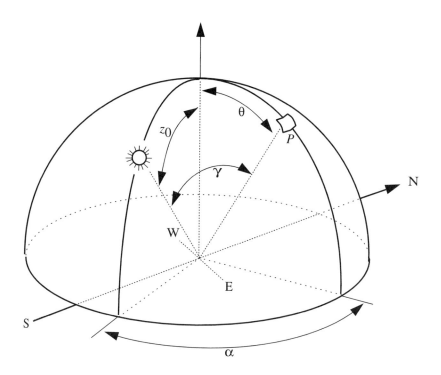

Figure 10.2: *Geometry for skylight.*

10.1.5 Spot Lights

Spot lights, as commonly defined for computer graphics, are a special case of the general luminaire where the intensity distribution is defined implicitly by a simple function (see Figure 10.1 (e)). The most common functional form is a cosine of the angle away from the axis, raised to an exponent, $S(\vec{\omega}) = \cos^n \theta$. As for the general luminaire above, if the spot light is specified by its maximum power per steradian, $I_{\max}$, in the direction of the axis, and the power of the cosine distribution is n, then the form factor is given by

$$F_{ij} = \int_{A_j} \frac{\cos^n \theta_i \cos \theta_j}{r^2} V(\mathbf{x}_i, \mathbf{x}_j) \, dA_j \qquad (10.11)$$

10.1.6 Sky Light

Illumination from the sky (as opposed to the sun) can be considered as light emanating from a hemisphere of infinite radius (see Figure 10.1(f)). The appropriate units in this case are again power per solid angle (power/steradian), but in this case the solid angle is not *from* the source but rather the solid angle *to* the source (see Figure 10.2). This does not present a problem, due to the reciprocity relationship.

The CIE[1] provides a number of formulae for estimating the luminance of a point P on the sky hemisphere, depending on cloud cover and sun position. For a completely overcast sky the luminance is given by

$$L(\theta) = L_z \frac{1 + 2\cos\theta}{3} \qquad (10.12)$$

where L_z is the luminance at the zenith. In this simple empirical model, the sky luminance is assumed uniform in a circle at any given height, so the luminance is a function only of the angle θ between the zenith and the point P. The sky in this model is brightest at the zenith and darkest near the horizon. The value of L_z is itself a function of the height of the sun. It should be noted that this model is generally not accurate for low-lying cloud cover.

For a clear sky, the CIE gives the following function:

$$L(\theta, \gamma) = L_z \frac{(0.91 + 10e^{-3\gamma} + 0.45\cos^2\gamma)(1 - e^{-0.32\sec\theta})}{0.274(0.91 + 10e^{-3z_0} + 0.45\cos^2 z_0)} \qquad (10.13)$$

where L_z and θ are as above, z_0 is the angle between the zenith and the sun, and γ is the angle between the sun and P (see Figure 10.2). The angle γ can be computed from the angle α formed by the projections of the sun and P onto the ground plane (see Figure 10.2), using $\cos\gamma = \cos z_0 \cos\theta + \sin z_0 \sin\theta \sin\alpha$ [1].

If the zenithal luminance L_z is converted to radiance R_z (see Chapter 2), then the form factor term can again be derived. This requires an integration over the sky dome hemisphere, Ω, as well as over element j. $S(\vec{\omega})$ is again defined as the ratio of the radiance in direction $\vec{\omega}$ to R_z (zenithal radiance).[2] The form factor to the sky is then given by:

$$F_{ij} = \int_\Omega \int_{A_j} \frac{S(\vec{\omega})\cos\theta_j}{2\pi} V(\vec{\omega}, dA_j)\, dA_j\, d\omega \qquad (10.14)$$

Takagi *et al.* [229] provide a valuable discussion of sky light in the context of the photo-realistic rendering of automobiles in exterior scenes. Nishita and Nakamae [176] discuss sky light specifically in the context of radiosity. In particular, they address the issue of determining occlusion with respect to sky light, as well as techniques for interiors that receive sky light through windows.

---

[1]Commission Internationale de l'Éclairage

[2]$S(\vec{\omega})$ may return a value greater than one near the sun in the clear sky model.

10.1.7 Normalization

The use of the standard Lambertian diffuse area sources requires the specification of the source in terms of radiosity, or power/area. Thus, if the area of the light source is changed and the radiosity is held fixed, the total power will change in proportion to the area. Similarly, the above derivations of the form factors for general luminaires and spot lights required the source to be defined in terms of power/sr. As a result, if the maximum power/steradian of a spot light is held fixed and the exponent n is allowed to vary, the total power of the light will fall as n grows.

It is often desirable to specify an area source in terms of *total* power, thus allowing the size of the diffuse source to vary without affecting emission. It is also useful to have spot lights or more general luminaires specified in terms of total emitted power, with the spotlight function or the goniometric diagram defining only the *relative* intensity distribution.

This requires a *normalization* to replace the scaling function $S(\vec{\omega})$ (just 1 for Lambertian sources) with a *probability density function* that by definition integrates to 1 over the sphere for directional sources and over the area for area sources. The advantage in this system is that as the area of a diffuse source or the distribution of the spot light or general luminaire changes, the total amount of energy emitted by the source remains constant. This provides a much more intuitive system for modeling lights and determining their relative contributions to the illumination of the environment. An additional advantage is that Monte Carlo sampling, as described in Chapter 4, becomes straightforward.

Providing this normalization in source specification requires the derivation of a *normalization scaling factor* based on the size and/or distribution of the source.

Lambertian Diffuse Area Source: This is straightforward in the case of the diffuse source. The source i can be specified in terms of total power, and the scaling factor is simply $1/A_i$.

Spot Light: In the case of the spot light, the normalization factor is determined by integrating the distribution function over the hemisphere:

$$\int_0^{2\pi} \int_0^{\pi/2} \cos^n \theta \sin \theta \, d\theta \, d\phi \qquad (10.15)$$

Note that in polar coordinates, a differential element on the hemisphere is given by $\sin \theta \, d\theta \, d\phi$. The above integral has an analytic solution:

$$-\frac{\cos^{n+1} \theta}{n+1} \Bigg|_0^{\pi/2} = \frac{1}{n+1} \qquad (10.16)$$

Thus the normalization factor is simply $n + 1$. In other words, to specify a 100-watt spotlight with a spot size defined by $n = 30$, the maximum power/sr in the direction of the axis should be given as $100 \times (30 + 1) = 3100$ watts/steradian.[3]

General Luminaire: A similar result can be obtained from a general spatial distribution by scaling the power by the reciprocal of the integral of the distribution over the hemisphere. A nonanalytic distribution will require numerical integration over the distribution in polar coordinates.

10.1.8 Light Source Data

Data for electrical light fixtures can be obtained from catalogs such as [3]. The IES Lighting Handbook [2] is a good general resource for interpreting these sources. Directional data for light fixtures given by a goniometric (i.e., directional) diagrams are often available from luminaire manufacturers, but online versions are not yet widely available.

The emission spectrum for a light source is determined primarily by the type of bulb, (e.g., incandescent, low pressure sodium, etc.). Relative power spectra for different types of lamps are given in several sources (e.g., [2, 127]). These spectra may be characterized by smooth curves, as for incandescent lights, or by narrow spikes, as for mercury lamps. Spectra characterized by spikes may need to be filtered before use, depending on the color model adopted.

Smooth emission spectra are generally characterized as *black body emitters* parameterized by temperature T. For a given temperature T, the blackbody spectral radiance distribution is given by Planck's distribution:

$$
\begin{aligned}
I_b(\lambda) &= 2C_1/[\lambda^5 \{\exp(C_2/\lambda T) - 1\}] \\
C_1 &\sim 0.595 \times 108 \, \text{W} \mu\text{m}^4/\text{m}^2 \\
C_2 &\sim 14388 \, \mu\text{mK} \,, \quad \lambda \text{ in } \mu\text{m} \,, \quad T \text{ in K} \quad (10.17)
\end{aligned}
$$

The spectral distribution and luminance for natural (sky) light depends on time of day, latitude and sky conditions (e.g., clear or over cast). The different spectral values for direct (direct line to the sun) and indirect (from the hemisphere of the sky) can be found in the [2] or [177]. A rough approximation of a clear sky is a blackbody at 15000K, and for an overcast sky, a blackbody at 6500K. The luminance of indirect natural light is generally in the range of 1000 to 5000 cd/m^2. Direct sunlight is well represented spectrally by a blackbody at 5800K with a magnitude of approximately 1300 W/m^2.

---

[3]Note that wattages given for light bulbs represent consumed power, not emitted light energy. Most of the consumed power is converted to heat. A typical tungsten filament converts only a small fraction (about 5 percent) of the consumed power to visible light.

10.2 Directional Reflection

As described in Chapter 2, the reflective behavior of a surface is described by a bidirectional reflectance distribution function (BRDF) defined over the hemisphere of directions above the surface. The BRDF represents the complex interactions of incident light with the surface and has a complicated shape, in general.

It is convenient to treat this complicated function as the sum of three components: Lambertian (or ideal) diffuse, glossy, and ideal (or mirror) specular [118] (shown in Figure 2.12). Radiosity is limited to BRDFs consisting only of the Lambertian diffuse component. Models for radiosity thus consist entirely of surfaces with matte finishes.

Since the non-Lambertian components of reflection play an important part in everyday visual experience, radiosity images, although compelling, are often not completely realistic. The absence of highlights (the glossy reflection of light sources) not only reduces realism, but removes an important visual cue to shape and curvature. The restriction to matte finishes is also a serious limitation for design applications where the evaluation of surface appearance is important.

Before discussing methods to incorporate ideal specular and glossy reflection into the radiosity solution, we will introduce the notion of *transport paths* and a notation that will simplify the discussion and comparison of algorithms.

10.2.1 Classifying Transport Paths

Producing an image requires accounting (approximately) for all photons that leave the light source and eventually enter the eye. The sequence of surface interactions encountered by a photon on its way from the light to the eye describes a *path*.[4] Global illumination algorithms can be characterized by which paths they consider and how they determine them.

Kajiya first makes the connection between the Neumann expansion of the rendering equation (equation 2.52) and the sequences of surface interactions encountered during the propagation of light [135]. The rendering equation is an integral equation that can be expressed in terms of an integral operator, $\mathcal{K}$,

$$u = e + \mathcal{K}u \tag{10.18}$$

In the case of the rendering equation, u corresponds to the radiance function and e to the emission term. A solution to integral equations of this type (an exact

---

[4]In practice, algorithms more typically take each path as representing a *packet* of photons (a *ray* or *beam*). Each packet starts from the light carrying a certain power, which is reduced at each interaction to account for absorption [214].

solution in the case of the rendering equation) is given by the Neumann series

$$u = \sum_{i=0}^{\infty} \mathcal{K}^i e = e + \mathcal{K}e + \mathcal{K}^2 e + \mathcal{K}^3 e + ... \qquad (10.19)$$

Each term of the series corresponds to an additional application of the operator.

Kajiya points out the following physical interpretation of this series: each application of the operator, $\mathcal{K}$, corresponds to an additional surface interaction, or bounce, along a path from the light to the eye. Thus, the term $\mathcal{K}^2 e$ accounts for paths in which light reaches the eye via two bounces. This interpretation provides a useful way of comparing illumination algorithms, which Kajiya undertakes for several classic shading techniques.

The usefulness of such a comparison can be increased by formally including the split of the BRDF into components, since algorithms can often be characterized by how they account for these components. Several authors have taken this approach; the following discussion is based on Heckbert [120], who also introduces the use of *regular expressions* to provide a compact notation for describing paths.

For simplicity, the BRDF will be split into a Lambertian diffuse and a specular component, as in Heckbert's presentation. The specular component subsumes the glossy and ideal specular parts. The kernel of the rendering equation can then be split into diffuse and specular components. Similarly, the integral operator becomes the sum of diffuse and specular operators $\mathcal{K} = \mathcal{D} + \mathcal{S}$.

Expanded in terms of these operators, the Neumann series becomes

$$\begin{aligned} u &= e + (\mathcal{D} + \mathcal{S})e + (\mathcal{D} + \mathcal{S})^2 e + (\mathcal{D} + \mathcal{S})^3 e + ... \\ &= e + \mathcal{D}e + \mathcal{S}e + \mathcal{D}\mathcal{D}e + \mathcal{D}\mathcal{S}e + \mathcal{S}\mathcal{D}e + \mathcal{S}\mathcal{S}e + ... \quad (10.20) \end{aligned}$$

Each term in this equation represents a subset of the infinitely many paths that start at the light source and enter the eye from a particular direction. The first term, e, is the path leading directly from the light to the eye. The second term, $\mathcal{D}e$, consists of paths that start at the source and are diffusely reflected once before entering the eye, while the third term, $\mathcal{S}e$, represents paths that contain one specular reflection, and so on. In all, light reaching the eye from a given direction may have traveled from the source via paths that include any number and combination of diffuse and specular interactions (see Figure 10.3). Since the series is infinite all possible light paths are accounted for. Similarly, an algorithm that accounts (correctly) for all paths provides a solution to the integral.

Heckbert suggests the use of regular expressions[5] to simplify the description of paths. With the addition of L to indicate emission from the light and E to

---

[5] A regular expression describes a *language* consisting of words constructed from a

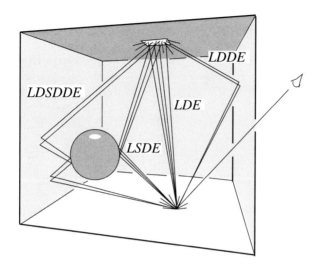

Figure 10.3: *Some of the paths contributing to the radiance for a particular direction leading to the eye.*

indicate absorption by the eye, any particular type of path can be represented textually by a string of symbols from the *alphabet* consisting of the letters $\{L, D, S, E\}$. As an example, light arriving via one bounce from a diffuse surface follows the path LDE, and that arriving by one bounce from a specular surface follows the path LSE.

The regular expression $L(D|S)^*E$ expresses the set of all possible paths for the two-component reflection model. This expression simply states that light leaving the source and reaching the eye may follow a path containing any number (including zero) of diffuse and specular reflections in any order. Algorithms can be characterized compactly by expressions that describe the subset of all possible paths that they attempt to account for.

The most common type of local illumination model, called the *Utah approximation* by Kajiya and widely available in graphics hardware, is characterized by the expression $L(D|S)E$. This expression contains the paths LDE (lo-

---

given *alphabet*. The expression formally expresses the set of words that can be realized in the language and consists of a string of characters constructed from the alphabet plus the superscripts $*$ and $+$, the symbol $|$, parentheses $()$, and the empty string $\emptyset$. The superscript $*$ indicates any number (including 0) of repetitions of the superscripted term. For example, D^* indicates the set $\{\emptyset, D, DD, DDD, DDDD, ...\}$. The superscript $+$ is similar to $*$ but does not include the empty string (i.e., there must be at least one of the superscripted term). The symbol $|$ means *OR*, and the parentheses have the obvious meaning.

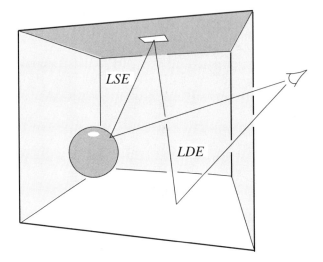

Figure 10.4: *Paths handled by the Utah approximation.*

cal diffuse shading) and LSE (the Phong highlight), as shown in Figure 10.4. In addition to ignoring paths involving multiple reflection, such models often ignore shadowing, and thus include nonphysical paths. Classical ray tracing handles the paths $LDS^*E \mid LS^*E$, but with some restrictions (see Figure 10.5). The sequence LS in any path approximates glossy reflection using the Phong model, but subsequent specular reflections ignore all but ideal specular reflection. Distribution ray tracing extends ray tracing to account for all paths in $LDS^*E \mid LS^*E$. Radiosity is limited to the paths LD^*E since in its traditional form it cannot handle specular reflection (see Figure 10.6).

10.2.2   Tracing the Transport Paths

A complete global illumination algorithm must account for all paths that start at the light and end at the eye. However, because of absorption and directional reflection, all paths do not contribute equally to the radiance reaching the eye. An efficient algorithm distributes computational resources among the paths appropriately, expending the greatest effort on paths that contribute most to the image.

Eye-Ray Tracing

For portions of paths consisting of the sequence S^*E, the BRDF provides an a priori basis for estimating the importance of various paths. The eye position and

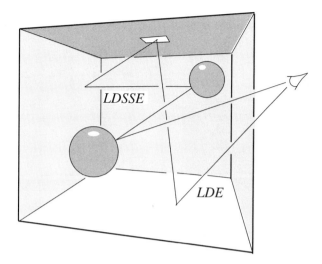

Figure 10.5: *Representative paths handled by classical ray tracing.*

the pixel location determine the outgoing direction for the final S interaction, and the shape of the BRDF provides a guide as to which incoming directions are likely to contribute significantly.[6] (In the case of ideal specular reflection, the outgoing direction determines the *only* contributing incoming direction.) Working backwards from the eye, each subsequent S interaction along the path can be treated similarly. This provides the basic strategy for Whitted-style ray tracing and distribution ray tracing.

The utility of this strategy hinges on the ability to distinguish a limited number of incoming directions as important. As the BRDF becomes increasingly diffuse, the relative importance of different incoming directions becomes correspondingly closer to equal and an increasing number of incoming directions must be considered for an accurate estimate (see Figure 10.7). At some point this strategy becomes prohibitively expensive. In such cases, most ray tracing algorithms give up and determine importance based on the location of the luminaires rather than the BRDF.

Light-Ray Tracing

Specular reflection also provides an a priori importance estimate when working forwards from the light source, for portions of paths consisting of the sequence

---

[6] A posteriori sampling is also useful, since the actual contribution coming from various incoming directions cannot be estimated until some samples have been taken. The graphics literature contains a great deal of discussion of such strategies [71, 135, 140, 147].

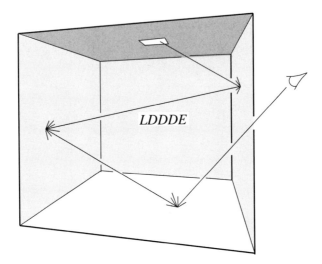

Figure 10.6: *Paths handled by radiosity.*

LS^*. In this case, a path starting at the light intersects a surface, which determines an incoming direction, and the BRDF provides a basis for weighting the importance of all possible outgoing directions. This is the motivation for light-ray tracing, which is often used to find what are loosely referred to as *caustics*.[7] Light-ray tracing for this purpose was first described by Arvo [12], although it was applied to shading by Appel very early in computer graphics [8]. Many subsequent algorithms have also used this approach [120, 214, 272]. As with eye-ray tracing, this strategy loses its utility once a D interaction is encountered (see Figure 10.7).

Bidirectional Ray Tracing

If there is only one D interaction, light-ray tracing and eye-ray tracing can be combined to account for all paths by having them meet in the middle at the diffuse surface (an approach often called *bidirectional ray tracing*). Light rays that end on the diffuse surface typically have their power deposited in "bins" into which the surface is subdivided. Eye rays ending on the diffuse surface then interpolate the stored power to approximate contributions that would be obtained by tracing the path farther (see Figure 10.8).

---

[7]Although the term *caustic* has a very specific meaning in optics, in image synthesis it has often been used more generally to refer to the illumination of diffuse surfaces by light reflected from a specular surface. Mitchell and Hanrahan discuss caustics in detail in [168].

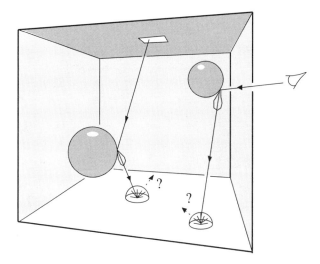

Figure 10.7: *Light-ray tracing and eye-ray tracing. Neither provide an advantage for path segments containing a diffuse interaction.*

Bidirectional ray tracing handles the paths LS^*DS^*E. Paths are effectively "broken" at the diffuse surface by averaging together the effect of many paths landing within a certain bin. This takes advantage of the fact that the ideal diffuse component of radiance usually changes fairly slowly, a consequence of the fact that incident illumination is integrated over the entire hemisphere of incoming directions — essentially a filtering operation.

Radiosity and Transport Paths

In one sense, radiosity is simply a generalization of the bidirectional ray tracing strategy to multiple diffuse interactions. Radiosity restricts the number of paths to be considered by agreeing to minimize the error over a region (Galerkin method) or at discrete points distributed over surfaces (point collocation). The interactions between the regions or points are then computed using numerical integration. In effect, the form factor between two elements (or basis functions) averages together the effect of paths that directly join the two elements.

Conventional radiosity handles the paths LD^*E. When combined with eye- and light-ray tracing, it can be extended to the paths $LS^*(D^*)S^*E$ (see Figure 10.9). In this case, light rays are traced until their power is deposited on an ideal diffuse surface. A radiosity solution is then performed with initial radiosities determined from the deposited power. Finally, eye-ray tracing is used to render an image, tracing paths from the eye through (potentially) several

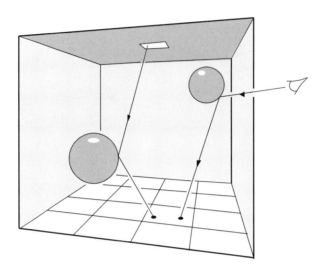

Figure 10.8: *Bidirectional ray tracing with a single diffuse interaction.*

specular interactions to reach a Lambertian diffuse surface.

The inner sequence D^* in the above expression, which is handled by the radiosity step, is incomplete, since it is only a subset of the correct sequence, $(D^*S^*D^*)^*$.[8] This is because radiosity does not account for light that travels from one diffuse surface to another via specular reflection by intermediate surfaces.

The next sections will present methods for accounting for these missing paths in the radiosity solution. Such methods can be classified as either *implicit* or *explicit*. In an explicit method, the global illumination problem is formulated in terms of the radiance $L(\mathbf{x}, \phi)$. An approximation of $L(\mathbf{x}, \phi)$ is computed and stored for all surfaces, including those with a BRDF containing glossy or ideal specular components.

In an implicit method, the problem formulation remains the same as in the radiosity method, with the effect of reflection from ideal specular or glossy surfaces included only to the extent that they affect Lambertian diffuse surfaces. This is accomplished by modifying coefficients of the operator $\mathbf{K}$. The glossy and ideal specular components are never actually computed or approximated.

---

[8]The string $LS^*(D^*S^*D^*)^*S^*E$ is equivalent to the string $L(S|D)^*E$.

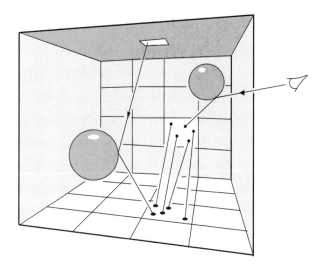

Figure 10.9: *Radiosity with eye-ray tracing and light-ray tracing.*

10.2.3 Implicit Methods

Extended Form Factors

The discretized radiosity equation expresses the radiosity for each element as a linear sum of the radiosities of all other elements. Somewhat surprisingly, it is possible to rewrite the equation, leaving out certain elements and still form a correct solution for the remaining elements. The new system will be correct as long as the coefficients of the radiosity equation, the form factors, account for *all* paths between the elements of interest. This can be used to incorporate the effect of glossy and ideal specular surfaces into the radiosity solution.

As an example, if there are four elements $\{a, b, c, d\}$ (see Figure 10.10) element b can be eliminated from the computation by computing *extended* form factors from all other elements to all other elements *via* element b. In the case of constant basis functions, the extended form factor F_{dba} represents the fraction of energy leaving element d and arriving at element a after reflecting from element b. If all surfaces are diffuse, then $F_{dba} = F_{db} * \rho_b * F_{ba}$. An equivalent system of form factors can thus be constructed given all extended form factors with b as the intermediate element, by

1. adding F_{ibj} to the term F_{ij}, for all pairs ij, and

2. eliminating the bth row and column from **K**.

The resulting system is equivalent to the original system, insofar as the included

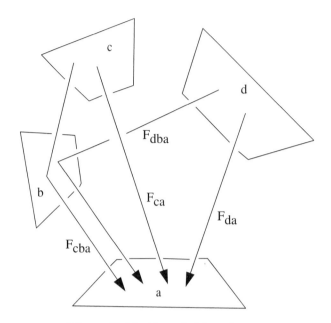

Figure 10.10: *Extended form factors.*

elements are concerned. Eliminating element b is much like the *elimination* involved in linear equation solvers such as Gaussian elimination.

The extended form factor is a natural generalization of the notion of a form factor, which simply expresses the fraction of energy leaving one element that will arrive at another element. Eliminated elements provide additional multi-bounce paths along which energy can be transported between the remaining elements. The additional paths are accounted for by increasing or *extending* the form factors between the other elements.

When does it make sense to exclude certain surfaces from the solution? Whenever it is difficult or expensive to store an approximation of the radiance for those surfaces. This is certainly the case for surfaces with a highly directional BRDF, since an adequate approximation requires storing a detailed directional distribution at closely spaced nodes. It may also be useful to exclude procedurally defined objects, like fractal surfaces, for which it may be impractical to generate a mesh. When excluded surfaces are rendered in the final image, their radiance is computed using another algorithm such as eye-ray tracing, with the radiosity solution providing the approximation of the ideal diffuse component where needed.

The basic theory for extended form factors was introduced to image synthesis by Rushmeier [197, 201]. Rushmeier provides an algorithm for computing extended form factors for paths that contain a single ideal specular bounce (DSD) from a planar surface (i.e., a mirror). With these limitations it is possible to compute extended form factors using the hemicube algorithm. Mirrors are simply treated as openings into a virtual mirror world, which consists of the entire scene flipped about the plane of the mirror. The form factor to an element in the mirror world is added to the form factor to the element in the normal world, to obtain the total extended form factor. Rushmeier's *mirror* form factor algorithm provides the first pass of the two-pass method described by Wallace *et al.* [246]. Hall [114] provides pseudocode for the mirror form factor algorithm.

Malley, Sillion, and others [142, 157, 218] compute extended form factors using recursive ray tracing. This allows multi-bounce DS^*D paths to be followed and BRDFs with a glossy reflection component to be included. It also extends the method to nonplanar surfaces. In addition, ray tracing can be used to compute extended form factors that account for transparent, refracting surfaces. Shirley [212] has demonstrated the use of extended form factors to eliminate a Lambertian diffuse surface from the solution. In this algorithm, the radiosity of the excluded surface is computed during rendering using Monte Carlo ray tracing.

Color plates 43 and 44 provide a comparison of images computed with and without the use of extended form factors. Note the light missing from the top of the table in front of the mirror in the "before" image.

10.2.4 Explicit Methods

Implicit methods, like extended form factors, do not provide an approximation of the directional component of the radiance, which must be computed by other means during rendering. By contrast, in an explicit method the more general rendering equation is solved to produce an approximation of the radiance, $L(\mathbf{x}, \vec{\omega})$. The approximation must thus represent the directional as well as spatial variation of the radiance.

The Global Cube

One straightforward approach to approximating both the directional and spatial variations of the radiance is to use two sets of basis functions. The directional radiance distribution at each node can be approximated using one set of basis functions defined over direction, with the spatial variation interpolated across elements using a different set of basis functions.

Immel *et al.* [132] approximate the directional radiance distribution at each node using a *global cube*, in which the radiance for discrete directions over finite solid angles is approximated by a constant value. The directional discretization is determined by uniformly subdividing the faces of a cube (see Figure 10.11).

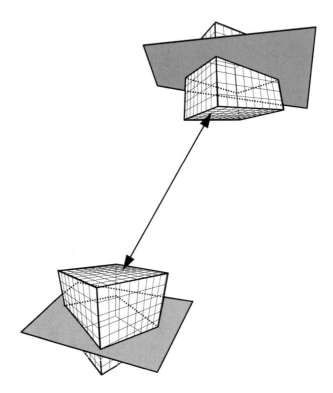

Figure 10.11: *Discretization of directions with the global cube.*

This allows the surface visible in each direction to be determined quickly, as in the hemicube algorithm. If the number of nodes in the environment is n and the number of discrete directions represented on the global cube is m, there are now $n \times m$ unknowns representing the radiance, $L(\mathbf{x}, \vec{\omega})$, at n positions in each of m directions.

The radiance for a given outgoing direction at a node can then be expressed as a function of the radiance for every outgoing direction for every other node in the environment.

$$L(\mathbf{x}, \vec{\omega}) = E(\mathbf{x}, \vec{\omega}) +$$
$$\sum_{x'} \sum_{\Omega} \rho(-\vec{\omega}', \mathbf{x}, \vec{\omega}) \, k(\mathbf{x}', \vec{\omega}', \mathbf{x}, -\vec{\omega}') L(\mathbf{x}', \vec{\omega}') \, \Delta\vec{\omega}' \Delta A' \qquad (10.21)$$

The $k(\mathbf{x}', \vec{\omega}', \mathbf{x}, -\vec{\omega}')$ terms are similar to form factors in that they specify the fraction of energy leaving point $\mathbf{x}'$ in direction $\vec{\omega}'$ and arriving directly at $\mathbf{x}$ from

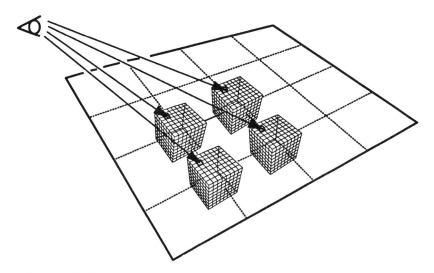

Figure 10.12: *Rendering using the results of the global cube algorithm.*

the opposite direction $-\vec{\omega}'$. Note that the reflectivity terms now also depend on direction.

The resulting $(n \times m)^2$ matrix can be formulated and solved as in the conventional radiosity method. The matrix is very large but extremely sparse, since a given node can interact with another node via only a single pair of incoming and outgoing directions. Immel *et al.* anticipate progressive radiosity by solving for the element radiosities in roughly the order of light propagation.

During rendering, Immel *et al.* obtain the radiance at a node for the view direction by linearly interpolating between the sampled outgoing directions that bound the view direction (see Figure 10.12). Radiances on the element interiors are obtained by linear interpolation from the resulting nodal values. Hall [114] provides pseudocode for the global cube algorithm, with discussion of some related practical issues.

While the global cube algorithm approximates all paths in $L(D|S)^*E$, the algorithm runs into trouble for highly directional BRDFs, as shown in Figure 10.13. The fine details of the reflection in the floor of this image are poorly approximated and display obvious artifacts. An accurate approximation of a highly directional radiance distribution requires an extremely fine mesh, as well as a high resolution global cube, which results in impractically high storage requirements and solution times. Furthermore, increasing the cube resolution everywhere is inefficient, since high resolution is principally required for portions of paths ending at the eye.

Figure 10.13: *An image produced using the global cube algorithm. Courtesy of David Immel, Program of Computer Graphics, Cornell University.*

Iterative Refinement

Shao *et al.* [210] address ideal specular and glossy reflection using the conventional radiosity equation by changing the meaning of the form factor. As in conventional radiosity, the form factor from a directionally reflecting surface A_j to a second surface A_i is the fraction of the total energy leaving A_j that reaches A_i. For directional reflection, however, the amount of energy reaching A_i from A_j will depend on the actual distribution of outgoing radiance for A_j. For a glossy surface, this is a nonuniform distribution that depends on the BRDF and the distribution of incoming energy. Thus, unlike a true form factor, Shao's form factor is not purely geometric and cannot be computed a priori.

Shao's modified form factor is computed using the hemicube to determine which elements are visible in all directions. The delta form factor for a receiving element seen through hemicube pixel p depends on the radiosity of other elements contributing incoming energy through other hemicube pixels. The contribution of the incoming energy for hemicube pixel q to the delta form factor for pixel p is weighted using the BRDF for the element. Thus, the form factor to a given receiving element will depend on the radiosity of elements contributing incoming energy from other directions.

Clearly, Shao's form factor cannot be computed a priori, since it depends on already knowing the element radiosities. Instead, he uses an iterative approach to refine the estimate of the factors gradually. The initial step is to compute a conventional radiosity solution, ignoring directional reflection. Form factors can then be computed with respect to all directionally reflecting elements, using the initial radiosity solution to provide an estimate of the incoming distribution of light for those elements. The radiosity matrix is reformulated and resolved with the new form factors. The improved estimate can be used again to refine the form factors further. To save time, the hemicubes are computed only once, and then stored to be reused during later iterations.

The converged solution accounts for light arriving at diffuse surfaces via directional reflection from other surfaces. Shao's approach is an explicit method, in that approximations of the directional radiance distribution are computed when needed during the solution. However, these approximations are not suitable for rendering, for the same reasons noted for Immel's algorithm, and distributed ray tracing is instead used to determine the directional component at image resolution.

Hall and Rushmeier [113] describe improvements to Shao's basic approach, including adaptive subdivision for directionally reflecting surfaces and extensions to progressive radiosity.

Spherical Harmonic Basis

In the global cube algorithm, the use of constant basis functions of a fixed width to represent the directional radiance distribution means that a very large number of directions must be evaluated and stored for each node to ensure that small features are captured. Sillion *et al.* [217] observe that, just as with functions defined over a surface, higher-order basis functions defined over the sphere of directions should allow the distribution to be approximated with fewer samples. Since the BRDF and the directional radiance distribution are functions defined over the hemisphere, Sillion proposes the use of spherical harmonics as a basis. The first three terms in the series are plotted in Figure 10.14.

Spherical harmonics are an infinite series, analogous to the Fourier series, that can represent a large class of functions defined over a sphere. The first three sets of spherical harmonics are shown in Figure 10.14. Slowly varying functions can be approximated relatively accurately using only a small number of terms from the series. Sillion *et al.* find that if the ideal specular term is removed, the remaining radiance distribution due to glossy and Lambertian diffuse reflection can usually be adequately approximated by computing coefficients for the first 100 or so terms of the series.

Representing the BRDF, as opposed to the directional radiance, is more complex, since the outgoing distribution represented by the BRDF varies as a function of incoming direction. Sillion *et al.* approximate the distribution for a single incoming direction using approximately the first 80 spherical harmonics. However, since this outgoing distribution changes as a function of the incoming direction, the distributions must be represented for all incoming directions. Assuming isotropic reflection, this variation depends only on a single value, the angle between the incoming direction and the surface normal. The variation of the distribution with this angle is interpolated using a one dimensional cubic

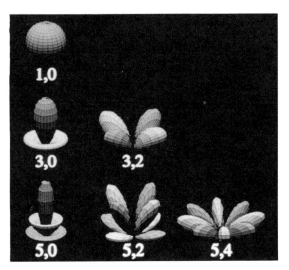

Figure 10.14: *The first three spherical harmonics. Coutesy of François Sillion, Cornell University Program of Computer Graphics.*

spline to approximate the function describing the variation of each coefficient with incoming direction.

Given this method for approximating the distribution, the solution process itself is a straightforward generalization of a progressive radiosity approach. At each solution step, the directional radiance distribution of every node is updated based on the directional distribution of a selected shooting element. Sillion *et al.* use a point collocation approach to approximate the spatial variation of the radiance function. Thus, energy is transferred from elements to nodes. Each node then has a directional radiance distribution represented by a finite number of coefficients for the spherical harmonics.

The contribution of a shooting element with area A' to the radiance distribution, $L(\mathbf{x}, \cdot)$, for a receiving node located at $\mathbf{x}$ is given by

$$L(\mathbf{x}, \cdot) = \int_{A'} L(\mathbf{x}', \vec{\omega}') \frac{\cos \theta \, \cos \theta'}{r^2} \rho(\vec{\omega}, \cdot) V(\mathbf{x}, \mathbf{x}') \, dA' \qquad (10.22)$$

where the dot "·" represents the hemisphere of directions, $L(\mathbf{x}, \cdot)$ is the radiance distribution at $\mathbf{x}$ and $\rho(\vec{\omega}, \cdot)$ is the bidirectional reflectance function for incoming energy from direction $\vec{\omega}$.

Numerical integration over the element i is performed, as in Wallace *et al.*'s ray-shooting form factor algorithm [247], by breaking the element into N

```
for ( each delta area, ΔA_i ) {
    Compute direction ω⃗ from x to sample point x' in ΔA_i ;
    Shoot ray from x to x' ;
    if ( no occlusion ) {
        Evaluate radiance L(x', ω⃗') leaving x' in the direction toward x ;
        Compute resulting incident energy flux ΔΦ at x ;
        Retrieve BRDF coefficients from B-spline approximation for
            incoming direction ω⃗ to x ;
        Scale BRDF by incident energy flux ΔΦ to obtain
            contribution to outgoing radiance distribution ΔL(x, ·) ;
        Add ΔL to the node's cumulative radiance distribution L(x, ·) ;
    }
}
```

Figure 10.15: *Pseudocode for updating radiance at a point.*

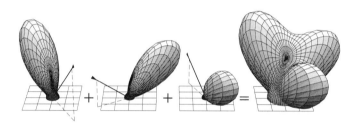

Figure 10.16: *The summation of radiance distributions due to multiple contributions from shooting elements. Coutesy of François Sillion, Cornell University Program of Computer Graphics.*

smaller delta areas, $\Delta A'$. The resulting summation over the delta areas is

$$L(\mathbf{x}, \cdot) = \sum_{j=1}^{N} L(\mathbf{x}'_j, \vec{\omega}'_j) \frac{\cos \theta_{\mathbf{x}} \cos \theta_{\mathbf{x}'_j}}{r_j^2} \rho(\vec{\omega}_j, \cdot) V(\mathbf{x}, \mathbf{x}'_j) \Delta A'_j \qquad (10.23)$$

The visibility of each delta area from a node i is determined by shooting a ray. The steps for updating the radiance distribution at a node at $\mathbf{x}$ due to the current source element i are given in Figure 10.15.

The addition of several contributions to a node's cumulative radiance distribution is shown in Figure 10.16. Since the radiance distribution and the BRDF

are approximated by spherical harmonics, scaling, addition and other operations on these distributions are operations on the spherical harmonic coefficients
themselves. These are described in detail in [217].

Spherical harmonics are not appropriate for approximating ideal specular
reflection since the BRDF in this case is a Dirac delta function. In fact, explicit methods in general encounter difficulties for ideal or near-ideal specular
reflection, due to the expense of approximating the highly directional radiance
distribution. In the case of the ideal specular component, Sillion uses extended
form factors computed using ray casting (see section 10.2.3). During rendering, the ideal specular component is added using recursive eye-ray tracing. The
glossy reflection component is obtained from the stored directional radiance
distributions and interpolated linearly across elements.

Images computed using Sillion's algorithm are shown in color plates 46 and
49. Note the diffused highlight on the cabinet doors of the kitchen in color plate
49. In color plate 46 the object on the left has an aluminum finish. The bright
illumination in the upper left-hand corner of the containing box is due to light
bounced directionally from the top of the aluminum object.

In addition to spherical harmonics and Immel's global cube data structure,
several other schemes for storing the directional radiance distribution have been
proposed. La Saec and Schlick [148] use a hemisphere discretized along merid-
ians and parallels. For a progressive radiosity approach, Chen [49] stores the
energy incident from each shooting source in a queue. The radiance distribution
is not actually resolved until the receiving element is called on to shoot its energy in the progressive solution. Buckalew and Fussell [40] describe a system
in which a network of links is constructed along parallel rays in space, for a
distribution of directions. Energy is then transferred along these links based on
the reflection of the intersected surfaces.

10.2.5   Non-Lambertian Reflection and Hierarchical Methods

Aupperle and Hanrahan [14] have made a thorough theoretical examination of the
issues related to the use of notions similar to extended form factors. Significantly,
they have also included these notions into the framework of hierarchical radiosity
methods.

In their work, the radiance distribution is not represented in terms of position and direction, but rather through two positions. The second position is
interpreted as *"in the direction of."* In other words, L_{ij} specifies the radiance
of area i in the direction of area j. Note that there is no explicit specification
of direction; instead the direction is defined by the relative positions of areas i
and j. This redefinition of the radiance distribution provides the framework for
applying hierarchical methods similar to those outlined in Chapter 7.

Constant basis functions can be defined over any $(area \times area)$. In other words, the radiance from area i to area j is approximated as constant over the two areas. Given this approximation of the radiance field, one can derive the relation,

$$L_{jk} = E_{jk} + \sum_i L_{ij} R_{kji} \qquad (10.24)$$

where, E_{jk} is the emitted radiance from area j to area k and R_{kji} is the *area reflectance* of area j in direction k due to light from area i. Putting the definition of *area reflectance* aside for a moment, the above relation can be stated as: *The radiance of area* j *in the direction of area* k *is equal to the emitted radiance of area* j *in the* k *direction plus the sum of the radiance of ALL areas* i *in the direction of area* j *multiplied times the area reflectance* R_{kji}.

Equation 10.24 is analogous to the original radiosity equation for diffuse surfaces. The biggest difference is the area reflectance term, R_{kji}, which accounts for the BRDF as well as the geometric and visibility relationships between areas j and k and between areas j and i. The derivation of this term is not pursued here; the reader is referred to [14]. The result is given as

$$R_{ijk} = \frac{\int_{A_i} \int_{A_j} \int_{A_k} f_r(\mathbf{x}, \mathbf{x}', \mathbf{x}'') G(\mathbf{x}, \mathbf{x}') G(\mathbf{x}', \mathbf{x}'') \, d\mathbf{x}'' d\mathbf{x}' d\mathbf{x}}{\int_{A_i} \int_{A_j} G(\mathbf{x}, \mathbf{x}') \, d\mathbf{x}' d\mathbf{x}} \qquad (10.25)$$

where f_r is the bidirectional reflectance distribution function and G is a geometric term similar to the form factor (without the normalizing π in the denominator).

One can now ask what the optimal choices of areas i, j, and k are in order to have as few R_{kji} terms as possible, while maintaining a given level of accuracy. Aupperle and Hanrahan develop a hierarchical algorithm based on arguments similar to those underlying the hierarchical form factor algorithm of Hanrahan *et al.* (described in Chapter 7) [116]. The resulting algorithm can be found in [14].

10.2.6 Transmission

Although only reflection has been discussed so far, surfaces may also transmit light. Transmission can be described by a bidirectional transmission distribution function (BTDF), analogous to the BRDF for reflection, defined over the hemisphere on the reverse side of the surface. As in the case of reflection, transmission can be separated into Lambertian diffuse (translucency), glossy, and ideal specular parts.

Note that the BTDF describes the interaction only at the interface between the two transport media (for example, the air and glass). It does not take into account absorption within the transmitting material, which depends on the

length of the transmission path. Absorption of a fixed fraction at the interface
is a reasonable approximation for thin transmitters like windows, but in general,
a correct treatment of absorption requires an illumination model that includes
participating media.

Transmission can be incorporated into a radiosity solution using implicit
or explicit methods, just as for reflection. In an implicit method, for example,
refraction could be included by using recursive ray tracing to compute extended
form factors. In explicit methods, which construct an approximation of the
reflected radiance distribution, transmission can be incorporated by constructing
a similar approximation of the transmitted radiance distribution.

Translucency

Translucency, or Lambertian diffuse transmission, is analogous to Lambertian
diffuse reflection and is particularly easy to add to a conventional radiosity solution [197, 201]. In translucency, a fraction of the energy incident on one side
of a surface is reradiated by the other side of the surface in a Lambertian diffuse
distribution. Thus, energy incident on the back of a translucent element contributes to the radiosity of the front of the element (see Figure 10.17). Likewise,
the back of a translucent element will have a radiosity that is partially due to
energy incident on the front. Since the transmission distribution is constant for
translucency, it can be represented by a single scalar value, just as for Lambertian diffuse reflection. Only two modifications to the radiosity algorithm are
required.

First, the radiosity equation for a translucent element now includes a contribution due to light arriving on the back side of the element,

$$B_i = E_i + \sum_{j=1}^{n} (\rho_i B_j F_{ij} + \tau_i B_j F_{kj}) \qquad (10.26)$$

where ρ_i is the coefficient of Lambertian diffuse reflection, τ_i is the coefficient
of Lambertian diffuse transmission, element k is the back side of element i, and
F_{kj} is thus the form factor from the back of element i to element j. The second
change is to recognize that there are now more elements since the front and
back sides of a surface may act independently. Thus n is the total number of
elements, counting the back sides of translucent surfaces as separate elements.

Aside from computing the extra radiosities and form factors, the radiosity
solution proceeds normally. The image in Figure 10.18 was computed using
translucent elements to model the lampshade. The image was rendered using Monte Carlo eye-ray tracing to compute the direct illumination (see section 9.3.1).

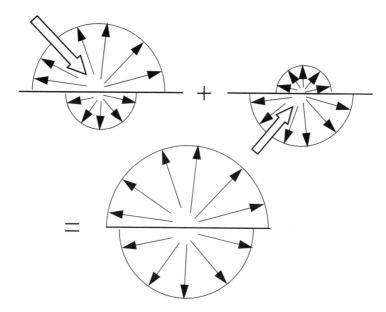

Figure 10.17: *A fraction of the light arriving at the front of a translucent surface is transmitted and radiated from the back of the element with an ideal diffuse distribution. Similarly, a fraction of light arriving at the back of a translucent element is radiated from the front.*

10.2.7 Two-Pass Methods

It is possible to account for all paths in $L(S|D)^*E$ using only eye-ray tracing or only a finite element approach. Kajiya's path tracing algorithm provides an example of the former approach, while Immel's global cube radiosity algorithm is an example of the latter. Neither is entirely satisfactory. Eye-ray tracing has the advantage that the number of paths to be traced is reduced based on the eye direction. Directional reflection can be sampled as finely as desired with no storage penalty. However, for diffuse reflection, a large number of paths must be sampled, and images tend to be noisy (see the Monte Carlo image in color plate 1, for example).

The finite element approach reduces the number of paths that must be traced for diffuse reflection by averaging the effect of paths over the surface. However, this approach requires excessive storage for highly directional reflection, as demonstrated by [132] (see Figure 10.13).

Two-pass methods abandon strict adherence to a single strategy; instead, they use each strategy to handle the category of paths for which it is most

Figure 10.18: *Image computed using translucent elements to model the lamp-shade. Courtesy of Peter Shirley, University of Indiana.*

efficient. Because of the linearity of light transport as modeled by the rendering equation, it is possible to sum the independently computed components to get the final result. Such approaches are often called two-pass methods, because the total solution typically consists of a radiosity and/or light-ray tracing pass followed by an eye-ray tracing pass.

The two-pass approach has been used prior to its application to radiosity (and prior to the origin of the term *two-pass*). For example, Kajiya and Von Herzen [136] use a two-pass method to compute images of clouds and other volume densities. Other examples of nonradiosity-based two-pass methods include Arvo's backwards ray tracing algorithm [12], Heckbert and Hanrahan's beam tracing algorithm [124], and Chattopadhyay and Fujimoto's bidirectional ray tracing algorithm [48]. Watt [259] also describes a two-pass method in which caustics are rendered by tracing beams forward from the light source.

Radiosity Plus Reflection Frustum

A two-pass method incorporating radiosity is first described by Wallace *et al.* [246]. The first pass consists of a Gauss-Seidel radiosity solution with stored form factors. Extended form factors are computed using Rushmeier's hemicube based mirror form factor method. The second pass traces eye-rays by recur-

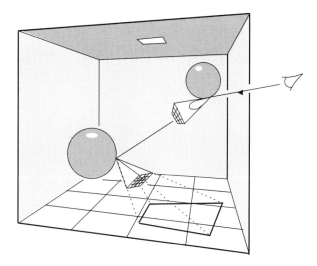

Figure 10.19: *Use of the reflection frustum during the rendering pass to sample a highly directional BRDF.*

sive application of a Z-buffer-based sampling algorithm, called the *reflection frustum*. The reflection frustum algorithm samples a number of incoming directions using scan conversion and Z-buffer hidden surface removal to evaluate the glossy component of reflection (see Figure 10.19). The sample directions are selected as grid points on the cross section of a square frustum oriented in the specular direction. The contribution of each sample is then weighted by the non-Lambertian components of the BRDF in that direction. This combination of algorithms accounts for the paths $L(D^*|D^*SD^*)S^*E$, with the restriction to ideal specular reflection in the D^*SD^* sequences (which shows how difficult it can get to figure out which paths are actually accounted for in any particular algorithm).

Radiosity Plus Ray Tracing

The two-pass algorithm described by Sillion and Puech [218] differs from that of Wallace *et al.* in that recursive ray tracing is used to compute extended form factors in the first pass, which allows the inclusion of DS^*D sequences (see Figure 10.20). Eye-ray tracing is used to handle ideal specular reflection in the second pass. Sillion and Puech point out that distribution ray tracing could be used to include paths containing glossy reflection as well.

The algorithm of Sillion *et al.* [217] (described earlier in section 10.2.4) in which glossy reflection is approximated using spherical harmonics, is also

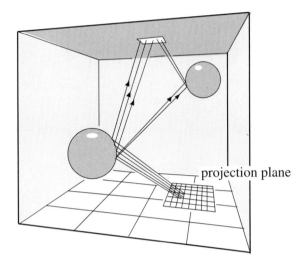

Figure 10.20: *Use of recursive ray tracing to compute extended form factors during the first pass of Sillion's two pass algorithm. Sillion uses a single projection plane rather than the five-faced hemicube to compute form factors.*

incorporated into a two-pass method. In this case completing the solution requires only the use of eye-ray tracing in the second pass to handle S^*E path segments consisting of ideal specular interactions. This algorithm accounts (approximately) for all paths in $L(S|D)^*E$.

Bidirectional Ray Tracing

Bidirectional ray tracing, described above in section 10.2.2, is a two-pass method, although as originally formulated it traces power from the light only until it lands on a Lambertian diffuse surface. However, it can be extended to handle multiple Lambertian diffuse interactions, using an approach similar to progressive radiosity in which light rays are propagated further into the environment through successive bounces from diffuse surfaces [213, 214].

Although equivalent to progressive radiosity, this approach does not explicitly compute form factors. Instead, power-carrying light rays are shot out into the scene from the light emitter. When a ray hits a surface its power is deposited and stored in an array of bins (analogous to elements). Light rays are then shot in a cosine distribution from the diffuse surface reflecting the most energy, and so on, for each reflecting surface (see Figure 10.21). As for progressive radiosity, the shooting step is repeated for other reflecting surfaces until the energy falls below a certain level.

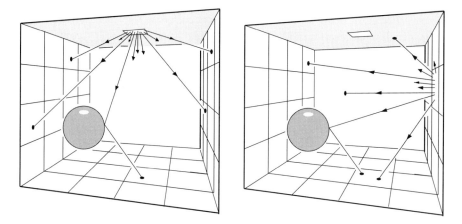

Figure 10.21: *Light-ray tracing extended to handle diffuse interreflection. These are two steps from the first pass of a two-pass algorithm.*

Glossy and ideal specular reflections can be incorporated into the first pass using an approach analogous to extended form factors. Instead of computing and storing the radiance for directionally reflecting surfaces, rays that encounter specular surfaces are traced recursively until they reach a diffuse surface. During the second pass, eye-rays are traced to account for segments of paths that start at a diffuse surface and interact with specular surfaces before reaching the eye (DS^*E path segments).

Color plate 42 was produced by Shirley using this approach. Note the caustics on the table top, which are produced by S^*DE path segments refracted through the wine glass. These are computed during the light-ray pass. The refractions and reflections visible in the wine glass itself are DS^*E path segments followed during the eye-ray pass. In addition to tracing eye-rays to follow specular reflection, Shirley also computes LDE paths, i.e., the direct illumination of diffuse surfaces, at each pixel during rendering (this approach is discussed in greater detail in Chapter 9). Shirley uses Arvo's illumination map data structure [12] to store incident power on diffuse surfaces.

Heckbert's rex algorithm uses the same basic light-ray tracing strategy as Shirley's algorithm, as well as a more powerful adaptive version of the illumination map data structure (this algorithm is described in more detail in Chapter 8). The images in Figures 8.30 and 8.31 were computed using Heckbert's bidirectional ray tracing algorithm.

The *multi-pass* algorithm of Chen *et al.* [52] uses both extended form factors and light-ray tracing. A radiosity solution using extended form factors is first performed to provide an initial low-frequency approximation of all $L(D|S)^*E$

paths. Light-ray tracing is then used to produce a more refined high-frequency approximation of caustics produced by LS^*D path segments. A key point, mentioned by Chen, is that the contribution of LS^*D paths initially computed using extended form factors must be subtracted before the higher-quality approximation of the *same* paths made by light-ray tracing is added in. *When combining algorithms in two-pass or multi-pass approaches, care must be taken to avoid counting the same paths more than once.*

Radiosity Plus Phong

Where absolute accuracy is not an issue, satisfactory images can be obtained relatively quickly by adding specular highlights to the radiosity shading during hardware rendering. This is accomplished by defining light sources for the graphics hardware prior to sending down the radiosity elements for Gouraud shading. Shading parameters are passed to the hardware along with the radiosity elements, with the specular component specified as needed and the diffuse component turned off. The vertex colors representing the radiosities can typically be included in the shading equation in the ambient component, by turning on a white ambient light source. The computed specular shading is then simply added to the ambient component by the hardware shader. Naturally, highlights produced by this method will not take shadowing into account. The image of the boiler room in color plate 40 was produced using this technique.

10.2.8   Surface Reflectance/Transmittance Data

Spectral and bidirectional reflectance and transmittance (BRDF/BTDF) data for the huge variety of materials found in typical environments is difficult to come by. Since image synthesis depends on this data, there is growing recognition of the need to develop fast and inexpensive techniques for making the necessary measurements. The reflectance of a material depends on its chemical constituents, surface finish, and often subsurface characteristics. In addition, these characteristics may vary over the surface.

One existing source for spectral data is [202]. This text includes spectral data for some building materials such as asphalt and brick, and plants such as lichen. (Also included is the reflectance for assorted foods, including the crust of baked bread parameterized by thickness!) Some information can also be found in [237] and [47]. However, these are primarily limited to materials with important thermal engineering applications rather than common architectural materials. Other sources of material data ranging from metals to sea water to ripe peaches are [104] and [219]. Surface finish information and related data on the spatial distribution of reflectance for a few materials can be found in [104, 114].

Drawing on data from [2], Rushmeier [199] provides a sample of "reasonable" room values for,

- total diffuse reflectances (i.e., averaged over the visible spectrum)
  - ceiling: 0.60 to 0.90
  - walls: 0.50 to 0.80
  - floor: 0.15 to 0.35
  - furniture: 0.30 (dark wood) to 0.50 (blond wood)
- specular reflectances
  - polished mirror: 0.99
  - polished aluminum: 0.65
- transmission coefficients
  - clear glass: 0.80 to 0.99 (basically "specular")
  - solid opal glass: 0.15 to 0.40 (basically "diffuse.")

Research is also being conducted to develop new methods for measuring the BRDF of surfaces and for generating the BRDF from simulated surface models [253, 263].

10.3 Participating Media

The radiosity equation, and the rendering equation from which it is derived, assumes that light interacts only with surfaces, ignoring the absorption or scattering of light by the medium through which it travels. The assumption of a nonparticipating medium, normally clear air or vacuum, is reasonable for many applications. However, clouds, humidity, fog, or smoke are often important factors in the illumination of exterior environments. For interiors, participating media may be required in order to simulate phenomena of particular interest, or for aesthetic reasons (as with the beams of light in the cover image).

A medium affects light transport through absorption, scattering and emission.[9] These may decrease or increase the radiance at any point along a path through the medium. A fraction κ_a of the radiance L will be absorbed per unit length along the path. Another fraction, κ_s, of L will be scattered out of the path (out-scattering). The radiance may also be increased when light incident on the point from other directions is scattered into the path (in-scattering), or if the medium itself emits light as in a flame. These phenomena are summarized in Figure 10.22.

---

[9]This exposition follows that of Rushmeier in [198].

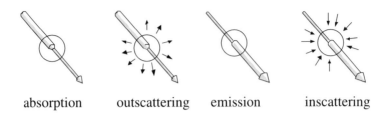

absorption   outscattering   emission   inscattering

Figure 10.22: *Phenomena affecting the radiance entering and exiting a differential volume along a path through a participating medium.*

10.3.1   Path Integrals

The effects of these interactions on the radiance along the path are described by the differential equation

$$\frac{dL}{d\mathbf{s}} = -\kappa_t L + \kappa_a L_e + \kappa_s L' \tag{10.27}$$

where κ_a is the absorption coefficient, κ_s is the scattering coefficient, κ_t is the extinction coefficient $(\kappa_a + \kappa_s)$, L is the radiance along the path, L_e is the emitted radiance, and L' is the radiance incident on the path.

The last term of this equation, which accounts for in-scattering, requires integrating incident radiance over the sphere of incoming directions. The scattering *phase function*, $f(\theta)$, specifies the fraction of the radiance arriving from an incident direction, θ, that is scattered into the path. With the inclusion of the integral over incoming directions, the equation for radiance in a participating medium becomes

$$\frac{dL}{d\mathbf{s}} = -\kappa_t L + \kappa_a L_e + \frac{\kappa_s}{4\pi} \int_0^{2\pi} \int_0^{\pi} L'(\theta)\, f(\theta) \sin\theta\, d\theta\, d\phi \tag{10.28}$$

A number of algorithms have been developed to solve this equation numerically, based on various simplifying assumptions. These are well summarized in [198]. The following section will concentrate on the generalization of the radiosity equation to handle media that scatter or emit light isotropically, that is, with equal radiance in all directions. This reduces the phase function to a constant in a similar fashion to the BRDF reducing to a constant for diffuse surface reflection. This approach was first introduced to image synthesis by Rushmeier in [200].

The radiance for a given direction leaving a point in space includes not only incident light scattered into the path but also light that is just passing through the point with no interaction at all. The complete radiance at a point is thus expensive to approximate accurately, since the light just passing through a point typically varies extremely rapidly with direction.

This problem can be avoided by formulating the solution to equation 10.28 in a way that separates out the contributions of in-scattering and emission along the path. This observation is essentially the same as that used to separate surface reflection into ideal diffuse and mirror specular terms. Solving equation 10.28 for $L(\mathbf{s})$ gives the integral equation

$$L(\mathbf{s}) = L(0)\tau(0, \mathbf{s}) + \int_0^{\mathbf{S}} \tau(\mathbf{s}', \mathbf{s}) J(\mathbf{s}') \kappa_t(\mathbf{s}') \, d\mathbf{s}' \tag{10.29}$$

where $J(\mathbf{s}')$ is a function describing the radiance added to the path at each point $\mathbf{s}'$ due to emission and in-scattering, and $\tau(\mathbf{s}_1, \mathbf{s}_2)$ is the integrated extinction coefficient κ_t along the path from $\mathbf{s}_1$ to $\mathbf{s}_2$.

$$\tau(\mathbf{s}_1, \mathbf{s}_2) = e^{-\int_{\mathbf{S}_1}^{\mathbf{S}_2} \kappa_t(\mathbf{S}) \, d\mathbf{S}} \tag{10.30}$$

For an isotropic medium with constant κ_t, $\tau(\mathbf{s}_1, \mathbf{s}_2)$ reduces to

$$\tau(\mathbf{s}_1, \mathbf{s}_2) = e^{-\kappa_t |\mathbf{S}_1 - \mathbf{S}_2|} \tag{10.31}$$

The first term in equation 10.29 accounts for what is seen through the medium; it consists of the radiance of the surface at the beginning of the path attenuated by absorption and scattering along the path. This requires only an approximation of the radiosity at the surface at which the path begins, and thus eliminates the need to approximate that highly directional component at every point in the volume.

The second term in equation 10.29 accounts for energy accrued along the path as the result of in-scattering and emission, which are represented by the function $J(\mathbf{s})$. $J(\mathbf{s})$, called the *source* function, varies much more slowly over the volume than $L(\mathbf{s})$ and can be approximated relatively inexpensively. The problem is thus to compute $J(\mathbf{s})$.

10.3.2 The Zonal Method

Rushmeier's method of solving for $J(\mathbf{s})$ is based on the *zonal* method, which has its origins in the field of heat transfer [130]. The zonal method follows the development of the standard diffuse surface radiosity closely. $J(\mathbf{s})$ is approximated by subdividing the volume containing the medium into discrete volume elements across which the radiance due to scattering or emission is assumed to be constant. The surfaces are subdivided into surface elements as before (see Figure 10.23).

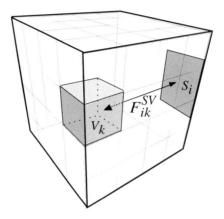

Figure 10.23: *Interaction of volume and surface elements.*

Assuming the participating media has been divided into m volume elements and the surfaces into n elements, then the radiosity of a *surface* element, i, includes contributions from all other surfaces, j, and all volume elements, k:

$$B_i A_i = E_i A_i + \rho_i \left\{ \sum_{j=1}^{n} B_j F_{ji}^{SS} + \sum_{k=1}^{m} B_k F_{ki}^{VS} \right\} \qquad (10.32)$$

where F_{ji}^{SS} is the surface-to-surface form factor and F_{ki}^{VS} is the volume-to-surface form factor. Likewise, the radiosity of a *volume element* V_k, includes contributions from all surface elements j and all other volumes l

$$4\kappa_t B_k V_k = 4\kappa_a E_k V_k + \Omega_k \left\{ \sum_{j=1}^{n} B_j F_{jk}^{SV} + \sum_{l=1}^{m} B_l F_{lk}^{VV} \right\} \qquad (10.33)$$

where F_{jk}^{SV} is the surface-to-volume form factor and F_{lk}^{VV} is the volume-to-volume form factor. The factor Ω_k is the *scattering albedo* of volume V_k, similar to the diffuse reflectivity term for surfaces. The computation of volume-to-volume and volume-to-surface form factors using the hemicube is shown in Figure 10.24.

The various form factors are similar to those for conventional radiosity, except that they include the effect of attenuation due to transport through the

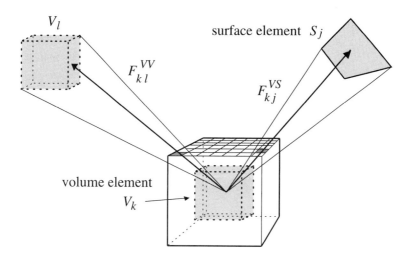

Figure 10.24: *Computation of volume-to-volume and volume-to-surface form factors using the hemicube.*

medium. The form factor F_{ij}^{SS} between two surface elements, S_i and S_j, is given by

$$F_{ij}^{SS} = \int_{A_i} \int_{A_j} \tau(\mathbf{x}_i, \mathbf{x}_j) \frac{\cos \theta_i \cos \theta_j}{\pi r^2} dA_j dA_i \qquad (10.34)$$

where $\tau()$ (see equation 10.30) reduces the transfer between the respective points on the two elements i and j. Note also, there is no division by area in this form. The volume-to-surface form factor is

$$F_{kj}^{VS} = \int_{V_k} \int_{A_j} \tau(\mathbf{x}_k, \mathbf{x}_j) \frac{\cos \theta_j \, \kappa_{t,k}}{\pi r^2} dA_j dV_k \qquad (10.35)$$

where $\kappa_{t,k}$ is the constant κ_t for volume k. The volume-to-volume form factor is given by

$$F_{kl}^{VV} = \int_{V_k} \int_{V_l} \tau(\mathbf{x}_k, \mathbf{x}_l) \frac{\kappa_{t,k} \, \kappa_{t,l}}{\pi r^2} dV_l dV_k \qquad (10.36)$$

The form factors may be computed using existing algorithms with little modification. The principle requirement is the evaluation of the path integrals. In Rushmeier's modified hemicube algorithm, τ is computed at each hemicube pixel, based on the distance to the surface or volume to which the form factor is being computed (see equations 10.30 and 10.31).

Rendering the solution of the zonal method is equivalent to the *volume rendering* methods developed for scientific visualization applications [75, 136, 149,

150, 264]. Volume rendering for hierarchical volumes is explored in [145]. During rendering, equation 10.29 is evaluated for each pixel. First, the contribution of the radiosity of the visible surface is computed, taking into account attenuation by computing τ as above. Then the contribution to the total radiance of every volume element through which the path travels is computed, also taking into account the attenuation based on the distance from the eye to the volume element. The final radiance for the pixel is the sum of all these contributions. Since J is computed independently of the view, rendering another view requires only recomputing these path integrals.

As in conventional radiosity, constant volume elements are not adequate for rendering. Trilinear interpolation can be used to smooth the volume radiosities during rendering. Results of this method are shown in color plates 1f and 48.

The zonal method has been extended by Rushmeier [198] to thin media exhibiting weak anisotropic scatter, where volume-to-volume interactions are assumed insignificant. It has been further extended by Bhate and Tokuta [28] to the case of more general anisotropic scatter, using spherical harmonics to approximate the directionally dependent phase function.

Chapter 11

Applications and Research

This chapter will explore the use of radiosity in design, engineering and scientific applications; the experimental validation of the radiosity method; and opportunities for research into improved models, numerical methods, and algorithms.

Applications and research are not as independent as they might seem at first glance. The incorporation of radiosity into an application precipitates a whole new set of requirements that can push research in unexpected and fruitful directions. The difference between algorithms suitable for specialists and algorithms for mainstream use is not trivial. Since image synthesis is often just a tool hidden inside a larger application, it is expected to perform robustly and predictably with little technical input from the user. This places great demands on the underlying algorithms. The development of automatic, accurate, and robust algorithms will provide research problems for a long time to come.

11.1 Applications

In general, radiosity is most useful in applications where ideal diffuse interreflection is important and the geometry is static. The view-independent approach is particularly valuable when the exploration of a three-dimensional model is required, rather than the production of a single static image.

When incorporating any global illumination algorithm into an application, it is important to insulate the user from the technical details of the procedure. Specifying a mesh resolution or adaptive subdivision criterion forces the user to learn entirely new concepts unrelated to his or her work. To the extent that the user is given control over the solution, results must be predictable. Radiosity solutions for complex environments are too expensive to allow trial and error as a reasonable approach.

These requirements have important consequences for the development of radiosity algorithms. Meshing algorithms must be extremely robust. Where parameters are necessary, they must map clearly to quality and cost. The time–quality tradeoff should be predictable, and quality should degrade gracefully with decreasing cost. For example, a lower-cost solution might provide less shadow detail, but should not contain disturbing artifacts.

In the next sections, several radiosity applications will be discussed. This will highlight some of the strengths of the radiosity approach, as well as some of the areas that need attention.

11.1.1 Architectural Design

Architectural design is in many ways an ideal application for image synthesis and the radiosity method in particular. Architects must communicate a design to clients, who may have difficulty visualizing the final building from abstract plans and drawings. As a result, architects currently depend on hand-drawn or painted perspectives, or on expensive physical models to provide a concrete representation. These media allow the designer to communicate a valuable emotional or aesthetic impression, but they also have limitations. For example, they can convey only a limited sensation of interior space, since they do not allow the client to look around or to explore the design from different viewpoints. Because they are time consuming to produce, they do not encourage the exploration of alternative materials, finishes, or lighting. For these reasons, the prospect of producing realistic three-dimensional renderings quickly and automatically has made image synthesis attractive.

Radiosity is particularly well suited to architectural design. Many interior surfaces (e.g., upholstery, textiles, matte paints) are reasonably well approximated by ideal diffuse reflection, and diffuse interreflection makes an important contribution to the illumination of interiors. Architectural models are usually static. The radiosity solution, when rendered on a graphics workstation, allows interactive walkthroughs of the shaded model, giving the designer and the client the opportunity to explore the interior space interactively.

Typical features of a radiosity application for architecture would include

- Translation from modeler data formats.

- Access to material libraries.

- Access to lighting libraries.

- Positioning of lights.

- Assignment of material properties.

- Positioning of texture maps.

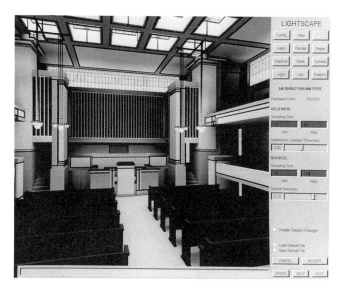

Figure 11.1: *A view of the Lightscape architectural design application. The model shown is Frank Lloyd Wright's Unity Temple, designed in 1904. Image courtesy of Stuart Feldman, Lightscape Graphics Software.*

- Control over the process of the solution. Progressive refinement is useful because it allows the user to evaluate the partial solution without having to wait for convergence.

- Camera control for interactive walkthroughs.

Radiosity simulations also have some limitations for architectural visualization. Although ideal diffuse reflection is a reasonable approximation for many common surfaces, many other common surface materials and finishes cannot be represented correctly (e.g., metals, polishes, glass). Two-pass methods and other approaches that incorporate specular reflection (see Chapter 10) are important in architectural visualization. An additional requirement for image synthesis in general is the availability of data describing materials, finishes, and lights. Routine use of image synthesis in design applications will require digital libraries of such data, preferably provided by the manufacturers, analogous to the large catalogues ubiquitous in design offices.

The cost and performance of radiosity simulation is another issue. Architectural models can be large; models in excess of 100,000 polygons are not uncommon. The $O(n^2)$ computation and storage cost makes current radiosity implementations impractical for problems of this size. The problem is intensified

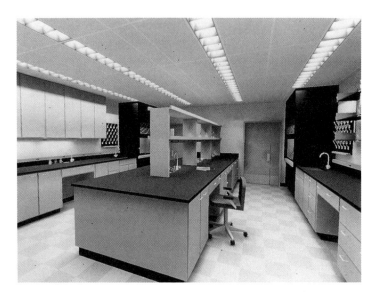

Figure 11.2: *An interior design study. Image courtesy of David L. Munson, Hellmuth, Obata & Kassabaum Architects, Inc.*

by the lack of computing power typically available to small architectural firms.

The time it takes to produce an acceptable image is particularly crucial because architectural presentation is often the first, rather than the last, stage of the design process. Presentations of a design proposal to a potential client are thus developed under pressing time constraints. For image synthesis to play a role, it must be fast and dependable. Radiosity methods are only beginning to provide this level of performance.

In spite of these issues, the compelling quality of radiosity images, the possibility of interactive walkthroughs, and the fact that it is physically based make radiosity an attractive alternative. An architectural design application using radiosity is shown in Figure 11.1 and in color plates 47 and 50. The images in Figures 11.2 and 11.3 were produced using software developed at the architectural firm of Hellmuth, Obata & Kassabaum, Inc.

11.1.2 Lighting Design

The accurate simulation of global illumination is also a useful tool for lighting designers. For conventional lighting situations, such as an office, designers often rely on tables, simple formulae or rules of thumb in deciding how many lighting fixtures to use and where to position them. For unique lighting designs, a three-dimensional model may sometimes be constructed and lit. Specialized software

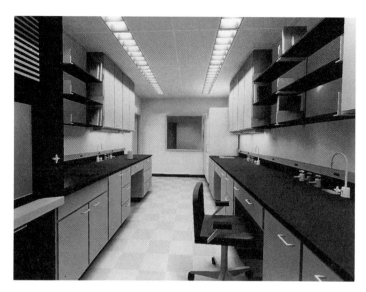

Figure 11.3: *A second view from the same interior design study. Image courtesy of David L. Munson, Hellmuth, Obata & Kassabaum Architects, Inc.*

is also becoming increasingly common. (Ward's experimental *Radiance* package is a particularly sophisticated general purpose example [252].) Physically based global illumination models and algorithms provide the possibility of more general quantitative results as well as realistic images for aesthetic evaluation.

Lighting manufacturers have also begun to develop their own radiosity based lighting design tools, often with the goal of distributing software along with digital catalogues of luminaires to architectural and lighting design firms. Companies ranging from Toshiba Lighting and Technology in Japan, to Philips Electronics and Zumtobel Licht GmbH in Europe (color plate 51) have begun to experiment with this technology.

Theatrical Lighting

Theatrical lighting is a special case of lighting design that has very particular requirements. Although light sources are limited to five or so basic types, a theatrical production typically uses hundreds of individual lights. These are turned on and off frequently in different combinations. The continuous variation of light intensity over time is often aesthetically important.

The circumstances under which the lighting for a particular production is designed are usually demanding. Sets are constructed at the last minute. As a result, the actual appearance of the lighted set cannot be fully evaluated until just

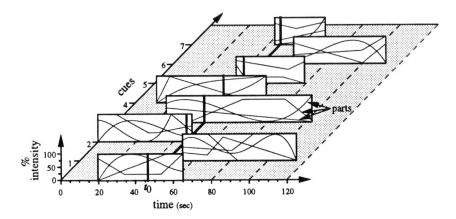

Figure 11.4: *Part of a lighting specification for a production at the Metropolitan Opera House. Each light or group of lights has its own time history of intensity. Provided by Julie O'B. Dorsey, courtesy of the Metropolitan Opera.*

prior to the first performance. Computer simulation thus seems ideally suited to the design of stage lighting.

Several features of the theatrical lighting design problem make radiosity a potentially useful tool. The model to be illuminated is normally static. The scene may need to be evaluated from a number of viewpoints throughout the audience seating. These views are taken from outside the scene, so there is a fairly well-defined limit to the shading detail required.

On the other hand, there are several aspects of the problem that require modifications to the conventional radiosity approach. For example, the light sources have very specific characteristics that must be modeled correctly. The sources are typically highly directional and thus quite different from ideal diffuse emitters handled by conventional radiosity. Dorsey [74fl]describes modified form factor formulae (similar to those discussed in Chapter 10).

Although the geometry of the scene is static, this is not true of the lighting. The complexity of the problem is suggested by the diagram in Figure 11.4, which specifies the lighting changes for different banks of lights over time for a production at the Metropolitan Opera House. Fortunately, most lighting changes involve changes in emitted power rather than repositioning or repointing of the light. The static positioning of lights allows the effect of various lights or combinations of lights to be computed independently. For any given lighting specification, the independent solutions can then be rapidly scaled appropriately and summed to provide the total radiosity [73fl].

Dorsey's program includes extensive tools for lighting specification (see

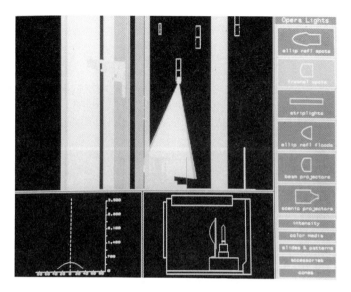

Figure 11.5: *The specification and pointing of lights in an application for operatic lighting design. Courtesy of Julie O'B. Dorsey, Program of Computer Graphics, Cornell University.*

Figure 11.5) and for viewing the solution. Color plates 53 and 54 and the image on the back cover show results generated by this application. The solutions were computed using progressive radiosity with ray traced form factors. Rendering was performed using a stochastic ray tracer. Texture mapping (discussed in Chapter 9) has also been used very effectively to add detail during rendering.

Lighting Optimization

Kawai *et al.* [137] have developed techniques that invert the radiosity simulation paradigm. Given a geometric description of an environment and the illumination requirements or a *desired appearance* for the scene, their algorithm addresses the question of how the lighting parameters should be set to achieve these goals. They describe a method for *designing* the illumination in an environment by applying optimization techniques to a radiosity-based image synthesis system. The user is able to specify the illumination in terms of subjective criteria such as "pleasantness" and "privateness." Other goals such as minimizing total energy consumption or maintaining a minimum illumination on a work surface can also be specified. An optimization of lighting parameters is then performed based on the user-specified constraints and objectives for the illumination of the environment. The system solves for the "best" possible settings for light-source emissivities, element reflectivities, and spot-light directionality parameters.

11.1.3 Remote Sensing

Satellite images of visible and near-infrared light are frequently used to survey land use and resources. From the point of view of a satellite, a forest or other region of vegetation is a "surface" with a characteristic BRDF that determines its appearance under various observation conditions. One way of determining this BRDF is to perform a series of measurements in the field.

Computer simulation provides an alternative means of determining the BRDF. For example, to compute a BRDF for a forest canopy, a simplified model of the canopy specifying its interaction with light can be constructed and evaluated. One such model treats the canopy as a system of homogeneous volume elements with a certain density. A model of radiative transfer is then used to compute the interaction of light with the volumes [99].

Radiosity methods have also been applied to this problem [34, 94]. Since radiosity requires explicitly modeled geometry, it can support a detailed canopy model constructed of individual leaves. It thus provides more control over the characteristics of the simulated vegetation. The view-independence of the radiosity solution is also an advantage. Although the reflectivity of any individual leaf is treated as ideal diffuse, the BRDF for the canopy as a whole can be highly directional, due to varying occlusion and anisotropic leaf orientation. Following the radiosity solution, the BRDF can be evaluated for a range of view angles by rendering an image of the solution for each view angle. The radiance is averaged over the pixels of the image, and the BRDF for that view angle is then determined by the ratio of the radiance to the incident irradiance.

Borel *et al.* [34] suggest other applications for radiosity in remote sensing, including modeling the scattering of light between topographic features like the sides of valleys and the effect of clouds on illumination of land features. They also envision the use of radiosity in plant biology to simulate light transport and photosynthesis in plants.

11.1.4 Visual Shape Understanding

The need for a better understanding of visual perception in developing more efficient and accurate image synthesis algorithms has surfaced a number of times in this book. Interestingly, image synthesis itself can play an important part in improving the understanding of visual perception. For example, texture mapping and ray tracing have been applied in research into visual *shape understanding* in experiments to explore how the eye and brain extract information about geometric shape from the visual field.

Information about geometric shape is provided by binocular vision, as well as by cues such as texture, shading, cast and received shadows, and highlights [29, 96, 128, 129, 274]. Wanger [250] has used texture mapping and cast shadows to explore the importance of these and other cues to positioning tasks in computer graphics applications. Synthesized images are valuable in investigating shape and positioning cues because they allow controlled experiments in which image features are isolated. For similar reasons, image synthesis is useful in testing algorithms and devices for machine vision. The machine vision field has relied mainly on edge finding algorithms for object recognition, but researchers have also investigated "shape from shading" techniques [128].

Although there is some understanding of how direct illumination provides shape information, illumination due to interreflected light complicates the problem [179]. Forsyth and Zisserman [85] have explored the applicability of the radiosity equation as a model of global illumination for shape perception. They argue that discontinuities in the radiance function, caused by shadows or surface creases, provide stronger shape cues than the smooth variation of the function due to surface curvature. The availability of discontinuity meshing may provide a means to investigate this possibility. Parker *et al.* [178] have developed radiosity code specifically for experimentation in shape understanding.

11.1.5 Infrared Signature Analysis

The goal of infrared signature analysis is the recognition of vehicles or other objects by their characteristic appearance or *signature* in images produced by infrared imaging systems. Computer simulation provides a valuable way to generate these signatures. An example of a simulated infrared image is shown in Figure 11.6.

An infrared sensor detects radiance leaving an object due to emission and reflection. Infrared imaging requires a complete heat transfer model incorporating the processes of convection, conduction, and radiative transfer (with shadowing) for ideal diffuse and specular BRDFs. Heat sources include engines, exhaust, solar illumination, and sky illumination.

Many of these requirements are outside of the concerns of normal image synthesis. However, the radiative transfer component can benefit from algorithms developed for radiosity as applied to image synthesis, particularly algorithms for computing form factors. For example, the hemicube algorithm has been used by Johnson *et al.* [133] for this application.

Figure 11.6: *A simulated infrared image. Courtesy of Keith R. Johnson, Michigan Technological University.*

11.1.6 Fine Arts

Computer graphics has already made an impact on the fine arts. Conferences such as SIGGRAPH include computer art and film shows in addition to technical presentations. Although much of this work is abstract, the ability to simulate realistic lighting effects can be an effective tool for conveying meaning in artistic works. Color plate 52 depicts a frame from an experimental video by Monika Fleischmann entitled "Home of the Brain," in which lighting effects are simulated with radiosity.

11.2 Experimental Validation

As applications turn increasingly to global illumination algorithms for design, engineering, or scientific problems, there is a corresponding need to verify that the algorithms produce valid results. Radiosity is a physically based model and purports to produce a physically accurate description of illumination. This is a claim that can be tested by comparing the results of a radiosity simulation with measurements of real models.

Experimental validation addresses two basic questions. First, does the mathematical model adequately describe the physical process of interest? For example, in the case of radiosity, one might ask whether the assumption of ideal diffuse reflection is too restrictive to be useful for modeling real environments. Second, experimental validation tests the accuracy of numerical methods and algorithms.

A further issue that requires experimental investigation is the quality of the visual experience provided by image synthesis algorithms. The perceived realism of images is very difficult to quantify, but this is nevertheless a crucial criterion in the evaluation of algorithms for certain applications.

Meyer *et al.* [167] have made preliminary efforts toward an experimental validation of the radiosity method. They have performed two sets of experiments with the familiar red, white, and blue box (similar to the boxes in color plate 1).

The first set of these experiments compares the results of a radiosity simulation to radiometric measurements of a physical model. These experiments were intended to evaluate basic assumptions of the radiosity method, particularly the assumption of ideal diffuse reflection and emission. Measurements of the integral of irradiance were made at intervals on the open face of a box whose interior faces were painted various colors. Illumination was provided by a diffused light source at the center of the top of the box.

The results of the experiment indicate that the assumption of ideal diffuse emission for the light source contributes significantly to errors in the simulation. The experiment also demonstrates that radiosity accounts well for the effect of diffuse interreflection or "color bleeding" and for the effect of occlusion, insofar as measurement by integrating irradiance can indicate.

The second set of experiments addresses the perceived quality of radiosity images, with the intention of seeing how close radiosity comes to creating a visual experience identical to that experienced seeing the real scene. Given the limitations of existing display devices, it was necessary to simplify the problem in several ways. For example, the light source was blocked from direct view in both the image and the actual scene so that the limited dynamic range of the display did not immediately give away the simulation.

In the experiment, a real scene and a simulated version were projected side by side onto frosted glass in the backs of two view cameras (see Figure 11.7 and color plate 5). Subjects were asked to determine which was the real scene and to rate the relative quality of features like shadows and color (color plates 6 and 7). The simulated image was chosen as the real scene approximately 50% of the time (for untrained observers), indicating that the synthesized image achieved the goal of perceptual realism in this highly constrained case. Color plates 8 and 9 are the result of exposing film placed in the view cameras. It should be noted that the reader is not getting the same visual experience as the subjects in the experiment. Film processing introduces its own distortions, as does the reproduction of the photograph in print. In addition, viewing light reflected from

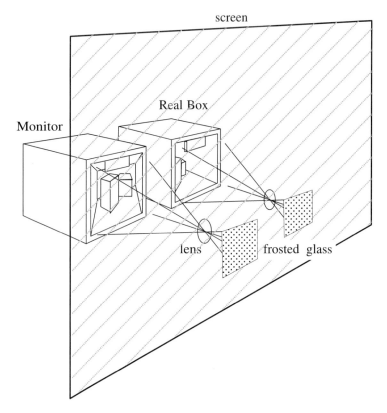

Figure 11.7: *The experimental setup for perceptual validation of a simple ra-diosity solution.*

the pages of a book is different than viewing light transmitted through frosted glass. Finally, the images presented to the experimental observer were upside down due to camera lens optics.

These experiments are clearly just a beginning. However, they raise many of the issues that any experimental validation must address and provide preliminary answers to some of them. These issues include the type of radiometric device appropriate for the physical measurements, the physical quantities that should be measured, and the problem of constructing a physical model and measuring its properties to define an equivalent computer model. For perceptual experiments, there are additional difficult questions, such as how to present the comparisons without biasing the result and how to obtain detailed information about what features contribute or detract from realism.

Ward [251] has also performed experimental verification of the *Radiance* lighting design program. Although this program does not use the radiosity method, the issues of experimental verification are essentially the same and a number of practical questions are addressed in this work. In spite of these contributions, experimental validation is clearly an area where much valuable work remains to be done.

11.3 Future Research Directions

Although developments over the last several years have demonstrated that radiosity is potentially a useful tool for image synthesis, fundamental improvements still remain to be made to ensure accuracy, achieve predictable results, and provide adequate performance. Several key areas for continuing work are described briefly in the following sections.

11.3.1 Error Analysis

The numerical evaluation of a mathematical model will rarely, if ever, produce an exact result. This is not necessarily a handicap, as long as the error can be characterized quantitatively and can be reduced to an acceptable level given enough computational resources. For radiosity applications, it would be ideal to bound the maximum error for the radiosity values in an image to, for example, to within 5%. In reality, this is very difficult to achieve, because error is introduced at many different points during the solution and propagates in a complicated manner.

Error is introduced by interpolation, the approximations made in discretization, numerical integration of form factors, the inability to converge the matrix solution fully, and the projection of the solution onto a new basis prior to rendering. Future work must develop a better understanding of where and how error is introduced into the radiosity solution, as well as how these errors accumulate to cause inaccuracies in the solution. This research will undoubtedly benefit from the existing literature in numerical methods and engineering analysis. Progress in placing global illumination analysis on a rigorous mathematical footing is also a prerequisite to understanding the sources and propagation of errors.

11.3.2 Perceptually Based Error Metrics

As a number of researchers have recognized [167, 238, 250], the image synthesis process does not end with an approximation of the radiosity or radiance function for the scene. The evaluation of a global illumination model is only a step in a process whose final outcome is a visual experience in the mind of the viewer.

Thus, although it is important to develop quantitative error measures, a full evaluation of the simulation must account for the perception of the image. In this respect, the job of image synthesis is more difficult than that of engineering, because the problem to be solved includes a perceptual process for which there are no complete and well-defined mathematical models.

The ability to measure the quality of the perceived image is important for more than evaluating the relative usefulness of different algorithms. A measure of accuracy is a key tool for any numerical algorithm that attempts to direct the course of the solution in order to minimize error and distribute computational resources efficiently. For example, a perceptually based error metric might direct the radiosity solution to focus effort on aspects of shadow boundaries that are important to perceived quality, while ignoring others. A purely radiometric measure might weight these characteristics equally. Currently, assumptions about which aspects of reality are perceptually important are most often built into the algorithm or the mathematical model on the basis of what is practical to compute rather than on firm perceptual grounds.

One goal of research in this area is to develop a better understanding of visual perception, with the ultimate aim of modeling the aspects of the process that are relevant to image synthesis. There is a large literature of perception research to be investigated. The literature of the fine arts is also a resource that should not be overlooked. Artists have struggled with many of these issues for centuries, and some of the discoveries of computer graphics research are available in art handbooks on the shelves of the local bookstore.

A related area for research is the development of algorithms that can incorporate image-based error measures into the solution process. The *importance* algorithm of Smits *et al.* [220] (Chapter 7) is a valuable first step in this direction.

11.3.3 Physically Based Emission and BRDF Data

The results of a physically-based global illumination algorithm are only as accurate as the data describing the model. Radiosity requires a geometric description of the environment, emission spectra for light sources, directional luminance data for light fixtures, reflectivity spectra for surfaces and, for more general algorithms, the BRDF for surfaces. The generation of geometric models is a field in its own right and is not covered in this text. However, the physically accurate specification of light emission and surface reflectivity is beginning to receive attention as a topic for research in the global illumination field. A survey of sources for data on a limited set of materials and lighting is given by Rushmeier [199].

Faced with the unavailability of the full range of data required for image synthesis, researchers have begun to investigate techniques for measuring the

BRDF of real surfaces and for generating the BRDF from simulated surface models. Ward [253] discusses an experimental setup for measuring the BRDF of real materials. Cabral, *et al.* [41] describe a method for computing the BRDF from bump maps specifying small scale surface geometry. Westin *et al.* [263] describe an algorithm for computing the BRDF based on detailed geometric models of materials such as cloth or brushed metal. As image synthesis algorithms become more accurate, their dependence on valid data will become more critical and this area of research will gain increasing importance.

11.3.4 Meshing

As evident from the discussion of applications, there is a great need for robust, fast, and predictable meshing algorithms. One of the largest hindrances to the adoption of radiosity for mainstream applications is the difficulty of specifying meshing parameters (and the trial and error required to get good results).

Meshing for radiosity has been until recently, to use Heckbert's words, something of a "black art" [120]. Although this state of affairs has improved, as demonstrated by the survey of meshing algorithms in Chapters 6 and 8, there are many techniques for finite element meshing that have yet to be investigated for radiosity.

Discontinuity meshing has made impressive gains in improving predictability and in eliminating the need for trial and error in setting mesh parameters. The development of discontinuity meshing algorithms that are efficient and practical for complex environments is an important direction to investigate. There is also room to improve a posteriori approaches, which may reduce the need to determine exact boundaries a priori.

11.3.5 Hierarchy

As noted in section 11.1.1, architectural models, for which radiosity is otherwise well suited, can easily exceed 100,000 polygons. Despite many improvements in efficiency, radiosity algorithms are still essentially $O(n^2)$ in the number of polygons. Fortunately, this does not seem to be an inherent lower bound on the efficiency of the technique.

The hierarchical methods described in Chapter 7 support the view that the cost of radiosity can be reduced. The basic concept underlying these methods is that the interactions between two widely separated groups of elements can be represented by a single average interaction. Current hierarchical algorithms always start with a polygon and subdivide downward. Thus elements can be grouped only within a polygon, and elements from different polygons cannot be grouped together to form larger *clusters*. As a result, current hierarchical methods reduce the cost of the radiosity solution in terms of the number of elements, but the cost in the number of polygons is still $O(n^2)$. Clearly, the next step is to cluster surfaces together, allowing interactions with multiple objects to be treated as a single interaction where appropriate. Preliminary work has begun in this area.

Xu [269] has used spatial substructuring to reduce the cost of the radiosity solution. In this approach, the volume containing the environment is subdivided uniformly to create *subscenes*. Elements within a single subscene interact normally, but interactions between elements in neighboring subscenes are mediated by special elements on the "surfaces" that define the subscene boundaries. These elements record directional information about the light reflected toward the boundary from inside the subscene. For the neighboring subscene, these boundary elements then provide an approximation of the illumination arriving from outside the subscene to the elements within. This approach has been used subsequently as a basis for the parallelization of the radiosity solution [10, 239], with each independent subscene handled by a different processor. A related approach has also been proposed by Neumann and Kelemen [172].

Although spatial subdivision reduces the cost of the radiosity solution, the subdivision must be specified a priori by the user. The hierarchy is inflexible and is limited to two levels, which does not fully exploit the potential of hierarchical methods to increase the efficiency of the solution.

Rushmeier *et al.* [196] describe a more flexible algorithm based on a two-pass method. In the first pass a radiosity solution is performed on a simplified version of the scene, in which complex objects are approximated by bounding boxes. The criterion for simplification is based on an approximation to the solid angle subtended by surfaces, objects, and groups of objects with respect to potential receiving surfaces. The rendering pass uses Monte Carlo ray tracing from the eye to compute direct illumination. Secondary rays are shot to compute the indirect illumination of visible surfaces. Beyond a certain neighborhood around the surface to be shaded, the illumination is provided by the radiosity solution computed in the first pass, which effectively clusters geometric detail into simplified representations. Even though the hierarchy of complex and simple geometric representation is limited to two levels, Rushmeier reports decreases of several orders of magnitude in solution time over conventional radiosity methods.

The clustering algorithms developed so far are only a first step. Future work should include automatic methods for generating the simplified geometry and generalization of the hierarchy to multiple levels. This remains perhaps the most important open problem for radiosity research.

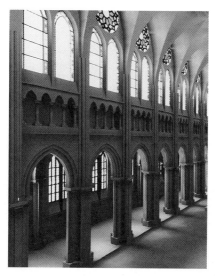

Figure 11.8: *A view looking down the nave of Chartres Cathedral. The model was produced by John Lin using Hewlett-Packard's ME-30 solid modeler.*

11.4 Conclusion

Architects have struggled to capture the grandeur of space and light in monumental structures. The renderings of such a structure in Figures 11.8 and 11.9 demonstrate that the radiosity method can produce compelling images based on the simulation of the propagation of light.

The goal of producing convincingly realistic images of nonexistent scenes is tantalizingly close to being achieved. However, many chapters in this exciting research endeavor have yet to be written. As computational speeds increase and the associated costs continue to decline, emerging applications will surely demand more of image synthesis algorithms. We hope that this text has provided a firm base upon which to build these future image synthesis systems and that it will encourage the reader to become involved in this quest.

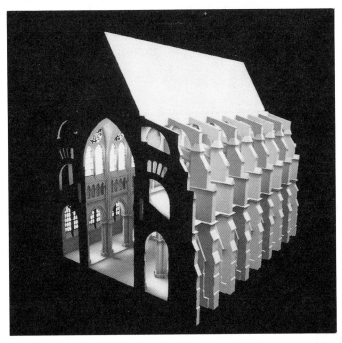

Figure 11.9: *An exterior view of the Chartres model.*

Bibliography

[1] *CIE Recommendations on Uniform Color Spaces, Color-difference Equations, and Psychometric Color Terms.* Bureau de la CIE, Paris, 1978.

[2] *IES Lighting Handbook.* 1981 Reference Edition, New York, 1981.

[3] *Sweet's Catalog File: Products for Engineering.* McGraw-Hill, New York, 1981.

[4] ANSI standard nomenclature and definitions for illuminating engineering. ANSI/IES RP-16-1986, Illuminating Engineering Society, 345 East 47th Street, New York, NY 10017, approved 1986.

[5] AIREY, J. M., ROHLF, J. H., AND BROOKS, F. P. Towards image realism with interactive update rates in complex virtual building environments. *Computer Graphics (1990 Symposium on Interactive 3D Graphics)* **24**:2 (Mar. 1990), pp. 41–50.

[6] ALA, S. R. Performance anomalies in boundary data structures. *IEEE Computer Graphics and Applications* **12**:2 (Mar. 1992), pp. 49–58.

[7] AMANATIDES, J. Ray tracing with cones. *Computer Graphics (SIGGRAPH '84 Proceedings)* **18**:3 (July 1984), pp. 129–135.

[8] APPEL, A. Some techniques for shading machine renderings of solids. In *Proceedings of the Spring Joint Computer Conference* (1968), pp. 37–45.

[9] APPEL, A. A. An efficient program for many body simulation. *SIAM Journal of Sci. Stat. Computing* **6**:1 (1985), pp. 85–103.

[10] ARNALDI, B., PUEYO, X., AND VILAPLANA, J. On the division of environments by virtual walls for radiosity computation. In *Second Eurographics Workshop on Rendering* (Barcelona, Spain, May 1991).

[11] ARVO, J., AND KIRK, D. Fast ray tracing by ray classification. *Computer Graphics (SIGGRAPH '87 Proceedings)* **21**:4 (Aug. 1987), pp. 55–64.

[12] ARVO, J. R. Backward ray tracing. In *Developments in Ray Tracing, SIGGRAPH '86 course notes*, Vol. 12. Aug. 1986.

[13] ATHERTON, P. R., WEILER, K., AND GREENBERG, D. Polygon shadow generation. *Computer Graphics (SIGGRAPH '78 Proceedings)* **12**:3 (1978), pp. 275–281.

[14] AUPPERLE, L., AND HANRAHAN, P. A hierarchical illumination algorithm for surfaces with glossy reflection. *Computer Graphics (SIGGRAPH '93 Proceedings)* **27** (Aug. 1993).

[15] BABUSKA, I., ZIENKIEWICZ, O., GAGO, J., AND DE A. OLIVEIRA, E., Eds. *Accuracy Estimates and Adaptive Refinements in Finite Element Computations*. John Wiley and Sons, New York, 1986.

[16] BARNES, J., AND HUT, P. A hierarchical $O(n \log n)$ force calculation algorithm. *Nature* **324** (1986), pp. 446–449.

[17] BARTELS, R. H., BEATTY, J. C., AND BARSKY, B. A. *An Introduction to Splines for Use in Computer Graphics and Geometric Modeling*. Morgan Kaufmann, Los Altos, Calif., 1987.

[18] BAUM, D. R., MANN, S., SMITH, K. P., AND WINGET, J. M. Making radiosity usable: Automatic preprocessing and meshing techniques for the generation of accurate radiosity solutions. *Computer Graphics (SIGGRAPH '91 Proceedings)* **25**:4 (July 1991), pp. 51–60.

[19] BAUM, D. R., RUSHMEIER, H. E., AND WINGET, J. M. Improving radiosity solutions through the use of analytically determined form-factors. *Computer Graphics (SIGGRAPH '89 Proceedings)* **23**:3 (July 1989), pp. 325–334.

[20] BAUM, D. R., WALLACE, J. R., COHEN, M. F., AND GREENBERG, D. P. The back-buffer algorithm: an extension of the radiosity method to dynamic environments. *The Visual Computer* **2**:5 (Sept. 1986), pp. 298–306.

[21] BAUM, D. R., AND WINGET, J. M. Real time radiosity through parallel processing and hardware acceleration. *Computer Graphics (1990 Symposium on Interactive 3D Graphics)* **24**:2 (Mar. 1990), pp. 67–75.

[22] BAUMGART, B. G. A polyhedron representation for computer vision. In *AFIPS Conference Proceedings* (1975), Vol. 44, pp. 589–596.

[23] BECKER, E. B., CAREY, G. F., AND ODEN, J. T. *Finite Elements, An Introduction, Volume 1*. Prentice Hall, Englewood Cliffs, NJ, 1981.

[24] BERAN-KOEHN, J. C., AND PAVICIC, M. J. A cubic tetrahedral adaptation of the hemi-cube algorithm. In *Graphics Gems II*, J. Arvo, Ed. Academic Press, San Diego, 1991, pp. 299–302.

[25] BERAN-KOEHN, J. C., AND PAVICIC, M. J. Delta form-factor calculation for the cubic tetrahedral algorithm. In *Graphics Gems III*, D. Kirk, Ed. Academic Press, San Diego, 1992, pp. 324–328.

[26] BEYLKIN, G., COIFMAN, R., AND ROKHLIN, V. Fast wavelet transforms and numerical algorithms I. *Communications on Pure and Applied Mathematics* **44** (1991), pp. 141–183.

[27] BEYLKIN, G., COIFMAN, R., AND ROKHLIN, V. Wavelets in numerical analysis. In *Wavelets and Their Applications*, G. Beylkin, R. Coifman, I. Daubechies, S. Mallat, Y. Meyer, L. Raphael, and B. Ruskai, Eds. Jones and Bartlett, Cambridge, 1992, pp. 181–210.

[28] BHATE, N., AND TOKUTA, A. Photorealistic volume rendering of media with directional scattering. In *Third Eurographics Workshop on Rendering* (Bristol, UK, May 1992), pp. 227–245.

[29] BLAKE, A., AND BRELSTAFF, G. Geometry from specularity. In *Proceedings of the Second International Conference on Computer Vision* (Tampa Springs, FL, 1988), pp. 394–403.

[30] BLINN, J. F. Models of light reflection for computer synthesized pictures. *Computer Graphics (SIGGRAPH '77 Proceedings)* **11**:2 (1977), pp. 192–198.

[31] BLINN, J. F. Simulation of wrinkled surfaces. *Computer Graphics (SIGGRAPH '78 Proceedings)* **12**:3 (Aug. 1978), pp. 286–292.

[32] BLINN, J. F., AND NEWELL, M. E. Texture and reflection in computer generated images. *Communications of the ACM* **19**:10 (1976), pp. 542–547.

[33] BOENDER, E. *Finite Element Mesh Generation from CSG Models*. PhD thesis, Dept. of Technical Math. and Informatics, Delft University of Technology, Netherlands, 1992.

[34] BOREL, C. C., GERSTL, S. A. W., AND POWERS, B. J. The radiosity method in optical remote sensing of structured 3-d surfaces. *Remote Sens. Environ.* **36** (1991), pp. 13–44.

[35] BOUGUER, P. *The Gradation of Light.* University of Toronto Press, 1960.

[36] BOUKNIGHT, J., AND KELLEY, K. An algorithm for producing half-tone computer graphics presentations with shadows and movable light sources. In *Proceedings of the Spring Joint Computer Conference, AFIPS* (1970), Vol. 36, AFPIS Press, pp. 1–10.

[37] BOUKNIGHT, W. J. A procedure for generation of three-dimensional half-toned computer graphics presentations. *Communications of the ACM* **13**:9 (Sept. 1970), pp. 292–301.

[38] BREBBIA, C. A., AND DOMINGUEZ, J. *Boundary Elements: An Introductory Course.* McGraw-Hill, New York, 1992.

[39] BU, J., AND DEPRETTERE, E. F. A VLSI system architecture for high-speed radiative transfer 3d image synthesis. *The Visual Computer* **5**:3 (June 1989), pp. 121–133.

[40] BUCKALEW, C., AND FUSSELL, D. Illumination networks: Fast realistic rendering with general reflectance functions. *Computer Graphics (SIGGRAPH '89 Proceedings)* **23**:3 (July 1989), pp. 89–98.

[41] CABRAL, B., MAX, N., AND SPRINGMEYER, R. Bidirectional reflection functions from surface bump maps. *Computer Graphics (SIGGRAPH '87 Proceedings)* **21**:4 (July 1987), pp. 273–281.

[42] CAMPBELL, A. *Modeling Global Diffuse Illumination for Image Synthesis.* PhD thesis, Dept. of Computer Sciences, University of Texas at Austin, Dec. 1991.

[43] CAMPBELL, A., AND FUSSELL, D. S. Adaptive mesh generation for global diffuse illumination. *Computer Graphics (SIGGRAPH '90 Proceedings)* **24**:4 (Aug. 1990), pp. 155–164.

[44] CATMULL, E. Computer display of curved surfaces. In *Proceedings of the IEEE Conference on Computer Graphics, Pattern Recognition, and Data Structures* (May 1975), Vol. 11, pp. 11–17.

[45] CENDES, Z. J., AND WONG, S. H. C^1 quadratic interpolation over arbitrary point sets. *IEEE Computer Graphics and Applications* **7**:11 (Nov. 1987), pp. 8–16.

[46] CHALMERS, A. G., AND PADDON, D. J. Parallel processing of progressive refinement radiosity methods. In *Second Eurographics Workshop on Rendering* (Barcelona, Spain, May 1991).

[47] CHANEY, J., RAMIDAS, V., RODRIGUEZ, C., AND WU, M., Eds. *Thermophysical Properties Research Literature Retrieval Guide 1900–1980.* IFI/Plenum, New York, 1982.

[48] CHATTOPADHYAY, S., AND FUJIMOTO, A. Bi-directional ray tracing. In *Computer Graphics 1987 (Proceedings of Computer Graphics International '87)* (Tokyo, 1987), Springer-Verlag, pp. 335–343.

[49] CHEN, H., AND WU, E.-H. An efficient radiosity solution for bump texture generation. *Computer Graphics (SIGGRAPH '90 Proceedings)* **24**:4 (Aug. 1990), pp. 125–134.

[50] CHEN, S. E. A progressive radiosity method and its implementation in a distributed processing environment. Master's thesis, Program of Computer Graphics, Cornell University, Jan. 1989.

[51] CHEN, S. E. Incremental radiosity: An extension of progressive radiosity to an interactive image synthesis system. *Computer Graphics (SIGGRAPH '90 Proceedings)* **24**:4 (Aug. 1990), pp. 135–144.

[52] CHEN, S. E., RUSHMEIER, H. E., MILLER, G., AND TURNER, D. A progressive multi-pass method for global illumination. *Computer Graphics (SIGGRAPH '91 Proceedings)* **25**:4 (July 1991), pp. 164–174.

[53] CHEW, L. Constrained Delaunay triangulations. In *3rd Symp. Comp. Geom.* (1987), pp. 215–222.

[54] CHIN, N., AND FEINER, S. Near real-time shadow generation using BSP trees. *Computer Graphics (SIGGRAPH '89 Proceedings)* **23**:3 (July 1989), pp. 99–106.

[55] CHIN, N., AND FEINER, S. Fast object-precision shadow generation for area light source using bsp trees. In *Computer Graphics, Special Issue (Proceedings 1992 Symposium on Interactive 3D Graphics)* (Cambridge, Mass., Mar. 1992), ACM Press, pp. 21–30.

[56] CLOUGH, R., AND TOCHER, J. Finite element stiffness matrices for analysis of plate bending. In *Matrix Methods in Structural Mechanics (Proceedings of the conference held at Wright-Patterson Air Force Base, Ohio, 26-28 October 1965)* (1966), pp. 515–545.

[57] CLOUGH, R. W. The finite element in plane stress analysis. In *Proceedings of the Second ASCE Conference on Electronic Computation* (Sept. 1960).

[58] COHEN, M. A radiosity method for the realistic image synthesis of complex diffuse environments. Master's thesis, Program of Computer Graphics, Cornell University, Aug. 1985.

[59] COHEN, M., CHEN, S. E., WALLACE, J. R., AND GREENBERG, D. P. A progressive refinement approach to fast radiosity image generation. *Computer Graphics (SIGGRAPH '88 Proceedings)* **22**:4 (Aug. 1988), pp. 75–84.

[60] COHEN, M., AND GREENBERG, D. P. The hemi-cube: A radiosity solution for complex environments. *Computer Graphics (SIGGRAPH '85 Proceedings)* **19**:3 (Aug. 1985), pp. 31–40.

[61] COHEN, M., GREENBERG, D. P., IMMEL, D. S., AND BROCK, P. J. An efficient radiosity approach for realistic image synthesis. *IEEE Computer Graphics and Applications* **6**:3 (Mar. 1986), pp. 26–35.

[62] COHEN, M. F., AND GREENBERG, D. P. The hemi-cube: A radiosity solution for complex environments. *Computer Graphics (SIGGRAPH '85 Proceedings)* **19**:3 (July 1985), pp. 31–40.

[63] COOK, R. L. Stochastic sampling in computer graphics. *ACM Transactions on Graphics* **5**:1 (Jan. 1986), pp. 51–72.

[64] COOK, R. L., PORTER, T., AND CARPENTER, L. Distributed ray tracing. *Computer Graphics (SIGGRAPH '84 Proceedings)* **18**:3 (July 1984), pp. 137–145.

[65] COOK, R. L., AND TORRANCE, K. E. A reflection model for computer graphics. *ACM Transactions on Graphics* **1**:1 (1982), pp. 7–24.

[66] COURANT, R. Variational methods for the solution of problems of equilibrium and vibration. *Bulletin of the American Mathematical Society* **49** (1943), pp. 1–23.

[67] CROW, F. C. Shadow algorithms for computer graphics. *Computer Graphics (SIGGRAPH '77 Proceedings)* **11**:2 (1977), pp. 242–248.

[68] DAVISON, B. *Neutron Transport Theory.* Oxford University Press, 1957.

[69] DELVES, L. M., AND MOHAMED, J. L. *Computational methods for integral equations.* Cambridge University Press, Cambridge, UK, 1985.

[70] DESAI, C. S., AND ABEL, J. F. *Introduction to the Finite Element Method.* Van Nostrand Reinhold, New York, 1972.

[71] DIPPE, M. A. Z., AND WOLD, E. H. Stochastic sampling: Theory and application. In *Progress in Computer Graphics*, G. W. Zobrist, Ed. Ablex Publishing, Norwood, NJ, 1991.

[72] DOCTOR, L., AND TORBORG, J. Display techniques for octree-encoded objects. *IEEE Computer Graphics and Applications* **1**:3 (July 1981), pp. 29–38.

[73] DORSEY, J. O. *Computer Graphics Techniques for Opera Lighting Design and Simulation.* PhD thesis, Program of Computer Graphics, Cornell University, Jan. 1993.

[74] DORSEY, J. O., SILLION, F. X., AND GREENBERG, D. P. Design and simulation of opera lighting and projection effects. *Computer Graphics (SIGGRAPH '91 Proceedings)* **25**:4 (July 1991), pp. 41–50.

[75] DREBIN, R. A., CARPENTER, L., AND HANRAHAN, P. Volume rendering. *Computer Graphics (Proceedings of SIGGRAPH 1988)* **22**:4 (August 1988), pp. 65–74.

[76] DRETTAKIS, G., AND FIUME, E. Structure-directed sampling, reconstruction, and data representation for global illumination. *Second Eurographics Workshop on Rendering* (May 1991), pp. 189–201.

[77] DRUCKER, S. M., AND SCHRÖDER, P. Fast radiosity using a data parallel architecture. In *Third Eurographics Workshop on Rendering* (Bristol, UK, May 1992), pp. 247–258.

[78] EMERY, A. F., JOHANSSON, O., LOBO, M., AND ABROUS, A. A comparative study of methods for computing the diffuse radiation viewfactors for complex structures. *The Journal of Heat Transfer* **113** (May 1991), pp. 413–422.

[79] ESSELINK, E. About the order of Appel's algorithm. Computing Science Note KE5-1, University of Groningen, 1989.

[80] FARIN, G. *Curves and Surfaces for Computer Aided Geometric Design.* Academic Press, San Diego, 1988.

[81] FEDA, M., AND PURGATHOFER, W. Progressive refinement radiosity on a transputer network. In *Second Eurographics Workshop on Rendering* (Barcelona, Spain, May 1991).

[82] FEDA, M., AND PURGATHOFER, W. Accelerating radiosity by overshooting. In *Third Eurographics Workshop on Rendering* (Bristol, UK, May 1992), pp. 21–32.

[83] FOCK, V. A. Illumination produced by surfaces of arbitrary shape. *Proceedings of the State Optical Institute* **3**:28 (1924).

[84] FOLEY, J. D., VAN DAM, A., FEINER, S. K., AND HUGHES, J. F. *Computer Graphics, Principles and Practice, 2nd Edition.* Addison-Wesley, Reading, Massachusetts, 1990.

[85] FORSYTH, D., AND ZISSERMAN, A. Shape from shading in the light of mutual illumination. *Image and Vision Computing* **8**:1 (Feb. 1990), pp. 42–49.

[86] FRANKE, R. Scattered data interpolation: Tests of some methods. *Mathematics of Computation* **38**:157 (Jan. 1982), pp. 181–200.

[87] FUCHS, H., KEDEM, Z. M., AND NAYLOR, B. F. On visible surface generation by a priori tree structures. *Computer Graphics (SIGGRAPH '80 Proceedings)* **14**:3 (July 1980), pp. 124–133.

[88] FUCHS, H., POULTON, J., EYLES, J., GREER, T., GOLDFEATHER, J., ELLSWORTH, D., MOLNAR, S., TURK, G., TEBBS, B., AND ISRAEL, L. Pixel-planes 5: A heterogeneous multiprocessor graphics system using processor-enhanced memories. *Computer Graphics (SIGGRAPH '89 Proceedings)* **23**:3 (July 1989), pp. 79–88.

[89] FUNKHOUSER, T. A., SEQUIN, C. H., AND TELLER, S. J. Management of large amounts of data in interactive building walkthroughs. In *Computer Graphics, Special Issue (Proceedings 1992 Symposium on Interactive 3D Graphics, Cambridge, Mass. 29 Mar, 1992)* (Mar. 1992), ACM Press, pp. 11–20.

[90] GASTINEL, N. *Linear Numerical Analysis.* Academic Press, 1970.

[91] GEORGE, D. W., SILLION, F. X., AND GREENBERG, D. P. Radiosity redistribution for dynamic environments. *IEEE Computer Graphics and Applications* **10**:4 (July 1990), pp. 26–34.

[92] GEORGE, P. *Automatic Mesh Generation.* Wiley, New York, 1991.

[93] GERSHUN, A. *The Light Field.* Moscow, 1936. Translated in Journal of Mathematics and Physics, Vol. 18, No. 2, 1939.

[94] GERSTL, S. A. W., AND BOREL, C. C. Principles of the radiosity method for canopy reflectance modeling. In *International Geoscience and Remote Sensing Symposium, 20–24 May 1990, Washington, DC, Proceedings IGARSS '90* (May 1990), Vol. 3, pp. 1735–1737.

[95] GIFFORD, S. *Data Parallel Two Pass Rendering.* Naval Research Laboratory Technical Report, Aug. 1991.

[96] GILSHRIST, A. L., AND JACOBSEN, A. Perception of lightness and illumination in a world of one reflectance. *Perception* **13** (1984), pp. 5–19.

[97] GLASSNER, A. S., Ed. *An Introduction to Ray Tracing.* Academic Press, San Diego, 1989.

[98] GLASSNER, A. S. Maintaining winged-edge models. In *Graphics Gems III*, D. Kirk, Ed. Academic Press, San Diego, 1992, pp. 191–201.

[99] GOEL, N. S. Models of vegetation canopy reflectance and their use in estimation of biophysical parameters from reflectance data. *Remote Sensing Review* **4**:1 (1988), p. 221.

[100] GORAL, C. M., TORRANCE, K. E., GREENBERG, D. P., AND BATTAILE, B. Modelling the interaction of light between diffuse surfaces. *Computer Graphics (SIGGRAPH '84 Proceedings)* **18**:3 (July 1984), pp. 212–222.

[101] GORTLER, S., AND COHEN, M. F. Radiosity and relaxation methods. Technical Report TR 408-93, Princeton University, 1993.

[102] GORTLER, S. J., SCHRÖDER, P., COHEN, M. F., AND HANRAHAN, P. M. Wavelet radiosity. *Computer Graphics (SIGGRAPH '93 Proceedings)* **27** (Aug. 1993).

[103] GOURAUD, H. Computer display of curved surfaces. Tech. rep., Dept. of Computer Science, University of Utah, Salt Lake City, Utah, 1971.

[104] GRAY, D. E., Ed. *American Institute of Physics Handbook.* McGraw Hill, New York, 1972.

[105] GREENBERG, D. P., COHEN, M., AND TORRANCE, K. E. Radiosity: A method for computing global illumination. *The Visual Computer* **2**:5 (Sept. 1986), pp. 291–297.

[106] GREENGARD, L. *The Rapid Evaluation of Potential Fields in Particle Systems.* MIT Press, 1988.

[107] GUITTON, P., ROMAN, J., AND SCHLICK, C. Two parallel approaches for a progressive radiosity. In *Second Eurographics Workshop on Rendering* (Barcelona, Spain, May 1991).

[108] HAINES, E. Essential ray tracing algorithms. In *An Introduction to Ray Tracing*, A. S. Glassner, Ed. Academic Press, San Diego, 1989, pp. 33–77.

[109] HAINES, E. A. Beams o' light: Confessions of a hacker. In *SIGGRAPH '91 Frontiers in Rendering course notes*. July 1991.

[110] HAINES, E. A. Ronchamp: A case study for radiosity. In *SIGGRAPH '91 Frontiers in Rendering course notes*. July 1991.

[111] HAINES, E. A., AND GREENBERG, D. P. The light buffer: A shadow-testing accelerator. *IEEE Computer Graphics and Applications* **6**:9 (Sept. 1986), pp. 6–16.

[112] HAINES, E. A., AND WALLACE, J. R. Shaft culling for efficient ray-traced radiosity. In *Second Eurographics Workshop on Rendering* (Barcelona, Spain, May 1991).

[113] HALL, D. E., AND RUSHMEIER, H. Improved explicit radiosity method for calculating non-lambertian reflections. *The Visual Computer (to appear)* **9**:5 (1993), pp. 278–288.

[114] HALL, R. *Illumination and Color in Computer Generated Imagery.* Springer-Verlag, New York, 1989.

[115] HANRAHAN, P., AND KRUEGER, W. Reflection from layered surfaces due to subsurface scattering. *Computer Graphics (SIGGRAPH '93 Proceedings)* **27** (Aug. 1993).

[116] HANRAHAN, P., SALZMAN, D., AND AUPPERLE, L. A rapid hierarchical radiosity algorithm. *Computer Graphics (SIGGRAPH '91 Proceedings)* **25**:4 (July 1991), pp. 197–206.

[117] HANRAHAN, P. M. Creating volume models from edge-vertex graphs. *Computer Graphics (SIGGRAPH '82 Proceedings)* **16**:3 (July 1982), pp. 77–84.

[118] HE, X. D., TORRANCE, K. E., SILLION, F. X., AND GREENBERG, D. P. A comprehensive physical model for light reflection. *Computer Graphics (SIGGRAPH '91 Proceedings)* **25**:4 (July 1991), pp. 175–186.

[119] HECKBERT, P. Adaptive radiosity textures for bidirectional ray tracing. *Computer Graphics (SIGGRAPH '90 Proceedings)* **24**:4 (Aug. 1990), pp. 145–154.

[120] HECKBERT, P. *Simulating Global Illumination Using Adaptive Meshing.* PhD thesis, CS Division (EECS), University of California, Berkeley, June 1991.

[121] HECKBERT, P. Discontinuity meshing for radiosity. In *Third Eurographics Workshop on Rendering* (Bristol, UK, May 1992), pp. 203–226.

[122] HECKBERT, P. Radiosity in flatland. *Computer Graphics Forum (Eurographics '92)* **11**:3 (Sept. 1992), pp. 181–192.

[123] HECKBERT, P. S. *Simulating Global Illumination Using Adaptive Meshing.* PhD thesis, University of California, Berkeley, 1991.

[124] HECKBERT, P. S., AND HANRAHAN, P. Beam tracing polygonal objects. *Computer Graphics (SIGGRAPH '84 Proceedings)* **18**:3 (July 1984), pp. 119–127.

[125] HECKBERT, P. S., AND WINGET, J. M. Finite element methods for global illumination. Tech. Rep. UCP/CSD 91/643, Computer Science Division (EECS), University of California, Berkeley, July 1991.

[126] HERMAN, R. A. *A Treatise on Geometrical Optics.* Cambridge University Press, 1900.

[127] HEWITT, H., AND VAUSE, A. S., Eds. *Lamps and Lighting.* American Elsevier, New York, 1964.

[128] HORN, B. K. P. *Robot Vision.* MIT Press, 1986.

[129] HORN, B. K. P., Ed. *Shape from Shading.* MIT Press, 1989.

[130] HOTTEL, H. C., AND SAROFIM, A. F. *Radiative Transfer.* McGraw Hill, New York, 1967.

[131] HOWELL, J. R. *A Catalog of Radiation Configuration Factors*. McGraw Hill, New York, 1982.

[132] IMMEL, D. S., COHEN, M., AND GREENBERG, D. P. A radiosity method for non-diffuse environments. *Computer Graphics (SIGGRAPH '86 Proceedings)* **20**:4 (Aug. 1986), pp. 133–142.

[133] JOHNSON, K. R., CURRAN, A. R., AND GONDA, T. G. Development of a signature supercode. In *Technical Proceedings 1938: Advances in Sensors, Radiometric Calibration, and Processing of Remotely Sensed Data (SPIE International Symposium on Optical Engineering and Photonics in Aerospace and Remote Sensing)* (Orlando, FL, Apr. 1993).

[134] KAJIYA, J. T. Anisotropic reflection models. In *Computer Graphics (SIGGRAPH '85 Proceedings)* (July 1985), Vol. 19, pp. 15–21.

[135] KAJIYA, J. T. The rendering equation. *Computer Graphics (SIGGRAPH '86 Proceedings)* **20**:4 (Aug. 1986), pp. 143–150.

[136] KAJIYA, J. T., AND HERZEN, B. P. V. Ray tracing volume densities. *Computer Graphics (SIGGRAPH '84 Proceedings)* **18**:3 (July 1984), pp. 165–174.

[137] KAWAI, J., PAINTER, J., AND COHEN, M. Radioptimization: Goal-based rendering. *Computer Graphics (SIGGRAPH '93 Proceedings)* **27** (Aug 1993).

[138] KINCAID, D., AND CHENEY, W. *Numerical Analysis*. Brooks/Cole, 1991.

[139] KIRK, D., AND VOORHIES, D. The rendering architecture of the DN10000VS. *Computer Graphics (SIGGRAPH '90 Proceedings)* **24**:4 (Aug 1990), pp. 299–308.

[140] KIRK, D. B., AND ARVO, J. R. Unbiased sampling techniques for image synthesis. *Computer Graphics (SIGGRAPH '91 Proceedings)* **25**:4 (July 1991), pp. 153–156.

[141] KOK, A. J. F., AND JANSEN, F. W. Adaptive sampling of area light sources in ray tracing including diffuse interreflection. *Computer Graphics Forum (Eurographics '92)* **11**:3 (Sept. 1992), pp. 289–298.

[142] KOK, A. J. F., YILMAZ, C., AND BIERENS, L. H. J. A two-pass radiosity method for Bézier patches. In *Photorealism in Computer Graphics*

(Proceedings Eurographics Workshop on Photosimulation, Realism and Physics in Computer Graphics, Rennes, France, Jun. 1990), Springer-Verlag, pp. 115–124.

[143] LAMBERT. *Photometria sive de mensura et gradibus luminis, colorum et umbrae.* 1760.

[144] LANGUENOU, E., AND TELLIER, P. Including physical light sources and daylight in global illumination. In *Third Eurographics Workshop on Rendering* (Bristol, UK, May 1992), pp. 217–225.

[145] LAUR, D., AND HANRAHAN, P. Hierarchical splatting: A progressive refinement algorithm for volume rendering. *Computer Graphics (SIGGRAPH '91 Proceedings)* **25**:4 (jul 1991), pp. 285–288.

[146] LE, K. H. Finite element mesh generation methods: A review and classification. *Computer-Aided Design* **20** (1988), pp. 27–38.

[147] LEE, M., REDNER, R., AND USELTON, S. Statistically optimized sampling for distributed ray tracing. *Computer Graphics (SIGGRAPH '85 Proceedings)* **19**:3 (1985), pp. 61–67.

[148] LESAEC, B., AND SCHLICK, C. A progressive ray-tracing-based radiosity with general reflectance functions. In *Photorealism in Computer Graphics (Proceedings Eurographics Workshop on Photosimulation, Realism and Physics in Computer Graphics, Rennes, France, Jun. 1990)*, K. Bouatouch and C. Bouville, Eds., Springer-Verlag, pp. 101–114.

[149] LEVOY, M. Display of surfaces from volume data. *IEEE Computer Graphics and Applications* (May 1988), pp. 29–37.

[150] LEVOY, M. Efficient ray tracing of volume data. *ACM Transactions on Graphics* **9**:3 (July 1990), pp. 245–261.

[151] LEWIN, L. *Dilogarithm and Associated Functions.* Macdonald, London, 1958.

[152] LEWINS, J. *Importance, the Adjoint Function: The Physical Basis of Variational and Perturbation Theory in Transport and Diffusion Problems.* Pergamon Press, New York, 1965.

[153] LISCHINSKI, D., TAMPIERI, F., AND GREENBERG, D. P. Improving sampling and reconstruction techniques for radiosity. Tech. Rep. TR 91-1202, Program of Computer Graphics, Cornell University, Aug. 1991.

[154] LISCHINSKI, D., TAMPIERI, F., AND GREENBERG, D. P. Discontinuity meshing for accurate radiosity. *IEEE Computer Graphics and Applications* **12**:6 (Nov. 1992), pp. 25–39.

[155] LOVE, T. J. *Radiative Heat Transfer.* Merrill Publishing Company, 1968.

[156] MACADAM, D. L. *Sources of Color Science.* MIT Press, Cambridge, MA, 1970.

[157] MALLEY, T. J. A shading method for computer generated images. Master's thesis, Dept. of Computer Science, University of Utah, June 1988.

[158] MÄNTYLÄ, M. *An Introduction to Solid Modeling.* Computer Science Press, Rockville, MD, 1988.

[159] MÄNTYLÄ, M., AND SULONEN, R. Gwb - a solid modeler with Euler operators. *IEEE Computer Graphics and Applications* **2**:7 (Sept. 1982), pp. 17–31.

[160] MARKS, J., WALSH, R., CHRISTENSEN, J., AND FRIEDELL, M. Image and intervisibility coherence in rendering. In *Proceedings of Graphics Interface '90* (Toronto, Ontario, May 1990), Canadian Information Processing Society, pp. 17–30.

[161] MAX, N. Smooth appearance for polygonal surfaces. *The Visual Computer* **5**:3 (1989), pp. 160–173.

[162] MAX, N. Optimal hemicube sampling. In *1993 Eurographics Rendering Workshop* (Paris, 1993).

[163] MAX, N. L., AND ALLISON, M. J. Linear radiosity approximation using vertex-to-vertex form factors. In *Graphics Gems III*, D. Kirk, Ed. Academic Press, San Diego, 1992, pp. 318–323.

[164] MAXWELL, G. M., BAILEY, M. J., AND GOLDSCHMIDT, V. W. Calculations of the radiation configuration factor using ray casting. *Computer-Aided Design* **18**:7 (Sept. 1986), pp. 371–379.

[165] METAXAS, D., AND MILIOS, E. Color image reconstruction from nonuniform sparse samples. In *Eurographics '90* (1990), pp. 75–86.

[166] MEYER, G. W. *Color Calculations For and Perceptual Assessment of Computer Graphic Images.* PhD thesis, Program of Computer Graphics, Cornell University, 1986.

[167] MEYER, G. W., RUSHMEIER, H. E., COHEN, M. F., GREENBERG, D. P., AND TORRANCE, K. E. An experimental evaluation of computer graphics imagery. *ACM Transactions on Graphics* **5**:1 (Jan. 1986), pp. 30–50.

[168] MITCHELL, D., AND HANRAHAN, P. Illumination from curved reflectors. *Computer Graphics (SIGGRAPH '92 Proceedings)* **26**:4 (July 1992), pp. 283–291.

[169] MOON, P. *The Scientific Basis of Illuminating Engineering.* McGraw Hill, New York, 1936.

[170] MORTENSON, M. E. *Geometric Modeling.* John Wiley & Sons, New York, 1985.

[171] NAYLOR, B. F. Binary space partitioning trees: An alternative representation of polytopes. *Computer-Aided Design* **22**:2 (Mar. 1990), pp. 250–253.

[172] NEUMANN, L., AND KELEMEN, C. Solution of interreflection problem for very complex environments by transillumination method. In *Second Eurographics Workshop on Rendering* (Barcelona, Spain, May 1991).

[173] NEWMAN, W., AND SPROULL, R. *Principles of Interactive Computer Graphics.* McGraw-Hill, 1979.

[174] NICODEMUS, F. E., RICHMOND, J. C., HSIA, J. J., GINSBERG, I. W., AND LIMPERIS, T. *Geometric Considerations and Nomenclature for Reflectance, NBS Monograph 160.* National Bureau of Standards, 1977.

[175] NISHITA, T., AND NAKAMAE, E. Continuous tone representation of three-dimensional objects taking account of shadows and interreflection. *Computer Graphics (SIGGRAPH '85 Proceedings)* **19**:3 (July 1985), pp. 23–30.

[176] NISHITA, T., AND NAKAMAE, E. Continuous tone representation of three-dimensional objects illuminated by sky light. *Computer Graphics (SIGGRAPH '86 Proceedings)* **20**:4 (Aug. 1986), pp. 125–132.

[177] OPTICAL SOCIETY OF AMERICA COMMITTEE ON COLORIMETRY *The Science of Color.* Optical Society of America, Washington, DC, 1973.

[178] PARKER, A., CHRISTOU, C., CUMMING, B., AND ZISSERMAN, A. Evaluation of a radiosity-based method for generating images of 3-d shapes. *Perception* **21**:(Supplement 2) (1992), p. 18.

[179] PARKER, A. J., CHRISTOU, C., CUMMING, B. G., JOHNSTON, E. B., HAWKEN, M. J., AND ZISSERMAN, A. The analysis of 3d shape: Psychophysical principles and neural mechanisms. In *Approaches to Understanding Vision*, G. W. Humphries, Ed. Blackwell, 1992, pp. 143–179.

[180] PEARSON, C. E., Ed. *Handbook of Applied Mathematics*. Van Nostrand Reinhold, New York, 1990.

[181] PHONG, B. T. Illumination for computer-generated images. Tech. rep., Dept. of Computer Science, University of Utah, Salt Lake City, 1973.

[182] PHONG, B. T. Illumination for computer generated pictures. *Communications of the ACM* **18**:6 (1975), pp. 311–317.

[183] POWELL, M., AND SABIN, M. Piecewise quadratic approximation on triangles. *ACM Transactions on Mathematical Software* (Dec. 1977), pp. 316–325.

[184] PREPARATA, F. P., AND SHAMOS, M. I. *Computational Geometry: An Introduction*. Springer-Verlag, New York, 1985.

[185] PRESS, W., TEUKOLSKI, S., VETTERLING, W., AND FLANNERY, B. *Numerical Recipies in C, The Art of Scientific Computing, 2nd Edition*. Cambridge University Press, Cambridge, 1992.

[186] PUECH, C., SILLION, F., AND VEDEL, C. Improving interaction with radiosity-based lighting simulation programs. *Computer Graphics (Proceedings of the 1990 Symposium on Interactive 3D Graphics)* **24**:2 (Mar. 1990), pp. 51–57.

[187] PUEYO, X. Diffuse interreflections. techniques for form-factor computation: A survey. *The Visual Computer* **7**:4 (July 1991), pp. 200–209.

[188] PURGATHOFER, W., AND ZEILLER, M. Fast radiosity by parallelization. In *Photorealism in Computer Graphics (Proceedings Eurographics Workshop on Photosimulation, Realism and Physics in Computer Graphics, Rennes, France, Jun. 1990)*, Springer-Verlag, pp. 171–181.

[189] RATLIFF, F. *Mach Bands: Quantitative Studies on Neural Networks in the Retina*. Holden-Day, Inc., San Francisco, 1965.

[190] RECKER, R. J. Improved techniques for progressive refinement radiosity. Master's thesis, Program of Computer Graphics, Cornell University, Jan. 1990.

[191] RECKER, R. J., GEORGE, D. W., AND GREENBERG, D. P. Acceleration techniques for progressive refinement radiosity. *Computer Graphics (1990 Symposium on Interactive 3D Graphics)* **24**:2 (Mar. 1990), pp. 59–66.

[192] REICHERT, M. C. A two-pass radiosity method driven by lights and viewer position. Master's thesis, Program of Computer Graphics, Cornell University, Jan. 1992.

[193] REWALD, J. *The History of Impressionism*. Museum of Modern Art, New York, 1973.

[194] ROCKWOOD, A., HEATON, K., AND DAVIS, T. Real-time rendering of trimmed surfaces. *Computer Graphics (SIGGRAPH '89 Proceedings)* **23**:3 (July 1989), pp. 107–116.

[195] ROGERS, D. *Procedural Elements for Computer Graphics*. McGraw-Hill, 1985.

[196] RUSHMEIER, H., PATTERSON, C., AND VEERASAMY, A. Geometric simplification for indirect illumination calculations. In *Graphics Interface '93 Proceedings* (Toronto, May 1993).

[197] RUSHMEIER, H. E. Extending the radiosity method to transmitting and specularly reflecting surfaces. Master's thesis, Program of Computer Graphics, Cornell University, 1986.

[198] RUSHMEIER, H. E. *Realistic Image Synthesis for Scenes with Radiatively Participating Media*. PhD thesis, Program of Computer Graphics, Cornell University, 1988.

[199] RUSHMEIER, H. E. Radiosity input/output. In *Radiosity, SIGGRAPH '92 course notes*, Vol. 11. ACM Press, July 1992, pp. 152–168.

[200] RUSHMEIER, H. E., AND TORRANCE, K. E. The zonal method for calculating light intensities in the presence of a participating medium. *Computer Graphics (SIGGRAPH '87 Proceedings)* **21**:4 (July 1987), pp. 293–302.

[201] RUSHMEIER, H. E., AND TORRANCE, K. E. Extending the radiosity method to include specularly reflecting and translucent materials. *ACM Transactions on Graphics* **9**:1 (Jan. 1990), pp. 1–27.

[202] SALA, A. *Radiant Properties of Materials*. Elsevier, Amsterdam, 1986.

[203] SALESIN, D., LISCHINSKI, D., AND DEROSE, T. Reconstructing illumination functions with selected discontinuities. In *Third Eurographics Workshop on Rendering* (Bristol, UK, May 1992), pp. 99–112.

[204] SAMET, H. *Design and Analysis of Spatial Data Structures*. Addison-Wesley, Reading, MA, 1990.

[205] SCHOENBERG, I. J. Contributions to the problem of the approximation of equidistant data by analytic functions. *Quarterly Applications of Mathematics* **4** (1946), pp. 45–99.

[206] SCHRÖDER, P., AND HANRAHAN, P. A closed form expression for the form factor between two polygons. Tech. Rep. CS-404-93, Department of Computer Science, Princeton University, Jan. 1993.

[207] SCHUMAKER, L. L. Triangulations in CAGD. *IEEE Computer Graphics and Applications* **13**:1 (Jan. 1993), pp. 47–52.

[208] SCHUMAKER, R. B., BRAND, M. G., AND SHARP, W. Study for applying computer-generated images to visual simulation, AFHRL-TR-69-14. Tech. rep., U.S. Air Force Human Resources Lab, 1969.

[209] SEGAL, M. Using tolerances to guarantee valid polyhedral modeling results. *Computer Graphics (SIGGRAPH '90 Proceedings)* **24**:4 (Aug. 1990), pp. 105–114.

[210] SHAO, M.-Z., PENG, Q.-S., AND LIANG, Y.-D. A new radiosity approach by procedural refinements for realistic image synthesis. *Computer Graphics (SIGGRAPH '88 Proceedings)* **22**:4 (Aug. 1988), pp. 93–101.

[211] SHEPHARD, M. S. Approaches to the automatic generation and control of finite element meshes. *Applied Mechanics Review* **41**:4 (Apr. 1988), pp. 169–185.

[212] SHIRLEY, P. *Physically Based Lighting Calculations for Computer Graphics*. PhD thesis, Dept. of Computer Science, U. of Illinois, Urbana-Champaign, Nov. 1990.

[213] SHIRLEY, P. A ray tracing method for illumination calculation in diffuse-specular scenes. In *Proceedings of Graphics Interface '90* (Toronto, Ontario, May 1990), Canadian Information Processing Society, pp. 205–212.

[214] SHIRLEY, P. Radiosity via ray tracing. In *Graphics Gems II*, J. Arvo, Ed. Academic Press, San Diego, 1991, pp. 306–310.

[215] SHIRLEY, P., AND WANG, C. Direct lighting calculation by Monte Carlo integration. In *Second Eurographics Workshop on Rendering* (Barcelona, Spain, May 1991).

[216] SIEGEL, R., AND HOWELL, J. R. *Thermal Radiation Heat Transfer, 3rd Edition.* Hemisphere Publishing Corporation, New York, 1992.

[217] SILLION, F., ARVO, J. R., WESTIN, S. H., AND GREENBERG, D. P. A global illumination solution for general reflectance distributions. *Computer Graphics (SIGGRAPH '91 Proceedings)* **25**:4 (July 1991), pp. 187–196.

[218] SILLION, F., AND PUECH, C. A general two-pass method integrating specular and diffuse reflection. *Computer Graphics (SIGGRAPH '89 Proceedings)* **23**:3 (July 1989), pp. 335–344.

[219] SMITH, F. W., Ed. *CRC Handbook of Marine Science.* CRC Press, Cleveland, Ohio, 1974.

[220] SMITS, B. E., ARVO, J. R., AND SALESIN, D. H. An importance-driven radiosity algorithm. *Computer Graphics (SIGGRAPH '92 Proceedings)* **26**:4 (July 1992), pp. 273–282.

[221] SPARROW, E. A new and simpler formulation for radiative angle factors. *Transactions of the ASME, The Journal of Heat Transfer* **85**:2 (1963), pp. 81–88.

[222] SPARROW, E., AND CESS, R. *Radiation Heat Transfer.* Hemisphere Publishing Corporation, Washington, 1978.

[223] SPENCER, S. N. The hemisphere radiosity method: A tale of two algorithms. In *Photorealism in Computer Graphics (Proceedings Eurographics Workshop on Photosimulation, Realism and Physics in Computer Graphics, 1990)* (1991), K. Bouatouch and C. Bouville, Eds., pp. 127–35.

[224] SPIVAK, M. *Calculus on Manifolds.* Benjamin/Cummings, 1965.

[225] STEVENS, S. S., AND STEVENS, J. C. Brightness function: Parametric effects of adaptation and contrast. *Journal of the Optical Society of America* **53**:11 (Nov. 1960), pp. 1139–.

[226] STOER, J., AND BULIRSCH, R. *Introduction to Numerical Analysis.* Springer-Verlag, New York, 1980.

[227] STURZLINGER, W. Radiosity with voronoi-diagrams. In *Third Eurographics Workshop on Rendering* (Bristol, UK, May 1992), pp. 169–177.

[228] SUTHERLAND, I. E. Sketchpad: A man-machine graphical communication system. In *Proceedings of the Spring Joint Computer Conference* (1963).

[229] TAKAGI, A., TAKAOKA, H., OSHIMA, T., AND OGATA, Y. Accurate rendering technique based on colorimetric conception. *Computer Graphics (SIGGRAPH '90 Proceedings)* **24**:4 (Aug. 1990), pp. 263–272.

[230] TAMPIERI, F. Accurate form-factor computation. In *Graphics Gems III*, D. Kirk, Ed. Academic Press, San Diego, 1992, pp. 329–333.

[231] TAMPIERI, F., AND LISCHINSKI, D. The constant radiosity assumption syndrome. In *Second Eurographics Workshop on Rendering* (Barcelona, Spain, May 1991).

[232] TELLER, S., AND HANRAHAN, P. Global visibility algorithms for illumination computations. *Computer Graphics (SIGGRAPH '93 Proceedings)* **27** (Aug. 1993).

[233] TELLER, S. J. Computing the antipenumbra of an area light. *Computer Graphics (SIGGRAPH '92 Proceedings)* **26**:4 (July 1992), pp. 139–148.

[234] TELLER, S. J., AND SEQUIN, C. H. Visibility preprocessing for interactive walkthroughs. *Computer Graphics (SIGGRAPH '91 Proceedings)* **25**:4 (July 1991), pp. 61–69.

[235] THOMPSON, J. F., WARSI, Z., AND MASTIN, C. W. *Numerical Grid Generation.* North-Holland, New York, 1985.

[236] TORRANCE, K. E., AND SPARROW, E. M. Theory for off-specular reflection from roughened surfaces. *Journal of the Optical Society of America* **57**:9 (Sept. 1967), pp. 1105–1114.

[237] TOULOUKIAN, Y. S., AND DEWITT, D. P. *Thermophysical Properties of Matter, Vols. 7, 8: Thermal Radiative Properties.* IFI/Plenum, New York, 1972.

[238] TUMBLIN, J., AND RUSHMEIER, H. E. Tone reproduction for realistic computer generated images. Tech. Report GI GVU-91-13, Graphics, Visualization & Usability Center, College of Computing, Georgia Institute of Technology, 1991.

[239] VAN LIERE, R. Divide and conquer radiosity. In *Second Eurographics Workshop on Rendering* (Barcelona, Spain, May 1991).

[240] VARSHNEY, A., AND PRINS, J. F. An environment-projection approach to radiosity for mesh-connected computers. In *Third Eurographics Workshop on Rendering* (Bristol, UK, May 1992), pp. 271–281.

[241] VEDEL, C. Improved storage and reconstruction of light intensities on surfaces. In *Third Eurographics Workshop on Rendering* (Bristol, UK, May 1992), pp. 113–121.

[242] VEDEL, C., AND PUECH, C. A testbed for adaptive subdivision in progressive radiosity. In *Second Eurographics Workshop on Rendering* (Barcelona, Spain, May 1991).

[243] VERBECK, C. P., AND GREENBERG, D. P. A comprehensive light-source description for computer graphics. *IEEE Computer Graphics and Applications* **4**:7 (July 1984), pp. 66–75.

[244] VILAPLANA, J. Parallel radiosity solutions based on partial result messages. In *Third Eurographics Workshop on Rendering* (Bristol, UK, May 1992), pp. 259–270.

[245] VILAPLANA, J., AND PUEYO, X. Exploiting coherence for clipping and view transformations in radiosity algorithms. In *Photorealism in Computer Graphics (Proceedings Eurographics Workshop on Photosimulation, Realism and Physics in Computer Graphics, Rennes, France, Jun. 1990)*, K. Bouatouch and C. Bouville, Eds., Springer-Verlag, pp. 137–150.

[246] WALLACE, J. R., COHEN, M. F., AND GREENBERG, D. P. A two-pass solution to the rendering equation: A synthesis of ray tracing and radiosity methods. *Computer Graphics (SIGGRAPH '87 Proceedings)* **21**:4 (July 1987), pp. 311–320.

[247] WALLACE, J. R., ELMQUIST, K. A., AND HAINES, E. A. A ray tracing algorithm for progressive radiosity. *Computer Graphics (SIGGRAPH '89 Proceedings)* **23**:3 (July 1989), pp. 315–324.

[248] WANG, C. Physically correct direct lighting for distribution ray tracing. In *Graphics Gems III*, D. Kirk, Ed. Academic Press, San Diego, 1992, pp. 307–313.

[249] WANG, Y., AND DAVIS, W. A. Octant priority for radiosity image rendering. In *Proceedings of Graphics Interface '90* (Toronto, Ontario, May 1990), Canadian Information Processing Society, pp. 83–91.

[250] WANGER, L. The effect of shadow quality on the perception of spatial relationships in computer generated imagery. In *Computer Graphics, Special Issue, (Proceedings 1992 Symposium on Interactive 3D Graphics)* (Cambridge, Mass., Mar. 1992), ACM Press, pp. 39–42.

[251] WARD, G. Evaluating a real lighting simulation. In *Radiosity, SIGGRAPH '90 course notes*, Vol. 21. ACM Press, Aug. 1990.

[252] WARD, G. The radiance lighting simulation system. In *Global Illumination, SIGGRAPH '92 course notes*, Vol. 18. ACM, July 1992.

[253] WARD, G. J. Measuring and modeling anisotropic reflection. *Computer Graphics (SIGGRAPH '92 Proceedings)* **26**:2 (July 1992), pp. 265–272.

[254] WARD, G. J., RUBINSTEIN, F. M., AND CLEAR, R. D. A ray tracing solution for diffuse interreflection. *Computer Graphics (SIGGRAPH '88 Proceedings)* **22**:4 (Aug. 1988), pp. 85–92.

[255] WARNOCK, J. A hidden-surface algorithm for computer generated half-tone pictures. Technical Report TR 4-15, Dept. of Computer Science, University of Utah, June 1969.

[256] WATSON, D. Computing the n-dimensional Delaunay tesselation with application to Voronoi polytopes. *The Computer Journal* **24**:2 (1981), pp. 167–172.

[257] WATSON, D. F. *Contouring: A Guide to the Analysis and Display of Spatial Data*. Pergamon Press, New York, 1982.

[258] WATT, A. *Fundamentals of Three-Dimensional Computer Graphics*. Addison-Wesley, 1989.

[259] WATT, M. Light-water interaction using backward beam tracing. *Computer Graphics (SIGGRAPH '90 Proceedings)* **24**:4 (Aug. 1990), pp. 377–385.

[260] WEGHORST, H., HOOPER, G. J., AND GREENBERG, D. P. Improved computational methods for ray tracing. *ACM Transactions on Graphics* **3**:1 (Jan. 1984), pp. 52–69.

[261] WEILER, K. Edge-based data structures for solid modeling in curved-surface environments. *IEEE Computer Graphics and Applications* **3**:1 (Jan. 1985), pp. 21–40.

[262] WEILER, K. *Topological Structures for Geometric Modeling*. PhD thesis, Computer and Systems Engineering, Rensselaer Polytechnic Institute, Troy, New York, Aug. 1986.

[263] WESTIN, S. H., ARVO, J. R., AND TORRANCE, K. E. Predicting reflectance functions from complex surfaces. *Computer Graphics (SIGGRAPH '92 Proceedings)* **26**:2 (July 1992), pp. 255–264.

[264] WESTOVER, L. Footprint evaluation for volume rendering. *Computer Graphics (SIGGRAPH '90 Proceedings)* **24**:4 (July 1990), pp. 367–376.

[265] WHITTED, T. An improved illumination model for shaded display. *Communications of the ACM* **23**:6 (1980), pp. 343–349.

[266] WILLIAMS, L. Pyramidal parametrics. In *Computer Graphics (SIGGRAPH '83 Proceedings)* (July 1983), Vol. 17, pp. 1–11.

[267] WILSON, P. R. Euler formulas and geometric modeling. *IEEE Computer Graphics and Applications* **5**:8 (Aug. 1985), pp. 24–36.

[268] WOO, T. A combinatorial analysis of boundary data structure schemata. *IEEE Computer Graphics and Applications* **5**:3 (Mar. 1985), pp. 19–27.

[269] XU, H., PENG, Q.-S., AND LIANG, Y.-D. Accelerated radiosity method for complex environments. In *Visual Computing: Integrating Computer Graphics with Computer Vision (Proceedings of CG International '92)* (Tokyo, Sept. 1989), Springer-Verlag, pp. 895–905.

[270] ZATZ, H. R. Galerkin radiosity: A higher order solution method for global illumination. Master's thesis, Program of Computer Graphics, Cornell University, Aug. 1992.

[271] ZHANG, N. Two methods for speeding up form-factor calculation. In *Second Eurographics Workshop on Rendering* (Barcelona, Spain, May 1991).

[272] ZHU, Y., PENG, Q., AND LIANG, Y. Peris: a programming environment for realistic image synthesis. *Computers and Graphics* **12**:3/4 (1988), pp. 299–307.

[273] ZIENKIEWICZ, O. C. *The Finite Element Method, 4th Edition.* McGraw-Hill, London, 1989.

[274] ZISSERMAN, A., GIBLIN, P., AND BLAKE, A. The information available to a moving observer from specularities. *Image and Vision Computing* **7**:1 (1989), pp. 38–42.

Index

A posteriori mesh 154
  limitations 222
A priori mesh 154
Adaptive subdivision 157, 169, 217,
    224
  BSP-tree 166
  quadtree 166
  tri–quadtree 214
  using templates 214
Advancing front 218
Ambient 122
Anisotropy 29
Antialiasing 244
Architectural design 332
Aspect ratio 145, 218
B 25
Barycentric coordinates 52, 247
Basis function 10, 46
  bilinear 52, 248
  box 49
  constant 49, 57, 244
  Haar basis 190
  hat 49
  hierarchical 167, 187
  higher order 52, 60
  linear 49, 144
  mesh 131
  order 142
  orthonormal 60
  rendering 244, 245
  spherical harmonics 313
  support 47–48
  wavelet 190
Bézier patch 252–253
  quadratic triangle 253

Bidirectional ray tracing 304, 322
Bidirectional reflection distribution
    function 28
Boundary element method 46
BRDF 28
  components 299
  data 324, 344
  remote sensing 338
  spherical harmonics 313
Brightness 269
BSP-tree 217, 238
  2D 166, 231
  3D 231
  balanced 218
  shadow volumes 230
B-spline 257
BTDF 317
Bump mapping 266, 267
C^∞ 143
Candela 27
Cathode ray tube (CRT) 3
Caustic 304
Clough-Tocher element 144
Color bleeding 341
Color 41, 109, 267, 273
  CIE XYZ space 278, 282
  emission spectra 298
  gamut 3
  luminous efficiency function 275
  matching functions 276
  metamers 274
  monitor 267
  perception 274–275
  RGB space 282
  sampling 280

spectral sampling 283
transformations 279
Conformance 147, 152, 214, 218
Constant elements 262
Continuity 143
Convexity 63
Coordinate
    barycentric 52
Critical surface 226
CRT 268, 279
Delaunay triangulation 217–221, 246
    constrained 220
Delta form factor 83
    nonconstant bases 99
Delta function 31
Diagonally dominant 110
Differential form factor 67
Diffuse reflection 32
Directional diffuse reflection 34
Discontinuity 139, 149, 164
    derivative 150, 224–228
    first derivative 224–228, 244
    shape perception 339
    value 147, 150–152, 222–224
Discontinuity meshing 154, 164, 222–
        233, 253, 259, 345
    critical surface 226
    reconstruction 256
    shadow volumes 229
    value discontinuities 222
    value 139
Dynamic environments 126
    geometry 127
    lighting 126
    reflectivity 127
E 40
Element 8, 46, 48
    aspect ratio 145, 218
    bilinear 52
    C^1 252
    Clough-Tocher 144, 253

concave 145, 251
conformance 147, 152, 214, 218
constant 49, 244–246, 262
continuity 244
hermite 144
isoparametric 144
Lagrange 143
linear 49, 143, 245–246, 256
master 61
order 142
orientation 146
parametric coordinates 247
quadratic 253
shape 144
size 139
standard 52
triangular 247
Emitted energy 26, 40
Error analysis 343
Error estimate
    gradient-based 160
    heuristic 160
    higher order 161
    min-max search 164
    residual 162
Error metric 48, 53
    finite 54
    function norm 133
    image importance 201
    image-based 135, 258, 344
    kernel-based 135
    local estimate 132
    oracle function 178–186, 201
    perceptually-based 136, 343
    residual 134
    true error 132, 134
    view-dependent 201
Experimental validation 340
Exposure 17, 23
Extended form factor 307, 323
    transmission 318

Fine arts 340
Finite element method 8, 45
    Galerkin 56
    history 8
    point collocation 55
    steps 46
    weighted residuals 56
Flatland radiosity 172
Flux Phi 19
Fog 325
Form factor 47, 58, 65–66, 167, 172
    algebra 72
    aliasing 84, 89
    area-to-area 69
    area-to-hemisphere 69
    closed form 71
    contour integral 70
    differential 39, 67
    disk approximation 146
    element shape 146
    error metric 135, 183
    extended 307, 318, 323
    general BRDF 312, 315
    geometry 68
    history 70
    matrix qualities 110
    Monte Carlo 94, 262
    non-area light sources 291
    nonconstant bases 98
    Nusselt analog 80
    occlusion testing 223
    per pixel 260, 262
    point-to-polygon 72
    polygon-to-polygon 74
    quadrature 77, 94
    ray traced 318
    reciprocity 68, 92
    sampling artifacts 262
    singularities 68, 100
    test environment 96
    translucency 318

    visibility 68
    volume-to-surface 328
    volume-to-volume 328
Form factor algorithms
    acceleration 103
    area sampling 90
    contour integral 95
    disk approximation 92
    hemicube 80
    Malley's method 90
    Monte Carlo 89–90
    numerical solutions 75
    simple shapes 72
    single plane 88
Fresnel formula 35
Function norm 133
Function space 42
    dimension 42
    finite 42, 52
Function subspace 42
Function
    continuity 143
    projection 42, 47, 196
$G(x, x')$ 39–41
Galerkin 56
    constant element 57
Gamma correction 268
Gathering 115
    super-shoot-gather 125
Gauss-Seidel 114
    algorithm 115
Geometric decomposition 216
Global cube 309
Global illumination 6, 38
Glossy reflection 33, 299, 313
Goniometric diagram 292–293
Goniometric 26
Gouraud shading 144, 249–251
Gradient 241
    analytic 164
    numerical differencing 164

tangent plane 164
Grid superposition 210
H-refinement 155
Hardware rendering 249, 284
    specular highlights 284, 324
    texture mapping 285
    visibility preprocessing 286
Helmholtz reciprocity principle 29
Hemicube 80
    acceleration 103
    delta form factor 83
    heat transfer application 339
    nonconstant bases 99
    resolution 85
    Shao's method 312
    volume form factor 328
Hierarchy 8, 167
    clustering 345
    geometric simplification 346
    glossy reflection 316
    importance-based 205
    multilevel 176
    patch subdivision 172
    quadtree 176
    spatial subdivision 346
    two-level 169, 175
Human perception
    error metric 136
Illuminance 24
Image synthesis 2
    goals 2
    history 4
    limitations 2
    tractability 42
    View-dependent 43
    View-independent 44
Importance meshing 201, 265
Importance sampling 78
Indirect illumination 38
Infrared signature analysis 339
Inner product 54

Integral equation 40
Intensity 25
Interpolation
    B-spline 253
    barycentric coordinates 247
    Bézier 252
    bilinear 247–248
    C^0 245
    C^1 252, 256
    Clough-Tocher 253
    quadratic 252
Irradiance 24
Isoparametric 62
Item buffer 82, 105
Iterative refinement 312
Jacobi iteration 182
Jacobi method 113
Joule 15, 27
K (see also Matrix) 56
    adjoint operator 202
    coefficients 66
    components 65
    flatland radiosity 172
    Galerkin 57
    matrix qualities 110
    matrix 171
    point collocation 56
    visualization 172
L 19
Lagrange basis 143
Lambertian diffuse 32
Leaf canopy simulation 338
Light leak 150
Light source
    emission spectra 298
    goniometric diagram 293, 298
    ideal diffuse assumption 341
    nondiffuse luminaire 293
    nondiffuse 289, 336
    normalization 297
    parallel 293

point 293
sky light 295, 298
spot light 295
time varying 336
Lighting design 334, 337
Lighting optimization 337
Light 14
    coherent 14
    electromagnetic spectrum 14
    flux 19
    incoherent 14
    particles 18
    polarized 14
    power 17
    spectral sampling 284
Linear equation solver
    direct 112
    Gauss-Seidel 114
    initial guess 113
    iterative 112
    Jacobi 113
    relaxation 113
    Southwell 116
Local illumination 5, 37
Lumen 16, 27
Luminance 19, 269
    pixel 268
Luminosity 25
Luminous efficiency function 275
Luminous intensity 25
Lux 27
M 60
Mach band 139, 143, 252–253
Machine vision 339
Master element 61
Matching functions 276
Matrix
    condition 111
    diagonal dominance 110
    sparsity 110
    spectral radius 111

    symmetry 110
Matrix solution 109
    gathering 181
    Gauss-Seidel 114
    Jacobi iteration 182
    shooting 181
    Southwell 116
Mesh 48
    a posteriori 154
    a priori 154
    artifacts 137
    aspect ratio 145
    BSP-tree 217
    boundary 211–212
    conformance 147, 152, 214, 218
    continuity 142
    density 139
    grading 147, 214
    hierarchy 238
    nonuniform 141, 147
    optimal 131
    quadtree 212, 214
    relaxation 155, 221
    shadow boundaries 163
    smoothing 210, 221–222
    template 210
    topology 218, 223, 231, 235–238
    transition 145
    uniformity 145
    uniform 137–139, 154, 166
    user parameters 331, 345
Mesh topology 234–238
    adjacency graph 234
    data structures 235
    Euler operators 236
    T-vertices 214–218
    traversal queries 238
Meshing algorithms
    adaptive subdivision 217
    advancing front 218

automatic 152
decomposition 216
Grid superposition 210
multiblocking 212
nodes-elements-together 217
nodes-first triangulation 219
quadtree 211
recursive subdivision 212
template mapping 211
Metamers 274
Monte Carlo 42, 77, 89, 99
importance sampling 78
quasi 42
ray tracing 309, 346
Multi-pass method 265, 323
Multiblocking 212
N_i 42, 48
N-body problem 177
Neumann series 111, 299
Nit 27
Nodal averaging 246
Node 46, 48
Nonuniform mesh 141
Norm 54
function 133
Numerical differencing 164
Numerical integration (see also Quadrature) 76
Numerical integration 76
adaptive ray shooting 314
Nusselt analog 80
Octree 241
Opera lighting 335
Optics 14
Oracle function 178–186, 201
Overrelaxation 124
P-refinement 155, 157
Parallel 129
fine grained 130
workstations 129
Parametric mapping 61

Participating media 318, 325
anisotropic 330
isotropic 326
phase function 326
zonal method 327
Patch subdivision 172, 175
Path tracing 319
Penumbra 149–150, 226, 229
Perception 267
evaluation of images 341
shape understanding 338
Phase function 326
Photometry 15
history 15
units 27
Photorealism 2
Pixel 5
luminance 268
Pi 40
Point collocation 55
occlusion testing for 223
Progressive refinement 8, 119
ambient 122
general BRDF 311, 314
overrelaxation 125
southwell iteration 120
Projected solid angle 24
Projection 42
Pseudocode
directional radiance 315
GatherRadShootImp 208
GatherRad 181
Gauss-Seidel 115
Hemicube 85, 86
HierarchicalRad 185
ImportanceDrivenRad 205
Monte Carlo 78, 95
Oracle1 183
Oracle2 186
progressive refinement 120
PushPullRad 182

Refinelink 186
Refine 179
SolveDualSystem 206
SolveSystem 180
Southwell iteration 118
Quadratic elements 253
Quadrature 76
    form factor 77
    gaussian 77
    importance sampling 78
    Monte Carlo 77
Quadtree 171, 176, 211–214, 233,
    238–239
    balanced or restricted 214, 217
    tri–quadtree 214
ρ 33
R-refinement 155–157, 221
RGB to XYZ 279
RMS error 133
Radiance program 241, 335
Radiance 19
Radiant exitance 25
Radiant intensity 25
Radiometry 15
    units 27
Radiosity
    definition 25
    diffuse assumption 40
    history 7
Radiosity equation 40, 41
    assumptions 289
    classical 59
    matrix form 56, 59
    singularities 247
    translucency 318
Radiosity function
    discontinuity 164, 222
    gradient 163, 164
Radiosity gradient
    analytic 163
Radiosity texture (Rex) 239

Raster graphics 5
Ray tracing 6, 43
    acceleration 106
    bidirectional 304, 322
    for vision research 338
    from the eye 302, 319
    from the light 303
    shaft-culling 106
Reciprocity 29, 59
Recursive subdivision 212
Reflectance 31
    biconical 31
    hemispherical 32
Reflectance equation 30
Reflection frustum 320
Reflection 28
    diffuse 32
    directional diffuse 34
    Fresnel 35
    glossy 33
    Lambertian 32
    microfacet 35
    mirror 30
    rough surface 34
    specular 33
Regular expression 300
Relaxation 113
Remeshing 155–157
Remote sensing 338
Rendering
    hardware 249
Rendering equation 8, 36
    definition 39
Residual function 47
Residual 54, 113
Shadow 149
Shadow boundaries 163, 226, 229
Shadow leak 150, 224
Shaft-culling 106
Shape function (see also Basis func-
    tion) 46

Shooting 117
    super-shoot-gather 125
Singularities 100
Sky light 295
    spectral distribution 298
Slave nodes 214–215, 218
Smoke 325
Solid angle 20
    projected 24
Southwell iteration 116
    algorithm 117
    residual update 117
Spectral luminous relative efficiency
    16
Spectral reflectance data 324
Specular reflection 33
Spherical harmonics 313
    volumes 330
Spot light 295
Steradian 20
Stoke's theorem 70
Subdivision
    adaptive 157, 169
    BSP-tree 166
    image-based 240
    patch 172, 175
    quadtree 171
Super-shoot-gather 125
T-vertex 214–218, 251
Table of Terms 41
Talbot 16, 27
Template mapping 211
Texture mapping 239, 266, 337–338
Theatrical lighting 335
Three-point transport 39, 316
Throughput 23
Tone reproduction 269
Translucency 318
Transmission 317
Transport paths 305
    double counting 265, 324

Transport path 300
Transport theory 17
Triangulation 166, 210, 214
    constrained Delaunay 220
    Delaunay 217–221
    Gouraud shading 251
    nodes-first 219
Two point transport 38
Two-pass method 259, 319, 322, 333
    direct illumination 264
    Monte Carlo 260
Umbra 149–150, 226, 229
Uniform mesh 137–139, 166
$V(x, x')$ 38
Vanishing moment 195
View coherence 104
View-dependent 43
View-dependent solution 201
View-independent 7, 44
Visibility
    acceleration 103
    preprocessing 286
    Z-buffer 82
Visual events 226
    critical surface 226
    EEE 226, 233
    VE and EV 231
    VE or EV 226
Visual shape understanding 338
Volume rendering 329
Voronoi diagram 221, 246
Walkthrough 284, 332
Watt 15, 27
Wavelet 190
    Haar basis 190
    detail function 190
    smooth function 190
    vanishing moment 195
Weighted residual method 54
Winged-edge data structure 218, 223,
    231, 235–238

    Euler operators 236
    performance 235
XYZ to RGB 279
Z-buffer 82, 105
Zonal method 327